James Cagney (signature)

Feb 2016.

encounters 1
architectural essays

Rakennustieto
www.rakennustieto.fi
P.O. Box 1004
00101 Helsinki
Finland
phone + 358 207 476 400

Editor:
Peter MacKeith

Editorial Secretary:
Marita Vehman

Graphic Design:
Juhani Pallasmaa
Teemu Taskinen

Translations:
Diana C. Tullberg
Michael Wynne-Ellis

Editorial Assistants:
Sean Twomey
Marianne Bellino

2nd edition

Paper: Multiart Silk, 130 g
© Juhani Pallasmaa and Rakennustieto Oy
Publisher: Rakennustieto Publishing
Printers: Meediazone, Estonia 2012
ISBN 978-952-267-022-9

Juhani Pallasmaa

encounters 1

Architectural Essays

Edited by Peter MacKeith

Rakennustieto Publishing

CONTENTS

experiences and questions.
Sigurdur Gudmundsson, *Collage*,
1979. Galerie van Gelder,
Amsterdam.

LANDSCAPES

Juhani Pallasmaa
In conversation with Peter MacKeith

"Alussa oli suo, kuokka ja Jussi [In the beginning, there was the swamp, the hoe, and Jussi]." The simple, eloquent first sentence of Väinö Linna's Finnish literary masterpiece, Täällä pohjantähden alla [Here Under the Northern Star], *delineates an appropriate image by which to begin our discussion. You have cultivated built and written work over many years as both an architect and as an architectural educator and critic, not least as Director of the Museum of Finnish Architecture, Dean and Professor of Architecture at the Helsinki University of Technology, and as chaired professor at several schools in the United States. Many of the essays now gathered here in* Encounters, *in fact, are the result of lectures given in schools of architecture, symposia or conferences around the world. Could you speak of your attitudes towards the teaching and writing of architecture?*

In considering this collection of essays, written across twenty-five years, it seems important to begin with a sense of creative uncertainty: I am doubtful whether architecture, musical composition, or writing poetry can be taught—in the sense that we teach the multitude of instrumental skills and crafts. This is so because all artistic work is fundamentally existential, I believe, and it revolves around the core of one's self-identity. The understanding of identity, the prerequisite for creative work, comes through a tolerance for—actually an engagement with—silence, solitude, even boredom...and uncertainty.

I share the view of Joseph Brodsky, the Russian writer, that before we become ethical beings, we are first aesthetic beings. The identification and enjoyment of beauty is the ground for ethical values.

Education is primarily about an aesthetical and ethical view of life, an internalization of a sense of responsibility and ambition. Thus, instead of trying to teach architecture or design, I try to teach *how to be an architect*: how to look at the world, perhaps, or how to think, and how to work with curiosity and humility.

You identify the engagement with silence, solitude, and uncertainty as fundamental to creative work. Indeed, the belief consistently emerges in these essays that 'silence' is a quality inherent in all significant architectural experiences. Writing about architecture, however, implies both the definition of thought and its vocalization—as well as an evolution and sharing of that thought through dialogue and public appraisal. In this paradoxical position, could you describe what compels you to write, and what you seek from such vocalization of thought?

In one collection of his essays, entitled *On Grief and Reason*, Brodsky also writes about the significance of uncertainty. "Poetry is a tremendous school of insecurity and uncertainty," he describes, "…writing it, as well as reading it, will teach you humility, and rather quickly at that. Especially if you are both writing and reading it!" The same applies to making architecture and writing about it, I feel. Engagement in the phenomenon of architecture is, for me, a balancing act between uncertainty and certainty, between a sense of security and a sense of helplessness. When one experiences architecture—or any of the arts—this way, it becomes inseparable from one's self-identity and way of life.

Perhaps in this way, writing for me has essentially and in fact been simply a continuous internal monologue—a form of continuing education; it is for me an extension of this desire to understand my situation, my identity. I do not write to have an audience or a readership, I write instead to clarify my own position and because of the joy of discovery. All work, in my view, is a form of reinforcing one's sense of self. As you start a design project or a writing project, you never know where you will end; this is the rewarding aspect of the essential uncertainty in the creative endeavor.

To what extent, then, do you understand yourself as a writer? Has this been less a conscious choice and more a 'fall' into such a vocation?

Yes, to begin another way, then, with an apparent contradiction: I never planned to become a writer in general, and certainly not a critic, let alone a theorist (by any definition), of architecture. I simply drifted into writing about art and architecture. Upon reflection, writing just seemed a natural extension of my interest in thinking through ideas, in intellectualizing architectural issues—out loud. My circle of friends in architecture school, and then when I set out to work in architecture, loved to speak about architecture and the arts, but I ended up being the one to write most extensively.

In this regard, I could say that I do not believe that one could, or even should, plan one's life; life is an open-ended process where one thing leads to the next, and the most enjoyable and rewarding moments are the ones that you never imagined in advance. This applies also to design work and writing; the joy does not arise from doing things you know, but from discovering things you have never considered. I feel that there is too much sentimentality over creative freedom. In my view, living and working is more a matter of seeing your way through from one impulse to the next, maintaining your basic sense of uncertainty and curiousity... that enables you to move in any direction.

You have moved productively in several directions within architecture and design, and within the larger circles of architectural culture (schools, museums, publications). Are these simultaneous and multiple spheres of activity intrinsic to your identity, and to your substantial architectural work? Education, and the transmission of thought in lectures and writing, may not always be prescriptive—as in an imposed ideology or order—but it does involve reflecting upon the nature, history, and possibilities of architecture. How do you understand, for instance, Vitruvius' Classical assertion that the architect's knowledge is "the child of practice and theory"?

Since the 1960s, I have simultaneously worked in design—throughout a range of scales and contexts—and design education, and speculated through writing and lectures on the nature of architecture. Initially, in writing about architecture, I thought of theoretical investigations as a precondition for design. For quite some time, however, I have regarded writing about architecture, and making architecture, as two relatively independent ways of working within the phenomenon of architecture.

Writing has sometimes made design work mentally very difficult for me; an analytical and critical attitude tends to confine and interrupt the emotional and self-motivated probing required in design work. In fact, analysis and synthesis call for two opposite mental states. One almost needs to develop a double personality, a kind of professional schizophrenia, in order to achieve significant work of either order.

I suppose everyone has competing and conflicting qualities in one's character, some of them conscious intentions, others unconscious reactions. Any artistic discipline consists of both instrumental and existential realms, the first being connected with conceptual knowledge and professional skills, the other with a sense of lived culture and life.

I see the dialectics of practice and theory in architecture in a similar way. A grasp of the historical, theoretical, and conceptual fields of architecture simply provides you with a kind of intellectual map, but it doesn't make you any better as a designer; design arises from lived and embodied reactions. In order not to drain the mental tension necessary for design work, one needs to keep theoretical thought and design work in different parts of one's mind. Teaching, for me, is primarily a matter of trying to open perspectives and views into the phenomenon of architecture. However, the phenomenon has to be seen and experienced, and eventually, understood by the student.

The word theory implies both a deep vision and an intense speculation, and writing on this basis can become self-conscious in ways that may paralyze the synthetic activity of design. How do you view this potential pitfall and maintain a balance of these activities?

Thinking and writing about architecture certainly raises the level of one's self-consciousness, but this can also turn into a problem in design work, which has to proceed from sub-conscious and embodied reactions. Design, or making art, is not a problem-solving situation, or an application of learned responses; I think it is more fundamentally about forgetting such tactics than it is about remembering established methods or agendas. Creative work of all kinds, I believe, is a matter of working on one's own self-understanding and life experience as much as on the concrete object of work. In this way, I do not think in terms of more or less important tasks. One needs to develop a rhythm of life and work, where moments of inspiration and excitement are embedded in everyday routines and even boringly repetitious tasks. The depth of any work, I believe, derives from this fusion and compression of things. This kind of introspection and speculation, which might be otherwise called theorizing, and then the process of design work, are the different and semi-autonomous rhythms in my life.

Often in these essays, you emphasize "the wisdom of the body," and the importance of direct experience, and further, the experience of our childhood, in forming our understanding of the world and consequently for work in architecture. To what extent have your attitudes of work—

and a consciousness of culture and design—emerged or been shaped through your upbringing . . . that is to say, before any formal education or employment in architecture?

As a young boy during the war years of 1939–45, I lived with my mother and my five sisters on my grandfather's small farm in Central Finland. My father, the chief accountant for a wood industry firm, was serving in the military. Farm life, and my farmer grandfather, shaped me in essential ways, I think; certainly the sincerity, the necessary economy, and the direct causality of farm life were impressed upon me. Since my sisters were younger than I, I spent my days with my grandfather in his daily work, and I came to understand and admire the scope of his skills. In those years, I never heard anyone ask another, "Can you do this?" It was simply self-evident in that way of life that everyone could do everything necessary in the daily life of the farm. I learned that everything in life is fully integrated and that one should attempt to do everything as well as one can, that the pride and joy of work is not in its position on the scale of social importance, but in one's personal respect for the work.

Perhaps out of this context, my initial ambition was to become a doctor . . . a surgeon, in fact. I suppose I was attracted by the unquestionable ethical dimensions of the medical profession. My high school art teacher may have awakened my interest in architecture, although I confess that I cannot recall the exact circumstance of that appeal. I had not met a single architect, nor did I know anything of architecture, as I entered the entrance examinations at the Helsinki University of Technology in 1957.

Can you recall your first architectural experience or place? At what point did you understand the vitality and value of the work of an architect?

Now, as an adult, I have been able to identify certain important childhood experiences of places and spaces—the courtyard of my grandfather's farmhouse, for example, delineated in a semi-open manner by the house proper, the sauna, the cow barn, the wood-shed, and the two-story storage hut for flour and meat. The attic spaces of the house, and the interiors of the barns, live vividly in my memory and still seem to constitute the ground of architectural experience for me. However, I only began to see architecture as an art form of conscious expression after I began my studies in architecture.

After the disasters of the war in Finland, the acts of designing, building, and constructing were emotionally and symbolically charged—a builder shared some of that fundamental goodness, that ethically responsible position, of the medical profession. Seeing Eliel Saarinen's original drawings on the corridor walls of the old School of Architecture building in Hietalahti (a Helsinki district) during the entrance examination days just ignited my passion for architecture. I was fortunate enough to be able to enter, and then more fortunate still in my first years of studies to encounter and befriend some of the best architectural minds in Finland. Since my first introduction to the discipline, I have never had a second thought.

Your admission in the mid-1950s into the School of Architecture in Helsinki brought you into contact with a number of colleagues, mentors, and professor role-models, as well as into the thick of post-war architectural culture in Finland through employment at the newly founded Museum of Finnish Architecture. The essays included in Encounters *on the work of Alvar Aalto and Aulis Blomstedt, for example, indicate that there is much that is formative and enduring in the relationships, experiences, and events of this time for you. Could you describe some of those friendships and figures, and provide a sense of the architectural atmosphere of the time?*

My friendship and professional collaboration with Kirmo Mikkola began at the onset of my studies; significantly, Kirmo brought the realm of the arts into my focus. Kirmo had been two years ahead of me at the School of Architecture—he was an exceptionally widely read person, who had mastered political and cultural history, philosophy and literature. He was also passionate about the arts and practiced painting and sculpture. Our intimate friendship and endless conversations were seminal for me, and, I believe, also for him. Kirmo was one of the very few architectural essayists in Finland in those decades with a philosophical and theoretical frame of reference, a perspective he maintained up until his death in 1986 at the age of 52. Kirmo was writing before I did, and in many ways I feel that I am carrying on his mission.

My long friendship with Kristian Gullichsen also began when I was a student in the School of Architecture. Our early professional collaboration resulted in several early projects: the Moduli 225 pre-fabricated housing system, and another housing system researched in concrete elements. Kristian remains for me the model of an architect, and the example of both the deep conscience and the lively sense of humor for our profession.

In 1958, during my second year of architectural studies, I began to work as an exhibition assistant at the newly founded Museum of Finnish Architecture in Helsinki. The founding director of the Museum, Kyösti Ålander, who in 1954 had written the passionate and influential *Architecture from the Renaissance to Functionalism* (published only in Finnish), became a father figure for me.

The Museum developed into an intellectual center of architecture, a kind of private academy, in Helsinki. In fact, it was the counterpoint to the School of Architecture at the Helsinki University of Technology, and to Alvar Aalto's own office 'Academy.' The members of the Finnish section of CIAM, a group identified by the Egyptian deity PTAH (the name was also the acronym for *Progrés Téchnique Architecture Helsinki*), would gather at the Museum—they had just established the journal *Le Carré Bleu* as a theoretical forum. The seeds of my thinking in architecture were sown in the old wooden villa in Kaivopuisto (a Helsinki park district) in which the Museum was initially located, in the excited afternoon tea conversations stimulated by the arrival of one of the *PTAH/Le Carré Bleu* members—conversations which often continued into the morning hours of the next day!

Throughout these conversations, both Ålander, and Aulis Blomstedt— who also became a close friend and strong influence—maintained a firm idealist and ethical tone in their thinking and contributions. Blomstedt's thinking, work, and force of personality had a particularly profound and lasting effect over the course of many years and repeated intellectual collaborations, beginning in 1960 when I assisted him in an exhibition design for the Moderna Museet in Stockholm. Later, in 1968, I assisted him in his early studies for a major exhibition on proportional harmony and modular coordination. This exhibition was never realized, as Blomstedt was commissioned to design the exhibition of Finnish architecture at the Louisiana Museum in Denmark, but we compiled material nonetheless and discussed extensively the history of ideas in proportional harmony.

In the meantime, in 1963, together with Blomstedt's eldest son Juhana, himself a painter, I assembled and designed an exhibition on Blomstedt's own studies in harmony for the Museum of Finnish Architecture… and ultimately curated yet another one in 1976, which went on to travel to the Le Corbusier Foundation in Paris and then to Tokyo and Warsaw. This sustained attention to these ideas of proportional harmony at a relatively early stage in my development as an architect was transformative: although I may not share Blomstedt's absolute convictions, the Pythagorean approach to numbers, proportion, and harmony in the arts and in the world remains a strong perspective in my thinking.

*The Museum conversations included a number of other younger archi-
tects, as well, each with their own perspectives and trajectories in architectural thought. What was the general appraisal of such conversations
and ideas by the larger group of Finnish professional architects?*

Yes, other architects attended the Museum conversations, each with
their own perspective and energy—and I owe extended intellectual debts
to them all. Keijo Petäjä, a devoted reader of Wittgenstein, introduced
connections between architecture and philosophy into those Museum
conversations. My association with Petäjä blossomed still further when,
in 1977, he began to host a conversation group in his home. The group
met roughly every second month to discuss a presentation given by one
of the members, or occasionally by an outside guest. The core group
consisted of a philosopher, a poet, a musicologist, a theologian, thera-
pists, and architects. Sadly, these conversations came to an end with
Keijo's untimely death in a bicycle accident in 1988.

But I was particularly influenced by the perspectives of therapeutic
theory and practice that were often the focus of our discussions. In my
view, the practices of therapy and architecture are closely related: one
is engaged with the inner space of the mind, the other with the outer,
lived space. But both focus on the mental and existential essence of
space and constitute a psychic continuum (as an extension, Alexander
Lowen's ideas of a bodily approach to therapy in order to bypass the
narrow verbal channel were also inspirational to me in the late 1970s).

However, in the 1950s and 1960s, architects in Finland who wrote
on architecture in such ways—or who simply expressed these more
speculative ideas in teaching or in conversation—were criticized and
even ridiculed by the pragmatic majority of the Finnish profession. In
the first place, collegial criticism was rare in those years among the
tight professional circles, and even small commentaries were over-
exaggerated in their importance.

For instance, while not included in this collection, my first published essay—in 1967—was a short critique of Reima Pietilä's Dipoli
Student Union building at the Helsinki University of Technology, a
piece with the word-pun title 'Vasta-poli' (meaning 'Counterpole').
Reima had brought linguistic ideas of morphology and semiology into
play in the early Museum conversations, even as his architecture at
that time built upon ideas of proportional harmonies. His development
towards a more expressionistic architecture as evidenced by the design
of Dipoli, and his increasingly idiosyncratic use of language, evoked
some confusion within the group of *Le Carré Bleu*. Unfortunately, the
critique set up a myth of animosity between Pietilä and myself, whereas

in fact we were friends regardless of our differing views of architecture, and corresponded until the last year of his life.

The irony here is that Pietilä was a prolific thinker and writer, subject to critique on that basis alone from those same tight professional circles. The pragmatic tradition in Finnish architecture is seemingly almost axiomatic, or tautological, by this point in time, although the essay included here, "The Two Languages of Architecture," was part of a larger effort you helped to mount at the Museum of Finnish Architecture indicating the range and depth of Finnish architectural thought and writing. Those readers who encounter Frosterus and Strengell's "Architecture: A Challenge" from 1904, for instance, understand quickly that there have been strong, critical voices earlier in Finnish architectural culture. Aalto's too often quoted remark on the value of paper that you respond to in this collection is the simplistic phrasing of a deeper and more broadly held set of beliefs. Where do the sources of this attitude lie? Why were the debates of the 1960s in particular so passionate?

A pragmatic, and one could say, even an anti-theoretical, stance is a long tradition in Finnish architecture. It probably reflects the peasant's unself-conscious attitude towards building, but it is also reinforced by the severely practical demands on construction in our climate. Even the fact that Finnish architects have generally enjoyed stable employment throughout the century could have contributed to this position; I mean to say that Finnish architects at large have been positively engaged in active construction, and have thus rarely had to question, or problematize, the conditions of their work—or develop an intellectual distance which might have led to a construction of theory alongside a practice of construction.

In the 1960s, there was a strong and evident opposition between the rationalist school of thought, emerging from the figures and conversations at the Museum of Finnish Architecture, and Aalto's 'Academy,' but these tensions actually had their origins in the previous generation of Finnish architects—the one that had been educated earlier in the century and had lived as adults through the Second World War. There were strong tensions between Aalto, on the one hand, and Ålander and Blomstedt, on the other.

The tensions arose from several differences of view: supporters of the Aalto 'Academy' expressed an independence from social issues and were critical of industrialization, as well as of a rational and theory-based approach to architecture. They also scorned writing about architecture. The group of conversants who had formed around the Museum—led by Ålander, Blomstedt, Petäjä, Pietilä, and Aarno Ruusuvuori—saw these positions as elitist and regressive attitudes. Proportional harmony and modular systems (Blomstedt), logic and philosophy (Petäjä), and morphology (Pietilä), were all in turn ridiculed by supporters of Aalto and by the pragmatists of the profession.

You place Aarno Ruusuvuori now into this context: could you situate him in the architectural and intellectual constellation of the time?

Ruusuvuori was influential in Finnish architectural culture, both through his tough and uncompromising architecture, which had developed towards an ever greater minimalism by the early 1960s, and through his role as a teacher, first as a studio instructor (1952–62) and then as Professor of the Basic Course in Architecture (1963–66) at the School of Architecture in Helsinki. His own office was also a kind of independent academy, where many of the most talented students and architects wanted to work—and indeed, did work. Ruusuvuori's confrontations were thus with Aalto's assistants more than with "the old man" himself. But as there was rather little open public criticism, or critical writing, of architecture, the tensions and discussions when they did occur tended to become emotionally heated… particularly after a few drinks, which often accompanied the encounters!

There was also a lot of ideological theater about Aalto's persona and genius that appeared unacceptably elitist in the idealistic democratic atmosphere of the 1960s. More to the extreme, from 1969 onwards, the Academician (as Aalto was in fact, but also as he was ironically labeled by his detractors) was scorned by the Stalinist intellectuals of the Finnish political and cultural left—their attacks applied to the entire architectural profession as supporters of 'Braggart Architecture.'

Readers with some knowledge of post-war architecture in Finland may be aware of your supposed reputation as an architectural radical at this time, along with Kirmo Mikkola, among other things due to your desire to intellectually engage the aging Aalto…

…But the truth is that the rationalists of the Museum conversations never wrote critically of Aalto, and neither I, nor Kirmo Mikkola, ever led an Aalto opposition, as Göran Schildt erroneously labels us in his biography of the architect; this view is simply not true. True, I was one of the few who dared to have a critical discussion with Aalto on his work in a direct way. One such discussion, in fact, remembered well by the many who were present, took place in 1963 at the Museum of Finnish Architecture in conjunction with an exhibition opening. Aalto's Helsinki Center Plan had just been published, and I approached and engaged him on this subject. Contrary to any sense of animosity to the discussion, Aalto seemed to like the confrontation and later in the evening, having departed once, he even returned to the Museum to continue it. Shortly after this event, I spent a week with the Aaltos in Mexico, in conjunction with another exhibition opening there, and in the midst of several friendly and rewarding days with the couple, this critical debate was never mentioned.

…and those opportunities were limited due to Aalto's own health and the intellectual climate of the time, as you describe above. Your analysis of the Villa Mairea included in this collection, and your references to him in several of the other essays indicates a great, and still growing, appreciation for his work and thought.

Yes, I admit with genuine regret that I, and probably most of my generation, read Aalto's writings thoroughly only after 1972, when *Luonnoksia,* the collection of his essays compiled, and edited by Göran Schildt (the collection was published in English in 1978 as *Sketches,* translated by Stuart Wrede), was published in Finnish. However, as I was one of the few who dared to have a critical discussion with Aalto, my later lectures and writings on Aalto's work have been viewed as opportunism…I should say, however, that as with all my essays, these critiques of Aalto's work have been commissioned by others, and I have welcomed the opportunities to consider and re-consider the dialogue which every Finnish architect invariably must have with Aalto and his legacy. I have learned much from these encounters with the master architect.

Perhaps as a consequence of shifts overall in architectural culture, and of an acquired critical distance now from the life and work of Aalto and Pietilä, it is possible to address architecture in both practice and theory—generally and in Finland. Your own thinking, too, has shifted in its attitudes and focus…although from essay to essay, ideas and references echo…how do you view this condition, with the full survey of the essays in front of you?

During the last several decades, the attitude towards theoretical investigations and critical examinations in general has become much more positive, and the interest of architects in theory has grown dramatically—in Finland, and of course, in architecture culture in general (I am critical, at this point, of a surplus of such interest, as the reader of this collection will find!). Most of these essays collected here began as lectures, for a number of different reasons and audiences, and consequently, my themes can seem arbitrary and unintentional, and often possess a certain repetition of ideas and references. If I remember correctly, every cell in our physical constitution is renewed in seven years; perhaps one's thoughts are renewed similarly in such slow transformation.

Throughout these years of lecturing and writing, alongside of professional work, my thinking on architecture has changed rather fundamentally a number of times. In my view, no serious artist, designer, or thinker operates in a vacuum. Thinking is contextual in the sense that the prevailing cultural situation conditions individual thought. An artist and architect has a vision of an ideal society, however vaguely and unconsciously recognized, and works to bring this ideal into being. Consequently, changes in the cultural and social atmosphere alter the course of one's thinking; in the long run, the ideas advocated may shift radically. For example, Aalto's ardent support of rationalism and 'non-synthetic' architecture at the end of the 1920s rapidly transformed into an outspoken criticism of this approach. For my part, instead of intellectual stubbornness and certainty, I support the attitude suggested by the Polish proverb: "only a cow does not change her opinion."

Is it possible to outline the trajectory of your thought, at least by the intellectual guides you sought?

During the 1960s, as I indicated, I was strongly influenced by my rationalist mentors. My early essays support the rationalist, technological, and futuristic stance parallel to the Utopian tone of the concurrent themes of the influential *Architectural Design* magazine in London. Buckminster Fuller was a personal friend and a strong influence, particularly through the *World Resources Inventory* publications he produced in collaboration with John McHale. Christopher Alexander's early writings and studies in the rationalization of the design process were also significant. At this time, too, I was also influenced by Marshall McLuhan, whose essays and books seemed to be based on excitingly novel observations and a radical argumentation.

Towards the end of the 1960s, I became interested in *Gestalt* and environmental psychology. These readings and discussions intersected with other events, for when I moved to Ethiopia in the early 1970s, my experiences there disillusioned my faith and confidence in rationality, the benefits of technology, and ideas of universality. I became interested in anthropological, structuralist, and eventually psychoanalytical ideas and writings. Erich Fromm's and Herbert Marcuse's books were particularly important and aided my understanding of the essence of collective psychic phenomena. Anton Ehrenzweig's two books on the unconscious dimensions of artistic creativity and perception gave, perhaps, the most important impulses to my way of thinking.

Through Christian Norberg-Schulz' writings, I was introduced to the 'ontology of place,' as well as to the philosophy of Martin Heidegger. A decade later I encountered a more full range of existentialist and phenomenological perspectives. My essays are clearly indebted to Gaston Bachelard and Maurice Merleau-Ponty. Anyone reading this collection will quickly see that Bachelard's writings are a kind of lodestone for me; I continue to be impressed by the sense of precision and authority that Bachelard's background in the philosophy of science projects onto his later investigations into poetic imagery. Merleau-Ponty is free of the cultural conservatism I sense in Heidegger's perspective; the Black Forest hut of Heidegger directs architecture backwards, I think, whereas Merleau-Ponty points my thoughts forward.

For the last decade at least, you have advocated the perspectives offered to architecture by the phenomenological approach, even as others in architectural culture pursue other possibilities—the eclipse of Euclidean geometry, the de-centering of the human subject, the undecidability of meaning. Could you identify the distinctions of this break point in your thinking? Even if, as you described earlier, writing is a form of internal monologue for you, to what understandings might the reader be directed throughout the breadth of these essays?

Paradoxically, I have grown increasingly skeptical about architectural theory; here my doubt reflects the late attitudes of both Aalto and Blomstedt. I have come to understand that artistic and architectural quality derives from unique and personal poetic encounters rather than from theories. The phenomenological approach appeals to me because of its intellectual innocence and its essence as an anti-theory. I wish I had been drawn to this line of thought decades earlier, although I probably would not have been ready for it. At a younger age, one seems to need rationalized explanations almost as intellectual crutches, whereas age and experience prepare one to accept uncertainty and undefinability. I have grown increasingly suspicious of persons who are sure of themselves and their work; in my own thinking, the realm of uncertainty constantly expands.

As a consequence of the shifting of my intellectual interests, my view of architecture has altered from a visual and formal focus to a multi-sensory, existential, and experiential understanding. I see this development as a rather consistent deepening of perspective and insight, as well as a strengthening of my personal encounter with architecture, as opposed to any given theoretical or dogmatic stance. In retrospect, I feel that the development of my thinking has been rather logical and inevitable; the shifts and slants are part of that very logic. I am a bit surprised to make this observation, as my writings on architecture have evolved as responses to externally given situations and impulses, rather than through a deliberate theoretical conception or project.

Throughout this conversation, you've spoken of the necessity for uncertainty, a form of creative doubt, a deepened intellectual curiosity. Alongside of this, many essays presented here seem to possess a declarative quality, even an imperative tone. "Architecture is...," and "Architecture must...," you often write. This tension between doubt and faith, between hesitance and exhortation is intriguing... how do you understand the tone you are attempting to sound?

I can identify an idealist and moral tone in my writing, a tone almost certainly derived from my early mentors Ålander and Blomstedt. It also reflects the polemical context of most of my lectures. More importantly, however, I see a definite moral imperative in the art of architecture. Architecture frames human existential experience and provides a horizon of understanding. As architects, we do condition others' lives; this definitively projects a decisive ethical dimension onto our work. Architecture also implies the significant allocation of collective resources—this is a serious responsibility. For me, the current course of Western culture—towards a surreal cult of materialism and consumption, temporary fashion and image—poses another moral imperative. The task of the artist and architect is to resist these forces, to prevent the erosion of value and meaning. As Italo Calvino saw the task of literature, so too I see the task of architecture: as the defense of the authenticity of human experience.

Yes, Italo Calvino speaks of "the rainfall of images" now inundating our minds without form or content; he might just as well have spoken of the rainfall of similarly undifferentiated words. In contrast, your lectures are usually accompanied by hundreds of carefully chosen images, each evocative in their own right, and your assertions are usually supported by a myriad of references and pointed quotations; both aspects reveal a collaborative reliance upon the intellectual and artistic work of others for inspiration and guidance.

Well, yes, in my view, all artistic work and thinking is achieved only through collaboration, not only in the obvious sense of the work, but in the sense of working in a historical continuum, and in an open exchange with a circle of friends, thinking in similar terms. You may never meet many of your most influential intellectual 'friends' because they happen to live on the other side of the world, or because they have passed away long before you were even born. Thinkers, writers, artists, and architects of all time create a brotherhood. These essays are such collaborations, fusing ideas adopted and transformed from others with my own experiences and perceptions.

I have been fortunate to have close friends among Finnish writers, painters, sculptors, and composers. I have collaborated with them in a number of ways, and these artist friends have made the realm of the arts familiar to me, introduced me to another way of working, and to the values of materiality and making; I am indebted to Tapio Wirkkala especially, for having revealed to me the thought and wisdom of the hand. From 1994 on, I have also participated in a conversation group consisting of a poet, a cultural historian, a theater director, a composer, a dramaturge, a painter, a photographer, and two literary critics; quite often, the group has met in my office library. These encounters, too, have inspired me, and made me believe in the shared task of all artists.

Many friends from outside Finland have also influenced my thinking throughout the years: Buckminster Fuller, as I have said, and Olivier Mourgue in the 1960s; Roland Schweitzer, Colin St John Wilson, Daniel Libeskind, Alberto Pérez-Gómez, and Kenneth Frampton fifteen years later; and Glenn Murcutt, Steven Holl, Tod Williams, Karsten Harries, William Curtis, and Dan Hoffman, to mention several, during the last decade. My list of sources of inspiration would be incomplete without mentioning the continuous stimulus and challenge provided by the many encounters, in many places, with teacher colleagues and students. The great benefit from teaching is that it keeps you intellectually moving. Besides, maintaining one's sense of curiosity is the most efficient way to resist the negative consequences of aging...

We've spoken across a series of intellectual landscapes: biographical, philosophical, pedagogical, and collaborative...but less so in terms of the physical geography of your Finnish birthplace, of the land and its forests, water, and light that figure so prominently in any real or imagined depiction of the country. Perhaps this is the cultivated 'silent' presence of this conversation?

I will put it in these words: across all these encounters with people, buildings, and ideas, I have been fortunate to travel widely, first making exhibitions of Finnish art and architecture, and later teaching and lecturing. As Brodsky also writes, "…the more one travels, the more complex one's sense of nostalgia becomes." My travels have strengthened my appreciation of individuals and achievements of other cultures, on all continents, but also reinforced my deep mental connection with the Nordic landscape. I can say sincerely that the more I have traveled, the more attached I feel to the Finnish natural and cultural soil. Often, in those fantastic destinations, before I fall asleep, I have an image of a view out onto a lake or deep into the Finnish forest.

2   Juhani Pallasmaa and Peter MacKeith in the office of Juhani Pallasmaa Architects, Helsinki, June 2004.

2

3 Zen Stone Garden, Ryoan-ji, Kyoto.
The garden is a microcosm, a
miniaturized landscape, with an
extraordinary image power.

4   Rhetorical alphabet of sign language,
     1644.
5   Peruvian 'pallares' beans used for
     communication.
6   A typical Italian gesture.
7   A characteristic Texas gesture.

THE TWO LANGUAGES OF ARCHITECTURE

Elements of a Bio-Cultural Approach to Architecture
(1980)

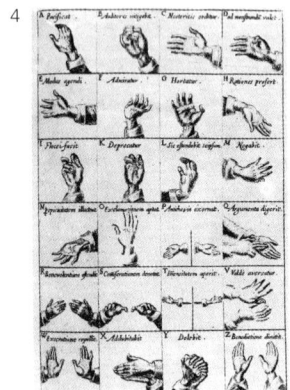

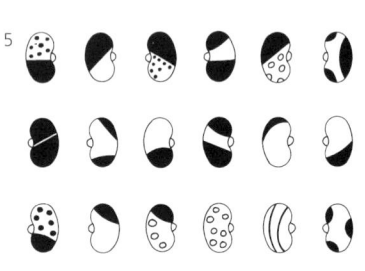

THE CRITIQUE OF MODERNISM:
AN ARCHITECTURE WITHOUT LANGUAGE

The past few years have been marked by an extreme criticism and judgment of Modernism, often verging on hostility. Critics cite the poverty of architecture's semantic content, due to the abstractness and rootlessness of the language of Modernism, as the main reason for its demise. This stereotyped architecture has lost its positive content, it is felt, and there is now a growing interest in the architectural history Modernism rejected. The search has begun for the ultimate roots of architecture and the linguistic essence of architectural expression.

Analogies borrowed from anthropological research have been used to shed light on the origin and evolution of expression—after all, until now our approach to architecture has consisted of limited samples from past and present cultures. Myths, rituals, and beliefs connected with building have been analyzed in order to discover how the worldview of each civilization is reflected in its architecture. Folk traditions in building have in turn been studied to elucidate the mutual influence of high and low culture, and the semantic levels of the architectural language. The idea of architecture as a language has gained ground among architects themselves, and conscious attention is being paid to the comprehensibility of architectural communication. Local dialects, anchored in local cultural heritage, have again begun to take over from the sterile architectural Esperanto of the International Style. The historical motifs and symbols abandoned by Modernism have likewise begun to return to the vocabulary of architecture, although architecture has all too often fallen into cheap pandering to romantic trends in public tastes.

The interpretation of architecture as a language has a long history, however. In the 18th century, architecture was understood as a self-evident language transmitting ideas carved in stone—in fact it was thought of as a form of writing anterior to the alphabet. However, the Functionalists' struggle for a unique expression, one deliberately dissociated from tradition—a sort of anti-style—has obscured our view of architectural communication. As Juan Pablo Bonta writes in *Architecture and its Interpretation: A Study of Expressive Systems in Architecture*: "But rather than a particular architectural language, it was the idea itself of linguistic communication in architecture that came under assault."[1]

6

ARCHITECTURE AS THE LANGUAGE OF REASON

The architectural theory of the Age of Reason possesses interesting affinities with the present-day plurality of values.[2] Ernst Kris, adopting the psychoanalytic approach of interpreting art, holds that great ambiguity in the meaning and interpretation of art is typical of periods of transition in behavioral ideals and social values; the French Revolution of 1789 and the period of cultural upheaval in the 1970s resemble each other in this respect.[3] The Utopian architecture of the French Revolution rejected inherited forms, and for the first time a conscious and calculated pluralism of architectural styles, an '*architecture parlante*,' was created. Today's Post-Modernism also strives for this quality.

The architectural writings of the late 18th and early 19th century regarded the language of architecture as dualistic. Some writers demanded that architecture should be abstract; it was to be 'the language of calculation.' Others took architecture to be an imitative art, whose signs of expression came directly from nature. In *Des signes et de l'art de penser*, published in 1800, De Gerando described all fine arts as systems of signs that imitate nature. Architectural communication, he stated, was based on its use of a universal, natural language: "… architecture even has its natural signs; because the signs of nobility, of majesty, depend in no way on human institution. It is in no way by virtue of a convention that grand and simple forms awaken in us all those impressions of meditation and respect, and engage us in deep and serious reflection."[4] The thought might just as well have appeared in Le Corbusier's writings.

These "natural signs" were presumed to appeal so powerfully to our imagination because of their immediate correspondence with the sensations and experiences to which they give rise. However, only a few of the basic ideas inherent in the architectural language could be expressed with a natural sign language; the more delicate messages tied to a single cultural context had to be transmitted by artificial conven-

7

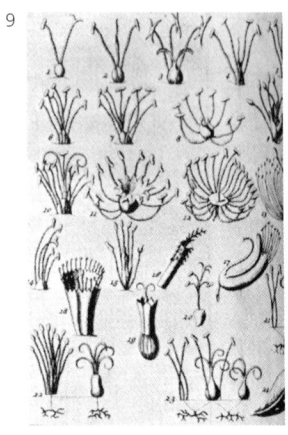

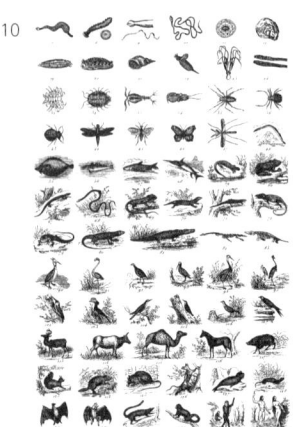

tional signs. Of these artificial signs, those that clearly correlated with natural signs were considered most effective.

A century later, the abstract language of Modernism was similarly assumed to be based on the universal effect of basic geometric forms. Amédée Ozenfant and Le Corbusier distinguished between primary and secondary sensations in the architectural experience.[5] Primary sensations are caused purely by form and color, they postulated, and are in essence both permanent and common to all of humanity. Secondary sensations are based on the genetic and cultural background of the individual. "Needless to say," they said, "anything that is of universal value is more valuable than something the value of which is purely personal."[6] Architectonic universalism did in fact come true on a massive scale in the following half century.

In the early 19th century, J.N.L. Durand developed a systematic architectural language similar to Lavoisier's classification of chemical phenomena or Linnaeus' classification of flora. The elements of Durand's system could be combined vertically as well as horizontally.[7] As with scientists of the period, Durand believed that every discipline could be reduced to a language, and that the future of architecture depended on the development of its specific language. He attempted to build his architectural canons on a solid foundation by keeping them apart from "the errors of religion, tradition and superstition."[8] The modern equivalent of Durand's systematic approach is Peter Eisenman's *Visual Syntax*.[9] A parallel, although dubious, aim of the 'rationalized' planning and control methods of our day is to liberate architecture from the mystique of creative intuition.

IS ARCHITECTURE A LANGUAGE?

Analogies, common in science, have great significance for the formulation of theories and methods. The language analogy is based on the assumption that it is useful to interpret various manifestations of culture as essentially similar to language. To call culture a 'code' or to say that behavior has a 'grammatical structure' is to make an analogy with language. In the same way, the 'vocabulary' of architecture, or the 'Grammar of Modernism,' are now commonplace architectural analogies.

Is there any point in saying that architecture is a language, or in essence, like language? The statement explains architectural communication as little as does the observation that poetry is language explains poetry. Both poetry and architecture convey, or give rise to, certain states of mind with their own systems of signs and symbols, each consisting of conscious and unconscious meanings, mental images, feelings, associations, flashbacks, sensory images, and psychological tensions. Language is a medium for storing and transmitting the message of poetry; material forms and the immaterial spaces determined by the forms, and their mutual relationships, are the means of architectural communication.

However, just as words as such do not constitute poetry, so the forms of architecture cannot be identified with the architectural experience. Architectural expression or communication can only be compared with language in metaphorical terms. The comparison is useful in that it emphasizes the communicative aspect of architecture along with its function, but it is misleading in that the influence architecture can have is much less formalized than language. That is to say, the architectural experience arises largely from unconscious and diffuse effects. Linguistic communication is for the most part conscious, although recent research has also stressed the importance of extra-linguistic spatial and physical factors.[10] The interference due to these extra-linguistic factors may rise to such a pitch that linguistic communication becomes impossible.

In contrast with language, the only messages communicated on a conscious level in architecture are the most obvious ones, based on conventional symbols, which communicate the meaning of the architect directly to the observer in the manner of speech. For the most part, architecture entails a unique experience and interpretation—a kind of free re-creation. Architectural communication takes place simultaneously on several levels: at the level of collective cultural conventions and meanings; at the level of automatic, biologically determined behavioral reactions; at the level of subconscious memories and experiences; and at the level of collective archetypes.

To contribute to the understanding of the nature of architectural communication, the linguistic analogy must be based on a deeper conception of the nature of language and the relationship between language and culture. Used superficially, the analogy serves only to distort our view of architecture as an art.

LANGUAGE ANALOGIES IN THE STUDY OF CULTURE

The various artistic manifestations of cultures inevitably reflect the same basic conscious and unconscious structures. Architecture is collective by nature—construction usually requires exceptional resources and general collective approval—and is thus particularly closely bound to the basic structures of culture. The study of cultures has proved useful for understanding architecture.

In the past twenty years or so, methods developed in linguistics have been widely applied to the study of other, non-linguistic, aspects of culture. Two fields of anthropological research that hold a special

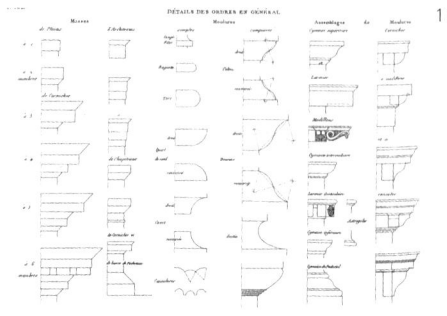

11

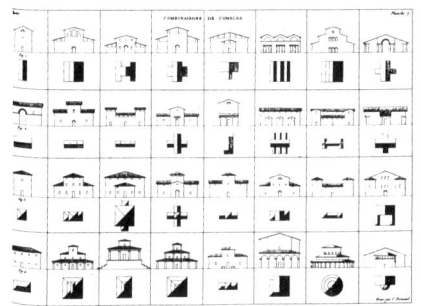

12

18th AND 19th CENTURY VIEWS ON CLASSIFICATION

8   The key to the generic system of Carolus Linnaeus' *Systema naturae*. Note the anthropocentric descriptions.

9   A generic system of plants. Numbers indicate Linnean classes.

10 Classes of organisms as represented in an illustrated encyclopedia of 1851.

J.N.L. DURAND'S SYSTEM OF ARCHITECTURAL ELEMENTS

11 Details of architectural orders.

12 Roof shape combinations

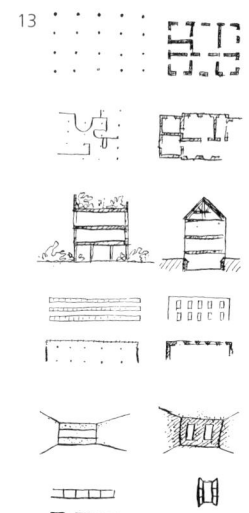

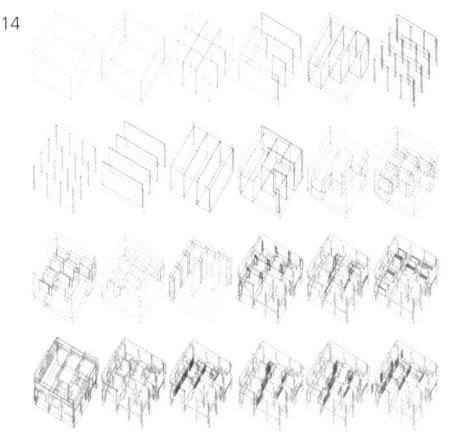

ALPHABETS OF THE LANGUAGE OF
MODERN AND CONTEMPORARY
ARCHITECTURE

13   Le Corbusier's characteristics of the
new architecture, *"Les 5 points d'une
architecture nouvelle* (1926)": free
plan solution, raised ground floor,
roof terrace, free articulation of
facades, and the strip window.
14   Peter Eisenman's "Visual Syntax":
analysis of the design for a residential
building, 1969.

interest for architectural theory, namely ethnoscience and structuralism, are likewise built on approaches developed within linguistics.[11]

Ethnoscience is an approach that has become especially popular in contemporary American research. Parallels for it are easy to find in the theory of architecture. Ethnoscience contends that the broad and complex field of all cultural behavior can be reduced to a small number of elements and rules that can be combined in different ways to produce cultural variation. This is reminiscent of Durand's idea of the language of architecture as a set of elements and rules. In contrast to Durand, however, it is not believed that these elements and rules are universal; they vary from one culture to the next. Culture is thus seen as a system of signs like language, a code that governs all observable human behavior. The aim of ethnoscience is to discover this sign system—in the same way as linguistics studies the elements and rules governing language—and to discover the grammar behind the culture being studied, in order to help predict how people behave in different situations. The "pattern language" for architecture developed by Christopher Alexander represents an effort to transfer the above approach to architecture. Alexander begins with the structural analysis of buildings or milieu intended for various purposes; from these structural patterns his goal is to evolve a kind of visual language to aid architects.[12]

ARCHITECTURE AND THE LANGUAGE OF THE BODY

Such analogies with language have great inherent limitations, however. For one thing, defining language as a schematic system of signs represents a very narrow view of language itself. It entails, for example, a denial of the effect of space and the body on communication, although all communication between people has been shown to require certain spatial relationships.

The language of space in general has not been understood by our civilization for three reasons: communication has been interpreted as one-sidedly linguistic; the regulation of spatial relationships takes place in the sphere of the subconscious; and our Western civilization as a whole is alienated from the corporeal. The anthropologist Edward T. Hall has investigated the subconscious spatial factors of communication; he has said that we have an extreme tendency to disassociate material from intellectual culture and as a result, our susceptibility to the language of our material surroundings has withered.[13]

Cultural behavior signifies a complex mutual influence of conscious and unconscious factors. The countless elements of culture, not belonging to language as such, may have a communicative function, but they contain features to which formal analysis is not applicable.

According to cerebrological calculations, the overall data processing capacity of the human brain may be of a magnitude of 10^{15} times the capacity of the conscious brain.[14] This ratio reveals how startlingly small the proportion of conscious brain operations is, and how completely this may disprove views which only take into account this part of behavior in communication, and in the mutual influence of man and the environment.

Paralinguistic studies of phenomena marginal to language have identified physical activities considered totally automatic and biological. Studies concluded that all parts of the body may communicate meaning in infinitesimal movements; our senses are extremely receptive to these parallel communications. The most bewildering discovery concerns synchronism, that is, the synchronization of the involuntary muscles and certain metabolic processes of communicating individuals. These studies show that communication also occurs on levels classed as biological—and that biological and cultural factors are thus inseparably linked. These new views also contribute to the understanding of the bio-cultural language of architecture.[15]

Architecture is experienced through many simultaneous sensations, and its meaning is communicated through an unconscious body language, not in intellectual, verbally articulated terms.

The importance of these subconscious reactions to architecture has been recognized recently; Edward T. Hall's famous studies of the spatial dimensions of behavior in various cultural areas were forerunners in the field. Among other things, Hall discovered the fundamentally insoluble problems involved in exporting architecture across cultural borders. Oscar Newman's controversial studies, for their part, have shown the importance of subconscious territoriality in social behavior.[16] His research has demonstrated the bio-cultural irrelevance of the idealistic but superficial ideas of town planning prevalent in this century. Studies directed by Professor Frode Strømnes on the links of spatial expression in the cinema with subconscious linguistic background structures have finally brought these ideas to the Finnish cultural scene. His views on language, behavior, and thought also provide stimuli for a theory of architectural communication.[17]

A new theoretical approach and method of treatment, based on the primacy of body language, has been developed in psychotherapy. In *The Language of the Body*, Alexander Lowen, an eminent representative of this school of thought, says: "The problem which psychoanalysis faces arises from the fact that the analyst deals with body sensations and body feelings on a verbal and mental level, for the subject matter of analysis is the feeling and behavior of the individual."[18] The way we

15

16

17

BASIC VISUAL ELEMENTS

15 Cover of the *Bauhaus* magazine, 1928.
16 Le Corbusier: "Three reminders to Messieurs les Architectes," *Towards a New Architecture*, 1923.
17 *The Universe*, painting by the 17th century Japanese Zen artist Sengai.

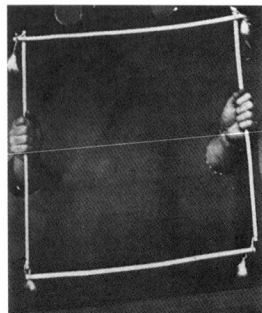

experience architecture is to such an extent indefinable by conscious linguistic expression that the planning control of the past ten years, aiming at 'scientific' accuracy by linguistic, mathematical, and statistical methods, has directly caused the disappearance of the artistic dimension of architecture. In *Body, Memory and Architecture*, Kent Bloomer and Charles Moore have incorporated body language—especially the 'body-image' and the subconscious memory—in their theory of architecture.[19]

THE GRAMMAR OF CULTURE

Certain central concepts of structuralism and transformational linguistics provide an excellent point of departure for a deeper interpretation of architectural communication. Structuralism, closely linked with the name of Claude Lévi-Strauss, is the most widely known application of the language analogy.[20] Lévi-Strauss' premise is that language of all social phenomena, is the only one that has been studied scientifically in the strict sense of the word. The study of phonemics, for instance, has made it possible to penetrate through the level of perceived speech into the laws underlying language that govern unconscious thinking.

Structuralism investigates other social phenomena in the same way as language is studied as an expression of the underlying universal laws that form the basis of the functions of the mind itself. In the structuralist view, the structure of language is similar to the structure of culture in general, as they both inevitably reflect the structure of the human mind. Thus, structuralism seeks to discover the general structure of the mind hidden behind the extraordinary diversity of cultural variation. It does not expect to find these universals in the everyday level of perception, but in hidden, unconscious regularities.

The nature of art, and of architecture as a specific language of art, is more clearly conceived if the general structuralist view of the nature of culture is supplemented by the basic premises of transformational linguistics, namely, that language is a two-level structure.

THE TWO LEVELS OF LINGUISTIC MEANING

Transformational grammar, as developed by Noam Chomsky, is itself a child of the structuralist approach to language. Chomsky starts with the observation that all grammars of all languages have a certain general structure in common. Language originates in the speaker's inner patterns of meaning, which he transforms into sound by speaking. The receiver, in turn, receives these sounds and transforms them into his own internal meanings. Chomsky calls these 'internal meanings' *deep structure*, and sound patterns he calls *surface structure*. He believes

THE SYMBOLISM OF BASIC FORMS

18 A square talisman of the Navajos, a ritual object which depicts the gap between the material and the spiritual world.

19 The position of the Buddha's fingers denotes perfection—a circle with neither beginning nor end.

20 *Universal unity* by the Japanese painter Yasuichi Awakawa.

that man has a genetic ability to generate surface structures and deep structures. The transfer from the speaker's deep structure to his surface structure and on to the receiver's deep structure takes place through transformation. In the act of transformation, the relationship between the deep structure and the surface structure corresponds to certain laws known as syntax. The aim of the discipline is to develop a set of rules for syntactic transformation to help the analysis of the transfer from the deep structure of meaning to the surface structure of sounds.[21]

The great advantage of the structuralist-transformationalist view is that it permits the simultaneous study of the diversity of cultures and universal identity. Previously, one or the other had to be omitted as they were considered mutually exclusive approaches. In the structuralist view, both occur simultaneously and are equally important, but are manifested on different levels of perception—diversity appears on the surface level of ordinary perception, whereas universality is to be found in the analysis of the processes of the human mind.

Deep structure constants can likewise be discovered behind the immense variation of architectural forms in all ages and civilizations. Structuralism and transformationalism together open up a manifestly useful approach to the characteristic features of architecture and its links with culture, as well as to the understanding of architectural communication. These ideas are further supplemented by the views of depth psychology on the subconscious language of art.

SURFACE STRUCTURE AND DEEP STRUCTURE IN ART

In his controversial memoirs Dimitri Shostakovich says, "Music will always have two levels."[22] The hypothesis of two levels of artistic expression also lies at the root of the analysis of art using the terms of depth psychology.

In accordance with the structuralist view, many scholars have similarly assumed that the main effects of the language of art are not to be found in its immediately perceived structure, that is, by the analysis of style or content, but in unconsciously delivered messages based on the immutable ways in which the language of art affects people. The same hypothesis can be made about the language of architecture.

Anton Ehrenzweig and others have shown that the conscious aims of a work of art are irrelevant for its artistic message; in fact, the essential message of a work of art is linked with the unconscious deep structure of art. Ehrenzweig has also noted that artistic structuring—in its creative and experiential aspects—primarily makes use of an unstructured and unconscious form of perception: the language of art is communicated through perception, which differs from our normal perceptions.[23]

21

22

23

24

THE CIRCLE AND THE SQUARE—
THE BASIC ORIENTATION

21 Hieroglyph representing an Egyptian city: *nywt.*
    The *Templum* sign indicates a space or cult site marked out by Roman augurs for religious purposes.
22 The *Templum* of Heaven.
23 The *Templum* of Earth.
24 Assurbanipal's Camp. Reliefs in Assurbanipal's palace at Nimrud, c. 900 B.C..

25 Cave drawing in Bohuslän, Sweden.
26 A square within a circle: map of the
    holy city of Benares. The squaring of
    the circle was also one of the great
    aims of the alchemists.
27 The Celtic cross, a universal symbol
    for perfect cosmic harmony. A
    Mexican fishing village in a lagoon,
    Pacific coast.

25

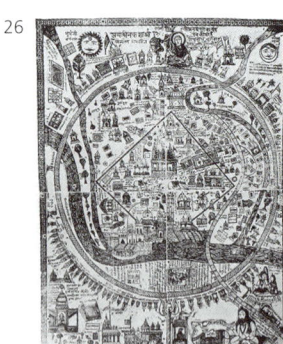

26

27

The language of art, then, has a surface structure and a deep structure, as in Chomsky's linguistic model. The surface structure contains
the artist's conscious intentions concerning style and content; these
are connected with the cultural conventions of the community. The
deep structure contains the artist's subliminal meaning and message,
based on the collective unconscious and archetypes. In *Architecture
and its Interpretation*, which approaches the artistic problem via the
study of semiotics, J. P. Bonta also distinguishes between the two levels
on which architecture can affect the viewer, labeling them signals and
indices. Signals are defined as signs produced for a fixed communicative purpose, whereas indices operate indirectly and unintentionally
in communication.[24] This view clearly corresponds to the distinction
between surface structure and deep-structure meaning in the language
of art.

The mainstream of architectural research has concentrated thus far
on the analysis of the surface structure of the language of architecture,
that is to say, comparisons of function and form, structural architectonic compositions and patterning of forms, and the use of conventional symbols. In ignoring the deep-structure meaning of the language
of architecture, this research has in fact been unable to discover anything relevant with regard to the nature of artistic communication in
architecture. The general analysis of architecture, in terms of conscious
aims and styles, typical of most architectural training and criticism, has
been unable to comprehend the level of artistic communication through
architecture.

Hans Sedlmayr, in his analysis of architecture based on "the
method of critical forms," says, "in the same way as the analysis of the
human mind, the analysis of art must ignore the surface structure of
ideals."[25]

Bonta also contends that the meanings consciously intended by
the architect are irrelevant: what is relevant in architectural communication is interpretation. The architect himself may be unable to
express his intentions verbally or he may strive for meanings that prove
insignificant for experiencing and interpreting the actual result. Bonta's
view emphasizes the dynamics of interpreting a work of art; here, different interpretations of the same work of architecture may also be in
complete contradiction with one another, but this superficial failure in
communication is part of the basic nature of art.[26]

Centuries and millennia later, it will in any case be impossible to
discern or comprehend the intended message of a work of art, connected
as it was with the cultural conventions current at the time of the work's
creation. The inevitable disappearance of the original surface meaning,

THE MANDALA

28 Nepalese mandala, c. 1700.
29 The phases of meditation according to Pali scriptures.
30 The way of the meditator through phases of meditation.
31 Plan of the temple of Barabudur.
32 The meditator's way drawn on top of a plan of the temple of Barabudur.

28

29

30

31

32

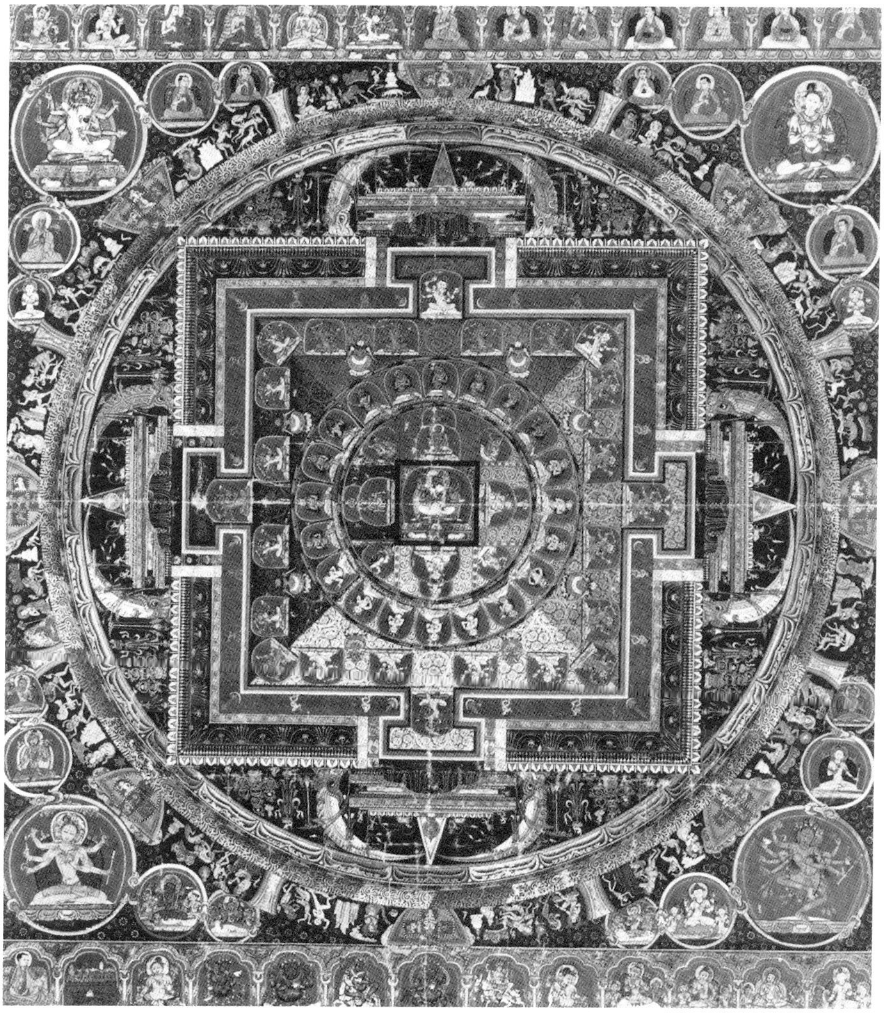

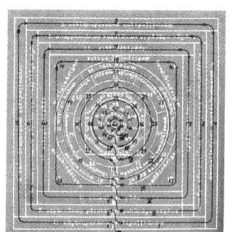

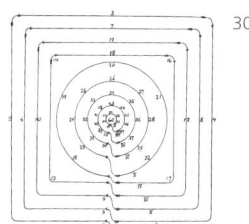

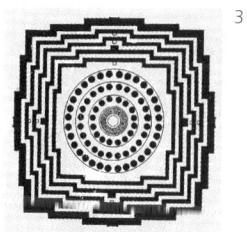

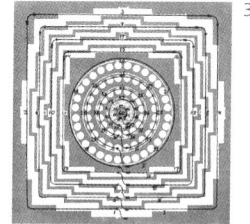

33

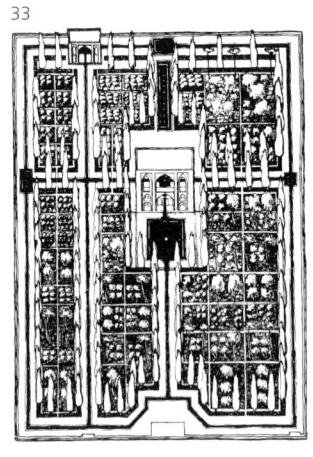

34

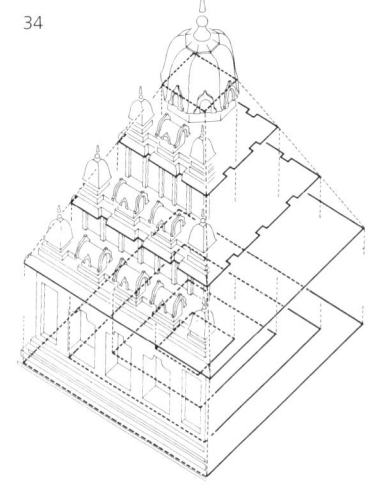

35

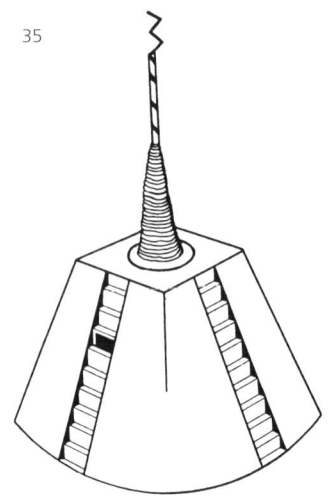

36

37

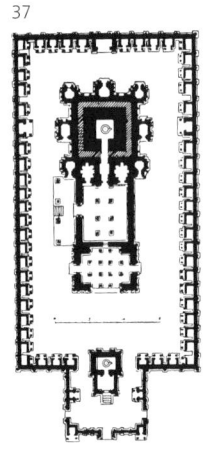

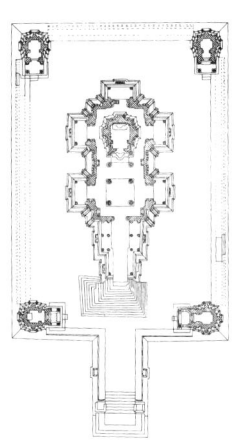

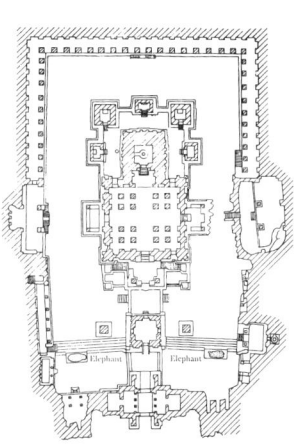

and the evolution of a new link in keeping with the spirit of each age, seem to be elements of the immortality of art. The deep-structure message of art speaks its archetypal language to all ages. The survival of art across fundamental cultural and temporal borders is incontrovertible proof of the existence of the permanent, universal language of art. The study of myths has in fact brought to light the existence and appearance of the same archetypal figures and experiences in the art of different civilizations.

THE SECRET LANGUAGE OF ARCHETYPES

Sigmund Freud described the images and associations arising from our dream as "archaic remnants of the mind"; correlatives of these remnants can be found in primitive thought, myth, and sacred rites. C.G. Jung later gave them the name 'archetype.'[27] These 'historical' associations operate as a link between the world of the intellect and the world of instinct. Jung defines archetypes as both patterns and emotions that tend to generate certain associations and meanings. In essence, archetypes do not have fixed, closed symbolic values, but instead act as generators of associations: they encourage constant reinterpretation. "They are pieces of life itself—images that are integrally connected to the individual by the bridge of the emotions," as Jung remarked.[28]

Archetypes are also the essential material of the formally simple language of architecture. Sinclair Gauldie expressly assumes the existence of an archetypal architectural language: "The building which, long after the fashionable idioms of its time have degenerated into clichés, still continues to contribute some memorable quality to human life is the building which draws its communicative force from the unchanging emotional associations in the architectural language, those which are most deeply rooted in the common sensory experience of humanity."[29]

Adrian Stokes' statement, "Architectural forms are a language confined to the joining of a few ideographs of immense ramification," also points towards the archetypal significance of the language of architecture.[30]

THE ARCHETYPAL MEANING OF BASIC ARCHITECTURAL FORMS

In the visual arts in general, and in architecture in particular, the basic forms dominate: the circle, the square, the triangle, and the basic orientation and numbers. The circle, for instance, is a symbol of the self, expressing all the dimensions of the psyche, including the man-nature relationship. In primitive sun worship and in modern religion, in myths and dreams, in the mandalas of Tibetan monks, in town plans, and in the circular systems of early astronomers, the circle always indicates

THE SPATIAL MANDALA

33 The spatial mandala of the Persian gardens symbolizes Paradise.

34 The spatial, cosmological, and ritual mandala of Dharmarajah-Ratha.

35 The "ark" of the Dogon tribe: "the granary of the Master of the Pure Earth," the tribe's condensed and complex mythological and cosmological symbol.

36 A spatial mandala in the ritual dance of the Nauatl, a Mexican Indian tribe. Four dancers descend by ropes from a revolving platform on the top of a column. After circling the column 13 times they touch ground. 4 x 13 = 52 rounds, symbolising the Indians' "century" of 52 years.

37 These plans of Indian temples are also yantra figures, objects of meditation.

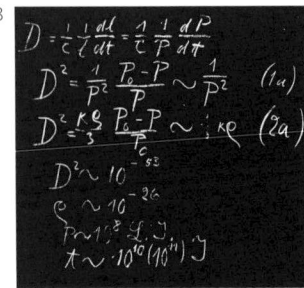

38

39

40

41

the unity of life.[31] The square, in turn, is an expression of earthbound static materialism, the body and reality.

Of the cardinal numbers, four is crucial, for instance, in Biblical exegesis.[32] The number four appears in multiple contexts: the four rivers of Paradise, the four Fathers of the Latin church, four-level exegetics, the four cardinal virtues, the four cardinal points, and the four quadrants of the world.

The mandala, an object of meditation that represents the cosmos in relation to divine forces, is a curious mixture of the basic forms. The mandala is usually associated with Oriental culture, but it also appears in Christian art. In architecture and town planning, the mandala is also of great significance. An interesting example of the squaring of the circle—the symbolic joining of the universe with the man-built world—is Plutarch's account of the contradictory founding rites of Rome, the *Urbs Quadrata*.[33] These rites were based on the circle. The founding rites and early maps of many other towns are based on overlapping circle and square images, regardless of geographical facts. The same archetypal significance of the basic forms was usually inherent in the orientation and siting of cult buildings. These rites achieved the ritual integration of the cosmos and man and the demarcation of the basic orientation and psychic center.

The Dogon tribe of Mali has condensed its creation myth and world picture, and its rules of conduct derived from them, into a symbolic granary or an ark forming a kind of three-dimensional mandala, consisting of a combination of circles and squares that functions as a key to the world.[34]

The abstract character of Modern architecture also acquires expressive power and emotional effect from the unconscious meanings of its basic forms.

THE AUTONOMY OF MODERNISM

In the history of art, the simplicity of abstract forms is linked with archetypal associations. By rejecting a programmatic representative subject and an immediately ascertainable descriptive link with the perceptual world, modern art has given rise to the basic misconception that abstract art is a mere formal game which appeals to the senses but has no links with external reality. As Anton Ehrenzweig says, however, "Scientific abstraction differs from an empty generalization in the way in which potent abstract art differs from empty ornament."[35] The essence of the abstraction is in condensing meanings on several levels, not in pure form devoid of significance. Many influential artists have made statements that have contributed to this fallacy. An illustrative example of this self-sufficient view is Frank Stella's contention that "practically always one winds up saying that there is something else besides color on the canvas. My painting starts from the premise that only what can be seen is there."[36] In spite of Stella's claim, his paintings awaken archetypal memories that seek formulation in the viewer's mind. This mutual influence of the abstract form and the unconscious memories and associations it arouses underlies the artistic effect of the painting.

The only content of Modern architecture, it has been assumed, is the abstract and self-contained message of beauty. The new architecture of our century was described by Le Corbusier's well-known credo as the "skillful, correct and magnificent interplay of interrelated building masses in light," with the implication that architecture is an autonomous visual construct.[37]

Nikolaus Pevsner, the influential architectural historian, voiced his belief in the independence of Modernism: "The Modern Movement is a genuine and independent style,"[38] and Philip Johnson made the rash claim that "the International Style was its own justification."[39] However, Johnson's most recent work shows that he, too, has lost his belief in the cultural independence of the language of Modern architecture. The recent condemnation of Modernism is distinctly due to the Modernists' programmatic repudiation of the historical content of the language of architecture. Both the redemptive function of architecture claimed by the pioneers of Modernism—"architecture or revolution"[40]—and the fashionable accusation that the inhumanity of our new environment is the architects' fault, are based on an ignorance of the links between architecture and culture.

THE SECOND LANGUAGE OF ARCHITECTURE

The general ideas in the various scientific fields described above give rise to the hypothesis that architectural communication also occurs on two levels—the level of consciously used stylistic material and that of the unconscious deep-structure systems. Following Chomsky, we may assume that architectural communication is only possible if the language of architecture—in this case consisting of sensory perception—has unconscious, deep-structure equivalents in the human mind. The deep-structure meanings unconsciously aroused by the architectural experience are memories and associations connected with the synesthetic mental images of early childhood, our spatio-kinetic experiences, and collective archetypes. These unconscious meanings, like dreams, have an independent expression apart from surface structure, an expression that can be interpreted just as dreams can be explained.

ABSTRACTION AND UNCONSCIOUS PERCEPTION

38 The famous blackboard Albert Einstein used when lecturing on relativity at Oxford in 1931.

39 A diagram of changes showing the working of the transcendental Tao and the links between the macrocosm and the microcosm. The Taoist Canon, Sung dynasty.

40 Subconscious interpretations infiltrate conscious perception. Henry Michaux, drawing, 1962.

41 Fifteen stones on a raked expanse of sand symbolize, among many possibilities, islands rising out of the ocean and the mountains of China. The rock garden of the Zen temple of Ryoan-ji in Kyoto.

42 A sign is a message based on an
    agreement. A sign always represents
    less than the object it signifies.

43 The content of a symbol is always
    greater than its immediate context
    of meaning, according to C.G. Jung.
    Christ and the four Evangelists, three
    of whom are represented in animal
    forms. The *vesica pisces* form used as
    a background for the Christ figure is
    derived from the circle constructions
    used in the temple orientation ritual.

44 The same symbolic representation in
    Egyptian mythology. The four sons
    of Horus—three of them likewise in
    animal shapes.

45 The Egyptian *ankh* sign stands for
    life, the universe, and man.

46 Female figure, the Cyclades,
    c. 2500 B.C..

47 Most of Henry Moore's sculptures
    take their power from rich emotional
    associations with the Great Mother
    and Mother Earth archetype. Henry
    Moore, *Sheep Piece*, 1972.

Responding to the sudden and deep impact certain buildings have on his mind, the architect Colin St John Wilson says, "It is as if I am being manipulated by some subliminal code, not to be translated into words, which acts directly on the nervous system and imagination, at the same time stirring intimations of meaning with vivid spatial experience as though they were one thing. It is my belief that the code acts so directly and vividly upon us because it is strangely familiar; it is in fact the first language we ever learned, long before words, and which is now recalled to us through art, which alone holds the key to revive it..."[41]

René Huyghe wrote in 1939, "Art is for the story of human societies what the dreams of an individual are for the psychiatrist... Many think of art as a mere diversion, a thing that is purely marginal to the real business of life, they do not see that it looks into life's very heart and lays bare its unconscious secrets, that it contains the most honest confessions, confessions that have within them the least element of calculation and must therefore be accounted exceptionally sincere."[42]

Adrian Stokes holds the same view—"Art is the face of mankind," he writes—and postulates that "Architecture, the most abstract of the visual arts, is specially adapted to stressing such experience with the smallest element of concealment."[43]

The unconscious language of objects, the environment, and architecture still awaits an interpreter, however. Hans Sedlmayr's study of the dehumanization of culture from the French Revolution to the present day gives rise to serious thought, even if his view of the message of modern art is conservative and one-sided.

A concealed yet jarring message is rising to the surface from beneath the seemingly elegant and controlled surfaces of techno-economical rationalism prevalent in the building of the past decade. On the level of style, the arrogant expression of total control masks an obvious cry of distress—after all, hubris was the great sin that finally destroyed even the mightiest of Greek heroes.

The standardized architecture of the post-1960s has lost the ability to communicate, it has been said, and has turned into a formal game with only internal rules defined by narrow dogmas. But are the town centers and housing areas of the last ten years, those monuments to industrial welfare and reason, really devoid of message? Do they not speak involuntarily, but pleadingly, of the alienation of industrial man, of the victory of materialism and objects, and of the shattered interaction between the ego and the world? To borrow the title of Richard Sennett's book, do they not testify to "The Fall of Public Man"?[44]

"Modern man's most urgent need is to discover the reality and value of the inner subjective world, to discover the symbolic life... The

42

45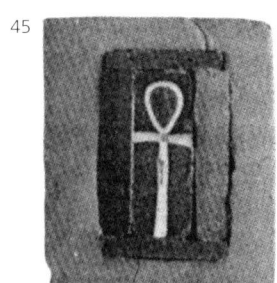

46

43

44

47

48

49

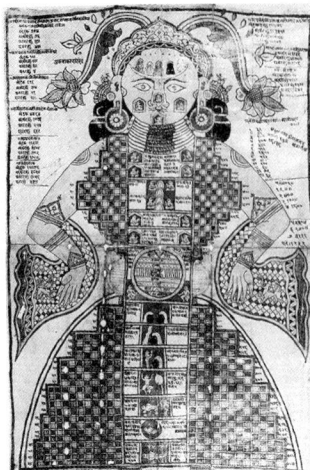

50

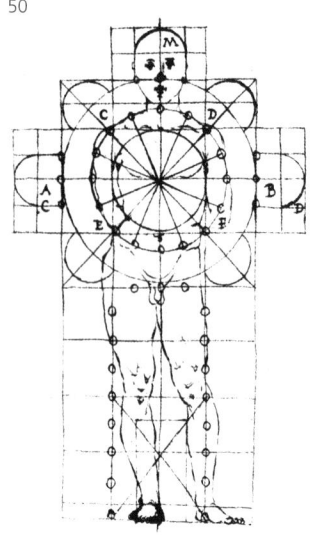

51

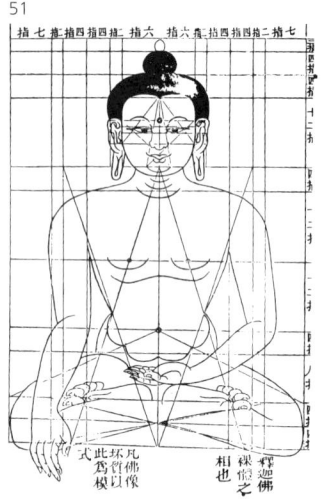

52

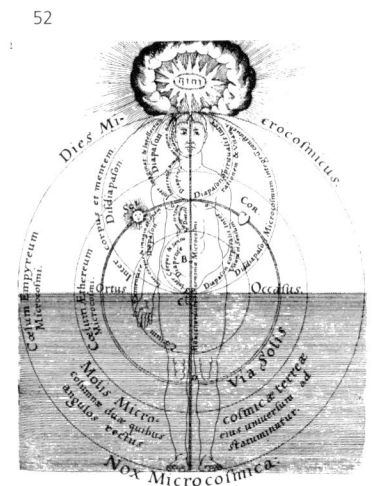

53

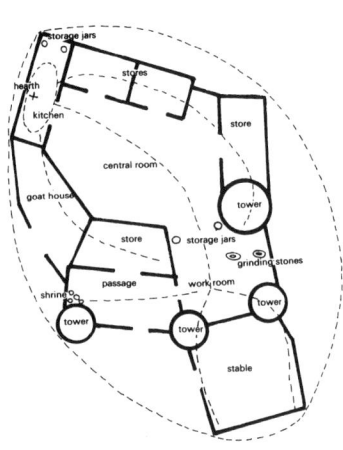

symbolic life in some form is a prerequisite for psychic health," says E. F. Edinger.[45]

It is as much a mistake to think that the language of architecture is lost, as to make the assumption that the language of architecture is independent of the other manifestations of culture. Sedlmayr's *Art in Crisis* should really be 'Art of Crisis.' Art and architecture always have an element of unconscious communication, but the message of this hidden language varies—it may express faith in a more human future, cynical submission to manipulation, defiant confidence in the power of reason to rule the world, or fear of the loss of our ties with nature or our own past.

Our age has lost the awareness that the act of building inevitably involves a metaphysical message, a reflection of a view of the world and man's relationship to the world. Buildings and other human acts are not dictated by purely practical needs—they always constitute a dialogue with the world and contribute to forming the relationship of the individual ego or the collective identity of a cultural community to time and the world.

We do not live in dissociated material and spiritual worlds; they interpenetrate fully. The way we articulate space is inseparable from our cultural articulation of other aspects of our world of experience and meaning. As Edward T. Hall remarks, we imperceptibly transform physical space into cosmological space.[46]

THE NOVELTY FALLACY

Art certainly strives for new, virginal expression, but the value of uniqueness resulting from the commercialization of art has made novelty the sole criterion of artistic quality. Art's more relevant ambition strives for an integrated experience of the world and for a return to the basic forms of human experience, understandings that our culture has lost. In the language of art, it is essential to differentiate between surface-structure surprises aimed at startling effects and timeless deep-structure messages. In our century, architecture, as with so many activities, has changed from a symbolic language bound to our cultural heritage, into an isolated image whose value is in its novelty, not in its adaptability to surroundings or its continuation of the cultural heritage. Change, novelty, and consumption have become obsessions to the point at which architecture has resigned its role in transmitting the relationship of people and culture to the world. The 'disposable styles' of the 1960s and 1970s are extreme manifestations of this development.

Ideas have also become commodities in our consumer society. The journalistic historiography of architecture, even more popular over the

54

55

56

57

past ten years, produces classifications and definitions at the rate of daily news. This obsession with novel categorization has turned architecture, too, into consumer information.

In the 1660s, Sir Christopher Wren wrote that architecture should bear "the Attribute of the eternal" and that it should be "the only thing incapable of new Fashions."[47]

The new expressions of art arise from individuals, but they should have the chance to take root in culture before they are swept aside. Expressions of art have their own characteristic period of development and growth. A new form of expression is born unconsciously from the internal compulsion of its deep-structure significance. Gradually this expression becomes part of the prevalent normative structures and begins to be used consciously. When it loses its potential for producing deep-structure associations, such expression also loses its communicative potential as art. The necrophilic impression created by the eclectic architecture of this decade is a result of the disappearance of the original creative forces underlying the expressions of both Modern architecture and any historically referenced order. Stylistic elements have been transformed into intentional calculation.

The communicative content of our contemporary language of architecture has suffered for two opposite reasons. The anarchistic Post-Modern renewal of historicized architectural expression has severed the ties of cultural comprehension to the language of architecture, while a stereotyped Modernist expression uses a vocabulary of architecture divorced from its psychological deep-structure meanings.

•

In the chapter entitled "Ceci tuera cela," which Victor Hugo added to the eighth edition of *Notre Dame de Paris*, the cathedral's archdeacon says cryptically that literature will kill architecture. Hugo analyzes the idea as follows: "The statement revealed a premonition that in changing shape the human idea would also change its form of expression, that the leading idea of each generation would no longer be recorded with the same substance and in the same form, that the firm and lasting book of stone would give way to an even firmer and more lasting printed book."[48] Hugo's prediction that architecture would lose its status to new media as the most effective means of cultural communication has come true. But new media have not taken over architecture's position because of greater firmness and durability; on the contrary, they have won precisely because they are fast and momentary. Now that styles, too, have become commodities in our consumer society, architecture has proved a

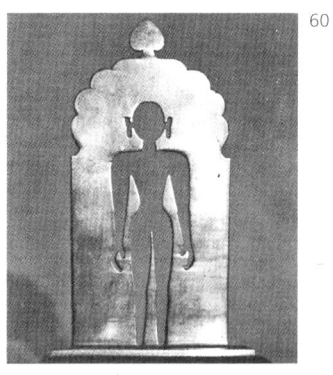

58 The *mihrab* of the Córdoba mosque is a spiritualised doorway.
59 The dramatic 'Moon Door' of the Wu-Shu monastery in China.
60 The liberation of spirit from matter. 18th century Jain bronze icon.

61

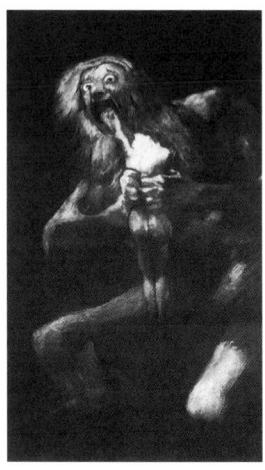

62

hopelessly clumsy medium for this era of disposable mass communication. Post-Modernism's cynically calculated use of shifting styles, and the adoption of genres utterly unprecedented in architecture—namely humor, parody, irony, and satire—may be interpreted as architecture's pathetic attempt to regain its lost status in today's meaningless flow of information.

Surely architecture possesses more dignity, more ambition. The purpose of architecture is to objectify and clarify the mutual relations of the members of the community, and their relationship with the institutions and the world in which they live. The great psychological task of architecture is to create a sense of cultural continuity. Thus, in its deepest significance, the art of architecture is ever on the side of preservation, not of change as an end in itself.

SELF-DESTRUCTIVE CULTURE AND THE CULT OF THE PAST.

Two false roads for architecture: a rootless recourse to the past, and a belief in the omnipotence of technology and science.

61 The cult of the past, archaism, promises a false flight into mythical memories of an idealized past. Kaiser Wilhelm I dressed as a Teutonic knight. Arnold Toynbee, *A Study of History*, 1972.

62 Francisco Goya, *Saturn eating his son*, painting, 1820–23, Museo del Prado, Madrid.

63 Detail of the rock surfaces of the Island of Hailuoto's harbor on which traditionally the fishing boats are painted.

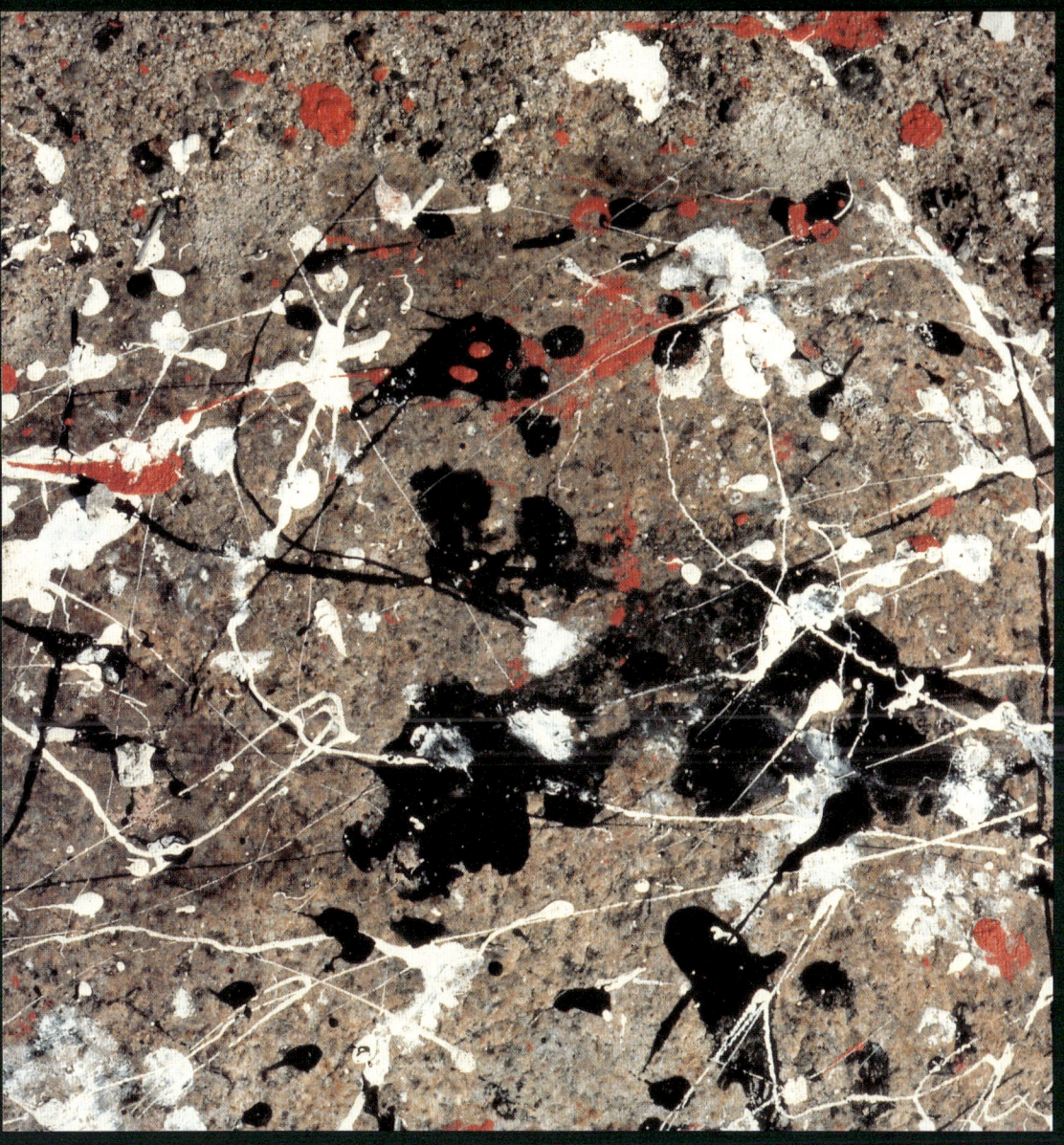

ARCHITECTURE AND THE OBSESSIONS OF OUR TIMES

A View of the Nihilism of Building
(1983)

THE CONDEMNATION OF THE MODERN MOVEMENT

Contemporary architecture has been condemned both by public opinion and by those architects who have lost faith in the Modern Movement. The two most notable pieces of confessional writing by such converted colleagues are *Form Follows Fiasco* by Peter Blake, the biographer of the Modern Movement's central masters, and *Farväl till funktionalismen (Farewell to Functionalism)* by Hans Asplund, son of Erik Gunnar Asplund, the Nordic pioneer of Modern architecture.[1] The same accusations have been echoed by many others, among them Leon Krier and David Watkins. Sweeping statements and generalizations are peculiar to these critics of the Modern Movement—Hans Asplund, for instance, mentions Hitler and Stalin as the two individuals who have most reinforced Modern architecture's position of power.[2]

In these recriminatory writings, the pioneers of the Modern Movement and the design concepts initiated by them, are named as being responsible for the environmental erosion of the industrialized world. The failure of Modern architecture is blamed on its false theoretical basis and formal limitations.

Behind this thinking lies an unpronounced presumption that architecture, as an idiom, is separate from all other cultural manifestations. But, is not the idea of one particular style of architecture being responsible for the miserable state of man's environment the reverse of the pioneering generation's Utopian view that 'correct' architecture can morally transform humanity—*"l'architecture ou revolution"* in the manner of Le Corbusier's program?[3] Whereas the Modern Movement believed in Modern architecture as the savior of our culture, today's accusers have declared it the scapegoat of environmental decay.

Ludwig Wittgenstein's *Culture and Value* contains a significant sentence concerning architecture: "Architecture immortalizes and glorifies something. Hence there can be no architecture where there is nothing to glorify."[4] Wittgenstein's serious interest in architecture, as well as his close friendship with Adolf Loos, lends credence to his words.

The philosopher's thought signifies that the content manifested in architecture fundamentally derives from outside the art form itself. Wittgenstein forces us to confess that the spiritual emptiness we experience in today's typical architecture reflects, after all, the emptiness of our collective spirit.

Architecture, like all other human activity, necessarily manifests the substance of its cultural context. Cultural structures affect all the material and intellectual manifestations of a particular age, and only "poets and criminals are able to free themselves from the conventions of culture," as Marshall McLuhan states.[5]

Therefore, to blame today's patently detrimental environment on a credo that was published half a century ago is simply without basis. To blame a handful of deceased architects for our own generation's inability to build humane cities is equally naïve.

THE MEANING OF BUILDING

Of course, the general drift towards a dreary, mechanical style of building cannot result from style itself, but from those collective factors regarding meaning that the form of building in question manifests and embodies. The real reasons for the inhumanity of our environment should be sought among the distortions of our imagery, our thinking, and our values. As I have remarked in another context, before their appearance on the edges of our cities, the concrete housing-boxes have existed in our own heads. The same mental distortions behind those aims, means of control, and methods of organization and production, are also the ones that cause our lives to become separated from humane values.

These distortions appear on the whole unconsciously, and even against our conscious efforts. All parties involved in building, for instance, earnestly assure society to act on the side of humane aims, whereas the final result only seldom bespeaks humanity.

Psychiatry uses a term called 'paradox intention,' for a distortion in behavior in which an intended action turns into its opposite, being driven into this by a motive suppressed from consciousness. The architecture of our day contains marked elements of this paradoxical and compulsive tendency. This unconscious and seemingly predestined drift towards inhumaneness gives rise to a need to name those responsible for this tendency.

THE OBSESSIONS OF OUR TIME

Erich Fromm and Herbert Marcuse, among others, have examined in their celebrated works the paradoxical distortions of industrialized man's thoughts and deeds. These social psychiatrists' literary works as a whole are inspiring reading for architects. [6]

As the title suggests, Marcuse's book, *One-Dimensional Man*, analyzes the disappearance of multi-dimensional and plastic qualities from our thoughts and consciousness. One sees an immediate and clear connection between Marcuse's thoughts and the problems of architecture. Building, after all, due to its existential directness and necessity, manifests most concretely the characteristics of our minds. One-dimensional man builds for himself one-dimensional architecture.

What mental distortions explain the fateful increase of inhumaneness in the architecture of our day? I have chosen the concepts of obsession and compulsion neuroses as the explanatory factors. [7] A compulsion neurosis can manifest itself in the form of a compulsion for extremely varied forms of behavior or thought. Many people have, for example, a compulsion to constantly wash their hands or to check that the door is locked. Other people are compelled by their neurosis either to step on the lines of the seams, or to avoid them, when walking on a surface of paving stones. Phobias are also compulsive forms of behavior, caused by involuntarily suppressed areas of the psyche, the troublesomeness or actual harmfulness of which the person in question may be quite aware of without being able to do anything about the compulsive behavior.

Certain reactions manifesting an obsessive quality appear in our culture on a collective level, and are manifested harmfully in our standardized architecture. This manner of building, regarded as 'rational' and now dominant throughout the world, in fact clearly contains obsessive features. Despite its supposed rationality, contemporary architecture seems to be guided by extremely irrational and negative forces. The inveterate continuation of a rigid architectural style, even after its harmfulness has been realized, reflects also an unconscious cultural compulsiveness.

This compulsiveness is manifested in certain of our psychological tendencies affecting architecture: our obsessed relation to time and tradition, our self-referential aspiration to freedom, our passion for manipulation, and our inclination to avoid hierarchy, to emphasize borders, and to fall into meaninglessness.

The Modern Movement is here examined as a standard style of industrial culture, and not as a set of the artistic masterpieces of our time. The Modern Movement has produced numerous works that in their forceful power of artistic expression compete with the architectural monuments of any era. But, having transformed over the course of fifty years into the building practice of the industrial world, the movement has lost both its visual force and spiritual content. Lacking an inborn quality characteristic of both vernacular and high-style historical tradition, the Modern Movement always requires a strong, innovative, and individual contribution. In fact, the greatest shortcoming of the Modern Movement is its inability to transform into a positive vernacular tradition.

Thus, despite its capacity for artistic expression, the Modern Movement has contained from its inception the potential seeds of its demise, those elements of impoverishment and dehumanization that the development of our industrial consumer society has highlighted to tragic proportions.

THE OBSESSION OF TIME

An essential mental motif of artistic expression is the unconscious fear of death. By transferring our world view and experience into a material shape we believe we can continue our limited existence. In architecture, this aspiration to immortalize man's life is particularly clear. "A house constitutes a body of images that give mankind proofs or the illusion of stability," Gaston Bachelard writes in his enigmatic but influential book *The Poetics of Space*.[8] The youthful Alvar Aalto, writing in his early journals, understood this as well, "Form is nothing else but a concentrated wish for everlasting life on earth."[9]

Time is an essential psychic dimension in art in another sense, as well. A work of art condenses both collective and individual history to the moment of artistic experience. Hence, an experience of art is a multi-dimensional time experience.

Industrial Man has a frustrated relationship with time. The frustration results from a repressed attitude towards aging and death. The conversion of the cyclical time concept into a linear view, with an absolute beginning and end, brought the frustration of irreversibility to our experience of time. Industrial Man tries to halt time in the present tense in order to live a timeless youth. Time is transformed into a materialized commodity. The natural and inevitable aging of people, buildings, and objects is repressed. In a welfare society, the elderly are transferred to the outskirts of consciousness, aging and deterioration are hardly regarded as design factors, and objects of use are utterly disposable. The requirement for modernity in the arts reflects the same irrational compulsiveness in our relation to the element of time.

In the American psychotherapist Gotthard Booth's view, "The natural satisfaction of life comes from a vigorous participation in the life that extends beyond the life of the individual."[10] A way of life that exceeds the limits of individual life is also a participation in the progression of tradition. Modernism has programmatically attempted to interrupt this progression. Having discarded tradition, and thus the possibility of participation in a supra-individual pattern of life, modern man has obliged himself to seek his psychically essential experience of continuity in the spatial dimension, in place instead of in time. Instead of works intended for eternity, expanding his grasp of time, Industrial Man attempts to expand his life by expanding his acts in space—today, all the way to outer space. Participation in the fabric of tradition has been replaced by a compulsive desire for universality.

The aspiration for universality has resulted in the loss of situational responses and in the emergence of an alienated intellectualism, a kind of universal neutrality, and a lack of context. As a materialistic ideology converts ideas into products of consumption, the nature of true artistic quality is obscured. The rejection of tradition results in the inherent value of novelty and uniqueness and a gradual privatization of culture. Modern art thus becomes entirely identified with the notion of novelty.

Igor Stravinsky, writing in *The Poetics of Music*, deliberates on the privatization of the language of art and the consequent loss of communication capacity: "The requirement for individuality and intellectual anarchy...constructs its own language, its vocabulary and artistic means. The use of proven means and established forms is generally forbidden and thus the artist ends up talking in a language with which his audience has no contact. His art becomes unique, indeed, in the sense that its world is totally closed and it does not contain any possibility for communication."[11] Stravinsky holds the concept as so central an ingredient to art that he concludes, "Everything that remains outside of tradition is plagiarism..."[12] By rejecting tradition, architecture drifts towards a deadening uniformity on the one hand, and towards a rootless anarchy of expression on the other. Architecture, as with art or language in general, can only progress meaningfully through an accumulative tradition, one that balances both reforming and preserving elements in expression.

THE DELUSION OF FREEDOM

Modern thinking, social ideals, and art aspire to freedom, understood as an unchallenged independence from nature, tradition, established conventions, and the limitations of matter. This desire for freedom has also developed into an inherent value.

The ultimate possibility of freedom is philosophy's eternal question, but Industrial Man is satisfied with the mere illusion of freedom.

Limitations on freedom—in the form of superstition, religious belief, or earthly tyranny—may indeed have disappeared, but the invisible forces directing industrial materialism even more unconditionally restrict our freedom. To a tragic degree, the illusion of freedom and choice has become the basic strategy of our consumption society.

Moreover, freedom may even prove to be a delusion. Marcuse observes, "Underneath its obvious dynamics, this society is a thoroughly static system of life; self-propelling in its obsessive productivity and its beneficial coordination."[13] Marcuse's thought is easily associated with the contemporary design contradiction: regardless of our neurotic appreciations of individuality, we produce environments without individuality.

At the same time as Industrial Man compulsively yearns for freedom, Erich Fromm demonstrates, he also has a panic-stricken fear of freedom.[14] In architecture, for instance, this is reflected in the discrepancy between our wonder at the unlimited possibilities opened up by technology and our fearful grasp of conventions.

Psychoanalytic theory includes the notion of defense mechanisms.[15] A defensive mechanism represses an undesired matter from our consciousness by transforming or shifting it into an acceptable guise. One psychic defense mechanism is called rationalization. As a psychoanalytical concept, rationalization means the unconscious explaining of deeds, or their motives, as something other than the actual facts.

The characteristic rationalizations of our society reflect a clear defensive behavior against an open and unprejudiced confrontation with reality. Today's popular attempts to explain the art of building by the construction of logic, measures, and figures are not only a positive search for clarity, but simultaneously, and perhaps more significantly, a defensive attempt to restrain the unconscious substance of art. This defensiveness appears frequently in the aggressive denial of artistic expression and value among technocrats.

The neurotic appreciation of freedom is reflected in the valuation of uniqueness, transforming art into another realm of fashion. The task of art ought to be a deepening of our experience of reality; the swift, fashionable shifts in artistic expression render it yet another medium of estrangement and alienation.

Great artists rarely speak of the dimension of freedom in their work. They emphasize the role of restrictions and constraints in the shaping of their personality and style. Rather than speak of any longing for freedom, they bring forth the disciplined, tradition-bound character of their art form.

Leonardo da Vinci considered resistance more important for an artist than freedom: "Strength is born from constraint and it dies in freedom."[16] In his humane memoirs, *My Life and My Films*, the film director Jean Renoir writes about the "resistance of technique,"[17] while Stravinsky speaks of "the resistance of material and technique."[18] Stravinsky scorns any yearning for freedom: "The ones who try to avoid subordination support unanimously the opposite (counter-traditional) view. They reject constraint and they nourish a hope—always doomed to failure—of finding the secret of strength in freedom. They do not find anything but the arbitrariness of freaks and disorder, they lose all control, they go astray…"[19]

Manifestos and histories of Modern architecture speak frequently of 'liberating' architecture. Le Corbusier's well-known and influential 'five points of new architecture' of 1926 exemplify this tendency to see the evolution of architecture as 'liberation.' Louis Kahn was the first to bring freedom's opposite to contemporary architectural thought: the eternal themes of construction. He was concerned by what "brick and vault themselves wanted to become."[20] The obsession with freedom in the name of liberating artistic expression has, however, led architecture to the unfortunate rejection of its timeless rules and its disciplinary structure. The 'liberation' of architectural expression has most often meant the mere denial and rejection of its deepest emotional means.

During the past decade, demands have again been frequently voiced to liberate architecture—on the one hand from 'the cul-de-sac of functionalism,' and on the other from 'the straitjacket of rationalism' or 'the chains of purist aesthetics.' In our era of ultimate confusion, should not architecture rather be reconnected with its tectonic and mythical substance, to the eternal traditions of construction?

THE HUBRIS OF MANIPULATION

The greatest sin of Antiquity was *hubris*, the sense of unmerited omnipotence by which man set about to compete with the gods. In his own omnipotence, industrialized man no longer seems to need either the higher forces or the wisdom of previous generations.

Our aspiration for freedom results in the compulsive manipulation peculiar to our scientific and technological culture. We no longer live as part of tradition and nature. Reality has become an object outside ourselves, a commodity that we fashion to suit our needs and passions. The world is not a part of our life's experience, but a resource outside ourselves. The subjects of manipulation include nature and natural resources, as well as thoughts and human relations. The manipulative attitude is equally manifest in both pedagogy and medicine, or in the subliminal conditioning characteristic of consumer ideology. However, the freedom gained through manipulation always turns into violence.

Industrial man has forsaken the accumulated wisdom of architectural traditions, while developing a universal method of building based on industrial technique. However, this universality is reached through a disregard for local conditions and resources, not to mention a disregard for culture.

The manipulative approach is characterized by the domination of operationalist thinking in all areas of life, even in such an area of human science as psychology. Operationalist thinking tends to use only such concepts that are explicable in terms of certain operable functions. Interfering concepts, those that cannot be proved by such operations, are eliminated. Marcuse calls this shift in thinking "the attack of radical empiricism."[21] Current construction is dominated by this way of thought and its resultant reduction of thinking to a single dimension. Today's Post-Modernist architecture extends such manipulation to history and its content. This so-called "avant-garde" architecture perhaps so often seems cynical for the very reason that, unlike genuine art, its character is not born from internal resources of cultural tradition and artistic responsibility, but from commercial speculation and manipulative appearances.

THE FEAR OF HIERARCHY

The prime archaic hierarchy is the division between the divine and the earthly. In removing the sanctified, mythical, and ritualistic layers of reality, modern man removes his sense of hierarchy.

Marcuse observes that thought becomes one-dimensional once "the other level of reality" and the tension between the ideal world and everyday reality disappear.[22] Our culture, he believes, has identified ideals with everyday reality and thus has done away with the role of art as an intercessor between these two worlds. In our profane and profit-seeking culture, art has been given the task of creating alternatives for everyday reality, instead of awakening an awareness of the metaphysical dimensions outside everyday consciousness. Building has become sheer technique and no longer provides a connection with the spiritual world through architectural symbols.

"Today's novel feature is the flattening out of the antagonism between culture and social reality through the obliteration of the oppositional, alien and transcendent elements in the higher culture by virtue of which it constituted another dimension of reality. This liquidation of two-dimensional culture takes place not through the denial and rejection of the 'cultural values,' but through their wholesale incorporation into the established order, through their reproduction and display on a massive scale."[23] Marcuse's thought here explains why the forceful principles and forms of early Modernist works, when grafted onto our everyday building practices fifty years later, have lost their content. The syntax of Modern architecture has turned into a usage lacking a message. Spiritual content is not transmitted by any stylistic paradigm; spiritual content must be created anew in each work of art.

Each spatial direction—up, down, in front, behind, right, left—has a separate meaning. The vertical has a fundamentally different meaning than the horizontal. "Even those who have long since ceased to believe in heaven and hell cannot interchange the words 'above' and 'below'," writes Erhart Kästner.[24] The psychoanalyst Fred Fischer has suggested that the unconscious significance of the different spatial directions is already imprinted in the human psyche at the embryonic stage.[25]

Modern man has rationalized space by homogenizing and equating spatial dimensions. The module grid of industrialized building spreads the meaningless and the uniform in all directions. As Gaston Bachelard points out, however, "A house that has been experienced is not an inert box. Inhabited space transcends geometrical space."[26]

Bachelard has noted the total disappearance of verticality from present day urban inhabitation and its transformation to pure horizontality. We have become Joë Bosquet's "one-storied people who have their cellar in their attic."[27] The disappearance of hierarchical composition and the standardization of space have promoted the disappearance of the experience of place.

The important difference of meaning between the top and the bottom of a building has disappeared. The roof-shape signifying the end of a building, its upward directionality, or the more general articulation of such outlines has disappeared, and the vertical and horizontal profiles of buildings have become identical. This homogenizing embodies the notion of extending the building elements in an undifferentiated structure, piling them beside, and on top of, each other.

The intrinsic difference between vertical and horizontal directions has also disappeared from contemporary structures. All structural elements—load-bearing or not—are similar rectangular section profiles. The origin, terminus, and joints of structural elements are left unarticulated. Structures, buildings, and townscapes have all become a mass-produced commodity available by the linear meter.

The obsessive idea of avoiding hierarchy also appears in architecture as an exaggerated demand for flexibility. Flexibility is not merely a conscious operative aim; it is also an unconscious means to avoid any hierarchical differentiation. We are apparently no longer able to create fixed rooms—we make optional 'possibilities.' A permanent spatial disposition is, however, the necessary basis of the language of architecture. Buildings and towns organize the world and reify cultural institutions. In their fanatical striving for flexibility, many of today's most ambitious buildings, such as the Centre Pompidou in Paris, have become mere showpieces of an architectural technique that does not evoke an architectural experience.[28]

THE EMPHASIS ON BOUNDARIES

In our contemporary perception and thinking, boundaries have become so emphasized that we find the simultaneous experience of unrelated phenomena unbearable. We have an anxiety-laden approach to polysemy. We possess an evident compulsion for separation and classification that produces a simplification and objectification of mental images. Our sensory contact with the world becomes 'colder' as visual remoteness gains supremacy over the intimacy of tactility. When man retreats from his unconscious, emotional, and osmotic reciprocity with the world, manipulation, the self-conscious fashioning of this relationship, steps into its place.

Demetri Porphyrios distinguishes between two different modes of thought, namely 1) homotopy, which is based on similarities, and 2) heterotopy, which is based on dissimilarities. The former has a limited capacity to tolerate disarray and confusion, whereas the latter is able to bear unspecified simultaneity. According to Porphyrios, the majority of 20th century architecture is clearly the outcome of homotopic thinking. He regards Alvar Aalto's architecture, by contrast, as an example of heterotopic thinking.[29]

The anthropomorphous columns of the Erechtheum, the interlacing of architectural and sculptural elements in Gothic cathedrals, or the gradual transformation of architectural themes into painted illusions in Baroque interiors; all represent a polysemy, an obscuring of boundaries, contradictory to modern man. In our own age, sculpture has been separated from the architectural elements to be isolated on its lonely pedestal, and painting has become pictures delineated by frames, detached from their environment. We are able to enjoy the unsegregated art of past eras because as observers we react on the subconscious and sensory level; now, owing to our defenses, the creation of a whole artistic experience without distinct boundaries has become almost impossible.

Whereas in Baroque space and in traditional town environments, places, being part of several hierarchies at once, are endowed with multiple meanings, the contemporary one-dimensional principle of organization has resulted in 'one-location' architecture, in which each space has only one meaning. The mainstream of modern art and architecture is characterized by a simplification of subjects and a disappearance of plasticity and depth. Stylistic reductionism has become dominant in the art of our day. Simplicity has become a surface mannerism devoid of any aim at artistic impact. In commercial building, on the other hand, an emphasis on the building's direct image has displaced the plastic-architectonic form. The building has become an advertisement.

Modern man's inability to tolerate indefinability and polysemy has been particularly destructive within town planning, where the orthodox separation of urban functions into mono-functional areas has impoverished urban life. The pigeon-holing of people with their social security pensions into standardized rooms, one on top of the other in grid-plan high-rise suburbs, represents a triumph of this one-dimensional system of organization.

THE IDEAL OF MEANINGLESSNESS

Modern man's compulsion for clarity rids both images and concepts of their secondary meanings. By using 'pure' concepts and images, industrialized man aspires towards meaninglessness. The art and architecture of our day is often accused of being too abstract. The argument is false, for abstract does not signify meaninglessness; on the contrary, it stands for a concentration of significance.

Different parts and motifs of buildings have their own ontogenesis, their own evolutionary history. The door has originally represented a dramatic opening between two worlds and also symbolized the mouth and the genitals; windows are the eyes of a house. An important feature of the apertures of a house is their capacity for closing. The symbolic means used for protecting doors and windows illustrate this urge. The Greeks applied pitch to their door and window frames in order to ward off evil spirits and demons; the Chinese used auspicious words or pictures of a portal deity; and the inhabitants of the Ozarks nail a horseshoe on their door, or use three nails forming a triangle that signifies The Father, The Son, and The Holy Ghost. Many cultures have even seen a need to protect the apertures of the human body in similar symbolic ways.[30]

In contemporary building, both the door and the window have been reduced to meaningless openings in the wall. We have 'rationalized' the parts of the house and purified them of their inherited mythical meanings. The architecture of our time is a psychologically empty visual composition, not meant to arouse in us any associations, memories, or feelings.

Modern architecture's stylistic cliché, the glass wall—at once both open and closed—reflects how far contemporary building has drifted away from its intrinsic archaic nature, and is, in its contradictions, now simply psychologically oppressive.

In his analysis of the phenomenology of the house, Bachelard states that the house is both an analogy, as well as an actual extension, of human memory. In Bachelard's view, a dwelling should contain a cellar and an attic, in addition to two inhabited floors, because these represent the unconscious of the human psyche—the attic signifying pleasant memories and the cellar experiences better left in darkness.[31] Are today's architects unable to tolerate a cellar and an attic due to the fact that these concepts represent an indistinct unconsciousness which architects are unable to rationalize?

•

The framework of this essay does not allow for a complete analysis of all the compulsive features of architecture. Additional psychological inhibitions in our architecture are reflected by the disappearance of plasticity and sensuousness, the avoidance of symmetry and axiality, and the refrainment from illusion, ornament, and framing. However, even this sketch-like examination of our collective psyche immediately highlights problematic aspects of our welfare society's architectural practices and results.

However, from this viewpoint, more light can be shed on the contradictory and negative nature of today's architecture than by the currently so popular incrimination of the artistic aims of the Modern Movement.

STAIRWAYS OF THE MIND

(2000)

ARCHITECTURE AS AN EXISTENTIAL METAPHOR

Our obsessively materialist and quasi-rational age has turned buildings into purely instrumental constructions, "machines for living," serving merely the practicalities of life.[1] Architecture's aspirations into the realm of aesthetics only seem to emphasize the understanding of buildings as visually beautified objects of utility. We have almost forgotten that the task of our houses is not only to provide physical shelter and bodily comfort. A house does not solely constitute our "third skin," an externalization of our bodily functions; it is also an externalization of our imagination, memory and conceptual capacities. The French philosopher Gaston Bachelard, whose phenomenological writings on the "poetics of space" have decisively inspired studies of the mythopoetic basis of architecture, gives a monumental task to our houses: "Our house is our corner of the world ... it is our first universe, a real cosmos in every sense of the word ... It is an instrument with which to confront the cosmos."[2]

Buildings and towns structure and articulate our existential experience. Maurice Merleau-Ponty's phenomenological analyses of the human encounter with the "flesh" of the world provide a stimulating basis for an understanding of the mental essence and functioning of works of art and architecture. He convincingly expresses the existential content of art: "How would the painter or poet express anything other than his encounter with the world?"[3] How could an architect do otherwise, we might ask with equal justification.

Similar to painting and poetry, architecture articulates and expresses the human existential experience. The art of architecture creates spatial and material metaphors of our fundamental existential

59

encounters. Today's constructed settings most often do not seem to have a meaning; these circumstances speak clearly of our disturbed sense of "being-in-the-world." An architectural metaphor, a highly abstracted and condensed ensemble, fuses a multitude of human experiences into a singular image. The most potent of these images continue to structure the course of civilization, and to make history comprehensible. The necrophilic architectural images of today are explicit, even if alarming, metaphors as well.

The philosopher Karsten Harries reiterates Bachelard's view of the mental role of architecture: "Architecture helps to replace meaningless reality with a theatrically, or rather architecturally, transformed reality, which draws us in and, as we surrender to it, grants us an illusion of meaning...we cannot live with chaos. Chaos must be transformed into cosmos...When we reduce the human need for shelter to a material need, we lose sight of what we can call the ethical function of architecture."[4]

A building is not an end in itself; it alters our experience of reality. A building frames, articulates, structures, relates, separates and unites, facilitates and prohibits. Deep architectural images are acts instead of objects. As a consequence of this implied activity, a bodily reaction is an inseparable aspect of the experience of architecture. A meaningful architectural experience is not simply a series of retinal images. The 'elements' of architecture are not visual units or *gestalt*; they are confrontations and encounters. A building is encountered; it is approached, confronted, related to one's body, moved through, utilized as a condition for other things. Architecture directs, scales, and frames actions, perceptions, and thoughts.

Consequently, the basic architectural experiences are best understood as *verb* forms rather than being *nouns*. Authentic architectural experiences consist, for instance, of approaching or confronting a building rather than the formal apprehension of a facade; of the act of entering, not the static appreciation of the visual image of the door; of looking in or out of a window, rather than the window itself.

Buildings relate us to the world in particular ways, and they redefine our being-in-the-world, both in terms of space and time. Architecture makes the continuum of space and the flow of time conceivable to the human mind.

THE HOUSE AND THE BODY

The authenticity of architectural experience is founded on the tectonic language of building and the comprehensibility of the act of construction to the senses. We behold, touch, listen, and measure the world with our entire bodily existence, and the experiential world is organized and articulated around the center of the body. Our domicile is the refuge of our body, memory, and identity. We are in constant dialogue and interaction with the environment, to the degree that it is impossible to detach the image of the Self from its spatial and situational context. "I am the space, where I am," as the poet Noël Arnaud states.[5]

There is a vivid and unconscious resonance, correspondence, and identification between our images of the house and of our own body with its sense organs and metabolism. The house is a metaphor of the body, and the body is a metaphor of the house.

In a description of a dream, Carl Jung gives an example of the identification of the Self and the oneiric house as well as the layered historicity of the human mind. He finds himself on the upper story of a house, in a salon furnished with fine old rococo furniture. Descending the stairs, he reaches the ground floor where the furnishings are medieval. Behind a heavy door, he discovers a stairway leading down into the cellar. The vaulted cellar apparently dates from Roman times. The floor is made of stone slabs and one slab is provided with a ring. Lifting the stone slab, he finds a stairway of narrow stone steps, which lead him to a low cave cut into rock. Scattered on the dust-covered floor, like the remains of a primitive culture, are bones and broken pottery.[6]

Place and event, space and mind, mutually define each other and fuse inevitably into a singular experience. The mind perceives the world and the world exists through experience. Experiencing a space or a house is a dialogue, a kind of exchange: I place myself in the space and the space settles in me.

Writers and artists, born phenomenologists, intuitively comprehend this fusion. "Today more than ever I feel that cell no. 461...has remained inside me, becoming the secret of my soul. Today more than ever, I feel like a bird that has swallowed his cage. I take my cell with me, inside me, as a pregnant woman carries her baby in her womb," writes Curzio Malaparte of the harsh memory of his prison experience,[7] Rainer Maria Rilke internalizes the memory of a childhood house in a surprisingly similar fashion:

Afterwards I never again saw that remarkable house...it is no complete building: it is all broken up inside me; here a room, there a room, and here a piece of hallway that does not connect these two rooms but is preserved, as a fragment, by itself. In this way it is all dispersed within me—the rooms, the stairways that descended with such ceremonious deliberation, and other narrow, spiral stairs in the obscurity of which one moved as blood does in the veins ...

THE DIALECTICS OF THE BODY AND THE HOUSE.

65 Louise Bourgeois, *Portrait of Jean-Louis*, 1947–49, bronze. Cheim and Read, New York.
66 Louise Bourgeois, *Femme Maison*, 1946–47, oil and ink on linen. Private Collection.

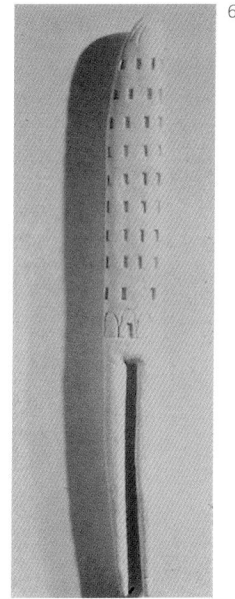

65

66

all that is still in me and will never cease to be in me. It is as though the picture of this house had fallen into me from an infinite height and had shattered against my very ground.[8]

The consistent parts of any house have their resonance with the human body. Windows are the fragile eyes of the house, observing the world and inspecting visitors. The eyes of the house pre-select and pre-view the landscape for the inhabitants' eyes. The world seen through a window is a tamed and domesticated world. A view through a window has already been given a specific meaning. A thunderstorm or a snowstorm loses its fearfulness when viewed through the window of a house. The house provides protection for the dreaming inhabitant, but windows enable them to dream. The polarized and darkened windows of contemporary houses, however, are eyes blinded by some horrible illness; these are malicious eyes that secretly control the inhabitants themselves.

The front door resists my body by its very weight; it ritualizes entry, and makes me anticipate the rooms behind it. Opening a door is an intimate encounter between the house and the body; my body meets the mass and surface of the door, and the door handle, polished to a sheen by long use, gives a welcoming handshake. The automated glass doors of today make entry physically convenient, but strip the act of any existential meaning. Excessive convenience and functionalization dilute the meaning of an architectural encounter. A proper door simultaneously protects and invites; it mediates gestures of privacy and welcome, courtesy and dignity. "How concrete everything becomes in the world of the spirit when an object, a mere door, can give images of hesitation, temptation, desire, security, welcome and respect," exclaims Bachelard perceptively.[9]

THE PHYSIOGNOMY OF THE STAIRCASE

In one of his lectures, Alvar Aalto recalls that one of the worst punishments in Dante's *Inferno* was a stair that had the wrong proportions.[10] Jorge Luis Borges presents the same ordeal: "I wandered up the stairs of and along the pavements of the inextricable palace (Afterwards I learned that the width and the height of the steps were not constant, a fact which made me understand the singular fatigue they produced)."[11] The proper dimensioning of the stair has been the concern of architectural theorists since Vitruvius of Roman Antiquity and the Renaissance architects Leon Battista Alberti and Andrea Palladio. The rule of thumb in today's architectural practice is simple enough for any architect to follow: 2 x the height of the riser + the width of the tread = 63 centimeters. Yet this practical rule only guarantees a certain average physical comfort. A dull stair makes the body feel heavy and clumsy, whereas a delightfully proportioned stair makes one glide up and down graciously and effortlessly. This qualitative difference is just as much a result of architectural ambience as of metric differences. Architecture qualifies physical measures and scales.

The fundamental imagery of stairs has remained virtually unchanged since prehistoric times. Although a stair's dimensioning is severely restricted, architectural stair ensembles throughout history project a surprising variety. Imagine the range of staircases: from medieval castles and Renaissance and Baroque palaces, to the designs of contemporary masters such as Mies van der Rohe, Arne Jacobsen, and Alvar Aalto. The imagery of stepped streets is equally varied, from those of Mediterranean vernacular towns to the Lipetta and the Spanish Steps, and the stairways of Santa Maria in Aracoeli and the Capitoline Hill in Rome. A stepped street provides us with a feeling of safety; our body knows that these are streets solely for pedestrians.

The mental significance and symbolic connotations of stairs are deeply rooted in our body. "The staircase is the symbolic spine of the house," writes the British-American film critic and semiotician Peter Wollen.[12] Stairs have the same significance to the vertical organization of the house as the spine to the structure of the body. There are buildings with externalized spines, Alvar Aalto's Baker House dormitory at MIT (1947–48), for instance, and the Centre Pompidou in Paris (Renzo Piano and Richard Rogers, 1970), but do we not experience today's office blocks, in which the staircases are concealed and used only for emergencies, as unreal and dreamlike, as if they were devoid of the proper physiognomy of a house? Are not these buildings without their proper spines?

According to Gaston Bachelard, the "oneiric house" of the mind has three or four stories: the middle ones are used for the normal activities of daily life, the attic is reserved for the purpose of storing pleasant memories, which we occasionally wish to revisit, and the cellar is meant for hiding unpleasant and frightening memories that we wish to bury forever.[13] The stair mediates between the different metaphysical realms of the house of our dreams.

THE STAIRCASE—DEVICE AND SYMBOL

Together with the door, the stair is that element of architecture that is encountered most concretely and directly by the body. As we ascend or descend a stair, our step measures its dimensions and our hand caresses the smooth surface of the banisters. To be precise, a stair is not an 'architectural element,' but rather one of the primary architectural

71　Pierre Chareau and Bernard Bijvoet,
　　Glass House (*Maison de Verre*), Paris,
　　1929. The stair leading from the fam-
　　ily room to the master bedroom can
　　be raised and folded into the ceiling.

72　Arne Korsmo, Korsmo House,
　　Planetveien, Oslo, 1953–55. Hinged
　　staircase leading from the living room
　　to the floor above.

images. Works of art in general are not composed of visual 'elements,' they are constituted by lived, tangible images and fantasies underlying our recollections, and the parts always acquire their meaning through the whole, not vice versa.

The staircase is the most important organ of the house. Without stairs, our houses would be without floors, cellars and attics; we would remain as Joë Bosquet's one-storyed man: "He was a man with only one story; he had his cellar in his attic."[14] As our modern houses have lost their attics and their cellars, they have also lost their memory; most of our houses have forgotten the mythological and poetic ground of architectural experience. The escalator and the elevator of the mechanical age maximize our physical comfort, but these technical inventions eliminate a central metaphor of the house. One of architecture's tasks is to reinforce and articulate the verticality of the human experience of the world; the inhabited towers of our age, however, served by mechanized stairs, have degenerated into virtual horizontality. A modern tower is a stack of flat floor plates, creating a sense of abstracted horizontality, alienated from gravity and the earth. Today's planning regulations, while admirably assisting the handicapped, tend to eliminate steps and stairs from the townscape and public buildings altogether, and thus deprive architecture of one of its most powerful expressive means. We are all becoming handicapped. Gustave Flaubert's exclamation, "Architects, all idiots; they always forget to put staircases in houses," assumes a new significance here.[15] In contrast to today's stairless towers, Pieter Brueghel the Elder's *The Tower of Babel* (1563) depicts a man-made mountain, hollowed out into countless chambers, connected by a labyrinth of stairs.

An intriguing special case of the stairless house is a multi-story house with a vanishing staircase. In Pierre Chareau's Glass House (*Maison de Verre*) in Paris (1931) the stair leading from the dayroom *(petit salon)* to the master bedroom above folds against the ceiling and literally vanishes by means of a complicated pivoting and balancing mechanism. Arne Korsmo devised a similar vanishing stair between the living room on the main floor and the bedrooms on the floor above in his Planetveien house in Oslo (1953–55). Such a vanishing stair evokes a sense of secrecy and concealment, but also an air of amnesia and a sense of an artificially extracted organ. The mechanistic gadgets of the Maison de Verre can be associated with the gynecologist owner's medical devices and instruments, and also evoke the image of Duchamp's bachelor-machine.

Stairs are responsible for the vertical circulation of the house in the same way as the heart pumps blood up and down the body. The

71

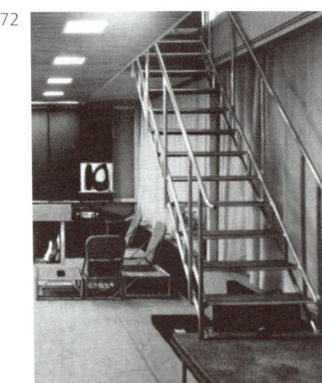

72

regular rhythm of stairs echoes the beating of the heart and the rhythm of breathing. Ascending a stair accelerates our heartbeat and breathing. Steep stairs address the heart, whereas gentle stairs echo the rhythm of our lungs.

According to Sigmund Freud, the regular rhythm of stairs also addresses our dream imagery through its essence as a sexual metaphor. The fact that certain words related with climbing stairs, such as 'to mount' and 'to tread' also signify copulation, lends support to Freud's analysis of stair dream symbolism. Freud commented on the sexual content of dreams of stairs at the turn of the century.[16] His later formulation of these observations makes the sexual symbolism of ascending stairs explicit: "We … began to turn our attention to the appearance of steps, staircases and ladders in dreams, and were soon in a position to show that staircases (and analogous things) were unquestionably symbols of copulation. It is not hard to discover the basis of the comparison: we come to the top in a series of rhythmical movements and with increasing breathlessness and then, with a few rapid leaps, we can get to the bottom again. Thus, the rhythmical pattern of copulation is reproduced in going upstairs."[17]

A phenomenological survey of architecture, however, does not seem to support this sexual content of the stair imagery. René Allendy suggests another gender reading of the two directions of the staircase: "Man climbs the stairs (activity), woman comes down them (passivity)."[18] Marcel Duchamp's seminal painting *Nude Descending a Staircase* (1912), and Rita Hayworth's seductive descent of a staircase in the film *Gilda* (1946), are two immediate examples supporting Allendy's observation.

Bachelard notes that the dream of the staircase is closely related with the dreams of flight and falling. On the other hand, these are two of the basic oneiric images. "Of all metaphors, metaphors of flight, elevation, depth, sinking and fall are the axiomatic metaphors par excellence. Nothing explains them, and they explain everything," he writes.[19]

The fear of falling in dreams does not arise from the terror of hitting the ground, but from the fear of not hitting firm ground at all. Significantly, Lucifer, cast out of heaven in Milton's *Paradise Lost*, falls for nine days.

SYMBOLIC STAIRS

The purely metaphoric, symbolic or conceptual purposes of a stair can supercede its practical function. Throughout history, the stair has represented cosmological ideas and spiritual aspirations, power and authority, prestige and status, hierarchy and classification. Steps and

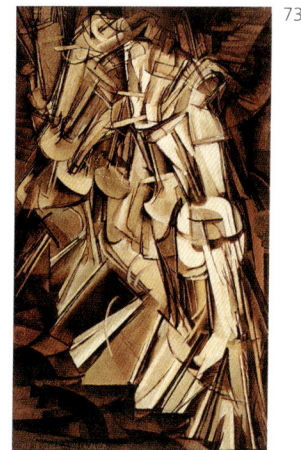
73

74

73 Marcel Duchamp, *Nude Descending a Staircase*, 1912. Philadelphia Museum of Art, The Louise and Walter Arensberg Collection.
74 Ralph Murphy, *Top of the Town*, 1937. John Harkrider, art director.

stairs conventionally symbolize the ascent to a higher spiritual plane, each step closer to Heaven. The climbing of steps reflects an archetypal psychic longing to approach the heavenly sphere of the cosmos. The temples of ancient cultures are often terraced to create an image of immense stairs: the ziggurat of Mesopotamia, the Stoup of South Asian Buddhism, and the pyramids of ancient Mexico. The temples of ancient Greece were built in a terraced formation to create a sense of elevation. This idea of an elevated terrace, a plateau approached by a great flight of steps, reappeared in contemporary architecture through the work of Jørn Utzon, most notably in his Sydney Opera House. Alvar Aalto also frequently used the symbolic effect of an artificially elevated ground level, and even a man-made hill-town, most notably in his town halls at Säynätsalo and Seinäjoki.

In Masonic symbolism, the steps depicted in allegorical tapestries represent the degrees of initiation into the chapter. Three steps correspond to moderation, justice, and benevolence. Seven steps represent the seven liberal arts of the medieval world, the seven ages of man, and the seven cardinal virtues, all believed to lead to self-knowledge, mastery and improvement. According to alchemical allegory, seven steps also lead up to the philosopher's stone.[20]

As architects, we tend to think that stairs are symmetrical with relation to the activities of ascending and descending. In the prosaic acts of daily life, the two directions may well appear equal. However, the specialized mental functions of the extreme floors of the oneiric house reveal the natural symbolism of above and below. Ascending stairs culminate in Heaven, whereas descending stairs eventually lead down to the Underworld. A characteristic image of the meaning of ascension is the theme of *The Presentation of the Virgin*, a popular subject in Renaissance religious paintings. The ultimate configuration of the ascending stair is expressed in Jacob's dream: "And he dreamed, and beheld a ladder set up on the earth, and the top of it reached to heaven; and beheld the angels of God ascending and descending on it. And, behold, the Lord stood above it, and said, I am the Lord God of Abraham thy father, and the God of Isaac."[21] Another image of stairs extending to Heaven is the Ladder of Judgment, from which the souls climbing the ladder are dragged off by devils and fall into the mouth of Hell.

STAIRS AS VERTICAL LABYRINTHS

The horizontal, vertical, and diagonal directions are interconnected in the design of a staircase, and this formal complexity transforms it into an architectural miniature, a microcosm, and an abstracted and condensed house within a house. The image of a staircase resembles that of the labyrinth; a staircase is a vertical labyrinth. A staircase can mediate the experience of getting lost, losing one's balance, or even one's mind. The endlessly criss-crossing stairs in the prison scenes of Giovanni Battista Piranesi's *Carceri* drawings create a spatial labyrinth that permits no exit: the haunted prisoners are doomed forever to ascend and descend this endless maze. M.C. Escher's drawings of 'impossible' staircases simultaneously leading upwards and downwards, creating endless loops, are further examples of labyrinthine stairs. Jorge Luis Borges describes similarly inconceivable stairs: "It [the palace] abounded in... incredible inverted stairways, whose steps and balustrades hung downwards. Other stairways, clinging airily to the side of the monumental wall, would die without leading anywhere, after making two or three turns in the lofty darkness of the cupolas."[22] The impossibility of actual descent or ascent creates an experience of hopelessness and suffocation. To ascend the confined and claustrophobic flight of steps into the Pharaoh's burial chamber, halfway up the great pyramid of Giza, is to paradoxically descend into Hades. Bachelard interprets the imagination of a fall as an *inverted ascent*.[23]

The library labyrinth in Borges' short story, "The Library of Babylon," creates a similar dizzying density of spaces, an architectural mist as it were, without a beginning, direction, or end: "Also through here passes a spiral stairway, which sinks abysmally and soars upwards to remote distances... they always arrive extremely tired of their journeys; they speak of a broken stairway which almost killed them; they talk with the librarian of galleries and stairs."[24]

CINEMATIC STAIRS

Staircases and stairways play a particularly important role in cinematic dramaturgy, forming simultaneously a stage and an auditorium. Cinema staircases reveal their innate asymmetry. Ascension implies an exit from the social stage and a withdrawal into privacy, but it can also signal movement into a prohibited realm, a way to disclose a secret, or the final journey to purification, judgment or amnesty. Descending a stair to the main floor in a film is usually related to entry into the public sphere and self-presentation. Curving stairs are particularly popular in cinema because they can present the descent of the protagonist first as a distant side view and finally as a close frontal view. Descending a staircase into a cellar signifies an entry into the realm of fear and menace.

Stairs in films are most often photographed looking upwards from below, so that an ascending person is consequently seen from behind and a descending character from the front. Stairs photographed from above express vertigo, falling, or panic-stricken flight. This preference

79

80

75 Pyramid of the Magician, Uxmal, Mexico.

76 An elevated platform with huge stairs reminiscent of Aztec or Mayan architecture. Jørn Utzon, Opera House, Sydney, 1957–73.

77 Alvar Aalto, Civic Center, Seinäjoki, 1958–87. Artificial mound and terraced steps next to the townhall.

78 Titian, *Presentation of the Virgin*, 1534–38. Gallerie dell' Accademia, Venice. Fragment.

79 A vertical labyrinth. Giovanni Battista Piranesi, *Invenzioni capric. di Carceri* (imaginary prison scenes), 1761.

80 An endless stairway of vertigo. M.C. Escher, *Relativity*, lithograph, 1953.

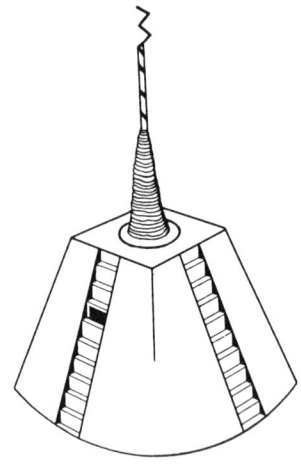

for showing staircases from below has its natural technical reasons—a stairway photographed from above seems to escape the picture—but this very fact reveals the psychological difference between the ascending and descending movements.

The Odessa Steps sequence in Sergei Eisenstein's *Battleship Potemkin*, the spiraling stairs of anguish in Fritz Lang's *M for Murder*, and the stairwell leading to the bell loft in Alfred Hitchcock's *Vertigo* are memorable examples of the cinematic dramatics of stairs. Why are the stairs in Hitchcock's films invariably to the right of the entrance door as perceived by the entering person? Is it because the stair stands for the heart of the house and consequently its proper location is to the left of the central axis?

STAIRS OF HIERARCHY AND CLASSIFICATION

Steps and stairs create a metaphor or an instrument of hierarchical classification. In *Liber de Ascensu et Descensu Intellectus*, the medieval Christian mystic Ramon Lull depicts the act of creation as a stair of ascent and descent. Each step represents one stage in the creation epic, ranging from the inanimate rock at the bottom to the flora, wild animals, humans, the firmament, angels, and finally, God and the House of Wisdom at the top.[25]

The same imagery appears in the cosmology of the Dogon people in Mali.[26] The key to the World Order of this legendary tribe is the mythological ark, "The Granary of the Master of Pure Earth," by means of which the first man, a smith, descended from Heaven to earth. Each of the four sides of the heavenly granary is equipped with a stair of ten steps. As the ark descended in 22 stages along a sevenfold spiral (note the emergence of mathematical wisdom: 22/7 is an approximation of Pi), various animal species were placed on the steps; the northern steps contained humans and fish, the southern steps domestic animals, the eastern steps birds, and the western steps wild animals, vegetables, and insects. The individual species were placed on the ten steps. For instance, the western steps contained, from the top downwards, antelopes, hyenas, cats (2 steps), reptiles and lizards, apes, gazelles, marmots, the lion, and the elephant. Thus, the steps of the ark constituted a primitive classification system of flora and fauna.

Today, winners of sports events continue to be awarded on a similar stair of classification.

THE NARRATIVE OF STAIRS

Great works of architecture, as all art, are saturated with images and inducements that direct our attention away from them as physical objects towards the metaphysical dimensions of human experience. A great stairway transcends its physicality and functionality, and becomes a microcosmic complex of images suggesting an epic narrative.

One of the most deeply touching stairways in the history of architecture is surely Michelangelo's stairhall in the Biblioteca Laurentiana, next to the Church of St. Lorenzo in Florence. The gray stone staircase, detached from the walls of its cubic spatial container, awakens the image of a dark stream solemnly flowing down from the level of the library itself. One can almost hear the rippling of the solitary stream. This is a liquid stairway. The oddly placed consoles of the lower portion of the walls, and the columns, all but devoured by the walls, create an experience of the pressure of being underwater. The stone stream becomes an underwater stream. Michelangelo's stairhall speaks of another dimension of time; it speaks of the metaphysics of time. This stairhall expresses the same melancholy, the same sorrow of loss, as Michelangelo's moving *pietás*.

Casa Malaparte is the powerfully metaphysical house of the Italian writer Curzio Malaparte, sited overhanging the sheer cliffs of Punta Massullo on the Isle of Capri, and made known outside the architectural profession by Jean-Luc Godard's film *Le Mepris* (1963). A straight flight of ever-widening steps leads to the roof terrace hovering over the Mediterranean, halfway between the earth and the sky. The absence of any balustrades or handrails induces sensations of fear and vertigo. The stairway is simultaneously part of the cliff and part of the house, but belongs absolutely to the sky. An experience of breathtaking beauty, flight, levitation, and the suffocating fear of falling, the stair makes one think of the tragic myth of Icarus, and the journeys of Ulysses across the sea below. One also recalls the maidens sacrificed to the Sun God at the top of the endless flight of steps of an Aztec pyramid; this is unavoidably the stage of Divine Judgment.

THE RE-ENCHANTMENT OF ARCHITECTURE

The buildings and townscapes of our time commonly lack a spiritual and emotional content. The sense of emptiness, distance, and rejection they do possess derives from the inability of modern settings to resonate with the unconscious sensibilities of the human mind. The progress of modern architecture has normalized human emotions, and consequently is unable to reflect emotional extremes such as ecstasy and melancholy. A work of art and architecture can touch our soul only if it touches something familiar in our collective memory. Technical ingenuity, novelty, formal inventiveness, or mere aspiration for aesthetic pleasure cannot move us. "Meaning cannot finally be made or

84

85

81 A stairway of violence. Sergei Eisenstein, *Battleship Potemkin*, 1925. The stairway of Odessa.

82 A stairway of terror. Alfred Hitchcock, *Vertigo*, 1958. The stairway leading to the bell tower represents the protagonist's vertigo.

83 The mythological Dogon Arch, "The Granary of the Master of Pure Earth." The four stairways of the image serve as a complex system of classification.

84 A stairway of melancholy. Michelangelo, Staircase of the Laurentian Library, Florence, 1524–57.

85 A stairway to the sky. Curzio Malaparte, Casa Malaparte, Capri, 1938–40.

invented; it can only be discovered, where such discovery will also be a self-discovery," as Karsten Harries acknowledges.[27] The art of architecture elaborates existential themes that echo the primordial depths of human experience.

As our existential experience continues to drift towards placelessness, insignificance and the absence of hierarchy, one of the most demanding tasks of architecture is to resist this erosion of mental value and experience. At the turn of the millennium, the great challenge for architects is the re-sensualization, re-mythologization, and re-poetization of the human domicile. The task of architecture is to resist the processes of psychological entropy. "One of the symptoms of alienation in the modern age is the widespread sense of meaninglessness ... Modern man's most urgent need is to discover the reality and value of the inner subjective world, to discover the symbolic life ... The symbolic life in some form is a prerequisite for psychic health," writes the psychologist E.F. Edinger, and this advice ought to be taken seriously by the architectural profession.[28]

Is it conceivable that our stairs could once again reawaken our awareness of Heaven and Hell?

86 Giorgione, *The Tempest*, c. 1506.
Gallerie dell'Accademia, Venice.
An eroticized architecture of the
painterly scene.

THE PLACE OF MAN

Time, Memory, and Place in Architectural Experience
(1982)

THE PSYCHE OF FORM

"For our house is our corner of the world…It is our first universe, a real cosmos in every sense of the work. The house is one of the greatest powers of integration for the thoughts, memories and dreams of mankind," writes Gaston Bachelard in *The Poetics of Space*.[1] Bachelard's subjects—drawers, chests and wardrobes, birds' nests, shells, nooks, and the phenomenology of roundness—and his research method—an analysis of primal experiences of houses through poetry—would certainly make many people limit their reading to a few pages were Bachelard not an authoritative philosopher of science.

However, Bachelard's book can certainly justify its inclusion in the source list for any respectable study of architectural theory. As the art of architecture sinks under the current payload of practical demands, Bachelard's phenomenological 'pure scrutiny,' or 'scrutiny of being,' pinpoints the heart of architectural experience. The increasing anonymity of building in the industrialized world, and its detachment from human experience, make one ponder the interaction between the human mind, culture, and building. As contemporary building seems to increase our sense of alienation, rather than offer a sense of home, there is good cause for analyzing the fundamental experiences related to buildings through thought and language.

With childlike freshness, *The Poetics of Space* concerns itself with the psychological elements that lie behind built forms. In simple terms, Bachelard analyzes the psyche of lived-in form. "All great, simple images reveal a psychic state. The house, even more than the landscape, is a 'psychic state'," he writes.[2] Alvar Aalto also uses the term "psyche of form" in his article about the Abbé Coignard, published in *Alvar*

Aalto: The Early Years, the first part of Göran Schildt's biography of the architect.[3]

This essay addresses the mental reflections of built form, the experience of place and time, and the interaction of environment and memory. Here, I do not intend to work out practical planning directives; I merely intend to point out certain basic experiences of the environment on the basis of literary sources and my own observations.

EGO, HOUSE AND UNIVERSE

A traditional community is both a built-up world picture and a concrete hierarchy of the corporate body, in which each member and institution has its place. Anthropological literature offers a vast number of fascinating examples of how this world picture, mythology, and a way of life are combined in building. The examples most often quoted in the literature are probably the Bororo village, made known by the structuralist Claude Levi-Strauss, and the type of village inhabited by the Dogon tribe in West Africa, which Aldo van Eyck's writings have made familiar to the architectural profession.

Traditional building grows unconsciously out of an interaction of landscape, soil, climate, materials, and type of culture. Just as a bird shapes its nest with its own body, so the traditional community shapes its habitat with its collective memory. Tradition is a centripetal force that prevents both the committing of errors and individual divergences. Through tradition, the overall interaction between physical conditions, a way of life, and psychological needs are developed towards a balance. However, the forms taken by the environment do not develop deterministically, without any choice. The determining factor in the equation is always a choice dictated by culture—the community's concept of the world—which building reifies. Building converts the community's cosmological view of the world into physical reality. Simultaneously, the temporal order is linked with the mythical order. In the end there is complete affinity between the individual and the community, between thinking and place.

The experience of place in an industrial culture, and the affinity between man and environment, are disappearing at the level of both local identity and man's sense of place on a human scale. Local forms of building culture are being eradicated by the entropic force of standardization exerted by industrial culture. Standardization is built into our culture, and furthered by technology's indifference to local factors. The latter allows us to break free from locality and to produce a synthetic environment independent of tradition, landscape, and climate. Having rejected the sense of continuity conferred by tradition in the time dimension, industrial man has started to expand his existence in place, instead of in time, by seeking a universal culture. Other characteristics of rationalized building also work towards a weakening of this sense of place on the human scale: over-scaled building complexes, excessive repetition, standardization dictated by production techniques, a lack of spatial organization due to need or flexibility, a flattening of shapes and surfaces called for by functional and economic considerations, and an overall erosion of form. Finally, an overall monotony of lighting, a lack of texture, and the eradication of individual detail complete the loss of sense of place.

In modern design, space is divided for the desired purposes as if a meaningless, valueless commodity. The modular grid of industrialized construction extends homogeneously and without differentiation in all directions. But, as the philosopher physician Viktor von Weizsäcker has pointed out, "Homogeneity of space kills sense of place."[4] Vertical elements creating spatial foci and giving rise to a sense of place have also withered away. Housing means inhabiting merely the horizontal plane.

Hans Sedlmayr uses the concept of man's 'inner catastrophe' in his thought-provoking book *Art in Crisis*, the original German name of which is *Die Verlorene Mitte (The Lost Center)*.[5] The loss of a center, a focal point, a specific gravity, and a sense of place in our environment cannot help but mean the loss of corresponding qualities in our minds. Man's external catastrophe stems only from an internal catastrophe.

THE ARCHITECTURES OF MAKER AND USER

In a specialist society, building is controlled largely by conscious and specialized views of the building trade. Although regulated by man's intellectual and cognitive powers—or rather limitations—the constructed building is actually mainly experienced emotionally, sensuously, and thus unconsciously. Designs implement ideal models and concrete images of order, which in turn offer only an impoverished and inhuman environment. Such building lacks the unity of thinking, action, and experience characteristic of traditional communities. In this, we can clearly see the disastrous dichotomy of industrial man and the consequent manipulation of self. With growing diversification and more advanced technology, the conscious dimensions of building gradually get the whip hand, in the end producing a paradoxical and pathological situation in which man builds an environment harmful to himself.

This duality also explains the designer's common choice of personal residence, which may often seem contradictory: although we design one-dimensional environments, we ourselves prefer to live in environments offering many chronological strata. As designers, we act within the limits of our intellectual and cognitive powers, but as residents and users of the environments we react with our whole personalities. To this extent, we may then find ourselves denying our own creations.

In judging and teaching architecture, most attention is given to matters connected with a design's artistic form. The art of building is analyzed as the art of organizing space, with neither conscious nor unconscious human significance. That environment and space are neutral concepts existing outside man is axiomatic. Yet it is precisely this separation of man and environment that anthropologist Edward T. Hall, for instance, views as one of the most destructive unconscious cornerstones of Western thinking.[6]

THE EXPERIENCE OF PLACE

The experience of the environment always involves several senses. One fundamental weakness of architecture today is in fact its exclusively visual quality, setting it outside our emotions. The intensity and tranquility of our experiences of a natural setting—or of a Japanese garden, for instance—stem from the fact that we are using all our senses. Through the various senses, man receives messages that reinforce each other. But the sensory stimuli provided by our buildings are usually one-dimensional or contradictory. Even a visually appealing building may well arouse emotional and motor feelings of rejection because of its angularity and the harshness of its forms.

In an environmental experience, there is an unconscious bodily identification with the object, a projection of the body pattern onto what is experienced, or a physical mimesis, an unconscious mimicry. "To at least some extent every real place can be remembered, partly because it is unique, but partly because it has affected our bodies and generated enough associations to hold it in our personal worlds," say Charles Moore and Kent Bloomer in their book *Body, Memory and Architecture*.[7] They consider the rejection of this bodily and sensory interaction one of the reasons for the poverty of the new environment: "What is missing from our dwellings today are the potential transactions between body, imagination, and environment."[8]

In moving architectural experiences, space, material, and time seem to unite into a single dimension that penetrates our awareness. In these experiences, space takes on more gravity, as it were—the character of light becomes tangible, time seems to stop, and space is dominated by silence. We identify with this place, the space, this moment, and they all become part of our body and consciousness. The experience of place returns the experience to ourselves: at bottom it is an experience of the self. An architectural space touches something deep and familiar in us. The sense of silence connected with an architectural experience is perhaps due to the fact that we are listening so intently to ourselves.

Here we see the importance of environment for our personalities and psyches. A properly organized environment—full of significance, finding echoes in the measurements of our body, and in the memories of our minds—expresses our relationship with the world, but at the same time reinforces our self-identity.

Towns, buildings, and objects are also metaphysical instruments. "The house is an instrument with which man confronts the cosmos," writes Bachelard.[9] But one could go further: the world we build makes us understand and remember who we ourselves are.

The phenomenological study of man's relationship with space and environment, which has become so widespread recently, is perhaps best articulated by the philosopher Martin Heidegger. Heidegger has paid special attention to the connection—or perhaps one should say the unity—between building, living, and thinking. He links space indivisibly with the human condition: "When we speak of man and space, it sounds as though man stood on one side, space on the other. Yet space is not something that faces man. It is neither an external object nor an inner experience. It is not that there are men, and over and above them space..."[10] Wallace Stevens, the poet, expresses the idea of the affinity of man and space in the ultimate simple form: "I am what is around me."[11]

One example of the affinity between environment and behavior is given by Herbert Marcuse, in his book *One-Dimensional Man*. Marcuse considers that buildings today are unerotic compared with the erotic images conjured up by the natural environment or traditional buildings.[12] Compare, for instance, the fantasies provoked by the meadow outside the city wall, or an old attic, to the numbing no-man's-land of a new housing area, or the anonymity of a flat crammed between concrete floors and walls. Marcuse thinks the flagrant sexuality of our time is one result of the growing lack of eroticism in our environment. (In the same way, juvenile delinquency is considered to be largely the result of a lack of stimuli in the environment, rather than a criminal turn of mind. The child quite simply compensates for the limits placed on his freedom by a greater desire for adventure.) When the environment no longer provides a sensitive, stimulating setting for our fantasies, our behavior becomes harsh and aggressive.

THE EXPERIENCE OF TIME

As well as experiencing place, we need to experience time. We need to reassure ourselves of our existence here and now, and of how we fit into time's continuum. This experience of continuity is one of our basic psychological needs, whose origins lie in an unconscious fear of death. "A house constitutes a body of images that give mankind proofs or illusions of stability," writes Bachelard.[13] Alvar Aalto, in turn, says, "Form is nothing else but a concentrated wish for everlasting life on earth."[14] Time is always the fundamental dimension of artistic experience, not so much in its physical sense of space-time, so often used in attempts to show the connection between modern architecture and the contemporary scientific concept of space, but rather in the form of an experiential mental dimension. The appreciation of art activates forgotten feelings in our mind and body. Earlier levels of awareness are awakened, ones that have retained images rooted in man's biological past. The time of artistic experience does not rush us into the future or open up the doors of the future, as we often think, but binds us to a past that civilization has forgotten. In the psychological sense, the basic essence of art is thus not an awareness of the never-before-experienced, but the reconstruction of a bio-cultural level of feeling.

The simultaneously alarming and calming strength of the great sculptor Henry Moore's art lies in its archaic quality. In Moore's sculptures we hear the voice of the geological past of nature and of the archaeological past of man. His sculptures are nature and artifice, flora and fauna, landforms and human shapes, material and imagery. The comforting and protective effect of Moore's sculpture stems from his eternal theme: the Great Mother or Mother Earth archetype. His sculptures, like all great art, return us to the all-embracing consciousness of the child, with its carefree identity between self and the world.

Bachelard writes of the 'primal image' as the cause of man's most powerful experiences.[15] The power of great poetry, and great art and architecture, stems from such primordial images, to which man reacts with the whole of his unconscious being. In *Water and Dreams*, Bachelard distinguishes between two areas of the imagination, 'formal imagination' and 'material imagination,' which he sees occurring both in nature and in the human mind.[16] In nature, the formal imagination produces 'unnecessary' beauty, such as flowers, whereas the material imagination creates what is primitive and eternal. The formal imagination of the human mind has led us into the innovative, the picturesque, the varied and the unexpected, whereas the material imagination is attracted by the permanence of things. The latter thus brings out the essence of the material or phenomenon itself. On this basis it is possible to speak about an art of form and an art of essence.

Modern architecture is blinkered in its faith in the potential of formal fantasy. It has grown remote from the essence of material, structure and phenomena and at the same time lost its strongest emotional content. Louis Kahn made it his life's work to restore to modern architecture the primal images of building—or, as he puts it himself, the institutions of man. His buildings do in fact speak with an unanswerable weight and authority: they are both primitive and noble at one and the same time.

Architecture in this century has been so dominated by the fascination with pure form and visual composition that it has increasingly ended up lacking in meaning and associative content. The growing attempts recently to enrich architectural expression with a diversity of form, external organic character, or elements with historical associations have not done much to give architecture more weight. These externals have no connection with the internal mental content. They do not give order to the world, and say nothing of things outside themselves, neither of the cosmos nor of man himself.

ARCHITECTURE, MEMORY AND DREAMS

Towns, buildings, and objects are an extension of the collective memory of the community and its individuals. "The individual is born in the village which existed before him. But slowly this village becomes his homeland, a place lived in, and full of memories," writes Rudolf Schwartz.[17] As well as containing a knowledge that guides us without our knowing it, the environment also tells us who we are. Architects have become immune to the poetic language of houses, rooms, and objects. I believe that architects, like poets, should be sensitive to the images provoked by things. We should re-learn naive seeing.

Finnish author Jarkko Laine writes of the things on his window ledge: "I like looking at these things. I don't seek aesthetic pleasure in them ... nor do I recall their origins: that is not important. But even so they all arouse memories, real and imagined. A poem is a thing that arouses memories of real and imagined things ... The things in the window act like a poem. They are images that do not reflect anything ... I sing of the things in the window."[18]

Like the poet, we could say that a house, too, arouses memories of things real and imagined. "How concrete everything becomes in the world of the spirit when an object, a mere door, can give images of hesitation, temptation, desire, security, welcome and respect," writes Bachelard.[19]

In the modern home, too, the fireplace, the dining table, and the bed all act as central foci around which our everyday lives revolve, and with which strong feelings are associated. Even modern planning senses their symbolic significance. The cupboard, on the other hand, is one of the most prosaic details in the home and its symbolic or psychological implications are rarely considered. But Bachelard gives us a complete chapter on drawers, chests and cupboards, giving these insignificant, if useful, objects an impressive role in the world of fantasy and daydream: "In the wardrobe there exists a center of order that protects the entire house against uncurbed disorder," he writes.[20] Cupboards and cabinets represent the functions of keeping and removing, storing and remembering. The inside of a cupboard is a highly intimate and secret place, not to be opened by just anyone. Small boxes and caskets are also hiding places for intimate secrets and as such, are of great significance for our imaginations. We have just as great a need to keep secrets as to know them. Our imagination fills the compartments of the places, rooms, and buildings with memories, and turns them into our own personal territories. Each great poem, painting, or building seems extraordinarily familiar and eventually makes us believe we have produced it ourselves, or at least could have done so. Herein lies the generous equality of art.

As an architect to be, I certainly should have been thrilled by the architectonic construct of my grandfather's farm yard in which the tight space between the sauna and the gable of the cowhouse defined a worthy entrance hall. But no: I only learned the value of the yard as an adult. On the other hand, one of the most lasting memories of my childhood is the house's attic: the overwhelming heat there in the middle of the summer, the chirping of the martins under the eaves, the smell of the moss and woodchips spread over the floor, the planks laid down for walking on, the yellowing piles of newspapers, the abandoned pots, oil lamps, and worn-out shoes. This museum-cum-library of my country childhood was roofed by an impressive construction of beams and roof tiles. The attic world was important to me, because it fed my imagination, and aroused images of past times and people. There, I could imagine myself as an adult.

A child's home should have unexplored corners that only reveal their secrets gradually; not everything should be clear at a glance or immediately obvious. A new block of offices or a housing area discloses its essence immediately, and simultaneously loses any interest it may have held: the poverty of our affluent society lies in its transparency, its obviousness, its lack of mystery. On the other hand, the society of increasing technology, control, and subordination grows shapeless and inaccessible to the senses. The control and ownership of our society have lost their human face. Our institutions are impersonal systems: the activities of everyday life take place outside the workings of our senses and beyond our understanding.

The menace represented by this brave new world lies in its lack of concrete quality. Even fear is acceptable as long as it has its understandable cause, or it symbolizes something, and as long as it is not cloaked in apparent order and well-being. The irrational fear in our cities grows out of the meaninglessness of the environment to our reason and its incomprehensibility to our senses. "Symptoms are intolerable precisely because they are meaningless. Almost any difficulty can be borne if we can discern its meaning. It is meaninglessness which is the greatest threat to humanity," says psychologist Edward Edinger.[21]

Architecture is often accused of excessive abstraction, but this is a misuse of the term. Abstraction is not a synonym for the lack of meaning, but its opposite. Abstraction is a condensation of meaning or imagery, a pregnant symbol. Mondrian's abstraction is not a game with the forms of elementary geometry, but a reflection of the painter's world, the sum of his experience of life. It gains its strength from all the Dutch landscapes that he saw and painted. "Scientific abstraction differs from an empty generalization in the way in which potent abstract art differs from empty ornament," says Anton Ehrenzweig.[22]

Obviously, even artistically ambitious design is often remote from the unconscious bio-cultural bases of behavior, and becomes an elegant and inventive, but psychologically empty, game with form. The current theoretical analysis and teaching of architecture deals with architecture simply as a visual play with form: "architecture (as) the masterly, correct and magnificent play of masses brought together in light," to borrow Le Corbusier's famous credo.[23] But architecture must also help man to exist by arousing feelings of home, safety, and continuity. The task of architecture is to "facilitate man's homecoming," as Aldo van Eyck often points out. Building in our industrial age lacks emotional substance, because it no longer provides images for our minds or nourishment for our dreams. Architecture aiming at simplicity does not reach the archetypal experience of our consciousness, and architecture trusting only to richness of form does not arouse our imagination. "Modern man's most urgent need is to discover the reality and value of the inner subjective world of the psyche, to discover the symbolic life," says Edinger.[24] Architecture transfers this symbolic life into material and spatial form.

Arousing images and dreams through design does not mean the promotion of architectural kitsch or nostalgic pastiche. These tendencies are degenerative; not just a deterioration in taste or morals, but also a weakening of the life force.

The environment should not offer sensory pleasure through a kind of architectural Muzak, but should operate as an external continuation of the human mind. Architecture is literally a biological and mental extension of man. The concentration on tradition implied by this perspective bears no resemblance to a simple nostalgia for history as a collection of superficial motifs. The condemnation of such eclecticism is not a moral attitude, but a question of the health of our collective mind, and thus a judgment both philosophical and biological. The manipulation of history always furthers estrangement, rather than stabilizing our identity. Distorting the time strata of the environment is a distortion of our consciousness. Do we want to distort our common memory in the name of momentary pleasure for the senses?

ARCHITECTURE IN PAINTING

Architecture is often considered the most important human deed, the art form from which other art forms derive life and strength. However, in our time architecture has lost its artistic autonomy and become sheer construction in the name of economic benefit and rationality. Although built architecture has lost its power to influence our emotions, inspiration may yet be gained by the study of the architecture of painting, poetry, and music. These art forms have not, after all, been drained to the same extent by our material and utilitarian culture.

I am fascinated by the artistic depiction of architecture. A painter chooses a natural, suggestive, and focus-giving setting for the depicted event, whether landscape, buildings, rooms, or merely objects. In doing so, the basic problems of experience posed by spatial and architectural phenomena are reduced to their essentials. In the language of painting, a city becomes a still-life and a still-life a city. Painting thus represents a phenomenological charting of architecture. The means by which artists have historically created the experience of place are exactly the same as those by which an architect today can achieve a sense of constructed place. While Cubism ultimately subordinated the subject, painting itself became a kind of architecture, a construction of images and associations.

The artist's architectural setting is often a compact miniature, in the manner of those painted by the medieval artists or Giotto and Fra Angelico. Their townscapes are as compressed as shrunken heads, depicting the entire city. They reflect the city's eternal role as a symbol of the cosmic order.

In its simplest form, the architecture of such painted worlds is presented as a background, a roofing, or an elementary space covered by a vault. Giotto or Fra Angelico's rooms are archetypes that speak as eloquently as any built rooms. The compact presentations of cities and architecture in Fra Angelico's works are particularly appealing. His *Annunciation* was held by Alvar Aalto to be the supreme presentation

94

95

96

97

of interior and exterior. Aalto's 1926 article, "From doorstep to living room," is an expressive description of the affinity between mind and space. His description, in fact, is an early phenomenological analysis of the architectural experience: "For very special reasons I have chosen as the picture of my title Fra Angelico's *L'Annunziazione*. There is a great deal of truth and nobility within its miniatures that are valid in this connection. It is a wonderful example of "entering a room". The distinct triad of human figure, room and herb garden, which is dominant in the picture, makes it an unattainable ideal of home culture. The smile on the Virgin's face comes out just as strongly in the sensitive detail of the building as in the gleaming flowers of the herb garden. However, two things are expressed here very clearly: the unity of the room, facade and garden, and a molding of these elements which makes them primarily bring out the human figure and reflect its states of mind. Anyone who really understands the secrets of Fra Angelico's picture can happily leave the reading of the rest of this article to others."[25]

Renaissance painters, fascinated by the new science of perspective, brought their architectural settings into line with normal observation. At the same time, their perspectively correct architecture took on the character of a stage-set.

In painting, both the natural landscape and the man-made artifice are reduced to their essentials. The scene presented may be a strange intermediate form of landscape and human construction, as in Arnold Böcklin's *Island of Death* or the ruin-like cave of Leonardo's *Madonna of the Rocks*. The cave, of course, as man's first shelter and a symbol of the womb, is particularly charged with emotion. In contrast to the darkness of the cave, one thinks of the ethereal light and color compositions of J. M. W. Turner and Claude Monet, which one could call 'caves of light.' The overgrown, moss-covered ruin, in Romantic painting especially, is often an eloquent reminder of the transience of man and all his edifices, or of the melancholy splendor of a past culture. A ruin always adds a plaintive note and an tragic dimension of time to a landscape.

In painting, architectural themes are often used as allegories that stimulate association, such as the puzzling, solitary fragment of a column in Giorgione's fascinating *Tempesta*.

A scale emphasis is achieved by studies and variations in lighting, as in Rembrandt and Vermeer's interiors, or the landscapes of other Dutch painters.

Interiors by Dutch masters such as Peter de Hoogh are true interior architecture, in which one can simultaneously see several rooms or a series of places, one visible through the other. This is literal transparency, without glass. The focal point of these interiors is often achieved using the constructions of external architecture, producing several layers of outside-inside-outside-inside images, each inside the other.

In painting, the setting and relations between persons are expressed by means of dramatic steps and differences in level, as in the historical spectacles of Paolo Veronese, Vittorio Carpaccio, or Gentile Bellini. In Baroque paintings, events are arranged into an undifferentiated space and the people themselves form the architecture.

In paintings, too, window and door openings have their original dramatic significance as the agents for a dialogue between two worlds, protagonists in the dialectic of interior and exterior. In these works of art, the most powerful emotional content is usually not connected with extremes of pure imagery, but with dual figures representing pairs of contrasts: interior and exterior, closed and open, darkness and light, light and heavy. The fact that a door or window is open only becomes dramatic when the possibility of its being closed is equally evident. In modern architecture, apertures have lost their evocative power, because they lack the potential activity of closing.

The everyday objects in paintings act as keys to the personality of the person depicted or as a symbolic framework adding to the depicted event. In René Magritte's paintings, everyday things actually gain supremacy and take possession of the architectural space. We no longer gaze at such things: they stare at us.

The focus of painted events is usually underlined by means of symmetry, but the mythical content may as well be hidden in the very abundance of everyday life, as is the case in Pieter Brueghel's *The Conversion of Saul* or *The Fall of Icarus*. The non-monumental staging of Brueghel's paintings is reminiscent of the way in which Alvar Aalto consistently distracts one's attention away from the entrance or other key elements of a building. Equally, emotional intensity may also be produced through a feeling of agonizing emptiness and desolation, or gain meaning by the anticipation or strangeness of an event, as captured by Carlo Carrà or Henri Rousseau.

The paradoxical quality of architectural scale or perspective in the case of metaphysicists such as Carlo Carrá and Giorgio de Chirico imbues the architectural scene with a menacing tension. De Chirico's paintings arouse palpable sensations of heat; the spatial experience is intensified by the sound of the distant train echoing through the townscape, drawing attention to the spatial depth of the scene. At the same time, the train points to a world outside (in the same way the angles in Mondrian's painting meet outside the picture) and confers a chilling sensation of the deserted town, full of evil premonitions, as the last link with life rushes away.

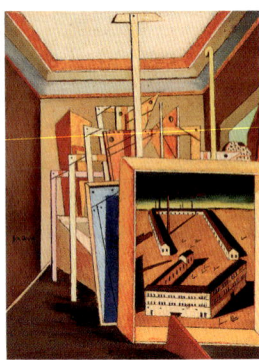

In Magritte's works, conflicting images—incompatible experiences, simultaneously night and day, life and death, reality and the interpretation of it, motion and static eternity—introduce a state of tension, of expectation and fear. But his paintings are not only horror: they also contain an awakening from nightmare and the element of recovery.

Metaphysical and surrealistic painters in particular have inspired architects recently, among them Aldo Rossi. As architecture has lost its power to give release to our fantasy, architects understandably seek inspiration in art forms in which repressed memories become an actual form of expression. In fact, the sole appeal of art lies in its power to tempt forth the archaic strata of our consciousness and to act as a projection for our feelings. The effectiveness of poetry lies in its ability to arouse such multiple and multi-layered images, repeatedly returning to the unsolved riddle of life with a sense of intense curiosity.

I have dwelt on this 'architecture of painting' because painting displays all the symbols, imagery, and reconciliations of opposites that have disappeared from modern architecture. Only in rare cases, such as in Aalto's texture collages, or Luis Barragán's metaphysical settings, or Louis Kahn's "ruins with windows behind which nobody lives" and Aldo van Eyck's house/city metaphor, has the architecture of our day attained the magical force equivalent to that depicted by painters.

The vanguard of architecture at the moment strives for effects that will provoke or shock us, sometimes with historical references, sometimes quite literally by shattering the entire image of the house, or by eliminating the effect of gravity. The new architecture possesses an alarming necrophiliac tone—the cemetery and the crematorium are favorite subjects. This architecture relies for its effect on the hypnotic endlessness and monotony of marching steps. Equally often, the message of such collaged historical architecture is frighteningly totalitarian. The use of historical motifs to make the environment more human and softer in fact often reveals itself to be a hidden desire for manipulation.

The architectural hybrids of our day are like the final shelters assembled from the ruins of a nuclear war, or architectural mutations produced by radiation, mutations which have broken loose from the natural order.

This essay emerged out of an address to a seminar entitled "Locality as an Element of Architecture," a theme embodying a fundamental dichotomy of thinking. The term 'element' gives the impression of a ready or given substance, which could be used or not used as the material of architecture. But is not local identity, or sense of place, among the most integral and comprehensive experiences of architecture? Is not the 'Finnishness' of Alvar Aalto's architecture, or simply what one feels when standing in a sacred place, the direct opposite of that concept 'element'?

The technique of dividing the architectural whole into elements has done much to produce a superficial view of architecture and to convert it into empty play with form. A work of art quite simply has no independent or ready-made elements; all the components acquire their meaning from the whole.

The recent search for roots, and efforts to tie architecture to local tradition, are indications of a welcome desire for change. But the idea of attaching traditional and local factors to architecture as conscious additives or loans is doomed to failure. For the same reason, design for another culture is ultimately bound to be artificial. A sense of locality can only emerge from within one's experience and a collective sense of culture. The estrangement and the weakening of the sense of our identity cannot be cured in a calculated way by means of a superficially 'localized' architecture. The inhuman environment of our age, which confers no sense of home, is a true image of our psychological rootless-ness and loneliness, and represents the sapping of our collective will. If architecture is to show the way forward to a more humane and stable world, it must be not merely the routine use of a design practice based on 'elements'; architecture must always embody a deep artistic imagery of a culture's traditions, the authentic expression of its culture.

94 Arnold Böcklin, *The Island of the Dead*, 1880. Öffentliche Kunstsammlung, Basel.

95 Leonardo da Vinci, *The Virgin of the Rocks*, 1483. The Museum of the Louvre, Paris.

96 William Turner, *Interior at Petworth*, c. 1837. Tate Gallery, London.

97 The Workshop of Rembrandt, *A Man seated reading at a Table in a Lofty Room*, 1628–30. The National Gallery, London.

98 Vermeer van Delft, *Interior with a Lady Reading a letter with her Maid (The Love Letter)*, c. 1669–1670. Rijksmuseum, Amsterdam.

99 Gentile Bellini. *The Miracle of the Cross Recovered from the Canal of S. Lorenzo*, c. 1500. Gallerie dell'Accademia, Venice.

100 Gianbattista Tiepolo, *Allegory of the Planets and Continents*, 1751–52. The Metropolitan Museum of Art, New York.

101 René Magritte, *Personal Values*, 1951–52. Private Collection, New York.

102 Pieter Brueghel, *Landscape with the Fall of Icarus*. c. 1558. Musées Royaux des Beaux-Arts de Belgique, Brussels.

103 Carlo Carrá, *Pine Tree by the Sea*, 1921. Casella Collection, Rome.

104 Giorgio di Chirico, *Metaphysical Interior with Workshop*, 1948. Private Collection, Rome.

THE GEOMETRY OF FEELING

The Phenomenology of Architecture
(1985)

106 Edward Hopper, *Manhattan Bridge Loop*, 1926. Addison Gallery of American Art, Phillips Academy, Andover, MA.

Why do so few modern buildings appeal to our emotions, when an anonymous house in an old town, or an unpretentious farm building, will give us a sense of familiarity and pleasure? Why is it that the stone foundations we discover in an overgrown meadow, or a dilapidated barn, or an abandoned boathouse can arouse our imagination, while our own houses seem to stifle and smother our daydreams? The buildings of our own time may arouse our curiosity with their daring or inventiveness, but they give us little sense of the meaning of our world or our own existence.

Efforts are being made to revitalize the debilitated language of architecture, through both a richer idiom and by reviving historical themes. But despite their effusive diversity, such avant-garde works are just as bereft of meaning as the coldly technical approach to building against which they rebel.

Architecture's impoverished inner meaning has also been considered in numerous recent writings on architectural theory. Some writers think our architecture is too poor in terms of form, others contend that its form is too abstract or intellectual. Philosophically, our culture of hedonistic materialism seems to be losing any meaningful dimension that might in general be worthy of perpetuation in stone. As Ludwig Wittgenstein argues, "Architecture glorifies and eternalizes something. When there is nothing to glorify there is no architecture."[1]

ARCHITECTURE AS PLAY WITH FORM

In becoming a specialist profession, architecture has gradually detached itself from its intentional background, evolving into a discipline more and more fully determined by its own rules and value systems. Architecture is now a field of technology that still ventures to believe itself a form of free artistic expression.

In *Architecture and the Crisis of Modern Science*, one of the most significant theoretical books on architecture in recent years, the Mexican architect and scholar Alberto Pérez-Gómez identifies the intellectual cul-de-sac into which architecture has thus entered:

"The assumption that architecture can derive its meaning from functionalism, formal games of combinations, the coherence or rationality of style understood as ornamental language or the use of type as a generative structure in design marks the evolution of western architecture during the past two centuries. Theory thus reduced to a self-referential system whose elements must be combined through mathematical logic must pretend that its values, and therefore its meaning, are derived from the system itself."[2]

It is not easy to argue against Pérez-Gómez's line of thinking, which is reinforced convincingly by historical evidence. Additional proof exists to demonstrate architecture's detachment from its proper background and purpose. I consider one viewpoint here: the relationship between architectural form and how architecture is experienced. Design has become so intensively a kind of game with form that the reality of how a building is experienced has been overlooked. We make the mistake of thinking of, and assessing, a building as a formal composition, no longer understanding that it is a metaphor, let alone experiencing the other reality that lies behind the metaphor.

We must consider, then, whether forms or geometry in general can give rise to architectural experience and emotion. Are forms the true and authentic elements of architecture at all? Are even such elements of architecture as walls, windows, or doors the real units of actual architectural effect?

THE ILLUSION OF ELEMENTARISM

The advance of modern science has been dominated by the principle of elementarism and reductionism. Every phenomenon so considered is divided into its basic elements and relations and is viewed as the sum of these elements. The early stages of this line of thinking are represented by Carl von Linné's classification of plants, and Antoine Laurent Lavoisier's classification of chemical phenomena, as well as J.N.L. Durand's system of rationalized architecture.

The elementarist view has also been dominant in the theory, teaching, and practice of art and architecture. At the same time, these arts have been reduced solely to arts of a visual sensibility. In the Bauhaus design pedagogy, architecture is taught and analyzed as a play with form, combining various visual elements of form and space. This form acquires a character, one that stimulates our visual senses by means of the dynamics of visual perception (as studied by perceptual psychology). A building is considered to be a concrete composition built up out of a selection of given basic elements. Yet such a composition is no longer in touch with the reality of any experience outside itself, not to mention any intention to depict and articulate the realm of our consciousness.

Pérez-Gómez writes to this effect: "The poetical content of reality, the *a priori* of the world, which is the ultimate frame of reference for any truly meaningful architecture, is hidden beneath a thick layer of formal explanations."[3]

But is not an artistic work actually the opposite of the entire elementarist idea? Surely the meanings of an artistic work are born out of the whole, from the poetic image that integrates the parts, and are in no way simply the sum of the elements.

The analysis of the formal structure of an architectural work does not necessarily reveal the artistic quality of the building or how it makes its effect. A formal analysis cannot reveal the building's artistic essence or its manner of impact. Le Corbusier's Convent at La Tourette, for instance, can, of course, be analyzed as a formal structure—and this is solely the type of analysis that has so far been applied—but this analysis does not reveal the metaphors of life's basic tragedy, man's simultaneous desire to live and to die, to achieve flight and to remain earthbound, which are forcefully mediated by the encounter with the building. The building is simultaneously a cave and a vehicle of flight. A formal analysis also uncovers very little of the concealed drama, "the melancholy of a titan"—to use Kyösti Ålander's expression of Michelangelo's emotional power—engraved in the walls of the Medici Chapel.[4] In this center of mythical power, gravity is denser than in the everyday world, and the metaphorical structures of the walls struggle against the pressure of the external world rather than against ordinary structural loads. Only the mental images, associations, recollections, and bodily sensations triggered by the work succeed in mediating the artistic message of the architecture. An authentic work of art always pushes our consciousness off of its commonplace track and focuses it onto reality's deeper structure.

THE ARCHITECTURE OF IMAGERY

The artistic dimension of a work of art does not lie in the actual physical thing; it exists only in the consciousness of the person experiencing that object. The analysis of a work of art is, at its most genuine level, an introspection by the consciousness subjected to it. The work of art's meaning lies not in its forms, but in the images transmitted by the forms and the emotional force that they carry. Form only affects our feelings through what it represents.

As long as teaching and criticism do not strive to clarify the experiential and mental dimensions of architecture, they will have little to do with the artistic essence of architecture. Current efforts to restore the richness of the architectural idiom through a greater diversity of form are based on a lack of understanding of the essence of art. The richness of a work of art lies in the vitality of the images it arouses, and—paradoxically—the simplest, most archetypal forms arouse the images open to the most interpretations. Post-Modernism's (superficial) return to ancient themes lacks emotive power precisely because these collages of architectural motifs are no longer linked with phenomenologically authentic feelings true to architecture.

In his *ABC of Reading*, Ezra Pound wrote a "warning" to the reader: "...music begins to atrophy when it departs too far from the dance;...poetry begins to atrophy when it gets too far from music..."[5] In the same way, architecture has its own origins, and if it moves too far away from them it loses its effectiveness. The renewal of an art means re-discovering its deepest essence.

The language of art is the language of metaphors that can be identified with our existence. If art lacks contact with the sensory memories that live in our subconscious and link our various senses, it could only be reduced to mere meaningless ornamentation. The experience of art is an interaction between our embodied memories and our world. As Adrian Stokes observes, "In a way all art originates in the body."[6]

If we are to experience architectural meaning and sense, it is vital that the effect of the building should find a counterpart in the world of the viewer's experience.

THE EIDOS OF ARCHITECTURE

As architects, we do not design buildings primarily as physical objects; we design with regard to the images and emotions of the people who live in them. "But all these delicate devices making for the permanence of the edifice were as nothing to those which he employed when he elaborated the emotions and vibrations of the soul of the future beholder of his work," as Paul Valéry writes in his magnificent dialogue *Eupalinos, or the Architect*.[7] Thus the effect of architecture stems from more or less shared images and basic emotions connected with building.

Phenomenology analyzes such basic responses, and its method has become a more common means of examining architecture, too, in the last few years. A philosophical approach initially attached most closely to the names of philosophers Edmund Husserl and Martin Heidegger, phenomenology is introspective in nature, in contrast to the postivist's standpoint's desire for objectivity. Phenomenology strives to depict phenomena appealing directly to the consciousness as such, without any theories and categories taken from the natural sciences or psychology. Phenomenology thus means examining a phenomenon of the consciousness in its own dimension of consciousness. That, using Husserl's concept, means a "pure looking at" the phenomenon, or "viewing its essence."[8] Phenomenology is a purely theoretical approach to research in the original sense of the Greek word *theoria*, which means precisely "a looking at."

The phenomenology of architecture is thus "looking at" architecture from within the consciousness experiencing it, through architectural feeling, in contrast to the analysis of the physical proportions and properties of the building or a stylistic frame of reference. The phenomenology of architecture seeks the inner language of building.

There is, on the whole, great suspicion of an introspective approach to art because it is thought to lack objectivity. But people do not seem to demand the same kind of objectivity from the artist's creative work. A work of art is a reality only when it is experienced, and experiencing a work of art means re-creating its dimension of feeling.

One of the most important "raw materials" of the phenomenological analysis of architecture is early childhood memory. We are used to thinking of childhood memories as products of the naive consciousness and imprecise memory capacity of the child, something with great appeal but with as little real value as our dreams. Both of these preconceived ideas are wrong. Surely the fact that certain early memories retain their personal identifiability and emotional force throughout our lives provides convincing proof of the importance and authenticity of these experiences, just as our dreams and daydreams reveal the most real and spontaneous contents of our minds.

In an untitled and unfinished essay, presumably written in 1925, Alvar Aalto describes young boys at a party, selecting their candy by the color and shape of the wrapping, while the adults chose "candies of the touristy kind" with pictures of castles and villages. He argues that the young boys acted through an instant instinct of beauty whereas the adult choices were purposeful. "There is hardly anyone who would seriously deny that instinctive joy is the response to an aesthetic experience. It is related to all intuitive activity, the joy of creation and the joy of work. Unfortunately modern man, particularly Western man, is so deeply influenced by methodical analysis that his natural insight and immediate receptiveness have been greatly weakened."[9]

107 Andrey Tarkovsky, *The Sacrifice*, 1986.
108 Walker Evans, *Coal Miner's House,
    Scott's Run, West Virginia*, 1936.
109 Balthus, *The Room*, 1952–54. Private
    collection.

The task of the phenomenology of architecture is to survey the natural and innocent consciousness so swiftly observed by Aalto.

ARCHITECTURE WITHOUT ARCHITECTS

Fruitful material for a phenomenological analysis of architectural experience is also offered by the ways in which architecture is presented and depicted in other branches of the arts. In poetry, images connected with buildings are common and these images are the actual materials of Gaston Bachelard's work *The Poetics of Space.* Bachelard has also written a phenomenological work on the poetics of daydreams, *The Poetics of Reverie*, which has many points of contact with the art of building in spite of its non-architectural subject.[10] In fiction, film, photography, and painting, the secret languages by which landscape, buildings, and objects influence people also often play a crucial role. Examples abound in the classics of Russian, German, and French literature, the films of Alfred Hitchcock and Andrey Tarkovsky, Walker Evans' photographs, or the architecture shown in paintings—from medieval miniatures to Edward Hopper's landscapes of metaphysical loneliness and Balthus' rooms full of erotic anxiety. A writer, film director, or painter has to give the human event he is presenting a setting, a place, and thus in fact performs a job of architectural design without a client, structural calculations, or a building permit. The presentation of architecture in other arts is a "pure looking," similar to a child's way of experiencing things, for the rules of architectural discipline do not regulate the experience of the way it is presented.

THE ARCHITECTURE OF MEMORY

The inner architecture of the mind emerging out of experiences and memory images is built on different principles than the architecture developed out of professional approaches. For instance, I cannot bring to mind a single window or door from my own childhood as such, but I can sit down at the windows of my many memories and look out at a *courtyard* that has long since disappeared or a clearing now filled with trees. I can also step through the innumerable doors of my memory and recognize there the dark warmth and special smell of the rooms on the other side.

The details of the roofs or hearths of the familiar buildings of my childhood have escaped from my memory, but I still recognize the pleasure on my skin when hearing the beating of rain under a sheltering roof, or when arriving at the warmth of the hearth with my limbs stiffened by cold.

I am not able to recall any longer the exact image of my grandfather's wooden table, but I can still imagine myself sitting next to it and

sense the power of the center of the farmhouse, integrating the family and occasional visitors. In my childhood, the table was an institution, the symbol of life's regularity and the family's hospitality. At Christmas time this center of everyday life was given a festive setting: a long and narrow table cover made of wax cloth was set on the table, one with colorful printed pictures of houses buried in snow that enticed my imagination.

THE TWO FACES OF THE DWELLING

One of Alvar Aalto's finest writings is the essay "From the doorstep to the living room," written in 1926 for the sample issue of the *Aitta* family magazine.[11] The essay is a subtle phenomenological study of a basic architectural experience. Aalto chose one of Fra Angelico's several *Annunciation* paintings to illustrate his essay. "We find in its miniature form a great deal of truth and refinement to illustrate our problem. The picture provides an ideal example of 'entering a room.'"[12]

Significantly, the experience pointed out by Aalto is not a visual or tectonic 'element' of the building, such as the loggia or the door, but rather an event possessing a verb form, rather than an noun.

Aalto also points out the essential metaphorical essence of architecture when speaking of the "two faces of the home." The first face is represented by the immediate connection with the outdoors associated with southern European traditions, whereas the second face, "the winter face," is expressed by "the furnishings of the inner rooms emphasizing warmth." The metaphorical meaning of architecture is also expressed in the reversed images of the garden as an interior and the hall as "the metaphor of free outdoors under the roof of the home."

The exceptional emotive power of Alvar Aalto's own architecture is undoubtedly based on the layered imagery revealed by this early essay.

I have analyzed the layered imagery of Aalto's Villa Mairea, especially the collage-like fusion of Modernist images and suggestions of the anonymous Finnish peasant tradition.[13] This intuitively articulated architectural 'painting,' with its local colors, foci, and zones of light and shadow, is closer to the way in which Giotto or Cézanne stage an architectural scene than to our established architectonic notions. In its design principles, the Villa Mairea is a Cubist collage rather than a structure organized according to a tectonic logic.

THE PRIMARY EMOTIONS OF ARCHITECTURE

I have said that architecture cannot be a mere play with form. This view does not spring from the self-evident fact that architecture is tied to its practical purpose and many other external conditions. But if a building does not fulfill its basic phenomenological conditions as a metaphor of human existence, it is unable to influence the emotions linked in our souls with the images a building creates. An architectural effect is based on a number of what we could call primary emotions. These emotions form the genuine "basic vocabulary" of architecture and it is by working through them that a work becomes architecture and not, for instance, a large-scale sculpture or scenography.

Architecture is a direct expression of existence, of human presence in the world, in the sense that architecture is largely based on a language of the body—of which neither the creator of the work nor the person experiencing the work is aware.

The following types of experience could well be among the primary emotions produced by architecture:

- The house as a sign of culture in the landscape; the house as a projection of man and a point of reference in the landscape;
- Approaching the building, recognizing a human habitation or a given institution in the form of a house;
- Entrance into the building's sphere of influence, stepping into its territory, being near the building;
- Having a roof over your head, being sheltered and shaded;
- Stepping into the house, entering through the door, crossing the boundary between exterior and interior;
- Coming home or stepping inside the house for a specific purpose, expectation and fulfillment, sense of strangeness and familiarity;
- Being in the room, a sense of security, a sense of togetherness or isolation;
- Being in the sphere of influence of the foci that bring the building together, such as the table, bed or fireplace;
- Encountering the light or darkness that dominates the space, the space of light;
- Looking out of the window, the link with the landscape.

Experiencing loneliness is one of the basic feelings given by architecture, similar to the experiences of silence and light often found in Louis Kahn's texts. A strong architectural experience always produces a sense of loneliness and silence irrespective of the actual number of people present or the surrounding noise. The experience of art is a private dialogue between the work and the person experiencing it, an encounter that excludes all other interaction. "Art is made by the alone for the alone," as Cyril Connolly writes.[14]

In the reality of emotive experience, that which is absent is as important as that which is present. What gives rise to the feeling of yearning when we encounter a beach casino closed for winter? Is it not the recollection of summer's joys? What causes the touching melancholy attending the sight of chairs turned upside down on tables in an outdoor restaurant? Does it not arise from the cheerful murmuring of people in our memory?

The natural landscape can never express solitude in the same way as a building. Nature does not need man to explain itself, but a building represents its builder and proclaims his absence. The harrowing feeling of solitude achieved by the metaphysical painters is based precisely on the constructed signs of man, reminders of the viewer's own solitude.

The most comprehensive, and perhaps most important, architectural experience is the sense of being in a unique place. Part of this intense experience of place is always the impression of sacred purpose: this place is for higher beings. A house may seem built for a practical purpose, but in fact it is a metaphysical instrument, a mythical tool with which we try to introduce a reflection of eternity into our momentary existence.

Alvar Aalto also identified this second reality of architecture. In the unfinished essay mentioned earlier, Aalto has Anatole France's figure, the Abbé Coignard, say:

> In front of us we see a town. Look at its towers, gates, houses and thoroughfares. What a fine and delicate picture of playfulness it shows us. What a flawless whole it seems to be. We rejoice to see a sight like this. Yet we know for sure that the people down there are just as vile, ludicrous, clumsy, mean and false as everywhere. This town is full of strife and deception. This is no harmonious community, it is a serpent's nest, just like all other societies of men…My son, here is something that has come from above, which atones for the imperfections of the inhabitants. God has laid down something which people do not have the intelligence to seek.[15]

In this essay Aalto uses the significant notion, "the psyche of form."

Architecture exists in another reality from our everyday life and pursuits. The emotional force of the ruins of an abandoned house or of rejected objects, stems from the fact that these artifacts make us imagine and share the fate of their owners. They seduce our imagination into wandering away from the world of everyday realities. The quality of architecture does not lie in the sense of reality that it expresses, but in quite the reverse, in architecture's capacity for awakening our imagination.

Architecture is always inhabited by spirits. People known to us may well live in the building, but they are only understudy actors in a waking dream. In reality, architecture is always the home of spirits, the dwelling place of metaphysical beings.

The defenders of the humanization of architecture today are completely mistaken when they claim that buildings should be designed for 'the needs of real people.' Every great building in the history of architecture was built for the idealized man. The primary condition for the production of good architecture is the creation of an ideal client for the commission at hand.

MULTISENSORY EXPERIENCE

An impressive architectural experience sensitizes our whole physical and mental receptivity. The structure of feeling is difficult to grasp because of its *vastness and diversity*. In each experience, we find a combination of the biological and the culturally derived, the collective and the individual, the conscious and the unconscious, the analytical and the emotional, the mental and the physical, the psychic and the embodied.

The symbols and associations in the language of art can be interpreted in many ways, and make our consciousness shift from one possible interpretation to another. Adrian Stokes refers, for instance, to the close connection between the experience of marble, the low relief technique, and water fantasies.[16] He also writes of "the oral invitation of Veronese marble."[17] I myself recall the strong oral invitation of the white marble threshold of the Gamble House in Los Angeles by the Green brothers.

Imagine now the sound-space created by drops of water falling occasionally in a dark, damp vault; the urban space created by the sound of church bells; the sense of distance that we feel when the sound of a night train pierces our dreams, or the smell-space of a bakery or sweet shop.

Why do abandoned and unheated houses have the same smell of death everywhere? Is it because the smell we sense is in fact the one created through our eyes?

THE BEGINNING

I once spoke with a church official about church design. He stressed the importance of understanding the liturgy, iconography, and other internal rulings of the church. He seemed upset when I said that only a heathen could design a truly expressive church. If the design of a church relies merely on the organization of given forms, I said, the effect would be empty sentimentality. In my view, the symbol of faith can only be fully transformed into stone by someone for whom the dimensions of faith are vivid, fresh, and direct.

After this conversation I remembered what Louis Kahn wrote about the significance of the beginning: "…It is good for the mind to go back to the beginning because the beginning of any established activity of man is its most wonderful moment. For in it lies all its spirit and resourcefulness, from which we must constantly draw our inspiration of present needs."[18]

THE ROOMS OF MEMORY

Architecture in Painting
(1985)

(Illustrations notes are on page 110.)

My miniature childhood world, with houses and landscapes scaled down to my own size, returns to me with a flood of emotion when I see medieval miniatures, icons, or early Renaissance paintings. Standing in front of Fra Angelico's murals in the monks' cells at the monastery of San Marco in Florence, I felt I was returning to the innocent world of my childhood. The houses and scenery depicted so long ago by the artist seemed to have the same significance and human face as in my earliest childhood recollections.

These paintings return me to the stage sets on which my childhood fantasies were played out: no mute spaces these, for they whispered to me about the play that was about to start. And just as these stage sets horizontally flattened my childhood's world to my diminutive measures, the world of these paintings is vertically reduced to the human scale. Are not these stage sets and painted landscapes, in fact, persons disguised as buildings?

In the world of the child and the artist, the constants of space, place, time, and dimensions lose their significance. A chair is a cathedral, for instance, and as well, an image of a cathedral can be found in the corner closet. The home is simultaneously a doll's house and the devout
111 symbol of human existence. Cities are reduced into objects, although they preserve their distinctive characteristics, just like shrunken skulls. No city ever built has the charm of the cities painted in the backgrounds
112 of Fra Angelico's *Descent from the Cross* and Piero della Francesca's
113 *Legend of the True Cross.*

In this world, man is always at the center, and even the houses take on a human visage. The top stories farthest from the spectator

114 are condensed as if an extremity of the body: the head of the house. The top floor of a building also represents the unconscious fantasies in
115 our memory. In the houses painted by Giorgio de Chirico and Edward
116 Hopper, the top floors seem to be straining their memory in order to bring some concealed, half-forgotten secret into the daylight; our daydreams and erotic fantasies are also stored in such attic rooms.

Clearly, as our houses have lost the memories and the associations which attract our fantasy, the attic, the symbol of these dimensions of the mind, has been lost altogether. Equally significant is the disappearance of cellars, stairways, and all the various obscure, superfluous spaces and recesses that occupy our unconscious spatial understanding. The cellar represents the final banishment of memories and mental
117 images from consciousness; the trapdoors of Hell in Fra Angelico's *Last Judgement* vividly communicate the idea of a realm of eternal oblivion buried in the bowels of the earth. But can we feel the existence of Hell under the floors of our modern houses?

118 Whenever I look at Pieter Brueghel the Elder's *The Month of August*, a childhood recollection takes hold of me: the excitement, mixed with fear, at crawling in the tunnels I had burrowed into a haystack. I have often pondered the powerful erotic feelings aroused by this painting and their association with haymaking and harvesting. Beneath its commonplace subject, is not Brueghel's painting a concealed erotic fantasy? Does not the path mown through the cornfield, so brimming with fertility, transform the entire landscape into giant labia; is not the harvesting of corn a hidden sexual metaphor in itself?

Brueghel's painted path and clean-shaven field are also architecture, human structures in the eroticized landscape. This is, in fact, the task of architecture: not simply to render the landscape comprehensible, but to eroticize the landscape, to fire our imagination with it. In his
119 *Venus*, Giorgione placed an ordinary farmhouse in contrast to the nude goddess as a symbol of earthliness, curiosity, and desire. Giorgione's enigmatic *Tempest* is another sensual allegory, in which fragments of architecture tell their nostalgic tale of a lost age of glory. But the architecture, illuminated by a flash of lightning before the storm breaks, is again strangely eroticized. Just look at that peeping eye of a house under a tree in the upper right-hand corner!

The architecture presented by such painters in their pictures is familiar and compelling because it approaches us through our earliest memories and experiences. The architecture of painters is an architecture of the human soul; it conveys the genuine inner poetry of architecture, a poetry independent of external style. The artist's architecture is an architecture of associations, and observes the laws of emotion, not of gravity.

In painting an imagined mythical or historical event, the artist defines the scene of the event pictorially. This definition of location is a basic task of architecture, whether it is defining a landscape, a townscape, a building, or a room. The artist conveys an image of architecture that makes the strongest emotional impact possible within the space and event he paints. One might say the artist creates phenomenologically genuine architecture, an art of building defined by his own emotion, rather than by the professional rules of the art of architecture. The house painted by an artist is a synopsis of innocent architectural experiences. In the phenomenological sense, architecture in painting is 'pure contemplation' or the 'contemplation of essence.'

120 Duccio's painting *Jesus Heals the Blind Man* is an illustrative example of the way in which a painter utilizes architecture as the sounding board of the depicted event or narrative characters. Here, a stately, distinct, nearly symmetrical palace with a chapel on its roof terrace forms the background to the depiction of Jesus and his disciples. The top floor has been vertically reduced to roughly a third of its 'correct' height. The two vaulted openings of the top floor governing the event suggest the image of eyes opened wide, the symbol of vision and benevolence. Behind the blind man, who appears as two separate figures, an asymmetrical structure echoes the man's disability, while the building's half blind side façade and partly closed window shutters seem to refer to his blindness.

121 Giovanni Bellini's *Religious Allegory* is another layered architectural metaphor which contains a number of architectural scenes, from the terrace in front with its dais, seats, and gates to the hermit's half-cave dug into the ground, or the village across the stretch of water and the castle on the top of the hill guarding the landscape—and even the castle has its guardians in the form of the mountain tops. The allegory contrasts the religious and the worldly, the planned and the arbitrary, high culture and the vernacular, and most importantly, the dual task of architecture as both shelter and symbol. The terrace, magnificently decorated with colored stone slabs, induces in the viewer a vision of the splendor of the palace behind, and this architectural hint shifts the enigma of the painting outside its very frame.

The architecture of painting is best illustrated graphically by a comparison of paintings from different ages: in this method, the narrative content loses significance and the purely pictorial and architectural message gains emphasis.

122 Giotto's *Annunciation of St. Anne* depicts the scene of a miracle. One wall of the building has been removed to provide a simultaneous view of the exterior, with a servant sitting on the porch outside spinning

124

125

126

127

thread, and the ascetic interior with the main characters. The everyday details and objects contrast with the pediment-like gables, suggestive of both home and temple. Although the presentation is as free from illusion as a structural drawing, the room is still as inexplicable and awe-inspiring as the supernatural event set in it.

123   The house in Edward Hopper's *High Noon* possesses an equally strong emotional charge. Both the human figure and the building express an identical atmosphere of drowsy sensuality. The sun is already high up in the sky when a woman appears at the front door; a half-open dressing gown is carelessly wrapped around her naked body. The half-drawn curtains and the phallic chimney strengthen the erotic hint contained in the woman's clothing. The erotic memory of the building again seems to belong on the top floor—we sense that the curtained windows of the attic rooms conceal the previous night's secrets.

124   In the archetypally perfect room depicted in Fra Angelico's *The Saints Performing a Miracle*, the saints are growing a leg for the legless deacon Justinian. This room has an extraordinary sense of concentration, protection, focus, and place. The frontally depicted room, with its architectonic dais bed, is an impressive prototype of the sheltered interior. Only the doorway to an adjacent room, shown at the right-hand edge of the image, establishes a slender link with the world outside.

125   In René Magritte's static room of *The Menaced Assassin*, the gramophone plays a wistful tune. An unknown previous event is all over; only a meaningless waiting is left. The room is bare but emotionally charged, its walls articulated only by a profile-molding. The perspective lines of the floorboards lead the spectator's gaze out from the room to the mountains in the background, the landscape a reminder of lost liberty. A powerful light is thrown on the scene from behind the spectator: the whole painting seems like a stage scene divorced from real life. The painting reminds me of the final scene in Antonioni's film *Profession: Reporter*, in which the camera indifferently observes a sunny courtyard from the window of a hotel room. Slowly, through the pace of the camera, the spectator begins to realize that while he is watching the meaningless events in the yard through the camera's eye, a murder is taking place behind his back.

    Often architecture's role in a depicted scene has been reduced to

126 a singular detail, as in Giovanni Bellini's *Presentation in the Temple*,

127 or in Raphael's *Lady of the Unicorn*. A mere edge of a balustrade or a partly framed opening stands for architecture in all its potential power and suffices to evoke an image of the space of a temple or palace.

    But the artist also creates nature, and in his hands even the landscape turns into architecture. A cliff painted by Sandro Botticelli in

128 *Pallas and the Centaur* has its own architraves, pilasters, and stereo-
129 bate foundation. Saint Jerome's cave in Gentile Bellini's painting *St.*
Jerome in the Wilderness is transformed into the facade of a Gothic
130 cathedral, and Mantegna's landscapes are reminiscent of arches, rostra,
and throne daises.

Architecture's true quality is not revealed until it is a ruin, after
everything superfluous has decayed, when only the faded skeleton of
the building remains. As it falls into ruin, a building reveals the core
of its idea, its innermost order, but it also loses its supernatural, inaccessible perfection; it humbles itself and starts to speak the familiar
language of mortals. A ruin, or the foundation of a lost building, or the
firewall of a smoke-blackened house—they all touch us by prompting us
to imagine the fate of their builders.

131 In Bramantino's *Adoration of the Magi*, the ruin of the surprisingly
'neo-classical' palace does not seem to have been caused by the devas-
tation of time or war. The building appears to have been intentionally
left unfinished in order to evoke associations with past times, and to
permit the blending of the mountains in the background with the architectural structure. Even the gifts in the foreground form an impressive
miniature architecture.

After these examples, it may be easier to understand why many
schools teach architecture today by analyzing presentations of architecture in the art of painting. The architecture of paintings offers a valuable phenomenological analysis of architecture similar to that offered
by childhood memories, poetry, novels, or films.

The architecture of painting is an incredibly rich subject; almost
every Renaissance painting contains themes of architecture in some
form. The architectural image of a single artist—Duccio, Giotto or
Fra Angelico—would provide substantial material for a fascinating
and stimulating phenomenological study, as would the architectures
depicted in conjunction with a single painterly subject, such as the
Annunciation or the *Nativity*, both of which have been depicted in
countless variations.

The history of painting provides numerous examples illuminating
the phenomenology of such basic architectural experiences as 'looking
out from a window,' 'separating,' 'isolating,' or 'climbing stairs,' and of
132 the silent speech of objects. In Caspar David Friedrich's *Woman at the*
Window, the window figures effectively as a regulator of the interaction
of external and internal space, for instance, and the cruel definitiveness
133 of isolation outside a wall is painfully portrayed in Brueghel's *Lepers*.

The feeling of place and the definition of space and focus achieved
by lighting has been the theme of many artists. Are there any more

133

134

135

136

137

stirring images of the spaces created by light than those depicted in Rembrandt's paintings? Can there be a more moving picture of nocturnal life in a sleeping metropolis than Hopper's *Nighthawks*? The richness of the metaphorical language of objects can be analyzed, for example, in Holbein's *Ambassadors*, with an anamorphic skull in its foreground, and in Quentin Massys's *The Banker and His Wife*, in which the mirror in the foreground reflects a window and a man behind the spectator. The banker's wife is sanctimoniously leafing through a prayer book, but at the same time she is avidly watching the weighing of the coins (according to certain psychoanalytical interpretations, the image of money refers to excrement).

Impressive definitions of man's position in the world appear in painting. Antonello da Messina's *St. Jerome* has a stage-like study built in an abandoned medieval church—the lack of window frames and the birds seen through the window openings suggest that birds inhabit the space. To the right of the human figure is a Gothic narthex and a lion, the saint's symbol, but on the left is a mysteriously everyday bedroom with no religious character. The study is seen through an opening in the wall that is neither a door nor a window.

Whereas Antonello's painting defines a refuge for man in the world, Hopper's *Office in a Small City* is a picture of harrowing solitude, where the individual is completely devoid of privacy, identity, and refuge in the cosmos of the city. The painting also shows that the modern window no longer regulates the interaction of the internal and external world—it discloses everything, without mercy.

Pieter Brueghel's *Netherlandish Proverbs* is a *tour de force* of architectural localization, a veritable encyclopedia of places. Over one hundred pictorially represented proverbs have been counted in the painting, and for each the painter has created its proper architectural setting. The condensation of different places represented in the painting is so unreal that the picture starts to writhe before the spectator's eyes, rather like Vasarély's multi-perspective geometrical figures 500 years later.

The backgrounds of paintings are often treasure troves of architectural motifs, and of depictions of landscape architecture, imaginary cities, or fantasy buildings. Piero della Francesca's paintings are majestic architectural compositions as such, but their backgrounds also include noble, expressive buildings and fascinating cities, such as those in the *Legend of the True Cross*. In the background cities of Mantegna's paintings, the man-made landscape rivals the imaginary architecture for dramatic impact.

The Roman city in de Chirico's *Roman Landscape* has been abandoned by its divine inhabitants, and taken over by ordinary mortals; the

138

139

140

141

142

143

144

145

146

147

148

149

grandiose architecture reveals the insignificance of the new inhabitants. The Romanità, or roman spirit, exuded by the painting reminds me of the opening of Fellini's *La Dolce Vita*, in which a helicopter carries a statue of the crucifixion above scantily dressed sunbathers lying on the roofs of Rome.

There are many painter-architects in the history of art, from Giotto, Michelangelo and Bramante to Le Corbusier, but usually the architecture of painters is based on the architectural conventions of their age. How these conventions are interpreted, and what canons of architectural style prove essential to those painters unversed in the internal rules of the building art, are the more essential issues.

142 The columns and arches of Fra Angelico have the same airy lightness as the weightless, gliding facade of Brunelleschi's Foundling

143 Hospital. In Masaccio's *Madonna Enthroned*, the monumental stone architecture of the throne is identical to the buildings of Brunelleschi and Alberti. But the painter has placed the Classical orders of columns in the wrong sequence, with the most archaic at the top and the most ornamental at the bottom. Hogarth, for one, considered this erroneous use of Classical orders to be the epitome of bad taste and ignorance. Painters, however, are not bound by the stylistic rules of architectural education.

The artist's transition from architectural realism to purely pictorial presentation can be illustrated by a comparison of the relationship of the painting's protagonist and the background. During the Renaissance, the standard procedure, especially in the *Sacra Conversazione* (Holy Conversation) type of character painting, was to place the protagonist

145 in a cockleshell recess, as in Fra Angelico's *Annalena altarpiece*. The arrangement is similar to the way in which medieval sculptures were

146 placed in their own niches. In Domenico Veneziano's *Madonna with Saints*, Mary is sitting on a dais in a kind of outdoor loggia, with a cockleshell niche behind her, but the niche is in fact far away behind

147 the courtyard. The chancel motif in Botticelli's *Adoration of the Magi* is no more than a purely pictorial recollection, a surface pattern marked off from the background sky by a ruined arch.

148 The accurate architectural space of Masaccio's *Trinity* fresco is believed to have been designed by none other than Brunelleschi, the great early Renaissance master of architecture and devotée of perspective (this is not difficult to accept if one compares it with the niche of

149 the Pazzi Chapel). Masaccio, however, made use of his artistic freedom by placing God standing on the profile of the back wall of the vault, although his hands support the hands of Christ on the cross in the foreground several meters in front of the wall (H.W. Janson has actu-

ally calculated the 'depth error' in the painting's carefully constructed perspective: 2.7 meters).

150

150 151 152 The most fascinating architectural inventions by painters include Giotto's architectural collages—so suggestive of present-day Post-Modernism—and de Chirico's urban visions, taciturn buildings, and menacing towers, so inspirational for the architecture of Aldo Rossi. The tower has long been a favorite architectural motif of painters—the analogy between the tower and the human body is so obvious that the anthropomorphization of the tower is a natural trick of the painter's trade.

151

153 154 Giotto's balcony and Piero della Francesca's arched canopy possess such architectural brilliance that one regrets that they were never actually built. Giotto was actually one of the few artists who was able to build his fantasies. He directed the construction of the Florence Duomo and designed its famous tower, the architectural themes of which many of his paintings presaged. Giotto has inspired many architects, and Alvar Aalto and Louis Kahn, at least, have paid tribute to him. Kahn's comment is telling in many regards: "Giotto was a great painter, because he painted the skies black for the daytime and he painted birds that couldn't fly and dogs that couldn't run and he made men bigger than doorways because he was a painter. A painter has this prerogative. He doesn't have to answer to the problem of gravity, nor to the images as we know them in real life."[1]

152

155 Architecture was a central theme of both early Renaissance art and of the Metaphysical painters of our own century. Gaston Bachelard clearly expresses the cause for the popularity of architectural motifs in these particular artistic movements: "…The house is one of the greatest powers of integration for the thoughts, memories and dreams of mankind."[2] The Renaissance was the first historical period to be aware of itself—the very concept of the individual and the self originated in the age. The Renaissance thus represents a kind of child's consciousness of culture; in its attempt to place man in the world, architecture—the image of culture and man perpetuated in stone—understandably became an important symbol and emotional factor.

153

In turn the Metaphysicals attempted to outline another reality of our consciousness, and they, too, gave architecture the principal role as the built image of human existence. Architecture evokes such powerful associations that the Metaphysicals often used it as a kind of second-hand subject, a painting within a painting. The experience of solitude, or of isolation, in Metaphysical painting is a way to turn the emotions on the spectator. Architecture—not nature—is a symbol of solitude. Solitude can be experienced intensely only if one is strongly reminded

154

155

156

157

158

159

160

of man's absence—in an empty house or city, for example, rather than in a natural landscape.

The task of architecture is to recreate 'the womb' and 'the mountain' in the mind, the former a closed, sheltering interior, and the latter an exterior landmark, a place visible from afar and with a wide view. This basic polarity of architecture has a psychoanalytical explanation, as Colin St John Wilson has described: "…It is uniquely the role of the masterpiece that it makes possible the supposedly impossible, namely the simultaneous experience of…two polar modes, envelopment and externality, fusion and otherness."[3]

161

The primal interior is the aedicule shelter supported by four pillars or columns, or the MA of Japanese architecture. The primal form of the mountain is a raised platform, the protagonist's pedestal. A kind of minimum form of the interior, 'the womb' is the vertical plane, whereas the ultimate form of 'the mountain' is the horizontal plane. The vertical surface is projected into the spectator's consciousness as a virtual interior advancing towards the spectator in front of the surface plane. The horizontal surface produces a 'mountain' by being projected upward. The experience of interior space created by the vertical plane is the theme of numerous paintings, such as Giovanni Bellini's *Madonna degli alberelli* and Fra Angelico's *Mocking of Christ*. Fra Angelico's painting also presents the 'mountain' in an exceptionally impressive way, making the painting the perfect minimum presentation of architecture in the phenomenological sense. A window opening placed in a vertical surface enhances the impression of interior space and in fact discloses the mental meaning of the vertical plane—see, for instance, the central panel of Bellini's *Pesaro altarpiece*.

162

After this diversity of imaginary architecture, an anti-climax: two very ordinary-looking houses, Paul Cézanne's *The Suicide's House* and Carlo Carrá's *The Abandoned House*. Architectural scenes appearing in the other visual arts are usually perfectly ordinary rooms and houses compared to the professional discoveries of architects. They represent the poetry of the commonplace. But the reality of symbols and metaphors lies hidden in these ordinary houses. Today architecture has narrowed into one-dimensional realism, losing its link with the symbolic life occurring backstage, in our unconscious world. The architecture of painting restores another, deeper reality, that dimension of poetry, symbol, and fantasy from which all art grows.

111 Duccio di Buoninsegna, *The Temptation of Christ on the Mountain*, painting on the predella of the Maestà altar. Frick Collection, New York.

112 Fra Angelico, *The Descent from the Cross*, ca. 1440, background detail from the left side. Museum of San Marco, Florence.

113 Piero della Francesca, *The Legend of the True Cross*, background detail of the left half of the painting. San Francesco, Arezzo.

114 Giotto, *Adoration of the Magi*, right half of the painting. Assisi, Lower Church.

115 Giorgio di Chirico, *The Enigma of Time*, 1911. Private Collection, Milan.

116 Edward Hopper, *Early Sunday Morning*, 1930. The Whitney Museum of American Art, New York.

117 Fra Angelico, *The Last Judgement*, 1432–35, detail of the lower central part of the painting. Museum of San Marco, Florence.

118 Pieter Brueghel the Elder, *The Month of August (The Corn Harvest)*, 1565. The Metropolitan Museum of Art, New York.

119 Giorgione and Tizian, *Sleeping Venus*, ca. 1510. Gemäldegalerie, Dresden.

120 Duccio di Buoninsegna, *Jesus Heals the Blind Man*. Predella of the Maestà altar. National Gallery, London.

121 Giovanni Bellini: *Religious Allegory* (Allegory of Souls in Purgatory), 1490–1500. Uffizi Gallery, Florence.

122 Giotto, *Annunciation to St. Anne*, ca. 1305. Arena Chapel, Padua.

123 Edward Hopper, *High Noon*, 1949. The Dayton Art Institute.

124 Fra Angelico, *Dream of Deacon Justinian*. Predella of the San Marco altarpiece.

125 René Magritte, *The Menaced Assassin*, 1927. Museum of Modern Art, New York.

126 Giovanni Bellini, *Presentation in the Temple*, 1460–64. Querini Stampalia Gallery, Venice.

127 Raphael: *Lady of the Unicorn*. Galleria Borghese, Rome.

128 Sandro Botticelli, *Pallas and the Centaur*, 1482. Uffizi, Florence.

129 Gentile Bellini, *St. Jerome in the Wilderness*. Contini-Bonacossi Collection, Florence.

130 Andrea Mantegna, *The Parnassus*, 1497. The Louvre, Paris.

131 Bramantino, *Adoration of the Magi*, 1501–03. National Gallery, London.

132 Caspar David Friedrich, *Woman at the Window*, 1822. National Gallery, Berlin.

133 Pieter Brueghel the Elder, *The Lepers*, 1568. Louvre, Paris.

134 Edward Hopper, *Night Hawks*, 1942. The Art Institute of Chicago.

135 Hans Holbein the Younger, *The Ambassadors*, 1533. National Gallery, London.

136 Quentin Metsys, *The Banker and His Wife*, 1541. The Louvre, Paris.

137 Antonello da Messina, *St. Jerome in His Study*. National Gallery, London.

138 Edward Hopper, *Office in a Small City*, 1953. The Metropolitan Museum of Art, New York.

139 Piero della Francesca, *The Legend of the True Cross*, San Francesco, Arezzo. Right half of the painting.

140 Andrea Mantegna, *St. Sebastian*, 1480. Detail of the right side background. The Louvre, Paris.

141 Giorgio de Chirico, *Roman Landscape* (Villa Romana), 1922, Private collection, New York.

142 Fra Angelico, *The Annunciation*, altarpiece, 1430–32. Prado Museum, Madrid.

143 Masaccio, *Madonna Enthroned (Madonna and Child)*, 1426. National Gallery, London.

144 Pieter Brueghel the Elder, *The Netherlandish Proverbs*, 1559. Berlin-Dahlem. Staatliche Museen.

145 Fra Angelico, *The Annalena altarpiece*. Museum of San Marco, Florence.

146 Domenico Veneziano, *Altarpiece of Santa Lucia dei Magnoli*, 1445. Galleria degli Uffizi, Firenze.

147 Sandro Botticelli: *The Adoration of the Magi*, ca. 1470–74. National Gallery, London.

148 Masaccio, *The Holy Trinity*, Fresco, 1427–28. Santa Maria Novella, Florence.

149 Filippo Brunelleschi, *The Pazzi Chapel*, Florence, 1429–61.

150 Giotto, *Presentation of the Virgin in the Temple*. Arena Chapel, Padua, ca. 1305.

151 Giotto, *Liberation of Peter the Heretic*. Assisi, Upper Church, late 1290s.

152 Giorgio de Chirico, *Mystery and Melancholy of a Street*, 1914. Private collection.

153 Giotto, *St. Francis before the Sultan (Trial by fire)*, left half. Assisi, Upper Church.

154 Piero della Francesca, *The Legend of the True Cross*. The Battle of Heraclius and Khosrow, 1460. Detail of the right side, San Francesco, Arezzo.

155 Giorgio de Chirico, *The Anguish of Departing*, 1913–14. Albright-Knox Art Gallery, Buffalo.

156 Giotto, *Presentation in the Temple*. Isabella Stewart Gardner Museum, Boston.

157 Andrea Mantegna, *The Crucifixion*, 1459–60. The Louvre, Paris.

158 Fra Angelico, *Mocking of Christ*, 1440–41. San Marino, Florence.

159 Giovanni Bellini, *Madonna degli alberelli*, 1487. Galleria dell' Accademia, Venice.

160 Giovanni Bellini, *Coronation of the Virgin*, Pesaro altarpiece, central panel, 1471–1475. Musei Civici, Pesaro.

161 Paul Cézanne, *The Suicide's House*, 1872–73. The Louvre, Paris.

162 Carlo Carrá, *The Abandoned House*, 1930. Galleria Annunciata, Milan.

164

165

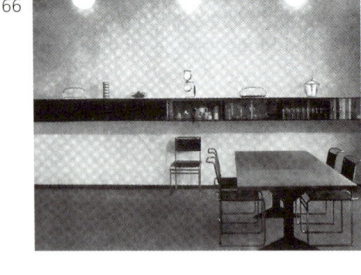

166

167

IDENTITY, INTIMACY, AND DOMICILE

Notes on the Phenomenology of Home
(1994)

HOMO FABER AND THE EXISTENTIAL VACUUM

Identity was the recurrent theme in the literary work of the Swiss writer Max Frisch, who, not so incidentally, was an architect by training. In his book *Homo Faber*, Frisch describes a Unesco expert, an engineer—the symbol of Modern Man—who continuously travels around the world on his missions. The engineer is a rational and realistic man whose life seems to be under perfect, rational control. However, gradually he loses contact with his locality and home, and, finally, with his own identity. He ends up falling in love with his own daughter—whom he does not recognize—as the tragic consequence of his loss of home and roots. Their indecent love leads to incest and ends violently in the daughter's death.[1]

Homo Faber's grave mistake was his conviction that man can exist without a stable domicile, that technology can so transform the world that it need not any longer be experienced through emotions.

Many of us in the consumer world today are suffering from Homo Faber's alienation. We have become homeless in our culture of abundance. This new homelessness derives from our inability to fuse the self with the world. Homelessness becomes synonymous with detached solitude and a perpetual present tense. Teilhard de Chardin focuses his writings on an enigmatic point *Omega*, "from which the world can be seen as a whole and correctly."[2] The closest earthly analogue of Abbé Chardin's *Omega* is surely the Home.

THE ARCHITECT AND THE CONCEPT OF HOME

Architects are concerned with designing buildings as philosophical manifestations of space, structure, and order, but we seem unable to touch upon the more subtle, emotional, and diffuse aspects of home. In our schools of architecture, we are taught to design houses, not homes. Yet the dwelling's capacity to provide domicile in the world is what matters to the individual dweller. The dwelling has its psyche and soul, in addition to its formal and quantifiable qualities.

The titles of architectural books invariably use the idea of 'house'— *The Modern House, GA-Houses, California Houses, Architects' Houses*—whereas books and magazines that deal with interior decoration and celebrities are engaged with the notion of 'home'—*Celebrity Homes, Artist Homes*. Needless to say, the serious architect considers the publications of the latter type sentimental entertainment and kitsch.

Our concept of architecture is based on the idea of the perfectly articulated architectural object, an artistic artifact devoid of life. The famous court case between Mies van der Rohe and his client, Dr. Edith Farnsworth, concerning the Farnsworth House, is an example of the contradiction between architecture and home. As we know, Mies had designed one of the most important and aesthetically appealing houses of the 20th century, but his client did not find it satisfactory as a home and sued for damages. The court decided in Mies's favor, and while I am not underrating Mies's architecture when recalling this particular case, I am pointing out the distance from life and the deliberate reduction of the spectrum of life that this architectural masterpiece displays. To give a more recent example: one of Peter Eisenman's early houses cuts the marital bed into two separate halves due to a formally dictated split in the floor and a column in the middle of the dining table on the floor below. When we compare the designs of early Modernity with those of today's avant-garde, we can immediately observe a loss of empathy for the dweller. Instead of being motivated by the architect's social vision or an empathetic view of life, architecture has become self-referential and autistic.

Many architects have developed a split personality; as designers and as dwellers we often apply different sets of values to the environment. In our role as architects, we aspire to a meticulously articulated and temporally one-dimensional environment, whereas as dwellers, we prefer a more layered, ambiguous, and aesthetically less coherent environment. The instinctual dweller emerges through the role values of the professional.

ARCHITECTURE VS. HOME

Can a home be an architectural expression? Home is not, perhaps, a notion of architecture at all, but of sociology, psychology, and psychoanalysis. Home is an individualized dwelling, and the means of this subtle personalization seem to be outside of our concept of architecture. A house is the container, the shell, for a home. The substance of a home is secreted by the dweller, as it were, within the framework of the dwelling. Home is an expression of the dweller's personality and his unique patterns of life. Consequently, the essence of home is closer to life itself than to the artifact of the house.

In this time of excessive specialization and fragmentation, the total fusion of the architectural dimension of the house and the personal and private dimension of life has occurred only in special cases: Alvar Aalto's Villa Mairea, for example, is a product of an exceptional friendship and interaction between the architect and his client. This home is an '*opus con amore*,' as Aalto himself confessed.[3] Equally, this residential masterpiece is an expression of a mutually shared Utopian vision of a better and more humane world. The Villa Mairea is simultaneously archaic and modern, rustic and elegant, regional and universal. Abundant in its imagery, the home consequently provides ample soil for individual psychic attachment.

In *The Poetics of Space*, Gaston Bachelard deliberates on the essence of 'the oneiric house,' the dream house of the mind.[4] He is undecided about the number of floors—either three or four—of this archetypal mental house. But the existence of an attic and a cellar is essential to this house. The attic is the symbolic storage place for pleasant memories, whereas the cellar is the final hiding place for unpleasant memories; both are needed for our mental well being.

The characteristics of the oneiric house are culturally conditioned, but the image also seems to reflect universal constants of the human mind. The oneiric house appears frequently in films, most famously, perhaps, as the neo-gothic Bates House in Alfred Hitchcock's *Psycho*. Modern architecture, however, has fiercely attempted to avoid or eliminate this oneiric image. Consequently, our arrogant rejection of history has been unsurprisingly accompanied by the rejection of the psychic memory attached to such primary images. The obsession with newness, the non-traditional, and the unforeseen, has wiped away the image of the oneiric house from our soul. We build dwellings that satisfy, perhaps, most of our physical needs, but which cannot house our mind. We have become travelers towards an unattainable Utopia, doomed to metaphysical homelessness.

THE ESSENCE OF HOME

Home is not merely an object or a building, but a diffuse and complex condition, integrating memories and images, desires and fears, the past and the present. A home is also a set of rituals, personal rhythms, and routines of everyday life. A home cannot be produced at once; it has its time dimension and continuum, and it is a gradual product of the family's and individual's adaptation to the world.

A home cannot, thus, become a marketable product. Current advertisements of furniture stores offering a chance 'to renew one's home at once' are absurd—they amount to a psychologist's advertisement to renew at once the mental contents of the patient's mind. A reflection on the essence of home takes us away from the physical properties of the house, into the psychic territory of the mind. We engage issues of identity and memory, consciousness as well as the unconscious, biologically motivated behavioral remnants, and culturally conditioned reactions and values.

POETICS OF HOME—REFUGE AND TERROR

The description of home seems to belong more to the realms of poetry, fiction, cinema, and painting, rather than to architecture.

"Poets and painters are born phenomenologists," as the phenomenologist J.H. Van den Berg has remarked.[5] In my view, so also are novelists, photographers, and film directors. That is why the essence of home, its function as a mirror and support of the inhabitant's psyche, is often more revealingly depicted in these art forms than in architecture. The Dutch filmmaker Jan Vrijman has made the thought provoking remark: "…why is it that architecture and architects, unlike film and filmmakers, are so little interested in people during the design process? Why are they so theoretical, so distant from life in general."[6]

The artist working in these other media is not concerned with the principles and formal intentions within the discipline of architecture and, consequently, he approaches directly the mental significance of images of the house and the home. Thus, artistic works dealing with space, light, buildings, and dwelling can provide valuable lessons to architects on the very essence of architecture itself.

Jean-Paul Sartre has written perceptively about the authenticity of the house as imagined and depicted by the artist: "[The painter] makes them [houses], that is, he creates an imaginary house on the canvas and not a sign of a house. And the house which thus appears preserves all the ambiguity of real houses."[7]

As well as being a symbol of protection and order, home can also become a concretization of human misery: loneliness, rejection, exploitation and violence. In the beginning chapter of Fyodor Dostoyevsky's *Crime and Punishment*, the protagonist Raskolnikov visits the home of the old usurer woman, his future victim. Dostoyevsky provides a laconic but haunting description of the home, eventually the scene of

HOME AND THE INHABITANT'S IDENTITY

168 John Wayne, the macho hero.
169 John Wayne's living room.

168

169

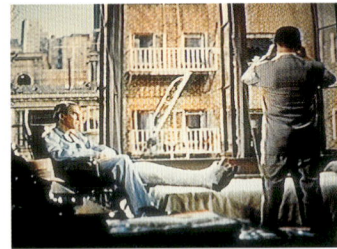

a brutal murder. Home transforms from the symbol of security into an image of threat and violence. The domestic interiors of Balthus (Count Balthazar Klossowski de Rola) reflect strange sexual tensions—the home has become eroticized—whereas Hitchcock charges the most ordinary home with extraordinary dangers, as in the films *Rear Window*, *Marnie*, and *Rope*.

The home is a multi-dimensional experience, one difficult to describe objectively. An introspective and phenomenological survey of the images, emotions, experiences, and recollections attached to the home seems to be a fruitful approach in the analysis of this concept.

THE HOME OF MEMORY

The word home immediately recalls for us all the warmth, protection and love of our entire childhood. Perhaps our homes of adulthood are only an unconscious search for the lost home of childhood. But the memory of home also awakens all the distress and fear that we might have experienced in our childhood.

"A house constitutes a body of images that give mankind proofs or illusions of stability,"[8] Bachelard asserts, "It is an instrument with which to confront the cosmos."[9] Here he speaks about home, a lived house, a house filled with the essence of personal life. The home is a collection and concretization of personal images of protection and intimacy, which help one recognize and remember one's identity.

In their influential 1963 book *Community and Privacy*, Christopher Alexander and Serge Chermayeff identified six spatial mechanisms between the polarities of private and public.[10] In his anthropological studies of our unconscious use of space, Edward T. Hall arrived at similar mechanisms and complexities.[11] The home is a staging of personal memory, a complex mediator between intimacy and public life. Personal space expresses the personality to the outside world, but equally importantly, personal space strengthens the dweller's self-image and concretizes his world order.

THE IMAGE OF HOME

Before I began high school, my family moved several times due to my father's job. Consequently, I lived in seven different houses during my childhood. In addition, I spent my childhood summers and most of the wartime period in my farmer grandfather's house. Regardless of having lived in eight houses as a youngster, I have only had one experiential home in my childhood. My experiential home seems to have traveled with me and constantly transformed into new physical shapes as we moved. My home was more in my memory and mind than

HOME AND FEAR

170 René Magritte, *The Tomb of a Wrestler*, 1960. Collection Harry Torczyner, New York.
171 Alfred Hitchcock, *Rear Window*, 1954.

in any particular physical setting, or perhaps more accurately, my mind transformed each one of the numerous settings into the unique image of home.

I cannot recall the exact architectural shape or layout of any of the eight houses that I have mentioned. But I do recall vividly the sense of home emanating from the feeling of returning home from a skiing trip in the darkness of a cold winter evening. The experience of home has never been stronger for me than when seeing the illuminated windows of our house in the dark winter landscape, and sensing the invitation of warmth already warming my frozen limbs. "Light in the window of the home is a waiting light," as Bachelard has observed.[12] An authentic home has a soul, a soul waiting for the inhabitant.

I cannot recall the shape of the front door of my grandfather's house, but I can still sense the warmth and odor of the air flowing against my face as I open the door in my dreams. The body remembers even when other sensory imprints cannot be retrieved.

In an essay entitled "The Geometry of Feeling," I have dealt with the properties of lived space as compared to common notions of architecture.[13] Emotions deriving from built form and space arise from distinct confrontations between man and space, mind and matter. An emotional architectural impact is related with an act, not an object or a visual or figural element. Consequently, the phenomenology of architecture is founded on verbs rather than nouns. The act of approaching the house, not its mere façade; the act of entering, not the door; the act of looking out of the window, not the window itself; or the act of gathering around the hearth or the table more than these objects themselves—all these verb expressions seem to trigger our emotions.

THE NOSTALGIA OF HOME

I remember the sadness and fear when leaving each home behind, as my family moved to another town. The most tragic experience was the fear of losing one's childhood friends and facing an unknown future.

The experience of home consists of, and integrates, an incredible array of mental dimensions, from that of national identity and of being a member of a specific culture to those of unconscious desires and fears. Unsurprisingly, sociologists have discovered that the sorrow for a lost home is very similar to the mourning for a lost relative.

There is a strange melancholy in an abandoned home or a demolished apartment house, a melancholy that reveals traces and scars of intimate lives to the public gaze. The remains of foundations or the hearth of a ruined or burned house, half buried in the forest grass, are touching in their melancholy. The tenderness of the experience results

172 Andrey Tarkovsky, *The Mirror*, 1975. The old Tarkovsky family house reconstructed for the film according to a family photograph. The director was born and spent his youth in the house.

173 Andrey Tarkovsky, *Nostalghia*, 1983. Throughout the film, set in Italy, the protagonist, a Russian poet, longs for his distant home outside of Moscow.

172

173

from the fact that we do not imagine the absent house, but instead the home, life, and faith of its inhabitants.

Andrey Tarkovsky's film *Nostalghia* is a touching record of the loss and grievance of home, of the nostalgia for an absent home—a typical Russian sentiment from Dostoyevsky and Gogol to Tarkovsky.[14] Throughout the film the poet Andrej Gorchakov fingers the keys to his home in Russia in the pocket of his overcoat as an unconscious reflection of his longing for home. All of Tarkovsky's films, in fact, seem to deal with the nostalgia of the absent domicile.[15] In the Communist state, the home often turned from a refuge into a place of surveillance, a condensed concentration camp. Consequently, the home became a mystical dream, one which countless Russian artists describe in their works.

HOME AND IDENTITY

The interdependence of identity and context is so strong that psychologists speak of a 'situational personality.' The concept is based on the observation that the behavior of a single individual varies more under different conditions than the behavior of different individuals under the same conditions.

The psycho-linguistic studies of Professor Frode Strømnes, the Norwegian-born Finn, have brought out further dimensions of the interdependence of identity and context. In his research on imagery as the basis of linguistic operations, Strømnes has revealed that even language conditions our conception and utilization of space.[16] Consequently, our concept of home is founded in language; our first home is in the domicile of our mother tongue. Language is strongly tied with our bodily existence; the geometry of our language articulates our being-in-the-world.

Language marks personal territory; I begin to think and speak of 'my room.' It is frustrating to be forced to live in a space which one cannot recognize or mark as one's personal territory. The minimum home of a child or a primitive is the mascot or the personal idol that gives a sense of safety and normality; my five-year old daughter, for instance, could not go anywhere without her scratching pillow. An anonymous hotel room is immediately personalized and taken into possession by subtly marking the territory—laying out clothes, books, objects, opening the bed. My American architect-assistant traveled to Finland with four books (James Joyce's *Ulysses*, T.S. Eliot's *Four Quartets*, and two books on American poetry, by the way), while another American friend travels with her set of kitchen knives, her magical instruments to recreate a sense of home.

INTIMACY AND HOME

We have private and social personalities and the home is the realm of the former, the private persona. Home is where we hide our secrets and express our private selves. Home is our safe place of resting and dreaming. More precisely, the role of the home as a delineator or mediator between the realms of public and private, the transparency of the home, as it were, varies greatly. There are cultures in which the home is the woman's domain. There are ways of life in which the home is a public showcase and the public gaze penetrates the secrecy of the home.

Generally, however, the intimacy of home is almost a sacred precinct in our culture. We have a feeling of guilt and embarrassment if, for some reason, we are obliged to enter someone's home uninvited when the occupant is not present. To see an unattended home is the same as seeing its dweller naked or in his most intimate situation.

In *The Notebooks of Malte Laurids Brigge*, Rainer Maria Rilke gives a powerful description of the intimate marks of the lives lived in a demolished house, lives to be seen in traces left on the wall of the neighboring building. These traces of life enabled the protagonist, Brigge, to recreate his own past. Rilke describes with staggering force how life penetrates dead matter; a history of life can be traced in the most minute fragment of the dwelling:

> But most unforgettable of all were the walls themselves. The stubborn life of these rooms had not let itself be trampled out. It was still there; it clung to the nails that had been left, it stood on the remaining handbreadth of flooring, it crouched under the corner joints where there was still a little bit of interior. One could see that it was in the paint, which, year by year, it had slowly altered: blue into moldy green, green into grey, and yellow into an old, stale rotting white. But it was also in the spots that had kept fresher, behind mirrors, pictures, and wardrobes; for it had drawn and redrawn their contours, and had been with spiders and dust even in these hidden places that now lay bared. It was in every flayed strip, it was in the damp blisters at the Tower edges of the wallpapers; it, wavered in the torn-off shreds, and sweated out of the foul patches that had come into being long ago. And from these walls once blue and green and yellow, which were framed by the fracture-tracks of the demolished partitions, the breath of these lives stood out—the clammy, sluggish, musty breath, which no wind had yet scattered.[17]

The extended quote demonstrates how life penetrates meaningfully into the verbal images of a great poem as compared to the often-sterilized

THE INTIMACY OF HOME

174 René Magritte, *The Month of the Grape Harvest*, 1959. Private Collection, Paris.
175 Edward Hopper, *Eleven A.M.*, 1926. Hirschhorn Museum and Sculpture Garden, Smithsonian Institution, Washington, D.C..

images of life in contemporary architecture. In its emotional power, Rilke's description is reminiscent of Heidegger's poetic description of the epic message of Vincent van Gogh's *Peasant's Shoes*.[18] (Meyer Shapiro's observation that van Gogh actually painted his own shoes in Paris does not diminish the poetic power of Heidegger's words). What is important, however, is the artist's extraordinarily dense imagery that reflects an authentic form of life.

In this intimate polarity, Bachelard points out an important bodily experience of the home: "Indeed, in our houses we have nooks and corners in which we like to curl up comfortably. To curl up belongs to the phenomenology of the verb to inhabit, and only those who have learned to do so can inhabit with intensity."[19] Home seems to be an extension of, and refuge to, both our body and constitution.

Our fascination with the world of personal intimacy is immense: in a small 1960s theater in New York City, through one-directional mirror-glass, the theater audience observed the daily life of a normal American family living in a flat they had rented, unaware of being on stage. The theater was open 24 hours a day and sold out continuously until it was closed by the authorities as inhuman.

INGREDIENTS OF HOME

A full conception of home consists of three types of mental or symbolic elements:

1) Elements that have their foundation on a deep, unconscious bio-cultural level (entry, roof, hearth);
2) Elements that are related with the inhabitant's personal life and identity (memorabilia, personal belongings, inherited objects of the family), and;
3) Social symbols intended to give certain images and messages to outsiders (signs of wealth, education, social identity, etc.).

Clearly, the structuring of home as a lived institution differs fundamentally from the principles of architecture. The architect composes a house as a system of spatial hierarchies and dynamics of structure, light, color, and so forth, whereas a home is structured around a few centers consisting of distinct domestic functions and objects. The following types of images may function as foci of behavior and symbolization: house front (front yard, facade, the urban situation), entry, window, hearth, stove, table, cupboard, bath, bookcase, television, furniture, family pictures and treasures, and memorabilia. Each of these ingredients forms the basis for individual phenomological examination and inspiration…a set of tasks beyond the scope of this essay, but which deserve, at least, some preliminary notes.

THE POETRY OF THE WARDROBE

Bachelard's analysis of the essential task of drawers, chests, and wardrobes in our mental imagery sets an inspiring example. He gives these objects—rarely considered as having architectural significance—an impressive role in the world of fantasy and daydream: "In the wardrobe there exists a center of order that protects the entire house against uncurbed disorder."[20]

Wardrobes, cupboards, and drawers represent the functions of putting away and taking out, storing and remembering. The inside of a cupboard is an intimate and secret space, and it is not supposed to be opened by just anybody. Small boxes and caskets are hiding places for intimate secrets and as such, they are of significance for our imagination. Our imagination fills out the compartments of rooms and buildings with memories and turns them into our own personal territories. We have just as great a need to keep secrets as we have to reveal and understand them.

One of the reasons why contemporary houses and cities are so alienating is that they do not contain secrets; their structure and contents are perceived at a single glance. Compare the labyrinthian secrets of an old medieval town or an old house, secrets which stimulate our imagination and fill it with expectation and excitement, to the transparent emptiness of our contemporary cityscape and apartment blocks.

HEARTH AND FIRE

The significance of the hearth or the stove for the sense of home is self-evident. The image of fire in the home combines the most archaic experience with the most contemporary necessity. The symbolic power of the hearth is based on its capacity to fuse together archaic images of the life-supporting fire of the primitive, timeless experiences of personal comfort with symbols of togetherness and social status.

Maurice Vlaminck, the Fauve painter, has written: "The well-being I feel, seated in front of my fire, while bad weather rages out-of-doors, is entirely animal. A rat in its hole, a rabbit in its burrow, cows in the stable, must all feel the same contentment that I feel."[21] The image of the hearth carries also immediate erotic connotations; Lewis Mumford discusses the influence of the invention of the oven on sexual behavior in his book *The City in History*.[22] Through the hearth and fire, the home reveals traces of our evolutionary past and biological impulses.

The fireplace is a bourgeois symbol of the separation of a fire for pleasure from the fire for preparing food, whereas the image of the

IMAGES OF FIRE

176 Teun Hocks, *Man at Fire*, 1990. The cold fire of contemporary life.
177 Antonio Gaudi, Casa Battló, Barcelona, 1904–06. The fireplace is integrated with a nest-like space.

176

177

stove has connotations of peasant life. Having spent my childhood in a farmer's home, I can still vividly recall the role of the stove in structuring family life, in marking the rhythm of the day, and in defining the male and female roles. The stove was the heart of the farmer's house.

In the modern home the hearth has flattened to an object with a distant and decorative function. The image of fire is so powerfully vivid that modern hearths are often solely built in the form of mantles—as symbols without any possibility of actual fire. Fire itself has been tamed and turned into a framed picture devoid of its essential task to give warmth and to sustain life. The fireplace has turned from a device addressing the skin into a medium of visual pleasure. We could speak of 'the cold fire of the modern home.'

THE TABLE

The structuring function and symbolic role of the table has also largely been lost in contemporary architecture. The significance of the table, however, is powerfully expressed in paintings and poetry.

Again, I recall vividly the heavy, unpainted wooden table of my farmer grandfather. The remembrance of the table is stronger than of the room itself. Everyone had his or her place at the table, my grandfather sitting at the inner end. The opposite end of the long table, closer to the entry, was left empty and was occupied only when there was an occasional guest. The table was the stage for eating, sewing, playing, doing homework, socializing with neighbors and strangers. The table was the organizing center of the farmer's house, marking the difference between weekday and Sunday, working day and feast.

DILUTED IMAGES OF HOME

Altogether, the over-functionalization and aesthetization of the home have stripped it of its deepest bio-cultural dimensions. Home has lost its metaphysical essence and become a functionalized and commodified product.

The image of the bed has been diluted, from a miniature house, a separate microclimate and visual territory, a house within the house, with physical and symbolic privacy, to a mere neutral horizontal plane, a stage of privacy. Bachelard's observation that the house, and consequently, our collective life, has lost its vertical dimension and become merely horizontal echoes in this circumstance.[23] Again, numerous images in historical paintings and drawings reveal the essence of the bed as the intimate core of home.

The window and, in particular, the act of looking out of the window of the home to the yard or to the garden is a poetic and essential experience of home. The home is particularly strongly felt when you look out from its enclosed privacy. My friend Bo Carpelan's poems and novels provide touching literary examples of this dimension. The tendency of contemporary architecture to use glass walls eliminates the window as a framing and focusing device and weakens the essential tension between the home and the world—the ontological essence of the door has been lost in the same way.

LACK OF CONCRETENESS

I live in an attic apartment under a tin roof. The strongest and most pleasurable experience of home occurs during a heavy storm when rain beats on the roof, magnifying the feeling of warmth and protection. At the same time, the beating of rain just centimeters away from my skin puts me in direct contact with the primal elements. These sensations are lost for the dweller of today's standard flat squeezed between concrete slabs.

Cooking by fire is immensely satisfying because one can experience a primal causality between the fire and the hearth. Again, this causality is lost with the electric stove—or even more with the microwave oven. Even food loses its connections with the natural world and turns into a synthetic and de-mystified matter.

In the contemporary home the function of the hearth has been taken over by the television. Both seem to be foci of social gathering and individual concentration, but the difference in quality is, however, decisive. The fire ties us back to our unconscious memory, to the archeology of images. Fire is a primal image, and it reminds us of the primary causality of the physical world. At the same time that flames stimulate meditative dreaming, they reinforce our sense of reality. The television alienates us from a sense of causality and transports us into a dream world that weakens our sense of reality, ourselves, and the ethical essence of togetherness. Instead of promoting togetherness, television reinforces isolation and privatization. The most shocking experiences of the negative impact of the television are the recent televised wars, telecast in real time around the globe as dramatized entertainment. An analysis of television as a structuring device of the contemporary home is, of course, essential for the theme of this educational project but further elaboration will have to wait.

Altogether, the weakening of the sense of causality threatens modern life. The menace represented by our brave new world lies in its lack of concreteness. Even fear is acceptable as long as it has its understandable cause or it symbolizes something, and as long as it is not cloaked in apparent order and well-being. The irrational fear in our cities grows

180

181

THE INTIMACY OF THE BED

180 Renaissance beds from Milan, about 1540. Bed as an intimate house within the house.
181 Hannes Meyer, Co-operative Interior, 1926. Bed as an open stage.

out of the meaninglessness of the environment for our reason and its incomprehensibility to our senses. We are losing the primary causality in our sensory experience of the world.

This meaninglessness, a hypnotizing emptiness, an absence of locality and focus, an existential vacuum, has become a recurring motif of contemporary art. The favorite, and alarming, theme of art today is the total isolation of man, disrobed of all signs of individual identity and human dignity.

AN ARCHITECTURE OF TOLERANCE

If architecture and home are conflicting notions, as it seems, what then is the architect's margin of facilitating 'homecoming,' a condition the Dutch architect Aldo van Eyck has so emphatically demanded?

In my view, architecture can either tolerate and encourage personalization or stifle it. We can make a distinction between an architecture of accommodation and an architecture of rejection. The first one facilitates reconciliation, the second attempts to impose an arrogant, divisive, and untouchable order. The first is based on images that are deeply rooted in our common memory, that is, in the phenomenologically authentic ground of architecture. The second manipulates images, striking and fashionable, perhaps, but ones that do not incorporate the personal identity, memories, and dreams of the inhabitant. The latter attitude likely creates architecturally more imposing houses, but the first provides the essential condition of homecoming.

Furthermore, there is a significant difference in how and to what extent an architectural design can allow and absorb aesthetic deviation without resulting in undesirable conflict. The architecture and furniture designs of Alvar Aalto are encouraging examples of design with great aesthetic tolerance, yet also without artistic compromise.

THE VIRTUE OF IDEALIZATION

My acknowledgement of a conflict between architecture and the intrinsic requirements of home could, perhaps, be interpreted as a signal that the architect should faithfully fulfill the explicit requirements and desires of the client. I want to say firmly that I do not believe in such a populist view. The uncritical acceptance of the client's brief only leads to sentimental kitsch; the architect's responsibility is to penetrate the surface of what is most often commercially, socially, and momentarily conditioned desire. The authentic artist and architect consciously or unknowingly engages in an ideal word. Art and exhilarating architecture are lost at the point that this vision and aspiration for an ideal is lost.

The South African writer J.M. Coetzee has said that taking the reader into consideration when writing is a deadly error for the writer.[24] Umberto Eco, for his part, has distinguished between two types of writers: the first type writes what he expects the reader to want to read, the second creates his ideal reader as he writes.[25] In Eco's view, the first writer will write mere kiosk literature, whereas the second writer is capable of writing literature that timelessly touches the human soul.

In my view, only the architect who creates his ideal client as he designs can create houses and homes that give mankind hope and direction instead of mere superficial satisfaction. Without Frank Lloyd Wright's Fallingwater, Gerrit Thomas Rietveld's Schröder House, Le Corbusier's Villa Savoye, Pierre Chareau's Maison de Verre and Alvar Aalto's Villa Mairea, to concretize the possibilities of human habitation, our understanding of modernity, and of ourselves, would be considerably weaker.

THE NECESSITY OF A HOMECOMING

Authentic architecture is always about life. Man's existential experience is the prime subject matter of the art of building. To a certain degree, great architecture is also always about architecture itself, about the rules and boundaries of the discipline itself. But today's architecture seems to have abandoned life entirely and escaped into pure architectural fabrication. Authentic architecture represents and reflects a way of life, an image of life. Instead, today's buildings frequently appear empty and do not seem to represent any real and authentic way of life.

Today's architectural avant-garde has deliberately rejected the notion of home. "Architecture must dislocate … without destroying its own being. While a house today must still shelter, it does not need to symbolize or romanticize its sheltering function. To the contrary: such symbols are today meaningless and merely nostalgia," Peter Eisenman has declared.[26]

Beyond the rejection of the phenomological approach to dwelling, today's avant-garde architecture has all but abandoned the problem of housing, which was central to the Modern Movement. Our post-historical era has ended historical narratives, the concept of progress, and closed our view of future. This loss of horizon and sense of purpose, this shortening of perspective, has turned architecture away from images of reality and life into an autistic and self-referential engagement with its own structures. At the same time, architecture has distanced itself from other sense realms and become a purely retinal art form.

Groundless nostalgia can wait: I still believe in the feasibility of an architecture of reconciliation, an architecture that can mediate man's

182 Interior of a Shaker House, Hancock.
183 Henry Matisse, *Goldfish* (*Les poissons rouges*), 1912. The Pushkin Museum of Fine Arts, Moscow.

182

183

"homecoming." We still need houses that reinforce our sense of human reality and the essential hierarchies of life. The art of architecture can still produce houses that enable us to live with dignity.

Bo Carpelan's poetic words provide a concluding lesson to architects:

> There are still houses with low ceilings,
> window-splays where children climb up
> and squatting, chin against knees,
> watch the wet snow falling
> peacefully over dark, narrow courtyards.
> There are still rooms that speak of lives,
> of cupboards of clean hereditary linen.
> There are quiet kitchens where someone sits
> reading with the book propped against the loaf of bread.
> The light falls there with the voice of a white blind.
> If you shut your eyes you can see
> that a morning, however fleeting, awaits
> and that its warmth mingles with the warmth in here
> and that each flake's fall
> is a sign of homecoming.[27]

184 A traditional Ethiopian house.

LIVED SPACE

Embodied Experience and Sensory Thought
(1999)

THE WORLD AND THE MIND

Art structures and articulates our being-in-the-world, or the "inner space of the world (*Weltinnenraum*)," to use Rainer Maria Rilke's concept.[1] Rather than mediating conceptually structured knowledge of the objective state of the world; a work of art renders possible an intense experiential knowledge. Without presenting any proposition concerning the world or its condition, a work of art focuses our view on the boundary surface between our Self and the world. "It is bewildering that while grasping what surrounds him, what he is observing, and giving shape to his perception, the artist does not, in fact, say anything else about the world or himself, but that they touch each other," writes the Finnish painter Juhana Blomstedt.[2] The artist touches the skin of his world with the same sense of wonder as a child touches a frosted window.

An artistic work is not an intellectual riddle seeking an interpretation or explanation. It is an image, an experiential and emotional complex that enters directly into our consciousness. Artists find their way behind words, concepts, and rational explanations in their repeated search for an innocent re-encounter with the world. Rational constructions provide little help in the artistic search because the artist has to rediscover the boundary of his existence, time after time. "In my work, I have never had any use for matters that I have known in advance," the great Basque sculptor Eduardo Chillida once said to me in conversation.[3]

The artist's exploration focuses on essences, and this aim defines their approach and method. As Jean-Paul Sartre states, "Essences and fact are incommensurable, and one who begins his inquiry with facts will never arrive at essences... understanding is not a quality coming to human reality from the outside; it is its characteristic way of existing."[4] Sartre's view defines the difference between the scientific and the artistic approach. The artist approaches this natural mode of understanding entwined in the very experience of being.

EXISTENTIAL SPACE

We do not live in an objective world of matter and facts, as commonplace realism assumes. The characteristically human mode of existence takes place in the world of possibilities, molded by our capacities of fantasy and imagination. We live in worlds in which the material and the mental, the experienced, remembered, and imagined completely fuse into each other. As a consequence, the lived reality does not follow the rules of space and time as described in the science of physics. We could say that the lived world is fundamentally 'unscientific,' when measured by the criteria of Western empirical science.

In order to distinguish the lived space from physical and geometrical space, it can be called 'existential space.' Lived existential space is structured on the basis of meanings and values reflected on it by the individual or group, either consciously or unconsciously; existential space is a unique experience interpreted through the memory and experiential contents of the individual. On the other hand, groups or even nations share certain experiences of existential space that constitute their collective identities and sense of togetherness. The experiential lived space is the object and context of both the making and the experiencing of art, as well as of architectural design. The task of architecture is "to make visible how the world touches us," as Maurice Merleau-Ponty wrote of the paintings of Paul Cézanne.[5] In accordance with Merleau-Ponty, we live in "the flesh of the world."[6]

In my view, the art form closest to architecture is not music—as is often thought—but cinema. The ground of both art forms is lived space, in which the inner space of the mind and the external space of the world fuse into each other, forming a chiasmatic bond.

THE REALITY OF IMAGINATION

Imagination is usually attached to a specific human creative capacity or to the realm of art, but our faculty of imagination is the foundation of our very mental existence and of our way of dealing with stimuli and information. Recent research by neuroscientists and psychologists at Harvard University show that imagined images take place in the same zones of the brain as visual perceptions, and that the former are as equally real as the latter.[7] No doubt, sensory stimuli and sensory imaginations in the other sensory realms are also similarly close to each other and thus, experientially equally real. Of course, this affinity of the external and internal experience is self-evident to any genuine artist without the proof of psychological research.

The experienced, remembered, and imagined are qualitatively equal experiences in our consciousness; we may be equally moved by something evoked by the imagined as by anything actually encountered. Art creates images and emotions that are as equally true as the actual encounters of life; fundamentally, in a work of art we encounter our own 'being-in-the-world' in an intensified manner. A work of art made thousands of years ago, or produced in a culture completely unknown to us still touches us because through the work we encounter the timeless present of being human. One of the paradoxes of art is that although all touching works of art are unique, they reflect what is general and shared in the human existential experience.

Art offers us alternative identities and life situations; this is its great educational task. Great art gives us the possibility of experiencing our existence through the existential experience of the most talented individuals. This is the miraculous and merciful equality of art. However, I do not experience the feelings of the gloomy protagonist of *Crime and Punishment*; I do not borrow his feelings. I lend Raskolnikov my feelings and my waiting; Raskolnikov's agonized waiting is *my* experience of *my* own frustration of waiting. All artistic effect and impact is based on the identification of the self with the experienced object, or the reflection of the self upon the object. We experience a work of art or architecture through our embodied existence and identification. An artistic experience activates a primitive mode of embodied and undifferentiated experience; the separation and polarization of subject and object is temporarily lost. Both the glorious beauty and the pitiful humility of the object of artistic representation are momentarily identified with our own embodied experience.

Can anyone look at Titian's painting *The Punishment of Marsyas*, *The Flaying of Marsyas* without experiencing the horrifying pain of one's own skin being stripped off? The viewer lends the tormented satyr, flayed by the vengeful Apollo, his own skin. Many of us can never mourn our personal tragedies with the intensity with which we suffer the fate of the fictive figures of literature, theater and film, distilled through the existential experience of a great artist.

THE REALITY OF ART

The manner in which art affects our mind is one of the great mysteries of culture. In our time, the understanding of the essence and mental workings of art has become confused and blurred by the superficial use of the notions of symbolization and abstraction. A work of art or architecture is not a symbol that represents, or indirectly portrays, something outside of itself; a work of art is an image-object that places itself directly into our existential experience.

Andrey Tarkovsky, for instance, whose films appear to be full of symbolic signification, strongly denies any intentional symbolization in his films. In his films, for instance, rooms are flooded with water, water soaks through ceilings and it rains constantly. "When it rains in my films, it simply rains," he writes, however.[8]

"Tintoretto did not choose that yellow rift in the sky above Golgotha to signify anguish or to provoke it," writes Sartre. "Not sky of anguish or anguished sky; it is an anguish become thing, an anguish which has turned into yellow rift of sky … It is no longer readable."[9]

A work of art may, of course, have conscious symbolic contents and intentions, but they are insignificant for the artistic impact and the temporal persistence of the work. A significant work of art is an image-condensation capable of mediating the entire experience of being-in-the-world through a singular image. In the words of Tarkovsky, "An (artistic) image is not a specific meaning expressed by the director; the entire world is reflected in it as in a drop of water."[10]

The poet Rilke gives a memorable description of the utter difficulty of creating an authentic work of art, and of its necessary density and condensation, reminiscent of the core of an atom: "For verses are not, as people imagine, simply feelings … they are experiences. For the sake of a single verse, one must see many cities, men and things, one must know the animals, one must feel how the birds fly and know the gesture with which the little flowers open in the morning."[11]

Rilke continues his list of necessary experiences endlessly. He lists roads leading to unknown regions, unexpected encounters and separations, childhood illnesses and withdrawals into the solitude of rooms, nights of love, screams of women in labor, and tending to the dying. But even all of this together is not sufficient to create a line of verse. One has to forget all of this and have patience to wait for the distilled return of these experiences. Only after all our life experiences have turned to our own blood within us, "not till then can it happen that in a most rare hour the first word of a verse arises in their midst and goes forth from them."[12]

UTILITY AND USELESSNESS

Architecture is an art form that serves commonplace utilitarian functions. But architecture does not simply emerge from the realities of use and usefulness; it arises from mental images outside the realm of utility. The impact of the art of architecture derives from the ontology of inhabiting space; architecture's task is to frame, structure, and give meaning to our being-in-the-world. We inhabit our world, and our particular way of inhabitation obtains its fundamental sense through constructions of architecture.

In general, art has a dualistic relation with technology. Various art forms accept and utilize inventions of technology, but, at the same time, they turn their back on technological rationality and utility. The most ingenious construction technique remains mere engineering skill if the structure is unable to illuminate our view of the enigma of human existence that lies behind technical rationality, and unless it creates a metaphor for our existence. Fundamentally, art always renders technology and rationality useless.

In Alvar Aalto's view, architecture is not at all an area of technology; it is a form of "archi-technology."[13] In other words, the art of architecture always returns technique to its ahistorical and archaic mental and bodily connections.

NEWNESS AND ETERNITY

"If you want to create something new, search for that which is ancient," my professor Aulis Blomstedt wisely taught me forty years ago.

The central ingredient of art is time, not as a narrative or futuristic interest, but as an archeology of collective and biological memory. Myths store the earliest experiences and mental themes of the human mind. Even the most radical art of our time derives its strongest impact from the echo of these timeless images of supra-individual memory. The time of art is regressive time, as Jean Genet expresses: "In order to achieve significance, every work of art has to patiently and carefully descend the stairs of millennia, and fuse if possible, into the timeless night populated by the dead, in a manner which allows the dead to identify themselves in this work."[14]

T.S. Eliot's *The Wasteland*, one of the greatest works of modern poetry, is a splendid example of the way in which a creative talent, aware of tradition, combines ingredients from completely different sources; the temporal origins and boundaries of Eliot's assembled images lose their meaning in the creative fusion. *The Wasteland*, as all great works of art, is an archeological excavation of images. The poem interconnects historical images and timeless myths with the common-place circle of life of the poet's own time. The poem combines references ranging from the Bible to Ovid, from Virgil to Dante, from Shakespeare to Wagner, Baudelaire to Hesse. The poetic work begins with a motto quoted from Petronius' *Satyricon* and ends in the reiteration of the final incantation of the *Upanisad*. A momentary reconstruction of the mind's evolution takes place in such an artistic experience.

ART AND EMOTION

Architecture also mediates and evokes existential feelings and sensations. The architecture of our time, however, has normalized emotions and usually eliminates such extremes of the scale of emotions as sorrow and melancholy, or happiness and ecstasy. The buildings of Michelangelo, on the other hand, represent an architecture of melancholy and sorrow. Michelangelo's buildings are not symbols of melancholy, they actually mourn. These are buildings that have fallen into melancholy, or more precisely, we lend these buildings our own sensation of metaphysical melancholia.

In the same way, the timeless buildings of Louis Kahn are not metaphysical symbols; they are a form of metaphysical mediation through the medium of architecture, leading us to recognize the boundaries of our own existence and to deliberate on the essence of life. They direct us to experience our very existence with a unique intensity. The masterpieces of early Modern architecture do not represent optimism and love of life through architectural symbolization. Decades after these buildings were conceived, they still evoke and maintain these positive sensations; they awake and bring forth the hope sprouting in our soul. Alvar Aalto's Paimio Sanatorium is not a metaphor of healing; even today it offers the promise of a better future—it heals.

The places and streets depicted in literature, painting, and cinema are as saturated with emotion and are as real as the houses and cities built of stone. The commonplace and desolate rooms of Edward Hopper, or the shabby room in Arles painted by Vincent van Gogh, are as full of life and affect as the 'real' rooms in which we live. The 'Zone' locale in Andrey Tarkovsky's *Stalker* exudes an air of inexplicable threat and disaster; it is certainly more real in our experience than the actual anonymous industrial area in Estonia where the film was shot. The landscape pictured by Tarkovsky contains more significant human messages and meanings than its physical original. The mysterious 'Room,' sought by 'the Writer' and 'the Scientist' under the guidance of Stalker, is finally disclosed as a very ordinary room, but the imagination of the travelers, as well as of the viewer of the film, has turned it into a metaphor and the center point of their metaphysical significance.

THE BOUNDARIES OF SELF

"Literature is made at the boundary between self and the world and during the creative act this borderline softens, turns penetrable and allows the world to flow into the artist and the artist to flow into the world," the author Salman Rushdie writes, and it seems possible in this regard to generalize from literature to art.[15]

All art articulates the boundary surface between the self and the world, both in the experience of the artist and the viewer. In this sense, architecture is not only a shelter for the body, but it is also the contour of the consciousness, and the externalization of the mind. Architecture—the entire world constructed by man with its cities, tools, and objects—has a corresponding mental ground. The geometry and hierarchy of the built environment, as well as the countless value choices that they reflect, have been mental structures before their materialization in the physical environment. Our most commonplace acts give evidence of our inner mental landscape, as inevitably as the rituals and monuments that we hold in high esteem. A landscape wounded by the acts of man, the fragmentation of the cityscape, and insensible buildings are all external landmarks of an alienated, shattered inner space.

"…like the Almighty, we make everything in our own image, for want of a more reliable model; our artefacts tell more about ourselves than our confessions," writes Joseph Brodsky in his book *Watermarks*, a work that touchingly analyzes the writer's experiences of Venice.[16]

"Architecture is constructed mental space," my late friend the architect Keijo Petäjä used to say. However, when a sense of gloom and anxiety is too often projected by the environments of our time, we are usually unwilling and unable to identify our own mental landscape in this dismal world. If we could learn to interpret the latent signals of our environment and architecture, we could certainly better understand our fanatically materialist culture and ourselves. A psychoanalysis of the environment could cast light on the mental ground of our paradoxical behavior—the adoration of individuality and our simultaneous unconditional submission to conditioned values, for example. The disappearance of beauty from the environment cannot mean anything else but the disappearance of the capacity for idealization, of reverence for human dignity, and of the loss of hope. Yet, man is able to construct only if he has hope: Hope is the patron saint of architecture.

George Nelson, the American architect-designer, foresaw the catastrophic fall of the Nazi regime by being able to read the suppressed message of Albert Speer's stone-clad architecture. Nelson understood that the architectural image projecting the one thousand-year future of the Third Reich in fact signified an unconscious fortification against its unavoidable self-destruction.[17]

THE TASK OF ART

Our technological, consumer, and media culture consists of ever-greater attempts to manipulate the human mind, in the form of thematized environments, commercial conditioning, and benumbing entertainment. Art has the mission to defend the autonomy of individual experience, and to provide the existential ground for the human condition. One of the tasks of art is to safeguard the authenticity of the human experience.

The settings of our lives are irresistibly turning into a mass produced and universally marketed kitsch. In my view, it would be ungrounded idealism to believe that the course of our culture could be altered within the visible future. But it is exactly because of this pessimistic view of future that the ethical task of artists and architects—the defense of the authenticity of life and experience—is so important. In a world where everything is becoming equal and, eventually, unavoidably, becoming insignificant and of no consequence, art has to maintain differences of meaning, and in particular, the criteria of experiential quality.

"My confidence in the future of literature consists in the knowledge that there are things that only literature can give us, by means specific to it,"[18] writes Italo Calvino in his *Six Memos for the Next Millennium*, and continues in another chapter, "In an age when other fantastically speedy, widespread media are triumphing, and running the risk of flattening all communication onto a single, homogenous surface, the function of literature is communicating between things that are different simply because they are different, not blunting but even sharpening the differences between them, following the true bent of written language."[19]

The task of architecture, similarly, is to maintain the qualitative articulation of existential space. Instead of participating in the process of further accelerating our experience of the world, architecture has to slow down experience, and fiercely defend that slowness.

Art is most often viewed as a means of reflecting reality through the artistic artifact. The art of our time often does reflect experiences of alienation and anguish, violence and inhumanity. But in my view, the mere reflection and representation of the prevailing reality is not sufficient as the mission of art. Art should not increase, or reinforce human misery, but alleviate it. The duty of art is to conceive new ideals and modes of perception and experience, and thus to open up and widen the boundaries of the world.

"Art is realistic when it attempts to express an ethical ideal," Tarkovsky writes, giving the notion of realism a surprising new meaning.[20] Along with creating a work of art, an authentic artist always creates his ideal reader, listener, and viewer.

I believe that authentic architecture can only be born through a similar process of idealization. An authentic architect imagines an ideal society or dweller as he designs. Only a construction that constructs something ideal can emerge as meaningful architecture.

"Only if poets and writers set themselves tasks that no one else dares imagine will literature continue to have a function," Calvino states. "The grand challenge for literature is to be capable of weaving together the various branches of knowledge, the various 'codes,' into a manifold and multifaceted vision of the world."[21]

Our confidence in the future of architecture can be based on the very same knowledge; existential meanings of inhabiting space can be wrought by the art of architecture alone. Architecture continues to have a great human task in mediating between the world and ourselves, and in providing a horizon of understanding to our existential condition.

The disappearance of beauty in our environment is alarming; can it mean anything else but the disappearance of human value, self-identity and hope? Beauty is not an added aesthetic value of the environment; the longing for beauty reflects a belief and confidence in the future, and it reflects the realm of ideals in our mindscape. "Beauty is not the opposite of the ugly, but of the false," as Erich Fromm wrote.[22] A culture that has lost its craving for beauty is already on its way towards decay.

KNOWLEDGE THROUGH ART

The prevailing view of our culture makes a fundamental distinction between the worlds of science and art; science is understood to represent the realm of rational and objective knowledge, whereas art stands for the world of subjective sensations. The world of science is understood to possess an operational value, whereas the world of art is usually seen as a form of exclusive cultural entertainment.

In a 1990 interview concerning the complexities and mysteries of the new physics, Steven Weinberg, who won the Nobel Prize for physics in 1979 for his discovery of the relationship between electromagnetism and the weak nuclear force, was asked: "Whom would you ask about the complexity of life: Shakespeare or Einstein?" The physicist answered quickly: "Oh, for the complexity of life, there's no question—Shakespeare." The interviewer continued: "And you would go to Einstein for simplicity?" "Yes, for a sense of why things are the way they are—not why people are the way they are, because that's at the end of such a long chain of inference…"[23]

Art articulates our existentially essential experiences, and also our modes of thinking, that is, our reactions to the world and our processing of information that take place directly as an embodied and sensory activity.

EMBODIED CONSCIOUSNESS

Our consciousness is an embodied consciousness; the world is structured around a sensory and corporeal center. "I am my world," as Wittgenstein writes.[24]

But the senses are not merely passive receptors of stimuli, and the body is not a mere point of viewing the world through a central perspective. Our entire being-in-the-world is a sensuous and bodily mode of being. The body is not the stage of cognitive thinking; in fact, the senses and our bodily being structure, produce, and store silent knowledge.

The knowledge of traditional societies is stored directly in the senses and muscles; it is not a knowledge molded into words and concepts. Learning a skill is not founded on verbal teaching, but rather on the transference of skill from the muscles of the master directly to the muscles of the apprentice through sensory perception and mimesis. This principle of embodying knowledge and skill—introjection, to use a notion of psychoanalysis—continues to be the core of artistic learning. Similarly, the primary skill of the architect is to convert the multi-dimensional essence of the design task into an embodied image; the entire personality and body of the architect becomes the site of the problem. Architectural problems are far too complex and too existential to be dealt with in an entirely conceptualized and rational manner.

SENSORY THOUGHT

The art forms of sculpture, painting, music, cinema, and architecture are all modes of sensory and embodied thinking characteristic to each particular artistic medium. Architecture is also a mode of existential and metaphysical philosophy, through its means of space, matter, gravity, scale, and light.

We structure our world on the basis of mental maps, and in the formation of these experiential schemes the structures of the environment play a central role. The existentially most important knowledge of our everyday life—even in a highly technological culture—does not reside in detached theories and explanations, but in a silent knowledge beyond the threshold of consciousness, fused with the daily environment and behavioral situations.

But a poet also speaks of encounters at the "threshold of being," as Gaston Bachelard writes.[25] Art surveys the biological and unconscious realms of our body and mind. Thus, art maintains vital connections with our biological and cultural past, with the soil of genetic and mythical silent knowledge. The essential time dimension of art points to the past rather than the future; art cultivates and preserves rather than uproots and invents.

THE THINKING HAND

Bachelard also considers the imagination of the hand: "Even the hand has its dreams and assumptions. It helps us understand the innermost essence of matter. That is why it also helps us imagine (forms of) matter."[26] Equally, Martin Heidegger connects the hand with our thinking capacity: "...the hand's essence can never be determined, or explained, by its being an organ which can grasp...Every motion of the hand in every one of its works carries itself through the element of thinking, every bearing of the hand bears itself in that element..."[27]

All the senses 'think' and structure our relation with the world without our being conscious of this perpetual activity. The sensory and embodied mode of thinking is essential in art and all creative work. Albert Einstein's well-known description of the role of visual and muscular images in his thinking process is an authoritative example of this: "Words and language, as they are written and spoken, do not seem to have any role in my thinking mechanism. Psychic entities, which seem to be the elements of thinking, are certain signs, and more or less clear images, which can be voluntarily repeated and recombined. The above elements are, in my case, visual in nature and, some of them, related with muscles. Ordinary words and other signs have to be laboriously sought only in the second phase, when the mentioned associative play has been sufficiently established and can be repeated if desired."[28] Einstein suggests that an emotional and aesthetic factor is equally central in scientific creativity as it is in the making and experiencing of art.

Using a hand analogy, the sculptor Henry Moore writes about bodily identification and the simultaneous "grasping" of multiple points of view in the sculptor's work:

"This is what the sculptor must do. He must strive continually to think of, and use form in its full spatial completeness. He gets the solid shape, as it were, inside his head—he thinks of it, whatever its size, as if he were holding it completely enclosed in the hollow of his hand. He mentally visualizes a complex form from all round itself; he knows while he looks at one side what the other side is like; he identifies himself with its center of gravity, its mass, its weight; he realizes its volume, and the space that the shape displaces in the air."[29]

Our educational philosophy should acknowledge the existence of sensory thinking and embodied intuition as counterparts and complementaries of conceptual thought, as a means of understanding the multi-dimensional and layered essence of art and creativity; or, I would like to say, in order to understand ourselves as human beings.

THE GIFT OF IMAGINATION

The uniqueness of the human condition is this: we live in the manifold worlds of possibilities created and sustained by our experiences, recollections, images, and dreams. The ability to imagine and daydream must be considered the most human and essential of our capabilities. But the deluge of excessive, nonhierarchical, and meaningless pictures in our culture of images today—"the rainfall of images" in Italo Calvino's words—flattens our world of imagination.[30] Television externalizes and passivates images when compared with the interior imagery evoked in us by reading a book; the effortless images of entertainment attempt to imagine on our behalf. The image industry detaches images from their historical, cultural, and human context and thus 'liberates' the viewer from investing emotions and ethical attitudes into what is experienced. Numbed by mass communication, we are already prepared to watch the most outrageous cruelty without the least emotional involvement. The deluge of images overwhelms our senses and emotions, suppressing our empathy and imagination.

The lack of horizon, ideals, and alternatives in today's political thought is a consequence of a withering of the political imagination. As our imagination withers, we are left at the mercy of an incomprehensible future. Ideals are projections of an optimistic imagination—but the withering of the imagination is bound to ruin idealism. The pragmatism and the lack of stimulating visions so evident today are surely consequences of an impoverished imagination. A culture that has lost its imagination can only produce apocalyptic visions as projections of its repressed unconscious. A world devoid of alternatives, due to the absence of individual and collective imagination, is the world of Huxley and Orwell's manipulated subjects.

The duty of education is to cultivate and support the human abilities of imagination and empathy, but the prevailing values of contemporary culture tend to discourage fantasy, suppress the senses, and petrify the boundary between the world and the self. Education in creativity today has to begin with a questioning of the absoluteness of the world and with the expansion of the boundaries of self. The main object of artistic education is not to be found in the principles of artistic making, but in the personality of the student and their image of the world.

Nowadays, the idea of sensory training is connected solely with artistic education proper, but the refinement of our senses and sensory thinking has an irreplaceable value for all of us, in many other areas of human activity. I want to say more: the education of the senses and of the imagination is necessary for a full and dignified life.

CITY SENSE

The City as Perceived, Remembered and Imagined
(1996)

The city, even more than the house, is an instrument of metaphysical function, an intricate instrument structuring action and power, mobility and exchange, societal organizations and cultural structures, identity and memory. Undoubtedly the most significant and complex of human artifacts, the city controls and entices, symbolizes and represents, expresses and conceals. Cities are inhabited excavations of the archeology of culture, exposing the dense fabric of societal life.

The city contains more than can be described. A maze of clarity and opacity, the city exhausts the capacity of human description and imagination: disorder plays against order, accidental against the regular, and surprise against the anticipated. Activities and functions interpenetrate and rub against each other creating contradictions, paradoxes, and an excitement of an erotic nature.

•

The contemporary city is the city of the eye. Rapid mechanized movement detaches us from a bodily and intimate contact with the city. As the city of the gaze passivates the body and the other senses, the alienation of the body again reinforces visibility. The pacification of the body creates a condition that is similar to the dulled consciousness induced by television.

Cartesian and perspectival, the city has gradually eliminated the specificity of place and detached verticality from horizontality. Instead of joining seamlessly to give rise to a plasticity of landscape, these two dimensions have become separate projections; the plan has been detached from the section. The visual city leaves us as outsiders, voyeuristic spectators, and momentary visitors, incapable of participation.

Visual alienation is reinforced by the inventions of photography and the printed image, which have created an ever-expanding Sargasso Sea of images. The camera has become the prime instrument of tourism. "The omnipresence of photographs has an incalculable effect on our ethical sensibility," writes Susan Sontag, describing a "mentality that looks at the world as a set of potential photographs."[1] As a consequence "…reality has come to seem more and more like what we are shown by cameras," she observes, and assumes that "taking photographs has set up a chronic voyeuristic relation to the world which levels the meaning of all events."[2]

Indeed, we can easily catch ourselves looking at a scene framed as a photographed image; the tourist's city is a collection of pre-selected visual images. The increasing use of mirror glass, a surface that returns our gaze without affect, contributes to the experience of superficial surfaces, as opposed to that of depth and opacity. The city of transparency and reflection has lost its materiality, depth, and shadow. We need secrecy and shadow as urgently as we desire to see and to know; the visible and the invisible, the known and what is beyond knowledge, have to obtain a balance. Opacity and secrecy feed the imagination and make one imagine life behind the city's walls. The obsessively functionalized city has turned too readily legible, too evident, leaving no opportunity for mystery and dreaming. As the city loses its haptic intimacy, secrecy and invitation, it loses its sensuality, its erotic charge.

•

The haptic city welcomes us as citizens, fully authorized to participate in its daily life. The haptic city evokes our sense of empathy and engages our emotions.

The image of the pleasurable city is not a visual experience, but an embodied percept based on a peculiar double fusion: we inhabit the city, and the city dwells in us. When entering a new city, we immediately start to accommodate ourselves to its structures and cavities, and the city begins to inhabit us. All the cities that we visit become part of our identity and consciousness.

The mental experience of the city is more a haptic constellation than a sequence of visual images; impressions of sight are embedded in the continuum of the more unconscious haptic experience. Even as the eye touches and the gaze strokes distant outlines and contours, our vision *feels* the hardness, texture, weight, and temperature of surfaces. Without the collaboration of touch, the eye would be unable to decipher space and depth, and we could not mold the mosaic of sensory impressions into a coherent continuum. The sense of continuity unites isolated sensory fragments in the temporal continuity of the sense of Self.

"My perception is therefore not a sum of visual, tactile, and audible givens: I perceive in a total way with my whole being; I grasp a unique structure of the thing, a unique way of being, which speaks to all my senses at once," as Maurice Merleau-Ponty writes emphatically.[3]

Thus, I confront the city with my body: my legs measure the length of the arcade and the width of the square, my gaze unconsciously projects my body on the facade of the cathedral, where it roams on the cornices and contours, groping for the size of recesses and projections, my body weight meets the mass of a door, and my hand grasps the door pull, polished to a sheen by countless generations, as I enter the dark void behind. The city and the body supplement and mutually define each other.

•

The final chapter of Steen Eiler Rasmussen's perceptive book *Experiencing Architecture* is significantly entitled "Hearing Architecture."[4] No doubt, every city has its specific echo, depending on the scale and pattern of streets, as well as on dominant architectural styles and materials. The most intimate encounter with any city is the echo of one's footsteps. The ears scan the boundaries of space, and determine its scale, shape, and materiality; the ears touch the walls. Rasmussen recalls the architecture of the echo in the underground tunnels of Vienna in Carol Reed's film *The Third Man*, starring Orson Welles: "Your ear receives the impact of both the length and the cylindrical form of the tunnel."[5]

The power of hearing in creating a sensation of space can be immediate and unexpected; waking up to the sound of an ambulance in a nocturnal city, we instantly reconstruct our identity and location. Before falling back to solitary slumber, we become aware of the immensity of the slumbering city with countless dreaming inhabitants.

Parks and squares silence the deafening rumble of the city, allowing us to hear the ripple of water and the twitter of birds. Parks create an oasis in the urban desert, enabling us to sense the fragrance of flowers, and the full smell of grass. Parks enable us to be simultaneously surrounded by the city and to be outside of it. Parks are metaphors of the absence of the city; at the same time parks are miniaturized still lifes, and images of constructed nature and Paradise.

Cities located by water are fortunate; the encounter of stone and water is entirely metaphysical. In the words of Adrian Stokes, "The hesitancy of water reveals architectural immobility."[6] The cosmopolitanism of harbors, and their juxtaposition of images of permanence and motion, stability and journey, ignites the imagination. The smell of seaweed makes one think of the depth of the ocean, of distant lands and exotic customs, of the excitement of travel, and the sweet longing for home.

•

The city is the art form of collage and cinematic montage *par excellence*; we experience it as an endless collage and montage of impressions. The contemporary obsession with collage reflects a fascination for fragment and discontinuity, and a nostalgia for traces of time. The incredible acceleration of speed—of movement, of information, of images—has collapsed time into the flat screen of the present, upon which is projected the simultaneity of the world. As time loses its duration, and its echo of the archaic past, man loses his sense of self as a historical being, and is threatened by time's shadows. "Long novels written today are perhaps a contradiction," writes Italo Calvino. "The dimension of time has been shattered, we cannot live or think except in fragments of time each of which goes off along its own trajectory and immediately disappears. We can rediscover the continuity of time only in the novels of that period when time no longer seemed stopped and did not yet seem to have exploded…"[7]

The city's structures capture and preserve time in the same way as literary and artistic works. Buildings and squares enable us to return to the past, and experience the slow healing time of history. The greatest of architectural monuments halt and suspend time for eternity.

•

We have an innate capacity for remembering and imagining places. Perception, memory, and imagination are in constant interaction; the domain of our present is merged with images of our memory and fantasy. We continually construct an immense city of evocation and remembrance, and all the cities we have visited are precincts in this metropolis of the mind. The "invisible cities" of Italo Calvino have forever enriched the urban geography of the world.

Literature and cinema would be devoid of their enchantment without our capacity to enter a remembered or imagined place. Memory returns us to distant cities, and novels transport us through cities invoked by the magic of the writer's words. The rooms, squares, and streets of a great writer are as vivid as any that we have visited. The city of San Francisco unfolds in its multiplicity through the montage of Hitchcock's *Vertigo*: we *enter* the haunting edifices in the steps of the protagonist, and see them through his widened eyes. We *become* citizens of St. Petersburg through the incantation of Dostoyevsky: we *are* in the room of Raskolnikov's shocking double murder, we *are* one of the terrified spectators watching Mikolka and his drunken friends beat a horse to death, we *are* frustrated in our inability to prevent the insane and purposeless cruelty.

There is, however, a difference between cities as visited and as imagined; details of the intangible cities of the imagination cannot be remembered, they fade away immediately as dreams drift away, and they can only be conjured again by the magical words of the writer.

•

There are cities that remain mere distant visual images when remembered, and cities that are remembered in all their vivacity. Memory re-evokes the delightful city with all its sounds and smells, and its interchanges of light and shade. I can even choose whether to walk on the sunny side or the shaded side of the street in the pleasurable city of my remembrance.

The measure of the sense of the city is this: in the city of your memory, can you hear the laughter of children, the flutter of pigeon wings, and the shouting of the peddler? Can you recall the echo of your footsteps? In the city of your mind, can you imagine yourself falling in love?

186 Renzo Piano and Richard Rogers, The
Centre Pompidou, Paris, 1971–78.

4 observing

FROM UTOPIA TO A MONUMENT

*The Centre Pompidou and the
Future of Modernism*
(1977)

Even before its completion, the Centre Georges Pompidou in Paris had probably attracted wider attention than any other building of this century. From the competition onwards, the project became the darling of the international architectural press as the fulfillment of the techno-romantic Archigram utopia of the 1960s. After the pioneering generation of Modern architecture, architecture has had no ideals or heroes; the Plateau Beaubourg project, however, contained the promise of a new example and inspiration. The design promised the total fulfillment of all the stylistic aspirations of Modern architecture—structural and technological expression, transparency, functional flexibility, temporality and aleatoricity, a machine-based building technique, and the exploitation of electronic communications technology. Under creation was the architectonic symbol of the 20th century, the heir to the Crystal Palace, the Galerie des Machines, and the Eiffel Tower—the herald of the culture of the 21st century.

FRANCE'S GREAT POWER COMPLEX

The Plateau Beaubourg project was a demonstration of supreme power, will and skill, as much in the realm of politics and culture as in design and technology. The latest manifestation in the French *tour de force* series—the steamship *France*, La Defense office city, the supersonic Concorde—the cultural Mecca, the Centre Pompidou, was a blatant effort to reinstate Paris as the artistic center of the world, a position it had lost to New York and London in the 1960s.

This was by no means an insignificant venture in the field of culture. The Centre has a surface area of 100,000 m², a staff of 900 and the average number of visitors to date has been 20,000 a day. The building cost 280 million francs and devours ten per cent of the annual cultural budget of the French Government.

By the time it was completed, the Centre Pompidou had become a historical monument, the capital's newest symbol and tourist attraction, receiving over a million visitors within seven weeks of opening. During the inauguration period, a tapestry of the Centre Pompidou was exhibited in one of the choirs of the nearby Church of St. Marie, the new building already an icon of the 1970s.

Symptomatically, the French exhibit simultaneously such contradictory traits as the preservation and destruction of tradition, entrenched conservatism and reckless avant-gardism, bigoted nationalism and openhearted universalism. In the Centre Pompidou, the conservatism against which Le Corbusier fought his entire life has now given way for the first time at an official, state level.

Unprecedented flexibility was shown in the exceptional freedom granted to the foreign designers to create this restoration of French cultural hegemony. As a foreigner was also appointed director of the Museum of Modern Art, so it can also be claimed that international forces were harnessed to create France's new cultural identity.

189

190

PER ARDUA AD ASTRA?

681 entries were submitted to the design competition by the time it closed in July, 1971. The winning designers (the British Su and Richard Rogers and the Italians Renzo Piano and Gianfranco Franchini) explained that they aimed at an idea that would be clearly distinguishable amidst the large number of entries. In the characteristic method of architectural competitions, to be successful one had to aim "over the goal." Taking into realistic consideration the countless number of requirements of an architectonic problem in a competition normally removes any possibility of a startlingly striking solution. The impact of a winning solution is mostly achieved through simplification, exaggeration, and indifference.

The winners were surprised by the decisiveness of the French, and by the urgency to implement the design directly on the basis of the winning entry. In order to carry out the project, it was necessary to draw up an agreement and commission procedure unique in France and even to legislate special laws. There were also legal attempts to stop the project. The Geste Architecturale Group, for instance, infuriated by the anti-monumental character of the design's architecture, brought several actions against the developer and even managed to stop work on the project for a brief period in July, 1974. President Giscard d'Estaing also

187 Joseph Paxton, The Crystal Palace, London World Exhibition, 1851.
188 Gustave Eiffel, the Bon Marché, Paris, 1876.
189 Dutert and Contamin, Gallerie des Machines, Paris Exhibition, 1889.
190 Gustave Eiffel, The Eiffel Tower under construction, Paris, June 1888. The plans were prepared by Eiffel in 1884–86, erection began in 1887.

191

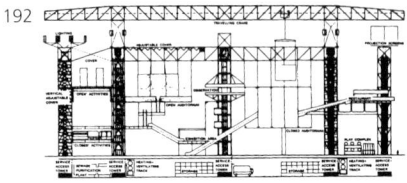

192

planned to halt the project, but succeeded only in changing the color of the ventilation ducts on the Rue du Renard façade from blue to white.

MYTH AND CRITISISM

Since the Centre's inauguration at the end of January, 1977, several special editions of professional journals have been devoted to the building and it quickly found its place in the annals of modern architecture.

However, even in professional circles the building's reception was contradictory, and the general view was that it was a disappointment. Rather than seeing the Centre as a preview of "tomorrow's architecture," the widespread feeling was that it was the terminal point of one major movement in Modern architecture. From being the architectonic symbol of the electronic age, the building has lapsed into a belated nostalgia for the steam engine culture of the preceding century. Post-war architectural fashions have been tragically ephemeral—a decade after its implementation, a late 1960s utopia is already a document of the past.

The Centre Pompidou is a descendent of 19th century cast iron construction, Russian Constructivism, and the neo-Constructivism of the 1960s. Nevertheless, despite its somewhat dated stylistics, the Centre ostensibly possesses a fanatical radicalism. However, the building lacks the obvious assurance of its illustrious predecessors; the language of Constructivism has degenerated into a style, *l'art pour l'art*. Even the technological grandiosity of the building is deceptive when compared to the great constructions of the preceding century. For instance, the Crystal Palace, with almost the same surface area, designed in seven days and built in twenty-eight weeks 125 years earlier, is certainly an achievement that eclipses the Centre Pompidou.

Although the architecture of the Centre resurrects the spirit of the pioneering generation's heroism, its efforts have now become a quixotic struggle on behalf of windmills. And yet, technology no longer needs such demonstrations, for technology has already become the despot.

Reviews in the professional journals to date (*Architectural Design* 2/77, for example) have discussed the building from the cultural, engineering, functional, and aesthetic points of view. This evaluation aims to illuminate the spiritual background of the building in order to discover the symbolic content and psychological effects of its architectural language.

The main contention of architectural criticism has been the building's battleship-like unsuitability to its environment. Within the scale of Paris and the city's historical stratification, the shock of the dimensional, structural, and color contrasts of the building are, however, understandable. In its brutal indifference, however, the composition

191 Alexander and Viktor Vesnin,
Competition project for the offices
of the Leningradskaya Pravda, St.
Petersburg, 1924.
192 Cedric Price, Fun Palace project, 1963.
Extreme expression of architectural
flexibility.

is truly thrilling and in fact relates well to the tradition of grandiose construction in Paris.

Yet simultaneously, the building project brought about a number of important environmental improvements. These included the implementation of the largest pedestrian precinct in Paris, the renovation of numerous dilapidated buildings in the vicinity, as well as a significant enlivening of urban activities, services, and the street scene.

The ambiguity of the Centre's architecture stems from the contradictory nature of its fashion-like superficiality, and its ideological and architectural basis, as well as from the negative psychological influence the building exerts. History rewards willpower and determination. On the other hand, history is gently forgetful of distorted social origins, economic foundations, technological failures, or artistic limitations. History punishes characterlessness by drowning it in the unfathomable depths of meaninglessness.

Obviously, the Centre Pompidou had become history before it was built: the future will see it as the heroic deed of both fanatical willpower and foolhardiness. The future will undoubtedly consider the Centre as one of the central monuments of post-industrialism, but equally, history is unlikely to forget the Centre's manifest violation of the basic laws of architecture.

As architecture throughout the world is at present in a chaotic state, this precocious monument offers a wonderful opportunity to diagnose the architecture of our time.

FRENCH CENTRALISM

The anthropologist Edward T. Hall's studies in the anthropology of space demonstrate that the basic structure of culture forms the warp into which all manifestations of culture are woven, from the individual's everyday subconscious behavior to the conscious, ceremonial manifestations of a culture. He has suggested, among other things, that the mental geometry of French thinking is centric, whereas American thinking, for instance, has a lattice structure. Hall sees this manifested in the French national road network, schools, and institutions, as well as the centric models of spontaneous space utilization followed by individuals.[1] The cultural conglomeration of the Centre Pompidou incontestably supports Hall's assumption. This concentration of cultural services is clearly in contradiction to present demands for democratic regionalism, a contradiction revealed by Michel Guy, André Malraux's successor, in calling the Centre "the center of decentralization."[2]

In principle, the concentration of cultural services—their production and distribution—in such a colossal factory is debatable. Is not the very

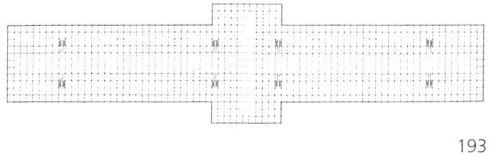

193

194

193 Joseph Paxton, The Crystal Palace, London World Exposition, 1851. Plan of the first story.
194 Renzo Piano and Richard Rogers, The Centre Pompidou, Paris, 1971–78. Plan in the same scale as the plan of the Crystal Palace above.

195 Joseph Paxton, The Crystal Palace, London, 1851. Covering the trancept, January 1851.

196 Joseph Paxton, The Crystal Palace, London, 1851. Glazing wagon using Paxton gutters as rails, December 1850.

197 Renzo Piano and Richard Roger, The Centre Pompidou, Paris, 1971–78. Transportation of one of the trusses at night time.

nature of artistic and spiritual culture closer to individualistic guerrilla warfare on the fringes of human knowledge, rather than a mass exhibition crammed into the center point of a nation? Does art not strive to extend the circle of knowledge by extending it and integrating it into reality? A gigantic aquarium placed in the very center of the metropolis is thus an alienated symbol of culture. Culture has been materialized, divorced from its roots, and exposed to the people's gaze. Culture has been turned into a mass-produced commodity, rather than a diversified view of reality and an indivisible part of life.

The Centre Pompidou is a cultural department store, a supermarket of the arts, where one can make hypocritical impulse purchases of the spiritual life. The programming and architecture of the Centre identify information and culture. Similarly, in recent years the border between data and spiritual content, quantity and quality, the ordinary and the exceptional, has become blurred.

The building's design group saw the Plateau Beaubourg as a living information center, which was to be "a combination of a computer-controlled Times Square and British Museum."[3] Significantly, the designers of France's cultural symbol use an Anglo-American metaphor; in other words, they never bothered to penetrate the nature and essence of French culture.

In one interview, the designers even expressed their disappointment with the numerous small art galleries and other "pseudo-cultural phenomena" that have sprung up in the vicinity of the building. Andrew Rabeneck cynically observed "there is certainly more information, more creative products and a greater trace of Gallic culture in a Paris flea market than can ever be expected from the Centre Pompidou."[4]

THE NATURE AND IDENTITY OF INSTITUTION

Louis Kahn often spoke of the nature of the institution in connection with architecture. In designing, he always wished to return to the basic, archaic form of each institution in order to understand and internalize the nature of the design task. Obviously, in the programming and designing of the Centre Pompidou, the nature of artistic and spiritual culture was not understood, but viewed instead as a part of material mass production and services. Actually, art should be a counterforce to materializing, fragmenting, standardizing, and alienating mass production.

Large art museums normally give rise to a sensory numbness in which the absorption of works of art is replaced by their superficial registration on our retinas. In size, the Centre Pompidou is so colossal, so rich in effect, and so diverse in content, that the events and objects presented lose their identity. The visitor automatically seeks protection from this excess by raising the threshold of stimuli. The small and the delicate are lost in the general cacophony—the eye fails to register any object smaller than a car. One's sensory numbness is completed by the intrusive exhibitionist architecture of the building.

The centralization of artistic events in the Centre is anticipated to lead to competition for public attention in the vicinity through the use of quantitative and sensationalist effects. One ominous portent of this is Jean Tinguely's steel-structured, colossal chocolate-coated vagina, under construction at the end of the building.

THE SYMBOLIC LANGUAGE OF ARCHITECTURE

The plastic, artistic language of architecture is simultaneously a symbolic language, one that shapes and communicates cultural meanings. The vocabulary of architecture, as with any language, has been molded by specific meanings, which cannot be arbitrarily ignored without the content losing its meaning. The Centre Pompidou uses the symbolic language of architecture anarchistically, in contradiction to the meanings ingrained into human consciousness. The exposed technical paraphernalia of the building is inevitably associated with the anti-humanistic environment of industry, an environment the architecture has failed to humanize. A rather arbitrary use of such symbols translate this form language into a symbol of a cultural institution, of human endeavor. This symbolic linguistic somersault is all the more surprising at a time when the entirety of technological culture has reached an impasse.

Is the Centre Pompidou a subconscious propagandist blow on behalf of technological culture? Is it an unconscious effort to persuade people to abandon their opposition and accept excessive techno-futurism as the only valid alternative? Does the architectural language of the building communicate a subconscious effort to sever the bonds of art with nature, biology, and the human cultural heritage?

In post-war architecture, technical equipment and installations have gradually become accepted as elements of a building's aesthetic composition alongside of its structures. The background to such an excessive exaggeration of technical equipment is clearly the stylistic enervation of the basic themes of Modernism. The designers seek neologisms for their language of expression that would still have a novel impact—but this endangers the basic hierarchy of architecture, the basic laws of architecture. The eternal purpose of architecture is to structure and communicate man's relationship to reality; by this, architecture is bound to articulate rather permanent requirements of biopsychic meanings. As Louis Kahn has observed, "A painter can paint square wheels on a cannon to express the futility of war. A

198

199

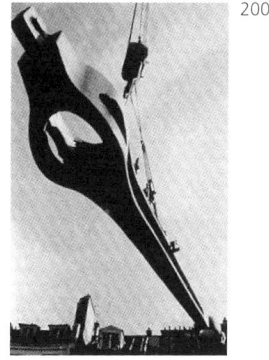
200

198 Renzo Piano and Richard Roger, The Centre Pompidou, Paris, 1971–78. Assembly of the structure.
199 Joseph Paxton, The Crystal Palace, London, 1851. Loading test of cast iron braced beams, March 1851.
200 Renzo Piano and Richard Rogers, The Centre Pompidou, Paris, 1971–78. Montage of one of the *gerberettes*.

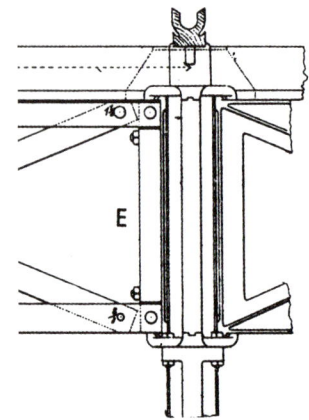

202

203

204

sculptor can carve the same square wheels. But an architect must use round wheels."[5] Parody and absurdism do not belong to the genre of architecture.

THE LANGUAGE OF ARCHITECTURE AND SPACE

In its visual themes, the Centre Pompidou may appear as the richest example of Modern architecture. The building is not, however, as visually exciting as one would expect. On the contrary, after recovering from the first shock, the abundance of motifs becomes monotonous and quantity negates quality. The architectural fault of the building is not in the methods used, but the accumulation of themes, *additio ad absurdum*, and an architectural hara-kiri to arouse the public's interest.

The recent installation of Aulis Blomstedt's exhibition, *Pensée et forme*, in Le Corbusier's Maison La Roche offered me an opportunity to make a comparison between two, quantitatively speaking, incomparable buildings.[6] Le Corbusier's early functionalist house is striking in its architectural poetry, with its accurate and meaningful economy of means. In actual fact, the building contains in miniature everything that can be expressed in architectural language.

The Centre Pompidou is garrulously verbose, but its cascade of motifs appears to contain no spiritual message. The building leaves one with a curiously empty feeling. In the Maison La Roche, the stylistic features and language of Modern architecture are more germinal, sensitive, and expressive. In the Centre, the language of architecture has become alienated into a noisy but meaningless statement.

Aulis Blomstedt's exhibition can also be viewed as direct criticism of the Centre's architecture. For Blomstedt, architecture is the art of restraint, reservation, and noble modesty: "Style is the result of an ethical stance and choice," he has written, "Elegance can only be achived through asceticism."[7]

The Centre Pompidou's architecture lacks a sense of hierarchy and counterpoint. In architectural composition—and in fact in all artistic structures—the essential element is the hypotaxis of the passive background motifs and active solo themes. In the Centre, the brilliantly developed multitude of themes produces a visual sameness. The building lacks an overall plastic rhythm and depth. The basic surface and mass of the building are not articulated, for then the form motifs would have been in front or behind, as protrusions or recesses, large or small. As the basic surface is not outlined, the facades and inner views appear as a network of sequential graphics whose position in space the eye cannot define. The endless wandering of the eye over the lines of the building brings on an attack of vertigo.

The Centre Pompidou is a concrete, although inverted, example of the primary importance of spatial articulation and relationships. In the absence of a spatial language, even the architectural effect disappears.

The creation of spatial localities has been deliberately avoided in the Centre's architecture. The building consists of five superimposed spaces, each the size of two football fields, which are secondarily divisible and flexible in nature. The building has space, but no spaces.

Through architectonic articulation, a space acquires a psychic meaning. In defining space, man commands and interprets it according to his experience of reality. The grandiose urban compositions of Paris, which give kilometer-long distances meanings of the projection of man's will, offer a continuously exciting and fresh experience.

INFLEXIBLE FLEXIBILITY

Modern architecture's aim to maximize flexibility is the consequence of rational thinking about efficiency, but at the same time this aim has weakened the expression of architecture. The psychic task of architecture is to visualize specifically the experience of reality, to return man to his environment and time, as well as to indicate his beliefs. In order to fulfill this basic psychic task, architecture must dare to make decisions and impose limitations. Complete flexibility, a game without rules, is not architecture. It is a means to efficiency, but not an expression of psychic structure.

Louis Kahn could not accept excessive flexibility as the starting point in his architecture (he would have much preferred to redesign the undivided space of the Yale University Art Gallery on the basis of fixed rooms). In his opinion, architects should always dare to express something final. The richness of an environment lies in its historical stratification, in what each period has dared to make final—and not what it has postponed to sometime later.

Unquestionably, the background to the exaggerated Functionalist aim for efficiency, aesthetic flexibility, and randomness lies in the basic arguments of Erich Fromm's work *Escape from Freedom*.[8] When the chaotic reality of despair provides no satisfactory artistic forms, one flees from creative freedom into biased rational arguments or leaves the frustrating making of decisions to chance.

Alan Colquhoun has noted that the complete flexibility of the Centre Pompidou has resulted in the total inflexibility of the furnishings and exhibits.[9] Conversely, the formal artistic inflexibility of Le Corbusier's and Alvar Aalto's architecture appears to offer maximum flexibility for the use of space. There is good reason to add to this paradox of architectural language another equally relevant contra-

201 Joseph Paxton, The Crystal Palace London, 1851. Joint between column and girders.
202 Renzo Piano and Richard Rogers, The Centre Pompidou, Paris, 1971–78. Assembly of the main structure.
203 Le Corbusier, Villa Stein-de Monzie, Paris, 1926–28.
204 Renzo Piano and Richard Rogers, The Centre Pompidou, Paris, 1971–78.

diction: rational ideas and environmental richness in architecture appear to be opposing values—the more clear and more masterful the idea of the building is, the more impoverished and more closed is its influence on the environment. The dominant idea in an experientially rich building will be difficult to define, due to its locally articulated and discontinuous logic. Complete flexibility does not lead to psychic freedom, therefore, but to a deteriorating identity and to a strengthening of the otherwise destructive development in our industrialized culture.

THE LANGUAGE AND LOGIC OF STRUCTURES

The Centre Pompidou is the fulfillment of the Constructivist dream of complete articulation and expression in construction. The construction is based on the bridge-building system developed by the German Heinrich Gerber in the mid-19th century, in which the main trusses are placed between short cantilevers in order to minimize bending. The most famous example of this principle is the railway bridge over the Firth of Forth in Scotland (1882–89). On the other hand, the escalators on the Place side of the Centre have been suspended from the ends of "gerberettes" cantilevers. Horizontal stability across the building has been achieved by combining the end trusses with diagonal braces.

In its construction, the Centre is altogether too complex visually. The viewer does not unconsciously and immediately understand the working principle of the building, and is left with a feeling of uncertainty and arbitrariness. Thus a person's perceptiveness appears to have its limits. The structural event should be simply and intuitively articulated in order to be understood. "Is there anything more solid and safe than a log balanced on two stones," wrote Aulis Blomstedt in his diary. In many of Blomstedt's other aphorisms he indicated that essentially, architecture has to do with primitive simple perceptions and semantic phenomena: "Architecture is of solid, restful earth,"[10] and "Architecture is geometry adapted to gravity."[11] Blomstedt was not as such opposed to the use of advanced technology in architecture, but, as I understand it, emphasized that the built environment should be viewed in relation to the biologically structured and tuned sensory complex.

Functionally speaking, the 48-meter giant span used throughout the Centre Pompidou is without any foundation. Only in the Forum on the ground floor does it make sense. Elsewhere, dividing the span would have reduced the whalebone-like structures and brought to the other floors a primary articulation facilitating the reading of scale.

In his article "The Triumph of Technology: 'Can' Implies 'Ought'," Hasan Ozbekhan asserts that industrial man justifies his deeds through imperatives beyond himself as his inner motives blur: "Thus feasibility, which has become a primary strategic concept, is raised to a normative position implying that whatever technology appears to be able to implement is seen as an obligation to implement it."[12]

The exaggerated spans of the Centre Pompidou, as much as moon landings and supersonic flights, are expressions of this technological imperative. Technology is no longer the means to fulfill man's objectives, but has become an objective in itself.

207

THE LOGIC OF OPERATION AND DETAILS

In designing an art museum or library, the lighting arrangements are a primary consideration. "A man with a book goes to the light. A library begins that way," noted Louis Kahn.[13] Alvar Aalto considered that light in an art museum is as important a design element as acoustics in a concert hall.

208

In the Centre Pompidou's topsy-turvy architectural language, the windows, too, have lost their original purpose as apertures admitting light and offering a view out. Instead, the glass surfaces offer only the possibility of looking in, turning the activities of the building into spectacles for the gaze of urban dwellers.

When the library and the art museum were pushed into sunless spaces, they simultaneously lost their opportunity of appearing in the cityscape as unique, clarifying symbols of communal structures. In the Centre, the particular has become the general, and the original has sunk into a standard solution.

As a building for exhibitions, the structures are too active. The presentation of the collections in the rooms of the Museum of Modern Art has been solved in the only possible way—by displaying them in neutral viewing areas through a system of low partition walls or lowered ceilings. Such an arrangement is naturally a direct criticism of the building design.

On the roof terrace, where it has not been possible to conceal the absurdly unnecessary lattice trusses, a viewing of the sculptures is quite impossible. The shining, sculptured structures steal the limelight. Insane in its repetitive series of movements and with its rusted joints screaming in agony, Tinguely's metamatic machine was the only work of art on the roof terrace that appears distinctly among the form cacophony of the building. One would almost expect to hear the building's machine-like structure accompanied by the sounds of chuffing and puffing and whistles blowing.

The construction details—such as the gerberettes and pillar joints—give the effect (but only the effect!) of movable structures, the

205 Le Corbusier, Maison La Roche, Auteuil, 1923. A rhythmic articulation of space and scale.
206 Renzo Piano and Richard Rogers, The Centre Pompidou, Paris, 1971–78. Library on the second floor.
207 Le Corbusier, Unité d'habitation, Marseilles, 1945–52. The roof terrace.
208 Renzo Piano and Richard Rogers, The Centre Pompidou, Paris, 1971–78. The roof terrace.

possibility of hydraulically raising and lowering the floor levels, which in turn strengthens the feeling of unreliable structures.

The steel-grille walkways of the external pedestrian levels, as well as the impermanent character of the stairs, railings and other details, all create a sense of fear. The lowness and fragility of the roof and balcony railings have a vertiginous effect, which distracts considerably from enjoying the view of Paris. In general, the detailing of the stairs and railings is careless and unrelated to the plasticity of the structures.

The apparent aim of the design was to give the impression of scaffolding in a continuous process of change. The result is an irritating confusion—the visitor is unable to decide what is the building, what is repair work, what exhibition is being erected, dismantled, or actually ready. The main exhibition for the opening of the building, the New York Hans Rücker Group's 800,000 franc "Urban Archaeology," appeared so unfinished that few among the dense throng of visitors actually realized it was an exhibition.

What is technically doubtful in such a building turned inside out is that the maximized external surface and delicate equipment have been exposed to the mercy of dust, rust, and pollution. The Centre's opening exhibition actually contained a portentous tinted façade drawing in which the Centre Pompidou was covered with Etienne-Louis Boullee's architecture.

THE PSYCHOANALYSIS OF MODERNISM

Architecture and the built environment reflect the subconscious hopes and fears of a culture, as much as its conscious intentions. At the end of the 1930s, the American designer George Nelson inferred the impending catastrophe of Germany from the subconscious expressions he observed under the veneer of Hitler's and Speer's pompous architecture. At a time when the world was experiencing the rise of Nazi Germany, Nelson interpreted the apparent strength of their stone architecture as an unconscious defense against inevitable self-destruction.[14]

The Centre's constructivism, now a speculative intellectualism, its meaningless symbolic language, its freedom now translated into uniformity, its flexibility that has paralyzed its identity and its culture that has become materialized, are all metaphors of the schizophrenia of industrial man. The building signals the divergence of intelligence and feeling, sense and thinking, the individual and the community, man and the environment, and self and the world.

An architecture that aims at identity, variety, and individuality through superficial formal means expresses the desperate attempt of psychically alienated man to clutch at a reality from which he is estranged.

The interaction between man and his environment is being severed, and the environment thus becomes a thing, a machine product, rather than a part of man's personality and culture, a part of the collective psyche.

The new suburbs of Paris already reflect the complete destruction effected by techno-culture. Those under construction are being built as though on the ruins of a nuclear or ecological disaster. In the hysterical forms of such contemporary building, the subconscious alienation, distress, and fear of industrial man are visible just below the surface.

Art and architecture constitute a counterforce to such alienation. Art unites the different realms of the mind and strengthens one's image of self. Art connects man to reality; it integrates. Architecture, for its part, connects the individual to the community, cultural structures, and the environment.

The Centre Pompidou again raises the question of the relationship between architecture, technology, and rationality—for in this building these have been fused together. Art and technology are by nature opposites. Art can use technique as a means or a subject, but their natures are fundamentally different—technology utilizes reality (material and natural laws), but art reflects the mental essence of reality.

Art and rationalist logic are likewise antithetical. Even in rationalist architecture, rationality itself does not turn into architecture. Rationality taken to its ultimate end, in fact, ceases to be architecture and becomes technology. The artistic dimension of architecture does not derive from rationality itself, but from an irrational level that is the non-logistic message of art.

In recent times, the rational character of architecture has been customarily blamed for the gloominess of our present environment. Rationalism, however, is one of the foundations of architectural thinking, and has by no means lost its importance or become a reason for environmental poverty. The reason for the atrophy of architecture in our industrial culture is the separation of rational thinking from the spiritual realm of the arts. Rational architecture ceases to be architecture when it relinquishes its function as the interpreter of the spiritual, unconscious essence of culture. Or perhaps, indeed, at this point it truthfully reflects the anti-humanism of our culture.

The standardized language of Modern architecture has indisputably lost its expressive capacity. The ability of language to communicate will not be improved by the invention of new words or the recycling of archaic ones, but by specifying the content of language and clarifying the history of its development. Irrespective of the divided state of architecture today, one should not abandon that which is permanent, but explicitly seek one's way to the original sources, to the place where the stylistic path of Modern architecture bifurcated. It is not necessary to flee back to the Baroque and Renaissance—as have Tafuri, Culot and Krier—for the Modern architecture of the 1920s provides a solid basis. The freshness and optimism that comes from a re-examination of Le Corbusier's early works offers the assurance that the foundations of Modern architecture are strong and healthy. Our task is to dismantle all that is spiritually rootless and alien atop these foundations, to rediscover the heritage of Modernism.

209 Daniel Libeskind, *The Burrow Laws*, architectural drawing, silkscreen, 1978. Exhibited in *Creation and Recreation: America Draws*, an exhibition of American architectural drawings presented at the Museum of Finnish Architecture in Helsinki in 1980.

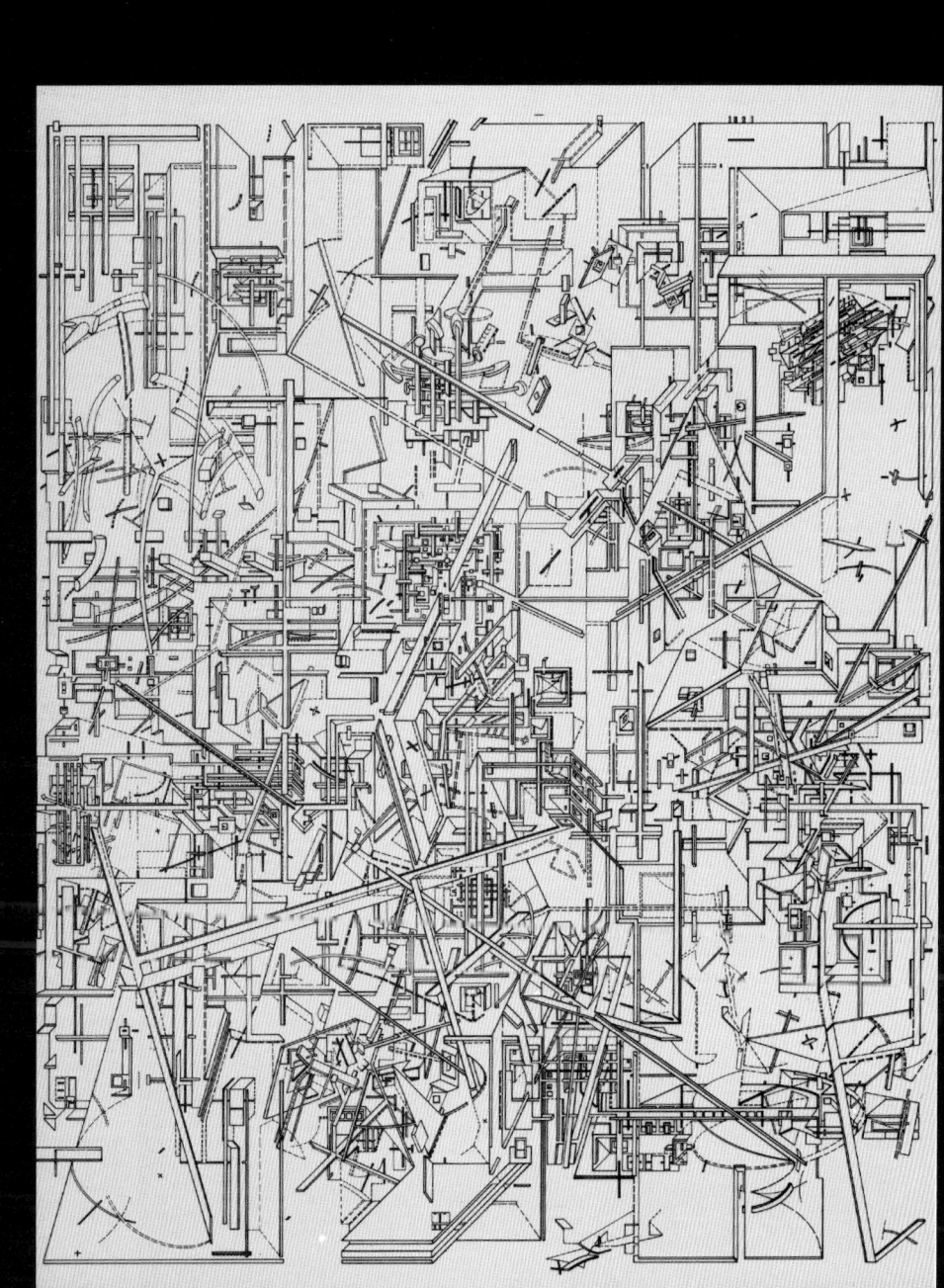

AVANT-GARDE VERSUS DERRIÈRE-GARDE

(1980)

There is general agreement on both sides of the Atlantic that Modern architecture is going through a time of crisis. This uncertain time clearly resembles the spiritual atmosphere of the early 1800s, as Hans Sedlmayr describes it: "The old certitude and self-assurance are gone and the new edifices lack the power to originate styles."[1] The cul-de-sac in the Modern Movement has resulted from the narrow orthodoxy of its doctrine, which did not allow scope for sufficiently varied expression. The loss of inspiration and meaning in architecture is less frequently seen in connection with our fading confidence in the Utopia of technological and rationalist civilization, the spiritual cornerstone of Modernist thought. "It is the fall of the ideal image that leads to the collapse of empires and the decay of cultures."[2] Only a few dare to believe in the continued vitality of the ideals of the Modernist approach; confidence in Functionalist principles does remain in Scandinavia, where architecture is pragmatically enrooted in its social task and rarely deviates into Utopian or stylistic speculation.

Since the pioneering generation of the Modern Movement, architecture has been considered a moral issue—the truth and nothing but the truth—of function, structure, materials, and the mythical Spirit of the Age. Each era is expected to have its true expression, and the task of the architect is to search for this hidden formula. Detaching forms from their historical origins and applying them in a new context is strictly taboo. Consequently, the Modern Movement has taken place in an absolute present tense, without a memory of the past, standardized into a closed doctrine and desiccated into lifelessness.

However, the grip of this high morality has weakened and an increasing number of Modernist disciples are abandoning the faith. Young American architects, in particular, seem determined to shake off the burdens of this morality and to create a "freestyle architecture" expressive of the American social and cultural context.[3]

Some of the most daring and extreme probing into the future of architecture today takes place in the United States. Beneath the surface of inventive and witty experimentation, however, a skeptical observer may also sense an unintentional architectural anticipation of the emerging socio-psychic problems prophesied by a host of social scientists. A Marxist critic would most likely interpret the American architectural avant-garde as a reflection of the alienation inherent in, or resulting from, the final phase of capitalism. The interdependence of architectural style and political doctrine is, however, one of the most confused issues of the profession today.

For me, it is somewhat difficult to accept the idea of art or architecture *in a state of crisis*—as if architecture could be an isolated expression, with an independent source of inspiration and life force. It makes more sense to speak of an architecture *of a state of crisis*, as the scattered spectrum of architecture today seems to anticipate fundamental changes in attitudes to nature, society, production, and ultimately, to life itself.

The arrogant confidence—perplexing, indeed, to a European unaccustomed to making finite historical evaluations of today—with which many American architects and critics are announcing the death of the Modern Movement and a beginning of a new age, is exemplified by Stanley Tigerman's article in conjunction with the exhibition of the "Late Entries to the Chicago Tribune Competition": "Our own generation has gained new vitality through its desire to find formal meaning in our cultural origins now that the barrenness of Modernism is behind us...It is Eros versus Anti-Eros; it is liberalization of the 1960s versus utopian dogma; and it is pluralistic design versus one single, right, legitimate way of making architecture...This exhibition takes place during a time of revisionism in which Modernism is being safely relegated to its place in history."[4]

The American architectural scene today is confusingly diverse and it is virtually impossible to make any general characterizations. Even the familiar formulas of the Big Firms are beginning to change under the input of young designers of this Transition Generation.

American architects themselves are far from agreement as to the future course of architecture. Various schools of thought and practice are in active—sometimes even hostile, it seems to an outsider—dialogue;

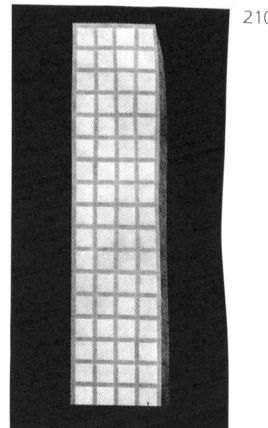

210

211

PROJECTS IN THE CHICAGO TRIBUNE TOWER "LATE ENTRIES" COMPETITION 1980

210 Tadao Ando.
211 Thomas Beeby.

212

the language of criticism is stunningly tough for a Finnish reader ed... cated in an atmosphere of collegial respect and politeness. Orthodox values and categories have been turned upside down and it is impossible to differentiate a revolutionary from a reactionary.

An excerpt from an article by Richard Plunz serves to illustrate the feeling of heated chaos: "A new academicism has assumed the facade of "avant-garde" aestheticism. Much of what is new might be characterized as exercises in 'formalism, graphism, hedonism and elitism'... Progressive and conservative causes have been interchanged and relabeled, using the guise of new terminology... The most regressive historicism can be promoted as progressive, hidden behind the claim to stylistic innovation and justified by the historical tradition of Post-Renaissance humanism."[5]

Many of the publicized American buildings and projects during the last decade, outside of Establishment Architecture, have seemed disturbingly elitist or anarchist to European eyes. They express hysterical individuality and an absence of social concern or historical enrootedness. Our noble concept of architecture has frequently been stretched to the point of insult. Often it has been difficult to judge whether a particular project should be taken as a sincere professional statement, an attempt at architectural humor, or simply as an expression of bad taste.

Are these strange and confusing ideas an expression of a particularly American—uninhibited and unbiased—way of looking at the contemporary world? Are we witnessing the emergence of a new architecture emancipated from the straitjacket of European tradition and morality?

Some one hundred and fifty years ago a French observer, Alexis de Tocqueville, described American pragmatism, "the American philosophical method" in his impressively sharp report *Democracy in America*: "...to accept tradition only as a means of information, and existing facts only as a lesson to be used in doing otherwise and doing better; to seek the reason of things for oneself, and in oneself alone; to tend to results without being bound to means, and to strike through the form to the substance... This disposition of mind soon leads them to condemn forms, which they regard as useless and inconvenient veils placed between them and the truth."[6]

Like de Tocqueville, I feel that a characteristically American way of looking at things is again emerging in architecture; in particular, a way of looking at history, style, and cultural context. The specific American cultural climate helps to make the recent architectural phenomena understandable—that which is otherwise so disturbingly enigmatic for a European observer. In the present phase of architectural thought, when

PROJECTS IN THE CHICAGO TRIBUNE TOWER "LATE ENTRIES" COMPETITION 1980

212 Helmut Jahn.
213 Charles Moore, John Ruble, Buzz Yudell.

we are all taking another look at history and the social relevance of architectural language, the American view may prove especially revealing.

In a recent article, Gerald Allen contrasts meaning with doctrine, and characterizes the architecture of the new era: "Architecture in the 1980s needs to learn to speak in many different tongues. In such a situation the issue of style becomes in some sense almost irrelevant ... Free-style architecture means architecture that is free in style in order to be freely expressive, not architecture that is free of style."[7]

The development of a 'free-style architecture' means the return of a deliberate architectural pluralism, akin to that of John Nash and Leo von Klenze in the early 1800s. In 1828, Heinrich Hübsch wrote an essay with a revealing title "In welchem Stil sollen wir bauen?", and Klenze, according to Sedlmayr, built a palace in the Renaissance style, a museum in the Greek style, a church based on the Capella Palatina, the Hall of Fame in the antique idiom, and an official residence in the Roman Baroque.[8] The American collages of styles today do not even stop here—they combine motifs of different styles within a single building.

The early working title for the 1980 exhibition of contemporary American architectural drawings at the Museum of Finnish Architecture was *Renewed Frontier*. The title referred to the mythical American concept of the frontier and suggested a new American frontline of the architectural avant-garde. The concept of the frontier is one of the guiding American myths. In his recent book *Disturbing the Universe*, Freeman Dayson suggests that the immense interest in space exploration in America has been yet another expansion of the frontier mentality.[9]

Frederick Jackson Turner, in his well-known paper, "The Significance of the Frontier in the American History" (read, incidentally, at a meeting of the American Historical Association in 1893 in conjunction with the Columbia Exposition of Chicago, a triumph of Beaux-Arts design over the dawning Modernism), thoroughly analyzed the specific American character, particularly the self-centered individuality molded by the frontier, "the meeting point of savagery and civilization":[10] "Each frontier did indeed furnish a new field of opportunity, a gate of escape from the bondages of the past, and freshness, and confidence, and scorn of older society, impatience with its ideas, and indifference to its lessons, have accompanied the frontier."[11]

Turner quotes the Italian economist and colonial historian, Achille Loria, a statement particularly intriguing in relation to the transitional phase of architecture today: "America has the key to the historical enigma which Europe has sought for centuries in vain, and the land which has no history reveals luminously the course of universal history."[12]

The Modern Movement has been declared emphatically dead by a few influential Anglo-American critics. The territory of Modern architecture seems to be fully exploited, these critics say, and it is now time to conquer and cultivate another frontier. Today American architects are searching for new architectural territory on several fronts: the revitalization of the Functionalist language—a kind of meta-Modern; the rehabilitation of American folklore; the fusion of Modernist and historicist language; the cultivation of American Industrial and post-industrial vernacular; the revitalization of American classicism and Art Deco—"Post-Modern Classicism"—among others.[13]

The American view of history is clearly different from ours. For a European, history appears as an inevitable continuum, and the evolution of history dictates its unquestionable patterns and logic. For us, history has a moral and didactic message, one we deal with in terms of patterns and context.

An American does not seem to be preoccupied by a respect for historical continuity—history can be fragmented and considered a depository of symbols, motifs, and forms, all of which can be re-used without shame. American cities, towns, and homes abound in reconstructed history and nostalgia for past glory. This American independence from the closed course of history enables American architects today to deal with the past and the present side by side without distinction. "The dividing line of using forms of the past and those of the present is no longer sharp. Designing in the manner of Palladio can be as legitimate as designing in the manner of Pelli," writes Juan Pablo Bonta.[14]

Another point arises: contrary to European aspirations, American architecture is rarely contextual. Due to the ethnic collage of the American people, a shared cultural context hardly exists. In the absence of a shared collective memory, the role of verbalized mythical notions—such as freedom, democracy, equality, and opportunity—has been important as a means of social cohesion for American culture.

214

American architecture—even the masterpieces—stands out and differentiates itself from the environmental setting rather than attempting to create consistency and continuity. The typical American urban scene is a collection of individual presentations rather than a coherent townscape.

American architecture provides striking examples of corporate architecture, but the collective social dimension is frequently missing. These demonstrations of corporate strength are impressive monuments to executive power, but the American scene in general seems to lack a collective coherence. Are we here witnessing "the fall of public man" in accordance with Richard Sennett's recent convincing book?[15]

American architecture has been characterized by technological advancement, perfection of execution, and professionalism. The new American architecture is often emphatically anti-professional and anti-technological—it regresses to intentional amateurisms and out-dated techniques, or ridicules technology by repressing it to mere pathetic gestures. Should this be interpreted as a stop sign for the technological dream? Or is it an unconscious revolt against the dictatorship of omnipotent rationality?

American architecture today has a distinct element of escapism, a desire to flee from the problems of the metropolis, of the post-industrial age, to a pastoral nostalgia. The romantic, naturalist, and historicist trends also seem to serve as defensive reactions. But, as Gerald Allen has stated, there is another meaning of the escape to the pastoral, to "the sylvan landscape of Arcadia": "But it is also important to point out that in fact the pastoral ideal does not portray flight so much as retreat, the temporary sojourn by on the whole very urbane people in a place where fundamental issues can be seen with clarity, and with any luck can be resolved. The pastoral landscape is the place for, in the broadest sense of the word, recreation."[16]

Much of current American architecture is a reflection of commercialism, sensationalism, and deliberate image-making: "the tendency to let image determine form rather than vice versa."[17] In the land of the advertisement, architecture has frequently taken on its function. Turner wisely added a word of warning in his analysis of the American character: "But...pressing individual liberty beyond its proper bounds has its dangers as well as its benefits."[18]

Until recently, architecture has been the art form that has excluded humor. There is an apparent contradiction between the requirement of permanence in architectural expression and the situational or temporal character of humor. However, recent American architecture has also introduced humor in buildings, sometimes in the form of such macabre symbolism as Stanley Tigerman's "Dog Killing Machine," a project for the SPCA (Society for the Prevention of Cruelty to Animals) in Chicago.[19]

The extreme consequence of these tendencies is, of course, the architectural terrorism of Philip Johnson. Through his exceptional status in the Establishment, Johnson has managed to turn skyscraper construction into his private architectural jokes. In the words of Dimitri Shostakovitch's much-debated memoirs, one might, however, ask the architect: "Do you think that history is really a whore?"[20]

An eclectic regression seems to occur at a speculative phase of cultural evolution, at a point when the *innere Notwendigkeit* (inner inevitability) defined by Wassily Kandinsky fades away, and style

215

PROJECTS IN THE CHICAGO TRIBUNE TOWER "LATE ENTRIES" COMPETITION 1980

214 Jorge Silvetti.
215 Cesar Pelli.

becomes a matter of deliberate choice. Sedlmayr writes of the pluralistic *'architecture parlante'* after the French Revolution: "...architecture shows for the first time the unmistakable characteristics of the artifact; art now speaks what is obviously a manufactured language, patched together out of various bits of the dead language of the past, the choice of these fragments being largely determined by a preference for the monumental and for simple geometric forms, the 'grammar' and 'syntax' that connects those fragments being reduced to a few very primitive rationalist connecting links..."[21] His description could just as well be of some of the Post-Modern attempts of recent years. There is a necrophilic aspect to such eclecticism due to the loss of architecture's primary unconscious creative force.

The fact that "verbal architecture" has become popular recently is another expression of the speculative dimension on the surface level. The Anglo-American "verbal architecture" has frequently been fiercely demagogic, confusing the functions of historian, critic, and creative designer. Instant classification and labeling has led to disposable styles. During the last decade, critics and promoters stole the scene from the designer, and the search for meaningful expression through architectural form became overshadowed by intellectual analyses and speculation *ad absurdum.*

"Nearly a hundred years ago Nietzsche prophesied that the end of the era of 'rational man' was at hand and that the coming age (our own) would be dominated by nihilists and 'last men'," writes Norris Kelly Smith, pointing to the nihilists and last men around us.[22]

The much-debated *Transformations* show at the Museum of Modern Art in New York in 1979 was a deliberate attempt to justify and canonize the banal and alienated tendencies in contemporary architecture. Today's architecture—in America and the rest of the industrial world—exists in an apocalyptic aura in which the unintentional message of disaster has become shockingly clear.

There is a growing foreboding that we have lost the metaphysical dimension in our personal, cultural, and architectural relation to the world. Today many architects are trying to re-establish ties with this lost dimension by reverting to the surreal, by sanctifying the banal, by interpreting our real misery as an expressive artifact, and turning nightmares into Elysium. With his writings on Las Vegas and the Strip, Robert Venturi has even attempted to justify the American tragedy: the fragmentation and dehumanization of the city, the physical expression of shattered social structures.

Is our Age of Communication doomed to turn into an Age of Isolation and Solitude? John Hejduk's *Thirteen Lonely Watchtowers of Cannareggio* and their inhabitants in their ritualized separation are an

PROJECTS IN THE CHICAGO TRIBUNE
TOWER "LATE ENTRIES" COMPETITION
1980

216 Robert A.M. Stern.
217 Tod Williams, Billie Tsien.

expression of the same contemporary metaphysical isolation as Edward Hopper's heartbreaking paintings.

In its deliberate attempts to break the paralysis of the Modern Movement, the architectural avant-garde today arouses fundamental questions concerning the social significance and responsibility of architecture: is the inner, collective coherence of the post-industrial society weakening? Is the ordered cultural pattern breaking into an assemblage of individual cultures, each one with its private language? Is the constantly innovative architectural language becoming anarchistic and, consequently, abandoning its communicative capacity? Or, is architecture seeking to recover its lost dimensions through the populist values of the 'great majority,' and, consequently, losing its spiritual insight, becoming mere recreation? Is the architecture of Consumerism and Commercialism, with its priority for novelty, moving dangerously far away from the permanent qualities in art? Are the calls for such an extreme variety of styles eliminating the fundamental task of architecture—to create a sense of continuity in our experience of the world?

I agree with Gerald Allen's view that architecture is inescapably an expression of its time—even in the case of "the Sun-Belt millionaire who is currently and lovingly bankrolling an authentic copy of a Louisiana plantation house in a Southern suburb."[23] No doubt architecture is unconsciously expressive of the state of the collective psyche regardless of, and independent of, its surface style. But this view shifts the fundamental issues from the scope of architecture to the human and social context. If this is the case, is there real hope for a new Humanism, or are we bound to create only monuments of a decaying culture? Or, finally, should we revive Le Corbusier's belief that architecture can truly replace revolution?

218 Daniel Libeskind, Jewish Museum,
Berlin, 1989–99.

THE CONTEMPORARY
AVANT-GARDE AND THE WISDOM
OF ARCHITECTURE

(1993)

Deconstructivism may well be the most deliberately fabricated and promoted architectural style in history. Instant history, in fact, was in the making at the Museum of Modern Art on the evening of June 22, 1988. The New York art world had been summoned to the opening of the *Deconstructivist Architecture* exhibition staged by the Arch-Deacon Philip Johnson himself, who had launched the International Style half a century earlier.

The exhibition projects appeared as extraordinary bursts of energy and creative imagination. The new movement was presented not only as another stylistic invention, but also as a new radical philosophy and method of making architecture. Deconstructivism was posed as the *avant-garde par excellence* of our time. Altogether, there was an air of breathless excitement and curiosity: were we witnessing a breakthrough in architectural thought, comparable to the Russian Constructivist avant-garde (whose works, predictably, were shown as a cunning introduction to the show)?

During the five years that have passed since that celebrated opening, a number of breath-taking projects and a few provocative buildings have dissected the very heart of architecture for inspection and diagnosis. At the same time, the Deconstructivist aesthetic has spread around the world to appear in museums and factories, gas stations, cafés, and 'follies' alike, as all styles do in our era of instant information.

In five years the Deconstructivist formal games have become secularized into the everyday household vocabulary of schools of architecture. One questions the degree of real depth and radicalism in the movement, and marvels at the incredible capacity of our consumer culture to accept, absorb, and suffocate any and all critical and subversive ideology. Whether any ideology or action in our culture can now create and maintain sufficient distance from convention in order to constitute an authentic opposition or avant-garde is highly questionable.

But did Deconstructivism really mean anything more than a name to conveniently package together practitioners of a certain retinal style? Has Deconstructivism at large redeemed its promise as a new philosophical and theoretical ground for the making of architecture?

THE END OF ARCHITECTURE?

The approaching turn of the century has resulted in extensive philosophical consideration of the concept of an End (end of art or art history, literature, or history itself, depending on the writer in question). Arthur C. Danto's Hegelian view is that it is with the discovery of its true philosophical nature that art attains the end of its history.[1] In Danto's view, art has already turned into its own philosophy and works of art now can exist only in coexistence with their projected theory.

Today it would be impossible to recognize certain works as works of art without being aware of their respective philosophical foundations. The entangling of philosophical formulations and architectural works is equally evident today. Architecture is frantically seeking its self-definition as much as responding to societal demands.

The amount of theorizing that has taken place in the field of architecture during the past decade is bewildering. We have seen theoretical concepts and constructions of various disciplines applied to architecture—from philosophy and linguistics, semiotics and psychoanalysis, to anthropology and genetics. Indeed, this fierce theorizing suggests a Hegelian interpretation: the End of Architecture. One cannot evade the feeling that through the Derridean method of deconstruction, in particular, architecture has sought a complete identification with its own theory. The making of architecture is turning into its own analysis and critique.

LOGOCENTRICISM AND THE EMBODIED METAPHOR

Today's avant-garde at large seems to have a logocentric obsession; architectural meaning is explained rather than experienced, and the significance of a building is seen to rest more in its conceptual and verbal aspirations than in the sensory and bodily encounter with the work itself.

Instead of being an embodied existential metaphor conveyed through the tectonic materiality of building, architecture is seen to derive and communicate its meaning through networks of verbalized explanations. There is a curious air of simultaneous over-intellectualization and mystification, of opening and closing, revealing and hiding. Much of today's theorizing seems to be a matter of achieving a distance from the reality of architecture, rather than attempting to closely understand its essence.

Deconstruction is primarily a philosophical method of deep reading and writing literary texts, a method of revealing layered meaning in existing literary texts, rather than a device of creating signification in matter and space.

Treating architecture as a language has caused more confusion than it has clarified the workings of the discipline. The linguistic analogy seems to offer a syntax for reading architectural meaning, but the idea should be approached cautiously. Architecture is fundamentally not a language; it affects us primarily through unconscious metaphors that interact directly with our body, senses, and memory.

"Buildings themselves constitute neither texts nor a true language; their complex of meaning and their subtle powers operate almost exclusively at pre- and non-linguistic levels," writes Michael Benedikt in his recent book *Deconstructing the Kimbell*. Benedikt applies the Deconstructionist method of literary analysis to Louis Kahn's masterpiece and concludes that a Derridean layering of meaning is inherent in the phenomenon of true architecture without any explicit Deconstructionist intention.[2]

THEORY VERSUS MAKING

The relation of architectural theory to the making of architecture is commonly confused; a theoretical position and explicit verbalized philosophical contents are now considered prerequisites for meaningful architecture. As a consequence, architecture has frequently turned into a medium of merely illustrating philosophical ideas.

All significant architecture is a product of serious thinking, or thinking through the medium of architecture. In the same way that cinema is a way of cinematic thinking and painting a means of articulating painterly ideas, architecture is a means of philosophizing through the embodied material act of constructing. Consequently art does not illustrate or mimic ideas of philosophy; it is a mode of such thinking in its own right. The ideas articulated by art—filmic, painterly, musical, and architectural thoughts—are conceived and expressed through the inherent medium of the particular art form, and these ideas are not necessarily ideational and translatable into the linguistic mode.

The correlation of theory and architecture is, however, far less interesting than the distance, tension, and dialectical interaction between a theoretical point of departure and the creative exploration. There is an inherent opposition between the two in art; art always wants to escape its definition. Theoretical analysis and the making of architecture are two parallel approaches to the art of building as well as to our existential reality, and not necessarily directly causally related. Simply put, true creative fusion can always achieve more than any theory is capable of projecting.

THE WISDOM OF ARCHITECTURE

In *The Art of the Novel*, Milan Kundera writes about "the wisdom of the novel."[3] He states that all real writers listen to this wisdom, a body of knowledge greater than the individual, and this is why all great novels are wiser than their writers. If a writer should feel smarter than his writing, he ought to change his profession, Kundera advises.

There is, no doubt, a similar wisdom of architecture to which all true architects listen. Consequently, all great architectural works are wiser than their designers. Authentic works of art always contain more than has been consciously put into them. Due to this silent wisdom of architecture, touchingly noble works have been created—and obviously will be created—on the basis of rather vaguely and naively formulated theoretical positions. Le Corbusier's polemical exclamations hardly explain the depth and poetry of his work. The silent authority and prestige of Louis Kahn's buildings can hardly be deduced from his esoterical pronouncements. Even such an extreme reductivist view as Hannes Meyer's ultra-materialist equation, ARCHITECTURE = FUNCTION x ECONOMICS, gave rise to such poetically charged architectural images as Meyer's own 1926 Peterschule in Basel.

This seeming paradox is conceivable because architecture is primarily not about theory, technique, or function, but about the world. Architecture creates pictures; it creates images that evoke the experience of life.

ARCHITECTURE AS IMAGE OF LIFE

Architecture provides our most important existential icons through which we can understand both our culture and ourselves. The important works of Modern architecture are images of a living reality and a new emancipated life-style; those of our own time are frequently self-referential pictures of architecture itself. Today's avant-garde works deal with the philosophical issues of representation more than with actual contents; they are discourses within the discipline itself and rarely true to life. In this respect, these works are empty retinal images and often convey (unintentionally) a necrophilic ambience.

If the first doubtful aspect of Deconstructivist theory as applied to the art of building is its intellectual and linguistic bias, the second is its underrating of the social and psychic dimensions of architecture. As a consequence of Deconstructivist architecture's outright declaration of autonomy and independence from cultural reality, it is a form of cultural critique more than an attempt to ameliorate the social condition. Due to the absence of social empathy, these works often exude the autistic air of abstract formalism, of a formal game that does not acknowledge man's need for domicile. Whereas Modern art and architectural projects secured their healing and poetic radiance from an innocent idealism and optimism, the formal brilliance of today's avant-garde often seems to express an air of calculation and a death of empathy.

Today's avant-garde works frequently appear as an architecture of exodus and exile, of a cosmopolitanism in the realm of ideas rather than a search for domicile on cultural and societal ground. A collective motivation and social idealization, a social vision—the very essence of the ethical dimension of art—all appear to have weakened. Significantly, today's avant-garde has hardly shown any interest in the social issues of architecture, whether framed by housing, or the refinement of industrial methods for mass production, or planning, all of which were core concerns of the Modern Movement.

While early Modern architecture sought to solve real social, technical, and economic problems, today's avant-garde appears as the style of the Society of Affluence and Abundance. The Pandora's Box of formal inventions has been opened up by the absence of constraints and limits.

This arrogance and self-centeredness was expressed by Peter Eisenman in his stunningly outspoken statement: "I never thought very much about what it (architecture) was doing to other people, because it was more important to work my own problems out."[4] This is certainly the ultimate reversal of the pioneer generation's societal morality.

Five years is certainly too short a time to make any valid or impartial judgment of a cultural phenomenon, but it seems that the fascination with the spatial and formal inventions of Deconstructivism is already fading; the yield of the "-ism" is being absorbed into the common means of contemporary architecture. However, we can certainly expect more architectural surprises from the architects that participated in the legendary exhibition at MoMA.

Whether it is responsible to categorize Daniel Libeskind's extension of the Berlin Museum, currently under construction, as a Deconstructivist work or not, the design possesses an exceptionally potent conceptual and symbolic idea, in addition to its brilliant

219 Daniel Libeskind, Jewish Museum, Berlin, 1989–99.
220 Daniel Libeskind, Jewish Museum, Berlin, 1989–99.

manipulation of form. The project attains its strength from the context of Berlin and from a sense of history that echoes the depths of the tragic past of humanity. Libeskind's work may likely redeem the promise of a radically new architectural thought. In any case, before making the final judgment about Deconstructivism, we should wait to see the finalization of this building.

221 Andy Goldsworthy, *Dandelion flowers / pinned with thorns to wind-bent willowherb stalks / laid in a ring / held above blue bells with forked sticks*, Morkshere Sculpture Park, West Bretton, 1 May, 1987.

FROM METAPHORICAL TO ECOLOGICAL FUNCTIONALISM

(1993)

222

223

THE CLOSING OF A CENTURY

The approaching turn of the century is already coloring our horizon. We are accustomed to view history in terms of a narrative of decades and centuries and, consequently, expect something dramatic to take place at this symbolically charged date. But whereas one hundred years ago the fin-de-siècle spirit, epitomized by the optimistic notions of The Gay Nineties, La Belle Époque, L'Art Nouveau and Jugendstil, was eagerly awaiting the opening of the new century, we seem to view the approaching date as the closing of our century. The Gay Nineties awaited a quick materialization of the budding promises of an exciting new future. But we, a century later, simply do not know what to expect and what to hope. We have lost sight of the horizon and our curiosity about the future. Instead of being excited, we are worried.

During the past two decades, the themes of 'closing' and 'coming to an end' have emerged remarkably frequently in many fields, from philosophy and historiography to the arts.

THE THEME OF THE END

The American philosopher Arthur C. Danto has announced the "End of Art,"[1] while Hans Belting, the German art historian, has assumed "The End of Art History."[2] Alvin Kernan, American professor of humanities at Princeton University, has recently published a book on the end of the Age of the Book with the gloomy title *The Death of Literature*.[3] Certain genres of music have also been judged to have reached their end, symphony and opera, in particular. "Blow up the opera houses!" advised

Pierre Boulez, the French composer and conductor, already in 1967; in his view, Alban Berg's *Wozzeck* was the ultimate achievement of the art of opera and, consequently, concluded the history of opera.[4]

The American political historian Francis Fukuyama brought the notion of an end into a wider context in his controversial essay entitled "The End of History."[5] Fukuyama's view, based on Hegel and Hegel's commentator Alexander Kojève, is that the worldwide victory of economic liberalism has exhausted the dialectical forces of the historical narrative and brought History to its end.

On earlier occasions, I have also questioned the feasibility of architecture in a consumer society, a condition that tends to detach architecture from its existential base and turn it into a disposable commodity and entertainment.[6]

Peter Eisenman brought the discussion of an end (of architectural thinking, at least) to its ultimate conclusion in his 1983 *Perspecta* article, "The End of the Classical: the End of the Beginning, the End of the End."[7]

THE END OF ART

I do not wish to sound an apocalyptic tone, but I feel that the notion of Utopia so dear to Functionalism and Modernism in architecture provokes consideration of the issues of a narrative and an end. The line of reasoning by Arthur C. Danto, in particular, casts light on the currently confusing and contradictory scene of architecture. Recent developments in art seem to bring forth the central issues of our culture, issues that are also reflected in architecture.

Before speculating on the future of Functionalism, of course, we better make sure that it has not already ended for good.

The idea of an art form coming to an end is not a product of our millennial neurosis. Aristotle assumed that the art form of tragedy had already reached its ultimate expression in his time: "Arising from an improvisatory beginning…tragedy grew little by little, as the poets developed whatever new part of it had appeared, and passing through many changes, tragedy came to a halt, since it had attained its own nature."[8]

The expression "attaining its own nature" seems to imply an exhaustion of essence or an arrival at self-knowledge, to use a Hegelian notion. Hegel, who introduced the idea of history coming to an end, reasoned that the historical process terminates in the consciousness of itself, in self-knowledge.

Giorgio Vasari, who shaped the narrative of Renaissance art through his *Lives of the most Eminent Italian Painters, Sculptors and*

Architects, saw that art had reached its ultimate perfection and limit in the work of the masters of High Renaissance. He could not see any way that art could improve after the achievements of Michelangelo (Vasari, of course, rounded off the narrative of art conveniently with his own biography).[9]

EXHAUSTING A STYLE

Obviously, the art of tragedy continued after the Greek poets and there has been art, even very great art, since the age of Vasari and Michelangelo. What these views of art coming to an end really implies is that a certain historical narrative, as viewed from inside that particular narrative, arrives at an exhausted endpoint. Every stylistic matrix has a limited field of variations; a style dries up once the potential for expression has been exhausted. In Danto's view, "coming to an end is almost a logical necessity, since narratives cannot be endless."[10]

Has the narrative of Modern architecture, or of Functionalism more specifically, come to an end? Have its unconscious motifs and forces already surfaced and turned into an external mannerism? If so, we can only view Modern achitecture now as outsiders and our creative attempts will flatten to mere repetition and mimicry.

Are we, perhaps, then obliged to follow Leon Krier's command: *"Vorwärts, Kameraden, wir Müssen Zurück"*?[11]

THE ART OF APPROPRIATION

The genre of portrait painting is usually offered as an example of an art form that has already exhausted its potential field of expression. The currently popular art of appropriation is given as another proof that art has lost its forward progression and become repetitive, because its only remaining option is the recycling of previously created imagery. "No matter where we look, it is becoming increasingly difficult to recognize an 'original' from a copy, or from a copy of a copy. Mimicry has replaced innovation as a creative value. We recycle everything," writes Thomas Lawson in his article "Nostalgia as Resistance" in a book entitled *Modern Dreams*.[12]

The art of appropriation is exemplified by the "Picassos" and "Morandis" painted by Mike Bidlo, by Sherrie Levine's rephotographed photographs of Walker Evans' photographs from the 1930s, by Malcolm Morley's painted copy of a postcard of Vermeer's *The Artist's Studio*, by Richard Prince's rephotographed details of meaningless images in magazine advertisements, and by Russel Connor's collage appropriations of historical masterpieces.

A GROWING DISTANCE

These examples of new art (last art) reveal a growing distance between the artist and the artistic subject.

The sensory and emotional force of Modern art sought to eliminate all distance between subject and object; it embodied and incorporated the object in the subject's experience. Today's art signals a disappearance of artistic empathy, sharing of experience, and responsibility—of the integrating function of art. The artist has become an outsider who self-consciously observes his own condition and very mission from an immense distance. Photo- and hyper-realism exemplify this chilling emotional separation.

The architectural magazines of the past two decades also abound in documents of frozen empathy and a calculated recycling of images. In addition to narcissistic tones, today's architecture often reveals cynical and necrophilic tendencies. This is a result of architecture having become alienated from its 'life-world,' to use the phenomenological notion of Edmund Husserl.

The contrary aim of eliminating all distance, the populist fusion of art and everyday life, was expressed twenty-five years ago in the pop ideology of Claes Oldenburg: "I am for art that is put on and taken off, like pants, which develops holes, like socks, which is eaten, like a piece of pie, or abandoned with great contempt, like a piece of shit…I am for art you can sit on. I am for art you can pick your nose with or stub your toes on…I am for an art that tells you the time of day, or where such and such a street is. I am for an art that helps old ladies across the street…"[13]

ART TURNS INTO ITS OWN PHILOSOPHY

Danto makes clear that what he means by art coming to an end is "not so much a loss of creative energy, though that might (also) be true, as that art was raising from within the question of its philosophical identity—was doing philosophy, so to speak, in the medium of art…"[14] In Danto's view, art has turned into its own philosophy and works of art exist only in coexistence with their own theory. Since the cave paintings of Lascaux, works of art have touched us directly through their magical capacity to evoke experiences of timeless humanity, without needing any explicit theoretical frame, or not even requiring any knowledge of the artist's conscious intention. Today certain works of art would be unrecognizable as works of art without being aware of their respective philosophical foundations.

The entangling of philosophical formulations and respective architectural works is equally evident today. Often, an intellectually

qualified stance is more essential than its sensory embodiment in the material language of building.

Avant-garde architecture today presents itself as a form of cultural critique, rather than a response to a social commission. But such forms of critique imply distance and estrangement. This attitude is expressed in the theme of a recent symposium held at the University of California, entitled "Postmodernism and Beyond: Architecture as the Critical Art of Contemporary Culture."[15]

THE BRILLO BOX DILEMMA

Danto considers Andy Warhol's 1964 exhibition of Brillo boxes at the Stable Gallery in New York as the philosophical turning point in the history of art: "(Warhol) brought the history to an end by demonstrating that no visual criterion could serve the purpose of defining art ... Why were these boxes art when their originals were just boxes? ... The meaning of 'work of art' could no longer be taught by example or understood through precedent."[16] Indeed, the foundations of the institution of art were shaken so forcefully in the 1960s that the art historian Hans Belting felt compelled to state: "There will have to be either a discipline for before 1960 and a discipline for after, or a history that has stopped forever a few years ago to be followed by ahistorical happenings."[17]

As the art forms of painting and sculpture have so clearly arrived at a decisive limit and an unavoidable paradigm shift, is it reasonable to expect architecture to continue unaffected on its Modernist and Functionalist path without its foundations being shaken and questioned in an equally fundamental way?

To me, architecture has evidently entered into the same self-conscious syndrome of autonomous self-definition and philosophizing on its essence. Characteristically, recent theorizing in architecture has not so much aimed at a comprehensive analysis of the internal structure and elements of architecture, as at defining its mere existence, its external boundary, its perimeter. The architectural discussion has not been concerned with what is *good* architecture, as much as with what is architecture *at all*. The criterion of authentic architectural quality as lived in its totality has clearly been replaced by the photographed image in the architectural press. Robert A.M. Stern exemplifies this loss, telling his students at Columbia University not to worry about their building after the day they had photographed it.[18]

SELF-REFERENTIALITY OF ARCHITECTURE

The art and architecture of the closing decade of the second millennium have become so self-referential, so concerned with their own existence and self-definition, that today art seems to be about artworks instead of being about the world, and architecture about buildings, not about life. Both deal more with the philosophical issues of representation than with their contents. The functional and utilitarian dimension of architecture has essentially been pushed to the margin.

This self-referentiality is exemplified by Peter Eisenman's isomorphic distortion of one of his houses in *The Idea as Model* exhibition. The axonometric of the three-dimensional model could be perceived correctly only from a single viewpoint, similar to the strange anamorphic skull in Hans Holbein's *The Ambassadors*. This architecture is solely interested in representation and has abandoned life completely.

Self-centeredness implies the vanishing of the social perspective. Indeed, it is difficult now to experience any epic scope to today's architecture or the desire to embrace the world, aspirations that rooted Modern architecture so vividly in its cultural context and made it radiant with optimism.

THE IMPOSSIBILITY OF UTOPIA

The current condition also implies the disappearance of the Utopian and visionary perspective. During the past two decades the architectural profession at large has not been concerned with the social dimension of architecture, in essence housing, or the refinement of industrial means for mass production, or issues of planning, all of which were core concerns of the Modern Movement. Can anyone name a significant architectural Utopia, urban vision, town plan, or a serious attempt at industrialization since the 1960s?

Japanese Metabolism, Yona Friedman's superstructure cities, the urban projects of Candilis, Josic and Woods, or the graphic utopias of the Archigram Group in the 1960s, may all appear naive to today's disillusioned eyes, but, nevertheless, they reveal the existence of a visionary horizon. We seem to have lost the naiveté and innocence that would enable us to project a Utopia. Consequently, we do not project our hope into the future; our melancholic Utopia is in the past. It resides in the unfulfilled promise of Modern architecture, which has acquired a mythical, if not erotic, appeal for us.

THE ANTI-UTOPIAN AGE

Our time is an anti-Utopian age. We have been disillusioned by the fall of the Utopia that inspired the pioneers of the Modern Movement. It has failed on all fronts, the technological and the cultural as well as the social. The justification of the aesthetic Utopia was severely questioned as early as the late 1960s, and the recent bankrupt failure of the great

226

227

228

229

social experiment (the Communist Utopia as well as American urban redevelopment efforts, for instance) completed the fall of ideals. But beyond this, the techno-scientific development that was expected to provide tools for the materialization of the Utopia has deprived reality of its poetic dimension. Norman Mailer's *Of a Fire on the Moon*, portraying man's first landing on the moon in 1964, expresses this clearly "as an assault by science on humanistic literature and the arts, preempting the God of poetry, Apollo, for the name of the mission, and transforming the traditional symbol of the romantic imagination, the moon, into a lifeless scientific object."[19] Whereas the Futurists' cry, "Down the moonshine!", only four decades earlier was a poetic evocation, the Apollo mission marked the end of poetic exploration and curiosity.

THE CRITIQUE OF ART

Recent Structuralist and Deconstructionist critiques have further contributed to this feeling of disillusionment and loss of horizon through questioning of the moral authority of great art.

"The traditional romantic and modernist literary values have been completely reversed," writes Alvin Kernan, continuing, "The author, whose creative imagination had been said to be the source of literature, was declared dead or the mere assembler of various bits of language and culture into writings that were no longer works of art but simply cultural collages or "texts."...What were once the masterpieces of literature, the plays of Shakespeare or the novels of Flaubert, are now devoid of meaning, or, what comes to the same thing, filled with an infinity of meanings...Rather than being near-sacred myths of human experience of the world and the self, the most prized possession of culture, universal statements about an unchanging and essential human nature, literature is increasingly treated as authoritarian and destructive of human freedom..."[20]

The questioning of the moral authority of the architect, if not his entire social mandate, already emerged in the Marxist-Leninist critique of architecture and the profession at the end of the 1960's. In Finland this ideological doctrine was particularly strong and severely shook the traditionally idealist self-identity of the architectural profession.

THE LOGIC OF FUNCTIONALISM

This swift survey of current philosophical issues in the arts seems necessary to understand why the future—or its very idea, so important to architecture—seems to have ended.

I am so deeply inspired by images of Functionalist architecture and by the poetics of Modern architecture in general, that my imme-

230 Le Corbusier, Villa Savoye, Poissy, 1930. The ideal of formal purity.
231 Frank Gehry, Vitra Design Museum, Weil am Rhein, 1986–89. The ideal of a collision of form

diate response to the central question of this Alvar Aalto Symposium "Functionalism: Utopia or the Way Forward?" was affirmative: yes, the Functionalist model not only provides a way forward, but it is our only way out. A Modernist dialectical position to reality, its perpetual questioning of its reading and interpretation of reality, is our only survival from universal kitsch, I thought. I realize now, however, that my conclusion was a bit hasty considering the current condition of art.

After having paused to consider the essence of Functionalism, I realize the extreme vagueness of the notion, both theoretically and historically. Functionalism does not seem to constitute any operative theory or method beyond mere slogans; neither does it provide a basis for a classification of architectural works beyond external stylistic characterization. Moreover, the notions of Modernism, Functionalism, and Rationalism overlap all too frequently, at any point in its theoretical explication throughout this century.

"'Functionalism' is a weak concept, inadequate for the characterization or analysis of any architecture…functionalism is a fiction—fiction in the sense of error," writes Stanford Anderson in his article "The Fiction of Function."[21]

Function as the focus of conscious design intention served as a useful lever in emancipating architecture from its historical stylistic burden, but what constitutes Functionalist theory is undoubtedly a misinterpretation or an over-simplification of architecture. Those few works of architecture explicitly labeled as Functionalist by their designers most often convey a deeply moving experience of a new world, a world of vibrant enthusiasm, hope and empathy. Even such an extreme reductivist Functionalist view as Hannes Meyer's ultra-materialist equation, ARCHITECTURE = FUNCTION x ECONOMICS, gave rise to poetically charged architectural images.[22]

ARCHITECTURE AS PICTURE

This paradox is conceivable because architecture is not primarily about theory, technique, or function, but about the world and life. Architecture creates pictures; it creates images that evoke an experience of a particular form of life. Architecture "makes a world that does not determine, but does allow us to live and think differently than if it did not exist," writes Stanford Anderson about the Villa Savoye.[23] Our experience of the scope of life in the modern world would be significantly dwarfed if we could not experience it through the Villa Savoye, the Maison de Verre, Fallingwater, and the Villa Mairea. This is what Martin Heidegger meant by his concept of *Vorverständnisch*, "pre-understanding," in

232

233

existential philosophy as the basis of the human condition. We are able to conceive only what our unique life condition makes possible, and architecture provides one of the most important horizons of experience and understanding.

THE MYTH OF FUNCTIONALISM

The architectural historian William Curtis, writing in his *Modern Architecture since 1900*, gives a very clear expression to this matter in the chapter dealing with the myth of Functionalism: "Even the most highly defined set of requirements may be answered in a variety of ways, and *a priori* images concerning the eventual appearance of the building will enter the design process at some point. Thus function could only be translated into the forms and spaces of architecture through the screen of a style, and in this case it was a style of symbolic forms which referred, among other things, to the notion of functionality."[24]

Architecture has a dual focus: it provides metaphorical responses on an artistic level at the same time that it solves the practical requirements of function, structure, execution, and economy. The purely Functionalist criteria seem to be at their strongest in the German and Swedish kitchen research of the 1920s and 1930s, and in the ergonomic design of chairs. But it is evident that not a single building has entered the history of architecture on its functional merits. The Functionalist stylistic matrix can be understood only by accepting its strongly metaphoric nature. This symbolic representation could refer simultaneously to the inherited language of architecture, and to imagery totally outside the traditional realm of architecture, such as combustion engines, ocean liners, or locomotives. Experiences of motion, force, transparency, or weightlessness were often more important than any functional or concrete aspects of the building.

"The bird's nest is absolute functionalism, because the bird is not aware of its own death," as Sverre Fehn once said touchingly and poetically.[25]

THE MACHINE AND THE VENUS OF MILO

234

As Modern architecture was born, the steamship replaced the Parthenon and the machine replaced the Venus of Milo as the aesthetic ideals. The admiration of the machine often took on a fetishistic and erotic character. Even man's self-image took the shape of the machine. "The object has to become the main character of modern painting and it has to throw the human figure from the throne. If the person, face or body turn into objects, a great freedom opens up to the modern artist ... to me the human face or figure does not have more meaning than a bunch of keys or a bicycle," wrote Fernand Léger.[26]

Paradoxically, regardless of its aesthetic admiration of the mechanical, Modern architecture (and art) radiates human empathy.

Although Functionalism is a myth as a generative theory, the works guided by this myth or conceived through its stylistic matrix continue to inspire us and to provide a horizon of hope.

Regardless of the evasive and mythical nature of the notion of Functionalism, I would want to continue using it. We know the timeless life of myths and their power over our minds. Myths generate responses and new interpretations. This, I believe, is the usefulness of the myth of Functionalism. The interrelation between an intellectually formulated theoretical stance and its respective sensory and artistic embodiment is related to deeper and less differentiated layers of our psyche than intellectual statements in words.

PSYCHOLOGICAL FUNCTIONALISM

The reductive rationalist theory of Functionalism was extended into the psychological realm in the 1930s, most notably by Alvar Aalto, who wrote: "In itself rationalization was not wrong in the first age of modern architecture, which we have now left behind. The fault is that rationalization has not gone deep enough ... Instead of fighting against the rationalist approach, the latest phase of modern architecture is trying to channel rational methods away from the technical sphere and into that of humanism and psychology."[27]

A decade later, Lewis Mumford elaborated the notion of Functionalism in much the same vein, in his article "Function and Expression in Architecture": "This (the self-imposed poverty of functionalism) does not mean, as some critics have hastily asserted, that functionalism is doomed: it means rather that the time has come to integrate objective functions with subjective functions; to balance off mechanical facilities with biological needs, social commitments, and personal values ... the doctrine that form follows function was (not) a misleading one. What was false and meretricious were the narrow applications that were made of this formula ... When the whole personality is taken into account, expression or symbolism becomes one of the dominant concerns of architecture ..."[28]

Richard Neutra's surprising notion of the "biorealist" is another example of the scope of Functionalist thinking.[29]

The Modern position, which continues to be strong in the Nordic countries, has widened the Functionalist point of departure during the last two decades, very much along the lines of Aalto and Mumford's views. Even the Post-Modern critique of the Modern Movement has been incorporated into contemporary Nordic neo-functionalism.

235

232 Le Corbusier, Villa Stein-de Monzie, Garches, 1928. Fish on the kitchen table.

233 Clinical virtuoso modernity with an air of modernist kitsch. Richard Meier, Douglas House, Harbor Springs, Michigan, 1971–73.

234 Fernand Léger, *Mona Lisa with Keys*, oil on canvas, 1930. Objects have the same value as the human figure.

235 Oscar Schlemmer, *Stick Dance*, Bauhaus School, 1927.

THE ORIGINS OF FUNCTIONALISM

The expansion of the notion of Functionalism to the biological, psychological, and symbolic dimensions advocated by Aalto and other Functionalists of the organic inclination invites us to review the origins of the idea of the interdependence of form and function. In later writings, Functionalist theory has often been given a purely mechanistic and deterministic tone, as if it had derived solely from the discipline of mechanics.

One of the first writers to make function the criterion of form was the 19th century American sculptor Horatio Greenough, who had studied biology as well as sculpture. On the basis of Lamarck's biological theorem that "form follows function," he published a series of papers that formulated the new aesthetic of the machine and extended its application to all forms of beauty. Greenough saw that this generalization applied to all organic and even man-made forms. Beauty, for Greenough, was seen as "the promise of function."[30]

THE DISAPPEARANCE OF THE SOCIAL MISSION

During the last twenty-five years, architecture has become alarmingly autistic as a consequence of its loss of social mission. In most industrial societies, architecture has been marginalized as a serious artistic endeavor. The architect's client has changed from the power elite to the cultural elite and, finally, today's avant-garde architect is his own client. Architecture is fortifying itself in the territory of artistic autonomy.

Vincent P. Pecora, for one, fiercely rejects this position: "In the end, these voices (of today's avant-garde) testify to nothing less than a massive (largely male) fantasy, a ubiquitous fear of socio-cultural castration that played itself out in the critical rhetoric of an architectural avant-garde and that hardly seems to have been exhausted."[31]

The real social challenge presented by the fate of humanity has been replaced by a self-centered interest in the institution of architecture itself as a niche of culture. The panorama of the terrifying quantitative problems awaiting mankind was momentarily opened at the end of 1960s, but the window of consciousness was hastily closed before a total panic could take over. The energy crises in 1973–74 shook the attitude of contemporary architecture again and produced experimental, ecologically motivated models. After the techno-romantic Archigram visions, the hippie communities, the solar heating experiments, the Whole Earth Catalogue, and the dome cookbooks all looked like an early apocalyptic nightmare, one quickly forgotten. Buckminster Fuller's Utopian program and his world resources inventory were dismissed as groundless idealism, techno-romanticism, and political naiveté.

TOWARDS AN ECOLOGICAL FUNCTIONALISM

Today, however, I cannot imagine any other desirable view of the future than an ecologically adapted form of life where architecture returns to its early, biologically-derived Functionalist ideals. This architecture must again take root in its cultural and regional soil; it could be called Ecological Functionalism. This is not the place to attempt a description of this future perspective, but in my understanding this view implies a paradoxical task for architecture: to become more primitive and more refined at the same time; more primitive, in terms of meeting the most fundamental human needs with an economy of expression and mediating man's relation to the world in an equally fundamental and literal way—and more sophisticated, in the sense of adapting to the cyclic systems of nature, both in terms of matter and energy. Ecological architecture also implies a view of building more as a process than a product. It suggests a new awareness of time—architectural time and human time—in terms of recycling and responsibility exceeding the scope of individual life. The architect's role between the polarities of craft and art has to be also redefined.

236

Whereas function in Modern architecture was dealt with primarily on a symbolic level, a metaphorical Functionalism will not satisfy the ecological imperatives of the 21st century. Functionalism has to be truly operative Functionalism. The current testing of the philosophical limits of architecture will be replaced by an authentic experimentation with new techniques (alternative energy sources, new materials, natural ventilation systems, and self-regulating building skins) and new concepts of living. The priority of representation will be replaced by the priority of performance.

237

After decades of affluence and abundance, architecture is likely to return to the aesthetics of necessity in which the elements of metaphorical expression and practical craft fuse into each other again; utility and beauty are again united. An ecological way of life brings forth a concomitant ethical stance: an aesthetics of noble poverty, as well as the notion of responsibility in all its philosophical complexity.

Lewis Mumford ended his 1968 article in a prophetic tone: "Man is the maker and molder of himself. In that process, architecture has been one of the chief means ... of transforming and making visible to later generations his ideal self ... the time has come for architecture to come back to earth and to make a new home for man."[32]

238 A child´s seat, Ahtävä, 19th century.
Pine, painted dark brown. The seat is
provided with a hole for the pot.

TOWARD AN ARCHITECTURE OF HUMILITY

(1998)

Architectural culture, in its social context and core values, has undergone significant shifts over the past half century. When I began my studies in the late 1950s in Helsinki, the heroic mission of Modern architecture still molded architects' collective ambitions. Architecture enjoyed high social status and positive symbolic connotations; architects were seen as the builders of our national identity. Then, beginning in the early 1960s, the postwar ideals of late-Corbusian plasticity and *gravitas* gave way to structural and modular clarity, prefabrication, transparency, and visual simplicity. Miesian structural classicism and traditional Japanese buildings were inspirations for an architecture of reduction and deliberate anonymity that sought to mirror industrialization.

During the decade following the Paris Spring of 1968, architecture shifted again, becoming politicized; the art of building was scorned as an elitist practice in the service of power and aesthetic yearnings were condemned. The 1980s saw a harsh questioning of the Modern ideology and a renewed interest in formalism. This decade witnessed efforts to reconstruct the identity of the architect, and the self-esteem and social role of the discipline; nothing less than a new paradigm was sought.

Today, architects in Finland have largely succeeded in reestablishing a sense of professional identity and mission. And yet the tumultuous changes of recent decades continue to be felt, for the architectural profession has lost much of its prestige, as well as its acknowledged position among the shapers of national culture. Indeed, the social significance of the art of architecture is now perilously tenuous. Competition over fees, new quasi-rational practices, the imperatives of cost and speed, and, perhaps most insidiously, the obsession with the image, are eroding the once-fertile soil of architecture.

This brief narrative of the changing values and fortunes of architects in a corner of the world where Modern architecture has played an undisputed social role forms the background to my critical views of recent developments. The tendencies I describe, however, are hardly confined to Scandinavia; they appear to be universal, although they vary from place to place. Aware of the dangers of generalization, I believe we must still try to identify cultural undercurrents that inevitably influence architecture. I should acknowledge that many contemporary architects and critics, professional journals, and educational institutions are working to resist the negative influences of our time. Poetic works of architecture continue to be created in this age of obsessive materialism. And in some sense negative cultural phenomena actually strengthen architecture's humanist mission: resistance to the decay of spiritual and cultural values is now the shared task of architects and artists.

The widespread rejection of the Modern Movement's orthodox doctrine and its emphasis on social morality has inspired impressive aesthetic diversity, but the rejection has also produced a climate of arrogance, cultural incoherence, and narcissism. As the understanding of architecture as a *social* art has diminished, the idea of architecture as a form of studio art has intensified: contemporary 'neo-avant-garde' works are presented today as products of individual genius. Yet paradoxically, the artistic authenticity and autonomy of architecture are today being undercut by three cultural tendencies: the commodification of buildings, the self-defeating search for newness, and the hegemony of the marketable image. These cultural tendencies are supported by both commercialized architectural journalism and the voracious global entertainment and tourism industries.

Is architecture relinquishing its potential to embody ambitious, idealistic cultural and collective values? Is it working to support ideological emptiness and commercial exploitation rather than a shared cultural and historical understanding? Is the emphasis on transient construction transforming architecture into disposable scenery?

Despite the current critical and media focus on celebrity designer-artists, architecture continues to be that art with the most irrefutable and unavoidable grounding in societal life. In addition to evaluating the mere aesthetic relevance of individual projects, architectural theory, criticism, and education should survey a now-neglected cultural ground—the *preconditions* of the art of architecture. Both education and practice would benefit from a rigorous cultural analysis of the prevailing state of architecture. What, for instance, is the collective mental background that informs the alarming conservatism—the nostalgic quasi-classicism—of American collegiate and corporate architecture? Is it cultural insecurity or a more serious suppression of the idea of (and hope for) progress? And what kind of mental defenses work to create our sickeningly regressive domestic architecture?

VISUAL IMAGES

Architectural publications, criticism, and even education are now focused relentlessly on the enticing visual image. The longing for singular, memorable imagery subordinates other aspects of buildings, isolating architecture in a disembodied vision. As buildings are increasingly conceived and confronted through the eye rather than the entire body—as the camera becomes the ultimate witness to and mediator of architecture—the actual experience of a building, of its spaces and materials, is neglected. By reinforcing visual manipulation and graphic production, computer imaging further detaches architecture from its multi-sensory essence; as design tools, computers can encourage mere visual manipulation and make us neglect our powers of empathy and imagination. We become voyeurs obsessed with visuality, blind not only to architecture's social reality, but also to its functional, economic, and technological realities, those which inevitably determine the design of buildings and cities. Our detachment from experiential and sensory reality maroons us in theoretical, intellectual, and conceptual realms.

HAPTIC EXPERIENCES

Recent dramatic changes in the temporal quality of experience have themselves affected architecture, which now must compete for immediacy of impact with today's frenetic forms of expression and communication—with fashion, advertising, and web culture. But while the visual image has an immediate impact, other dimensions of architectural experience require empathy and interpretation, an understanding of cultural and social contexts, and a capacity for envisioning the temporal endurance of buildings beyond momentary fashions. The appreciation of the sensory qualities of architecture requires slowness and patience (this is true for both the design process and the experience and judgment of the finished building). The impact of time, the effects of use and wear, and the processes of aging are rarely considered in contemporary design or criticism. Alvar Aalto believed that the value of a building is best judged fifty years after completion. The prospect that few new buildings will even last fifty years does not invalidate the significance of time and duration in architectural apperception.

Authentic architectural settings—fully realized microcosmic entities—strengthen our sense of reality; thus, a desire for haptic architecture is clearly emerging in reaction to ocular-centricity. The haptic
sensibility savors plasticity, materiality, tactility, and intimacy. It offers
nearness and affection rather than distance and control. While images
of architecture can be rapidly consumed, haptic architecture is appreciated and comprehended gradually, detail by detail. While the hectic
eye of the camera captures a momentary situation, a passing condition
of light, or an isolated and carefully framed fragment (photographic
images are a kind of focused *gestalt*), the experience of architectural
reality depends fundamentally on peripheral and anticipated vision.
The perceptual realm that we sense beyond the sphere of focused
vision—the event anticipated around a corner, behind a wall, or beneath
a surface—is as important as the camera's frozen image. This suggests
that one reason why contemporary places so often alienate us—compared with those historical and natural settings that elicit powerful
emotional engagement—has to do with the poverty of our peripheral
vision. Focused vision makes us mere observers; peripheral perception
transforms retinal images into spatial and bodily experience, encouraging participation.

SOCIAL RESPONSIBILITIES

The ocular, hedonistic, bias of contemporary architecture is exacerbated
by architects' loss of social empathy and mission. Issues of planning,
social housing, mass production, and industrialization—all-important to
early Modern architecture—are now rarely touched on in publications
or academic programs. Modernism sought to respond to the typical and
ordinary conditions of life; contemporary elitist architecture favors the
unique and the exceptional. This detachment of architectural language
from the ground of common experience has produced a kind of architectural autism. Compare, for instance, the fantasy projects so often
assigned in the design studios of the past decade with the socially
oriented design problems of the 1950s and 1960s.

Architectural design, as well as writing and criticism, should
acknowledge the need for civic responsibility. Architecture should
strengthen the reliability and comprehensibility of the world. In this
sense, architecture is fundamentally a conservative art; it materializes
and preserves the mythical and poetic ground of constructing and
inhabiting space, thus framing human existence and action. By estab-
lishing a horizon of existential understanding, architecture encourages
us to turn our attention away from architecture itself; authentic architecture suggests images of ideal life.

The mastery of structure and material, and the presence of skilled craftsmanship are essential to good architecture. The general weakening of our sense of tectonic reality—a weakening intimately related to the emphasis on surface and appearances—is caused partly by the diminishing role of craft in construction, but even more by the growing power of contractors, and by the increasing importance of short-term economics at the expense of architectural value. Architecture is too often viewed as a short-lived speculative commodity rather than as a cultural and metaphysical manifestation that frames collective understanding and values. Although projects that question or ridicule this large social role are now celebrated—both avant-garde and corporate projects often emit the fetid air of architectural necrophilia—architecture cannot escape its foundations in real, existential experience. In an age of simulated experience and virtual reality, we still desire an authentic, tangible home. The inherent language of architecture speaks of permanence, durability, faith, and human care.

CONTINUING VITALITY

Despite the general drift toward meaninglessness, some recent work offers glimpses of the continuous vitality of architecture. Much current building uses technology merely as a form of visual imagery; in contrast, Renzo Piano designs exemplary structures combining technological ingenuity with contextual concern and ecological morality. Such work underscores the fact that truly ecological architecture derives from invention and refinement, not from technical or aesthetic regression. Glenn Murcutt's delightful buildings are elegant blends of reason and modesty, common sense and poetry, technological sophistication and ecological subtlety; they are unique buildings—responses to a particular landscape—with universal applicability. Alvaro Siza's architecture fuses a contemporary formal and spatial complexity with a reassuring sense of tradition and cultural continuity. Sverre Fehn explores the mythical and poetic ground of construction. Steven Holl re-sensualizes space, material, and light. Peter Zumthor's recent projects convincingly unite opposites: conceptual strength with sensual subtlety, thought with emotion, clarity with mystery, gravity with lightness.

Western industrial culture values power and domination. Gianni Vattimo has introduced ideas of "weak ontology" and "fragile thought," a way of philosophizing that does not try to bundle the multitude of human discourses into a single system.[1] We can, I would argue, identify a "weak" or "fragile" architecture, or, more precisely, an architecture of the "fragile image," as opposed to the prevalent architecture of strong images. Whereas the latter strives to impress and manipulate,

239

240

239 Glenn Murcutt, Marika-Alderton House, Yirrkala Community, Eastern Arnheim Land, Northern Territory, 1991–94.
240 Renzo Piano, Beyeler Foundation, Riehen, 1992–97.

241 Lawrence Halprin, Auditorium
Forecourt Plaza, Portland, Oregon,
1961.
242 Carlo Scarpa, Museo Castelvecchio,
Verona, 1956–64.

the architecture of the fragile image is contextual, multi-sensory, and responsive, concerned with experiential interaction and sensual accommodation. This architecture grows gradually, scene by scene, rather than quickly manifesting a simple, domineering concept.

We can distinguish between an architecture that offers less in its real material encounter than its images promise, and an architecture that opens up new layers of experience and meaning when confronted in its built, contextual, and full reality. Any encounter with a building by Alvar Aalto, for instance, is a richer experience than viewing its image. His works are masterpieces of an episodic architecture, one that aims to achieve a specific ambiance rather than a formal authority. The paved pathways designed by Dimitris Pikionis that lead to the Acropolis in Athens, Lawrence Halprin's Ira's Fountain in Portland, Oregon, and Carlo Scarpa's meticulously crafted architectural settings, are further examples of an architecture whose full power does not rely on retinal imagery. The work of Pikionis is a dense conversation with time and history; Halprin's designs explore the threshold between architecture and nature; Scarpa's architecture creates a dialogue between concept and making, visuality and hapticity, artistic invention and tradition. Such architecture obscures the categories of foreground and background, object and context; it evokes a liberated sense of natural duration. An architecture of courtesy and attention, it asks us to be humble, receptive, and patient observers.

Focused on visual imagery, detached from social and contextual considerations, much of the architecture of our time—and the publicity that attempts to convince us of its genius—has an air of self-satisfaction and omnipotence. These buildings attempt to conquer the foreground rather than to create a supportive background for action and perception. Our age seems to have lost the virtue of architectural neutrality, restraint, and modesty. Authentic works of art, however, remain suspended between certainty and uncertainty, faith and doubt. Architectural culture, on the threshold of the new millennium, would do well to nurture productive tensions: cultural realism and artistic idealism, determination and discretion, ambition and humility.

The most significant thought for me during my architectural education was a single sentence by my professor, Aulis Blomstedt: "For an architect, more important than the skill of fantacizing space, is the capacity of envisioning situations of human life."

IMMATERIALITY AND TRANSPARENCY

Technique and Expression in Glass Architecture
(2003)

244

THE POETICS OF GLASS

As an architect, writer, and educator without any specialized knowledge of glass technology, it would be pretentious for me to address the historical evolution of glass as well as recent advances in this field. Rather, my aim here is to examine the experiential qualities and artistic expressions mediated by glass material and to point out distinct problems in this respect brought about by the current popularity of glass architecture. I will also attempt to valorize some of the mental, mythological, symbolic, and dream-like qualities of glass that unconsciously enter into our experiences of glass architecture. I wish to expand the discourse on glass technology to the realm of 'the poetics of glass' and the mental imagery evoked by it. After all, the ultimate success of architecture will always be measured by its experiential qualities and its psychic impact.

A number of art works illustrate my points; I believe that art opens a direct view into the heart of culture, including technology. As the famous art historian René Huyghe wrote already in 1939: "Art is for the story of human societies what the dreams of an individual are for the psychiatrist... Many think of art as a mere diversion, a thing that is purely marginal to the real business of life, but they do not see that it looks into life's very heart and lays bare its unconscious secrets, that it contains the most honest confessions, confessions that have within them the least element of calculation and must therefore be accounted exceptionally sincere."[1] Artistic and architectural works express hidden and repressed mental contents, dreams, desires, and fears. Regrettably, we have not learned to read these significant messages.

248.

247

246

245

GLASS AND MODERNITY

Glass is unquestionably the quintessential material of modernity; we could even say that in many ways it is synonymous with the imagery of the modern world. Michael Wigginton, the author of the seminal *Glass in Architecture*, begins his introductory text with a daring statement: "Glass is arguably the most remarkable material ever discovered by man... In the 4000 years of its known history, it has been drawn into use across the whole world of human endeavour."[2] Given the most recent advancements in structural glass, composite structures, and self-regulating, multi-functional, intelligent building skins comprised of glass (which regulate visibility, heat, light and glare, and produce energy), this super-cooled liquid, or 'transparent rock' promises to become the most flexible building material we have ever developed. The timeless task of authentic building is engaged with the polarities of enclosure and connectedness, privacy and visibility, protection and view, shadow and light—but the newest developments in glass technology seek to fuse these oppositions into each other by means of a singular material. Today glass is assimilating the properties of all other building materials.

ALL THAT IS SOLID MELTS INTO AIR

Beyond its utilitarian and technical qualities, glass is a material that has strong mythological, symbolic, and utopian connotations. The desire for simultaneous visibility and invisibility, materiality and immateriality, presence and absence is characteristic to the human psyche, and dreamlike images of houses and cathedrals of glass have persisted from the Middle Ages until the modern and post-modern era. Through a succession of visionary projects, Modern architecture has aspired to transparency, weightlessness, and immateriality. These aspirations are epitomized by, for example, the great greenhouse structures of the 19th century, in particular the fabulous Crystal Palace of the 1851 London Universal Exposition—in my view, the most revolutionary and progressive building of all time and an unsurpassed example of prefabrication and swift assembly. The crystalline structures of the German expressionists Paul Scheerbart, Bruno Taut, and Hans Scharoun prefigure Mies van der Rohe's 1920s all-glass tower projects and the utopian ambitions of the Russian Constructivists of the same period. The modern all-glass houses of Pierre Chareau, Paul Nelson, Mies van der Rohe, and Philip Johnson exemplify this ideal, along with the countless all-glass buildings of today's minimalist and 'high-tech' orientations.

A human existence caught within an invisible bubble of a transparent material has been an enduring dream—from Hieronymus Bosch's painterly vision of the Paradise in the early fifteenth century to Reyner

Banham's environmental bubble of the late 1960s. In Banham's influential essay of the late 1960s entitled "A Home Is Not a House," he argued that mechanical technology is gradually becoming more important than the traditional material components of architecture, and that the house will eventually turn into an environmental control device.³ With this, Banham implied the end of architecture as traditionally conceived. In his view, our understanding of architecture and its aesthetics need to be radically re-evaluated as a consequence of this development towards ever more refined and efficient technology and a gradually increasing invisibility. We can therefore appropriately speak of "an invisible architecture." In the utopian atmosphere of the 1960s, Hans Hollein actually proposed an environmental pill that would project the mental experiences of various architectural conditions by means of chemical induction.

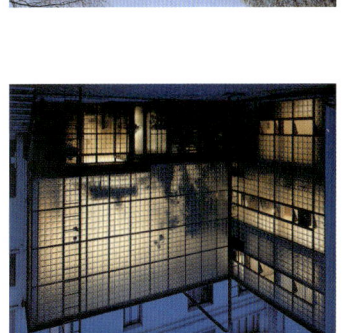

Buckminster Fuller, Yona Friedman, Frei Otto, and many others expanded the idea of an invisible environmental shelter to the grand scale of the metropolis and the landscape. Many of these futuristic images have already been realized in the contemporary architecture of Nicholas Grimshaw, Norman Foster, and Richard Rogers.

We tend to think that architectural forms derive from materials and technique, but geometry and form have their own independent lives granted to them by the human psyche. Even the pyramid, the ultimate image of weight, stability, and eternal durability has been transferred into glass material. Ecological architecture, too, after its first primitive and somewhat naïve earthbound applications, has increasingly turned towards the technological refinement, high performance, and efficiency offered by multiple qualities of glass. Indigenous buildings, as exemplified by the Eskimo igloo or the Native American tepee, utilize available natural materials and are highly ecological. These structures do not waste materials and energy, or upset the ecological balance; the materials used return back to their natural cycles of decay without a negative impact. The ecological constructions of the technological age imply careful strategies and planning, the consideration of the entire process of manufacture and construction, the complete cycle of use, demolition, and recycling, and the use of advanced technologies and materials, such as multi-functional and adjustable skins.

Glass has been and continues to be a utopian material. In the 1960s, Buckminster Fuller conceived the idea of transparent cities floating in the air; the air quantity inside the projected sphere is so immense that the elevation of the temperature inside the dome by one single degree above the outside temperature will elevate the entire city into the air. Futuristic images in literature, cinema, and painting, as well as cartoons

253

254

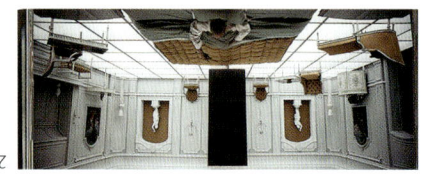

255

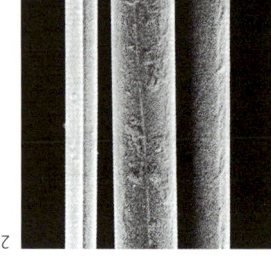

256

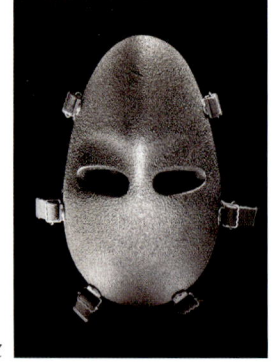

257

and the art of architecture itself have usually exhibited a crystalline geometry, transparency, and high reflectivity provided by glass. The final scene of Stanley Kubrick's 2001: A Space Odyssey, for instance, occurs within a room with a glass floor lit from below. Regardless of its utopian tone, this architectural image is quite disturbing, because it reverses our basic sensory constants of architecture. This observation presents an undeniable limit condition to architecture: man as a biological being with his senses and genetically induced reactions.

Overcoming material and temporal limits is the essence of utopian concepts—only dystopian narratives return back to the embrace of earth and darkness. Glass is the perfect material to create the experiences of abstract universality, agelessness, newness, and eternal youth—all obsessions of the human mind. "To be modern is to be part of a universe, in which, as Karl Marx said, 'all that is solid melts into air'," writes Marshall Berman in his influential book on the experience of modernity, which, in fact, has this credo as its very title.[4] The accelerated development of glass architecture during the past decades certainly makes one believe in Karl Marx's vision.

THE TECHNOLOGICAL IMPERATIVE

There is an unquestionable technological and economic imperative towards smaller size, lower weight, and higher efficiency—this is the very logic of technological advancement. Initially, the notion of the technological imperative referred to the human urge to realize and execute whatever has become theoretically possible. This inherent direction of development can also be identified in the evolution of structures in nature, even in the often stunningly efficient constructions of animals; it is evident that the evolutionary process in nature is parallel in its essence to techno-scientific advancement. The spider drag-line, for example, exemplifies the evolutionary tendency towards higher efficiency. Regardless of the miracles brought about by modern chemistry, the spider thread continues to be the toughest material on earth. Tougher even than polyaramid Kevlar, the material used in bulletproof vests and face-masks, woven spider thread can absorb an impact five times greater than the capacity of Kevlar without breaking.[5]

Beyond this imperative, which has its evident rational and economic motives, the human mind aspires for immateriality and transparency for metaphysical and metaphorical reasons. Overcoming the limits of place, time, gravity, and matter is an ancient human desire. Architecture's own development has been a continuous struggle to overcome gravity; this is one of the seminal narratives in the history of architecture. The evolution of construction is essentially the story of the

gradual reduction of mass through material and structural refinement. Ancient myths expressed the human fantasy of flying and levitation, and this quest continues in our modern era and finds its expression in architecture, as well. Experiential virtual movement—the vertical soar of the Gothic cathedral, the virtual flow along the undulating surface of a Baroque façade, or the horizontal Functionalist sensation of floating—creates a momentary liberation from the constraints of mass and weight. Ultimately, light is the most charged metaphor of all, and glass promises to liberate us from the dark and impenetrable opacity of matter.

"To live in a glass house is a revolutionary virtue par excellence. It is also an intoxication, a moral exhibitionism, that we badly need," writes Walter Benjamin.[6]

BETWEEN POLARITIES

Architecture is a balancing act between opposites: stability and movement, mass and void, opacity and transparency, shadow and light. The modern sensibility has primarily aspired the latter set of extremes to the dynamics of movement, weightlessness, transparency, and light. In fact, Louis Kahn was the first architect in the modern era to reintroduce stasis, weight, mass, materiality, and symmetry into contemporary architecture, a shift that altered the course of modern architecture. Kahn was hardly capable of designing in glass; in fact, he wrapped his buildings in images of ruins in order to eliminate the image of the glass window altogether. Significantly, however, the window has been eliminated by an opposite process, as well; it has been incorporated and fused into the wall of glass, the absent wall.

TECHNIQUE AND POETRY

Architecture is the art-form most directly and unquestionably engaged with the social, political, economic, and technological realities of contemporary culture. One line of argument, in fact, views the development of architecture primarily as a reflection of the development of technology and materials. I do not wish to question the central role of technology in architecture, but I do want to argue, however, that technical progress is not equal to architectural poetics. There is a fundamental difference between technological and scientific facts on the one hand, and mental and perceptual facts, on the other. Architecture as an art-form is primarily engaged with the latter. Technology aspires to solve problems, whereas art and architecture articulate the human experience of 'being-in-the-world', to use a Heideggerian notion. As with all art, architecture is fundamentally a reflection and a deliberate articulation of the human condition and the human experience of the world. Architecture, as

with all arts, structures and articulates our experience of the world by providing us with horizons of perception and understanding. In my view, the essence of all artistic expressions, including architecture, is the existential experience; art is primarily about life and the human confrontation with the world.

Pure utility and rationality, or even the most advanced technologies, cannot grant entry into the artistic realm. The realm of art is approached through metaphysical, existential, and poetic concerns. While I acknowledge the interdependence of science, technology, and architecture, the disciplines are also inherently different. This opposition needs to be pointed out—although here I hope that my point will not be misunderstood. I am not underestimating the significance of technology, I merely argue that the artistic dimension of architecture arises from other concerns and another mental ground. This reflects the fundamental difference between ends and means.

RETURN TO ANIMISTIC THOUGHT

The unorthodox French philosopher Gaston Bachelard's entire scholarly and literary work mediates between the worlds of scientific and artistic thinking. Bachelard began his career in the late 1920s as a philosopher of science, but halfway through his life he turned to a phenomenological survey of poetic imagery. He wrote penetrating studies of the classical elements—earth, fire, water, and air—and also investigated dreams and daydreams. Regrettably, Bachelard never addressed 'a phenomenology of glass', although it was well within the grasp of his thinking.

Bachelard's studies reveal that the poetic imagination is closely related to the pre-scientific image of the world. In *The Philosophy of No: A Philosophy of the New Scientific Mind*, written in the period when Bachelard's interest was shifting from scientific phenomena to poetic imagery, he described the development of scientific thought as a gradual transition from animism through realism, positivism, rationalism and complex rationalism, to dialectical rationalism.[7]

Significantly, however, Bachelard observes that artistic thinking proceeds in the opposite direction. Artistic thinking returns from the realist and rational attitude back towards a mythical and animistic understanding of the world. Science and art therefore seem to move past each other in opposite directions. The artistic logic is close to the alchemist's understanding of matter, and this observation is, indeed, the subject matter of James Elkins's recent provocative book entitled *What Painting Is*, which has an informative subtitle: *How to Think about Oil Painting Using the Language of Alchemy*.[8] We could explain architecture through the same metaphor. The greatest individuals in

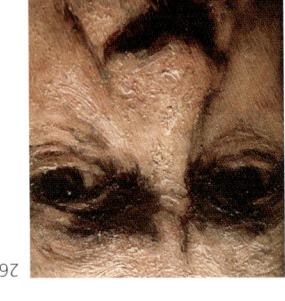

our profession are alchemists: they create transformations and meta-
morphoses of matter and image. In my view, understanding this fundamental difference between science and art enables the scientist and the
artist to understand and respect each other. Whereas scientific thought
progresses and differentiates, artistic thought seeks a return to an undifferentiated and experientially singular world. Artistic imagination
seeks condensed artistic images able to express the entire complexity
of human existential experience. This paradoxical task is achieved
through poeticized images, which are experienced and lived rather than
understood. A work of art or architecture is not a symbol that represents or indirectly portrays something outside itself; it is an existential
image or object that places itself directly in our experience.

This detour into the world of 'poetic chemistry',[9] to use an expression of Bachelard, emphasizes that the artist and the architect will look
at glass material with different eyes than the chemist and the engineer.
The poetic imagination differs fundamentally from technical virtuosity,
but this distinction has frequently been lost in our technical world.
Artistic imagery, in fact, is more concerned with the uncertainties and
ambiguities of things rather than with certainties and truths. By this
assertion, I mean to say more specifically that glass architecture needs
to sensitize itself to the realm of poetics in order to produce meaningful
and spiritually invigorating buildings.

ILLUSIONS AND REFLECTIONS

Glass encourages experiences of illusions and dreams. Glass' simultaneous transparency and opacity, reflection and fusion, presence and
absence—transforms its surface into a dream landscape, an experiential
collage. Indoors and outdoors, behind and in front, surface and depth,
are all fused into simultaneous and enmeshed images. Bachelard writes
about a special category of poets, the 'water poets'.[10] Being a super-
cooled liquid, glass evokes images that are directly related with those
of water. Consequently, we could speak of 'glass poets'. Indeed, there
are great glass poets among glass designers, artists, architects and
engineers, all capable of imagining enchanting and touching dreams of
glass. They are able to express the multiple essences of the material, its
simultaneous brittleness and maleability, hardness and fragility, immateriality and solidity, heaviness and weightlessness.

In the basic alchemy of architecture there are only two fundamental categories of matter: opaque matter and transparent matter. One
creates separation, privacy and shadow, the other provides connectedness, view and light. The first set of requirements can be fulfilled by a
variety of materials, leading to the characteristic architectures of brick,

262

261

261 Tapio Wirkkala, Padar's Ice, cast and
grinded glass, 1960.
262 Tapio Wirkkala, Glass vase, velvet
acidification and grinding, circa
1940. Decorative Arts Collection,
Bischofberger, Zürich.

concrete, wood, and steel. Glass, the material of transparency, is the unquestioned constant in our concepts of architecture—particularly since the beginning of the modern era. Other transparent or translucent materials—paper, alabaster, or plastics—are used rarely, and even they are usually associated with glass, the prime matter of transparency. Today we speak of 'plastic glazing', for instance, conflating the qualities of a synthetic material with the virtues of glass.

FROM FORM TO MATTER

Whereas Modernism was primarily concerned with form, structure, and space, the past three decades of artistic work have introduced a deepened interest in matter and time; the depth, opacity, weight, patina, and aging of materials have emerged in all forms of art. This development has been equally clear in painting, sculpture, and architecture. The Arte Povera Movement, the physical works of Richard Serra and Eduardo Chillida, as well as the material poetry and expressions of Jannis Kounellis and Anselm Kiefer all exemplify this new interest in materiality. This shift results from a change in our attitudes towards place and time, signalling a new desire for rootedness and perhaps, paradoxically, of an acceptance of our own mortality. The modern movement in architecture emphasized utopian universal values, an emphasis which led to placelessness and the eradication of the experience of time. Now, however, we have become concerned with our specific domicile and with the continuum of time as inescapable ingredients of our existential experience. We need to feel enrooted in our world and to experience our belonging to a specific place and time. Enrootedness, rather than the ideal of abstract and placeless generality, makes the thought of death tolerable.

This mental shift presents a challenge to glass as a building material and to large scale structures made of glass. Instead of its characteristic immateriality, glass is now required to present a recognizable density and materiality. Glass material creates sensory illusions and miracles of perception. But instead of drifting towards a world of suggestion and unreality, reinforced by the rapid expansion of the dream world of virtual reality, we increasingly desire experiences of causality and sensual reality. We desire an architecture of sensory and sensuous realism. We desire the eroticism of matter.

This observation suggests that in addition to glass technology's reach towards refinement, perfection, and increasing immateriality, it should also seek to develop applications of glass which offer comforting sensory pleasure instead of alienating perfection, applications which present a haptic and bodily invitation instead of mere retinal images. Architecture is fundamentally a haptic art-form and the atmosphere

263 Eduardo Chillida, *Harri II*, granite, 1991.
264 Richard Serra, *State Street Consequence*, forged steel, 1985.

263

264

265 Gordon Matta-Clark, *Window Blow-Out*, 1976. Institute for Architecture and Urban Resources, New York.
266 The aggressiveness of concealed sight. Image from the film *The Matrix*, 2003.
267 Foster Associates, Glass ramp, Crescent Wing, Sainsbury Center for the Visual Arts, Norwich, 1988–91.
268 Jean Cocteau, *The Blood of a Poet*, 1930.
269 Orson Welles, *Lady from Shanghai*, 1947.
270 Jacques Tati, *Playtime*, 1967.
271 René Magritte, *Evening Falls*, 1964. The Merill Collection, Houston.

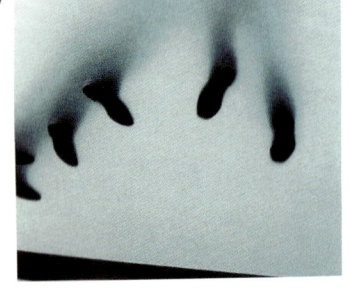

of alienation in today's architecture seems to arise from its exclusive visuality. We experience our being as an embodied haptic experience, not as a retinal picture.

THE SECRET LIFE OF BUILDINGS

In the animistic world of architecture, buildings gesture through their forms, their scale, and their materiality. Windows are the eyes of the house, and may be benevolent and inviting, or cruel and threatening. Broken windows are experienced as violated and blinded eyes. The eyes of the house may also be attacked by some frightening illness, as it were, or they may turn tragically blind; colored and polarized glass, when used without artistic sensitivity, often evokes the impression of an illness of the eye. No technical ingenuity can erase these unconscious readings from our experiences of buildings, because the reading of the environment is genetically programmed: we are conditioned to identify hostility and benevolence in a split second. We animate our buildings unconsciously; we encounter buildings the way we encounter creatures of the living world.

Initially, glass in architectural terms is the material of the window, and the entire story of architecture could be told through the narrative of the window. But glass has now also become the material of the wall, the roof, and the floor. Even the staircase, the fireplace, the bath, the bed, the table, and the chair have been turned into constructions and images of glass. The development of the window from a metaphysical device of focusing and mediating our perception into an entire wall of glass, a wall which evokes the total absence of the wall—as well as the disappearance of the window altogether—certainly also raises critical concerns. The entire house has now often turned into a window; we are invited to live in a window, as it were. Such inversions may be exciting and thrilling, but they may also impoverish architecture by annihilating its primary instinctual essence. The Mexican architect Luis Barragán, a true alchemist of our trade, argued that most modern houses would be more livable with only half of their window surface. In addition to satisfying our utilitarian and physiological requirements, buildings also have to satisfy the needs of our imagination, dreams, and embodied reactions. Moreover, concealed in our genetic information there is a primordial gatherer, hunter, and farmer, and architecture has to house also this primitive hiding in each one of us.

MIRRORS AND SYMBOLS

Glass is a material of enticement and seduction, but reflective and mirroring surfaces may also evoke displeasure, estrangement, and direct fear. "As a child, I felt before large mirrors that same horror of a spectral duplication or multiplication of reality...One of my persistent prayers to God and my guardian angel was that I not dream about mirrors," writes Jorge Luis Borges of his fear of mirrors.[11] Seeing the world and oneself as a reflection may be flattering and frightening, stimulating and alienating. Again, literature, painting, photography, and cinema offer us illuminating examples of the meanings of these experiences. In Jean Cocteau´s film *Orphée* (1949), the protagonist disappears from this world through a mirror. In Andrey Tarkovsky´s *Nostalghia*, the protagonist-poet looks into a mirror, but is unexpectedly confronted with the image of the mad mathematician Domenico. Orson Welles' *The Lady from Shanghai* (1948) ends dramatically with a duel in a reflecting mirror cabinet, with an effect that annihilates the distinction between the real and the unreal, friend and foe, embodiment and ghostly reflection. Jacques Tati's *Playtime* (1969) is the ultimate parody of the varied confusions and frustrations evoked by an excessive use of glass in modern life. And, too, in René Magritte's paintings, such as *Evening Falls* (1964), and *The Domain of Arnheim* (1949), the image of the world is shattered and the criteria of the real is questioned. In artistic contexts, a mirror is usually humanized by a scratched or corroded surface; its necrophilic perfection is thus violated. The corroded mirrors in Andrey Tarkovsky's films exemplify this suppression of perfection.

Glass is usually seen as a symbol of democracy, equality, and openness. But these experiential qualities depend entirely on the specific sensory qualities of the building, on its degrees of transparency, reflectivity, color, scale, and detailing, as well as on its interplay with the context and location. As a contrast to historical stone buildings, a contemporary glass building creates a totally different contextual interplay than when set among other contemporary glass buildings— although this is increasingly the case. A glass building may as well be symbolic of voyeuristic control, corporate power, secrecy, and even the loss of eyesight. New urban centers frequently evoke this air of alienation and exclusion. Darkened, colored, and polarized glass surfaces in particular tend to evoke this kind of negative reading, unless used with great artistic subtlety. Again, I wish to argue that a technology does not guarantee a distinct mental meaning; the experiential impact is a result of specific artistic intentionality and, finally, an interaction between the experiencing person and the architectural structure. The experiential impact cannot be calculated or theorized, resulting instead from an artistic imagination and the designer's capacity for empathy and compassion.

268

269

270

271

PERFECTION AND IMPERFECTION

I am suspicious of the currently popular tendency to identify architecture with technology, or architectural quality with technical perfection, as is so often the case in high-tech architecture by definition. I am not suggesting that superb technological ingenuity or perfection of execution would in any way be obstacles to architectural quality. I argue only that they are two different realms of experience. I also want readily to acknowledge that numerous engineer designers have created extraordinary architectural poetry in concrete and steel as well as in glass, by means of entering the world of architectural poetics.

Industry, naturally, aspires for perfection in its materials and products, but we have also our human desires for incompleteness and imperfection. Perfection tends to close imagination and prohibit participation; Leonardo's advice for artists was to stare at a crumbling wall in order to achieve the state of inspiration.[12] Both John Ruskin and Alvar Aalto even spoke of the value of a human error. "Imperfection is in some sort essential to all that we know of life. It is the sign of life in a mortal body, that is to say, of a process and change. Nothing that lives is, or can be, rigidly perfect: part of it is decaying, part nascent ... And in all things that live there are certain inequalities and deficiences, which are not only signs of life but sources of beauty," wrote Ruskin.[13] Aalto elaborated Ruskin's idea of the value of imperfection further when speaking about 'the human error,' 'sympathetic error,' and 'benign error,' and criticizing the quest for absolute truth and perfection, writing that, "We can say that architecture always contains a human error, and in a deeper view, it is necessary; without it the richness of life and its positive qualities cannot be expressed."[14]

THE RE-ENCHANTMENT OF ARCHITECTURE

Recent projects by Tod Williams and Billie Tsien, Steven Holl, Peter Zumthor, and Herzog & De Meuron, among a number of works by contemporary architects, are examples of a new orientation towards glass in architecture. Instead of structures that aspire to reduce the presence of matter, these architects utilize glass structures that possess the presence and authority of matter and real walls. Instead of a perfection and abstraction appealing only to our eyes, these buildings provide a sense of matter and craft, and the touch of the human hand. Glass material provides these options as well. In today's architecture, opacity and depth is often replaced by the enmeshing and layering of translucent, perforated, and transparent surfaces. The currently popular application of screening veils on top of glass surfaces is clearly an attempt to reintroduce mystery, ambiguity, fragmentation, and a distinct tactile

272

273

eroticism to all-glass facades. Even ornament and decoration have reappeared in entirely new forms—as images imprinted or engraved on sheets of glass. Glass is, again, transforming into the ideal material for this new layered and eroticized hapticity.

The increasing use of glass in architecture surely reflects the logic of technical rationality, but there are deeper psychological, symbolic, and unconscious motives in its popularity. Glass is a material of the alchemist and the magician; while being nearly invisible, and it isolates, separates, and unites at the same time. Glass material curiously unifies the four ancient elements by being born of earth and fire and resembling air and water. As a consequence, glass acquires cosmic and metaphysical qualities. The multiple, subtly changing, visual character of glass adds to its fascination; transparency transforms into a reflection, immateriality into mass, light into darkness.

•

"…I continue to inhabit my glass house, where one can see at every hour who is coming to visit me, where everything that is suspended from the ceilings and the walls holds on as if by enchantment, where I rest at night on a bed of glass with glass sheets, where who I am will appear to me, sooner or later, engraved on a diamond."[15]

272 Jacques Herzog and Pierre de Meuron, Institute for Hospital Pharmaceuticals / Rosetti Grounds, Basel, 1998.
273 Steven Holl, Stretto House, Dallas, Texas, 1992. "Melting Ice" fountain made of glass.
274 Glass panes with angle-selective films composed of a microscopic louvred grid structure.

274

275 Alvar Aalto, Villa Mairea,
Noormarkku, 1938–39. The main
staircase appears as a gazebo in a
garden.

5 learning

FROM TECTONICS TO
PAINTERLY ARCHITECTURE

(1992)

AALTO'S STYLISTIC PERIODS

Alvar Aalto, like most artists, moved through several stylistic phases during the half-century of his architectural career, at times reacting fiercely against his previous aims.

Having received his architect's diploma in 1921, Aalto started his career designing in the transformed Classical idiom in use at the time by a number of Scandinavian architects; architectural historians have come to identify this body of work more generally as Nordic Classicism. In later years, he glossed over his early neo-Classicist works, and historians paid little attention to them while he lived. Only with the reassessment of Modernism, which began in the late 1970s, and the concomitant revival of interest in history, did the individualistic Classicism of Aalto's early works become more widely known. In his Classicist youth, Aalto drew unabashedly from a variety of sources in his designs; his furniture of the 1920s reflects an eclectic multitude of 18th and 19th century European and American sources, for instance.[1]

Aalto's permissive attitude towards inspirations sought from history is clear enough at this early date: "And when we see how in times past one succeeded in being international, free of prejudices and at the same time true to oneself, we can with full awareness receive currents from ancient Italy, from Spain, and from modern America. Our ancestors will continue to be our masters."[2]

However, after taking part in the second CIAM congress in Frankfurt in 1929, where he struck up friendships with the leading names of the new architectural movement—particularly Walter Gropius and László Moholy-Nagy—and then closely observing the preparations for the Stockholm Exhibition of 1930, Aalto became an outspoken advocate of

276 The 14-year old artist Alvar Aalto in his studio.

Functionalism. After returning home from Stockholm in the summer of 1930, Aalto wrote enthusiastically of his new perceptions: "Motorboats, railway carriages, refrigerators, and gramophones have replaced that which was previously considered to be on a higher plane and called fine interior decoration…I take it as a highly commendable development that the artist, as it were, denies himself by venturing outside his traditional field of activity, and that he democratizes his product, transferring it from a narrow circle into the hands of the general public."[3]

Aalto's commitment to the principles of Continental Functionalism was short-lived, however. Only five years later, he presented a closely argued critique of Rationalism in a lecture entitled "Rationalism and Man": "…no doubt we agree that objects that could justly be called *rational* frequently suffer from a noticeable lack of humanity…In our time, when standardization is the principal of production, it should be seen that Formalism is most emphatically inhuman."[4]

Five years later, in "The Humanizing of Architecture," Aalto elaborated on this view: "Rationalism in itself was not wrong during the first phase of modern architecture, now in the past. The error was that it did not reach deep enough. Instead of fighting against Rationalist tendencies, the latest phase of modern architecture is seeking to transfer rational methods from the sphere of technology to that of the humanities and psychology…Technical Functionalism is correct only if it is extended to cover psychophysical considerations. That is the only way to humanize architecture."[5]

After the Second World War, Aalto's thinking—and his architecture—underwent yet another transformation. The technical problems inherent in the white-painted, rendered-surface, and flat-roofed Modern buildings led Aalto toward the use of more durable materials and constructions. During the 1940s, Aalto's Finnish regionalism began to take shape, with red brick, wood, and copper as its principal materials, and using for effect emotional images and vague historical references in combination with an otherwise Modern idiom. The historical dimensions of Aalto's buildings are so subtly concealed and tied to unconscious associations that one should speak of a presence of the experience of time to distinguish it from the Post-Modern use of historical references.

In the late 1950s, Aalto's works began to take on consciously monumental and Mannerist features, characterized by the use of marble, and formal and textural motifs of often Baroque richness. At about this time, Aalto stopped writing critically or speculatively about his architectural thinking. "God created paper for drawing architecture. All else—at least to me—is an abuse of paper. *Torheit*—as Zarathustra

277

would say," he wrote in 1958.[6] This jab actually gave rise to a general contempt for the theoretical analysis of architectural concepts among his Finnish colleagues for the next decade and beyond. Aalto's deliberate withdrawal from ideological discussions in the latter decade of his career also began to distance him from the emerging socially oriented ideals of the younger generation of Finnish architects.

The fact that Aalto had been one of the most prolific writers among the modern masters was all but forgotten until the publication of his articles, essays, and lectures in the book *Sketches*, edited by his friend Göran Schildt.

THE INGREDIENTS OF AALTO'S WORLD

Throughout Aalto's career, his architecture contained unusual and unorthodox characteristics. Certain themes reappear time and again, however, regardless of external stylistic features. Thus, the buildings of his neo-Classicist period evoke images of innocent applications of rusticity, as well as of rural Mediterranean traditions, and the golden ages of architectural history. The young Aalto was equally impressed by Brunelleschi and the rustic wood architecture of the Karelian peasant. Even the designs most closely in tune with Continental Functionalism, such as the Standard Apartment House (1929), and the Turun Sanomat newspaper offices in Turku (1928), reveal a softer touch and a more sensual profile than buildings by Aalto's Continental colleagues; his later, more individual Functionalist works contained a range of motifs outside the mainstream—all pointing towards themes on which he expanded in later works.

The Paimio Sanatorium (1928–32) and the Viipuri Library (1929–35) are undoubtedly the principal works of Aalto's Functionalist period. Regardless of their inventive technical vigor, both designs had the makings of a more personal, richer approach tied more closely to tradition; these elements continued to develop in Aalto's own house in Helsinki (1935) and the Paris and New York World's Fair Pavilions (1937 and 1939), and were expressed most convincingly in that architectural masterpiece, the Villa Mairea (1938–39). The most compact works of his postwar period, the Säynätsalo Town Hall (1950–52) and the Vuoksenniska Church (1958), took Aalto ever further away from the overt neo-Classicist and Functionalist ideals of his youth, into a fully independent synthesis which seems to include something of the essence of the Finnish tradition, difficult as this is to analyze or express.

Aalto's characteristic design preferences include non-orthogonal groupings of form, the fan shape, the use of free form and of wood as a material, sensual and ergonomically designed detailing, and a relaxed,

277 Alvar Aalto, oil painting, 32x40 cm, 1945.

liberated atmosphere free of all doctrinaire elements, with the occasional reflection of vernacular motifs. Aalto's architecture and design is characterized by a certain aesthetic tolerance, permitting many later changes or divergences from the original concept without any perceptible visual conflict. His working method also permitted the improvisation of details right into the final stages of construction.

AN ARCHITECTURE OF ASSOCIATIONS

The emotional impact of Aalto's architecture often arises from the subconscious sensual associations it evokes. Strict Functionalists tended to seek 'pure' expression, free from associations, by means of abstract composition. Yet just as abstract art acquires its significance against the background of tradition and memory, so too does Functionalist architecture and design. Aalto's characteristic use of associative images, however, was a conscious procedure; in fact, he referred to both pictorial and subconscious mental images in his writings already in the mid-1920s.

Aalto started his artistic career as a painter, and he continued to paint until the last years of his life. Göran Schildt, Aalto's biographer, has convincingly analyzed the influence of Cézanne's concept of painterly space on Aalto's ideas of an architectural space.[7] Painting was more than a hobby to Aalto; he seems to have been particularly fascinated by the way in which the painter composes and combines associations, building up an emotional impact in the process.

In a 1926 article, "From Doorstep to Living Room," Aalto analyzed the phenomenological content of Fra Angelico's *Annunciation*, comparing the painting with the balcony terrace in Le Corbusier's *L'Esprit Nouveau* pavilion (1925).[8] He considers Fra Angelico's painting the unsurpassed example of *entering* a house. The key idea of the article is the paradoxical inverse relation of enclosed and open space: the courtyard as an indoor experience and the interior as an outdoor experience (the hall "symbolizes the open air under the home roof."). "The hall as an open-air space can form a piece of the philosopher's stone, if correctly used," he writes.[9] The open-air effect of the interior appears frequently in Aalto's works, perhaps most clearly in the lobby of the Jyväskylä Workers' Club (1924), and in the stair hall of the University of Jyväskylä (1952–54). Conversely, the contrast of the red-brick courtyard of Aalto's own summer home with the house's white, rendered exterior creates the powerful impression of an interior hall under the open sky.

In the same article, Aalto refers to the symbolic nature of architecture in citing the "two faces" of the Finnish home. The first face

278

279

280

is represented by direct contact with the world outside, suggesting a more southern tradition; the other, the "winter face," is reflected in the home's interior design that "emphasizes warmth."

THE ARCHITECTURE OF PAINTING

In another 1926 article, Aalto analyses Andrea Mantegna's Paduan fresco *Christ in the Garden*.[10] He praises the painting as a brilliant analysis of the landscape, calling it "an architectural vision of a landscape," and "a synthetic landscape." "For me, 'the rising town' has become a religion, a disease, a madness, call it what you will," Aalto confesses.

In his own work Aalto was clearly involved with the image of the architectural or synthetic miniature landscape. A condensed miniature—similar to the hilltop town in Mantegna's painting, an imaginary collage of sorts—is evident in the form of the Säynätsalo Town Hall, a design which incorporates features of late medieval and early Renaissance depictions of towns, as exemplified by Giotto's painting *The Casting Out of Devils from the City of Arezzo*. The exceptional emotional impact and sensual richness of the tiny administrative building are fed by the associations with early urban culture; the image of a building turns into an image of a town, suggesting a world of its own.

A painterly device to which Aalto resorted frequently is the use of motifs suggesting temporal stratification and ruins. For instance, to illustrate his 1926 article concerning the inverse relationship of outdoor and indoor space, Aalto chose a picture of a ruined house in Pompeii. These motifs reappear just as much in his detailing—in the brick collage of his own summer home's courtyard; in the brick surfaces of his other buildings; in marble fragments, scattered about seemingly at random—as in the impression that the individual structures in his extensive building complexes are the product of different designers, perhaps even different architectural periods. Aalto's all but obsessive use of amphitheatres, of course, was directly associated with the ruined monuments of Antiquity and the institutions of the first democratic state. Weathering and the acquisition of patina also seem to be part of the positive content of Aalto's architecture. Many of his buildings have taken on an added depth and intimacy with age, in contrast to most contemporary architecture, on which aging usually has the negative impact of decay. Buildings will show their true quality only after fifty years, Aalto said repeatedly.

THE ASSOCIATIVE PAINTING OF THE VILLA MAIREA

Aalto's virtuoso display of the painterly collage technique in architectural design is the Villa Mairea, designed in 1938–39 in the brief period between his two World's Fair pavilions. The exhibition designs, which traced the various dimensions of Finnish traditions, craftsmanship, and industry, obviously had a profound impact on the amazing *tour de force* of architectural composition, formal invention, improvisation, and treatment of materials the architect achieved in the Villa. In Aalto's own words, the Villa Mairea was his "*opus con amore.*"

The intuitive associative 'painting' of the Villa Mairea seems to be closer to the way that, say, Giotto, Böcklin, or Cézanne 'staged' an architectural scene, rather than to the conventional tectonic principles of architecture. Similarly, the way that mental images are associated in the Villa is closer to the Cubist technique of collage than to the traditional structural logic of architecture.

In a text discussing the architectural principles of the Villa Mairea, Aalto referred directly to the similarity of his architectural approach with painting: "The unusual formal concept associated with the architecture also contains an intended link with modern painting…Modern painting may be bringing forth a world of forms connected with architecture and generating personal experiences instead of the historical ornament which once served prestige purposes."[11]

The building's abundance of motifs, rhythms, textures, and materials is overwhelming. Aalto accumulates and overlays motifs and textures in the same way a painter adds dots of color, light, and shade to a painting. The building is not unified by a single dominant architectural concept; instead, the conglomeration of ideas, impressions, and associations seems to be held together by a sensual atmosphere, in the same way as the disparate elements of a painting can be held together by a unifying quality of light.

THE TECHNIQUE OF COLLAGE

The architectural composition of the Villa Mairea is a collage that brings together the emblems of international Modernism, personal inventions, and references to anonymous rustic traditions. Instead of worshiping "the Spirit of the Age," the Villa Mairea points simultaneously to the Utopian Modern future and to the traditions of an indigenous heritage. With these dualistic associations, the building convincingly and beneficently attaches itself to the continuum of culture.

For the clients and the architect, the Villa was an experiment in the potential offered by the vision of a social utopia and the possibilities of industrial technology. They saw the special case of the luxury villa as a prototype with which to assist building the classless society of the future. The building married sumptuousness with rustic modesty and simplicity.

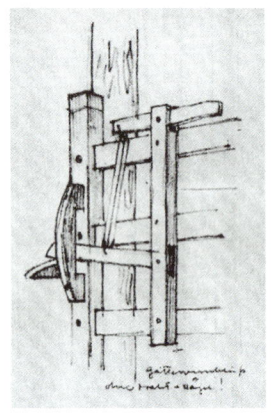

The collage technique employed by Aalto permitted irreverent combinations of antithetical elements: modern and rustic, the Continental avant-garde and prehistoric primitivism, homespun simplicity and the ultimate in refinement, handicraft traditions and industrial production methods.

The collage technique is evident in many deliberate contrasts. The first view glimpsed through the vertical filter of the pine forest shows a rectangular, dazzlingly white, Modern building, with a stereotypical white spiral staircase leading to a roof terrace. At closer range, the rustic entrance canopy supersedes this image. The canopy's asymmetrical outline, its columnar supports made of spruce saplings with the bark intact, and the columns' lashed connections, lend it the appearance of a primitive temporary structure. To its left, the image of a single building begins to disintegrate in the juxtaposition of white masonry surfaces, wood surfaces, projecting fragments of concrete beams, and wooden latticework.

On the courtyard side, the Modern element of a sliding glazed wall is played off against a primitive fieldstone-constructed combination of an open fireplace and stairs leading up to the roof. The flat graveled roof of the main building—another standard Modern feature—is opposed by the turf roof of the sauna wing; the white steel railing on the upper roof terrace, reminiscent of an ocean liner, contrasts with the lower terrace's irregular railing, made of thin saplings and suggesting a farm fence. The exaggerated thickness of the stone wall protecting the sauna terrace reminds one of the walls surrounding peasant farmhouses and old churchyards. Although the rest of the courtyard is walled off rather symbolically by bermed earth and plantings, the primitive force and weight of the stone wall projects an impression of protected peace everywhere. Behind the swimming pool, the courtyard ends in an artificial mound that brings to mind the "synthetic landscape" of Mantegna's painting. But, at the same time, the miniature landscape reminds one of Japanese gardens, such as those illustrated in Tetsuro Yoshida's influential book *Das Japanische Wohnhaus* (1935), that Aalto is known to have consulted during the time he was engaged in designing the Villa Mairea. The most amusing detail in the architectural collage is located by the corner of the sauna: the 'readymade' gate leading from the courtyard to the forest, complete with a wooden latch mechanism, borrowed from the sketchbook of Aalto's Swiss assistant's architect father.

Some surface textures and materials only appear once in the building, like a single brushstroke or a newspaper cutting, a braid of wickerwork or some other *objet trouvé* in a Cubist composition. The blue tiling on the outside corner of the Villa's dining room echoes the swimming pool surface and furnishes a cool and precise abstract contrast to the romantic stone external fireplace and staircase; a single brick surface gives a warm, homelike finish to the dining room, and the basket weave pattern of one half of the sauna door suggests a Finnish peasant's shingle basket. Other striking details entirely out of context include the slate roof of the studio wing and the glass brick used as wall infill in the service wing.

The interior also teems with collage-like details: the rattan-bound steel columns, the rough fiber facing of the studio staircase, the single concrete column in the library, the fireplace's fieldstone finish, and the variety of floor materials. The 'philosopher's stone' introduced by Aalto in his 1926 article—that inversion of external and internal space—here includes the transformation of the interior into a metaphorical forest punctuated by columns and wooden poles; conversely, the courtyard, a clearing in the pine forest, has a very sheltered atmosphere.

A special aspect of the collage principle consists of the many suggestions of Japanese traditional architecture, such as the juxtaposition of regular and irregular rhythms, the Japanese-type divided glass door leading from the living room to the winter garden, the shelving suspended from the winter garden ceiling, numerous wickerwork motifs, and the Oriental elegance of many details. Even the flat roof has been conceived as a kind of a Japanese garden, with scattered stone slabs marking an irregular footpath across the gravel roof.

AN ARCHITECTURAL DRAMA

Whereas Modern architecture generally sought the consistent development of a single, fixed leitmotif throughout a design, Aalto deliberately cultivated modulation, and a constantly changing rhythm, tempo, and key. He played opposites off against one another: Romantic and Rationalist, Modern and popular, new and traditional, shaped by nature and manmade, and free form and geometry. He subordinated the demands of logic and orthodox structural consistency in order to arouse poetic expectation, discovery, adventure, and intimate secrecy. The Villa Mairea is divided into separate thematic entities just as a play is divided into acts or a symphony into movements.

Aalto seemed to call into question the basic stylistic theses of the Modern Movement—clarity of form, unambiguousness, and the logic of thematic development—by engendering 'impure' collisions and by joining motifs that belong to different intellectual categories (e.g. fireplace + staircase). By diverging from typical expectations and stylistic norms, he denied self-evident and obvious solutions, experiences, and interpretations.

284

285

WOMAN AND STRINGED INSTRUMENT

284 Man Ray, *Violon d'Ingres*, 1925.

HOUSE AND STRINGED INSTRUMENT

285 Georges Braque, *Violin and Glass*, 1912–13.

286

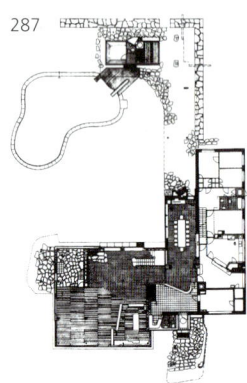

287

288

286 Pablo Picasso, *Guitar*, 1912–13.
Museum of Modern Art, New York.
287 Alvar Aalto, ground plan of the Villa
Mairea. The configuration resembles
a collaged image of a stringed
instrument.
288 The roof structure of the sauna wing
with the image of four guitar strings
cast in concrete.

"The building seeks to avoid artificial architectural rhythm," he wrote; for Aalto, the artificial seemed to mean a mechanically tectonic and linear logic.[12]

THE HOUSE AND THE GUITAR—THE MENTALITY OF PLAY

The free-form swimming pool of the Villa Mairea is usually interpreted as a metaphor of the Finnish forest pond. The pool's shape undeniably suggests the image, and the ingredients of 'Finnishness' were important to Aalto. But the swimming pool also suggests the secret female symbol of Cubist collages: the sound box of the violin, guitar, or mandolin. Cubist paintings often feature a stringed instrument—indeed, at a certain period in the work of Picasso, Braque, and Gris one would be hard put to find a still life that did not contain the motif. A particularly conspicuous detail in these instruments is the depiction of the strings.

The general plan of the Villa Mairea is reminiscent of the guitars painted or collaged by the Cubists, with the sauna complex forming the fingerboard and the swimming pool the sound box. At the corner of the main building's kitchen wing, crossing the underside of the sauna terrace roof, are four rounded beams, laboriously cast, which seem to have no structural or technical justification. Asked about their significance, Paul Bernoulli, Aalto's assistant architect in charge of the Villa Mairea building site, replied with a laugh, "They are part of Alvar's game."[13] It is plausible to take the beams as the guitar strings in Aalto's collage, and to imagine this as part of a game Aalto played with his Cubist friends Georges Braque and Fernand Léger. Some details of the Villa Mairea reveal Aalto's affinity with other European artistic work of the time and further my suggestion: the sculptured bronze door pull of the main door has similarities with Max Ernst's contemporary sculpture, and the rounded indentation of the fireplace appears as the negative casting mold for a piece of Jean Arp's sculpture. One of Aalto's earlier schemes for the Villa, however, gives specific support to the assumed guitar metaphor: the sauna roof was drawn suspended by four steel cables from the same corner of the kitchen wing.

My interpretation of the Villa Mairea as a Cubist collage is of course purely speculative, and its main purpose is to stress the way Aalto's work addressed the heritage of modern art while expressing his Finnish cultural background. In a later article, Aalto himself mentioned the "mentality of play" as an important ingredient of design "in our calculating, utilitarian age" by concluding: "Only if the constructive parts of a building, the forms derived logically from the parts and our empirical knowledge, are colored with something we could in all seriousness call the art of play, only then are we on the right track. Technology and economics should always be combined with a life-enhancing charm."[14]

289 Alvar Aalto, Villa Mairea,
Noormarkku, 1938–39. Collision of
two imageries of Aalto's architectural
collage at the corner of the sauna
structure.

THE LOGIC OF THE IMAGE

(1998)

The centenary of the birth of Alvar Aalto has already produced a spate of exhibitions, publications, and seminars, both in Finland and abroad.[1] In his home country, this adoration of the architect has reached surprising heights. In addition to Aalto's portrait and a picture of Finlandia Hall on the fifty-mark bank note as far back as 1986, a commemorative one-hundred mark silver coin has been minted this year. A theatrical play has been produced, depicting the time when, as a young reckless rebel in the early 1930s, Aalto was working on the Paimio Sanatorium.[2] More popular products of this veneration are the special bottling and labeling of Aalto's favorite Orvieto wines in the state wine stores, and a comic book of Alvar's colorful youth in the provincial town of Jyväskylä in Central Finland. All this certainly implies an unexpected position in the national consciousness for an artistic radical who even in mid-career named his motorboat *Nemo Propheta in Patria*.

At the same time as the idea of a '*Lex Aalto*' has been proposed in order to protect all of his immense *oeuvre*, Aalto's iconic Finlandia Hall has shed its Carrara marble facades to reveal an embarrassing yellow coat of mineral wool. For another year, this sad sight will continue to be the most visible evidence of a technical mistake by the prophet, as well as of the negative side of his adoration. Aalto's marble plates—quarried from 'Michelangelo's quarry', as he used to boast—hardly withstood the hardships of the Nordic climate for two decades before warping to a visually disturbing and structurally alarming degree.[3] After endless farcical polemics and repeatedly contradictory decisions by the various municipal and historical preservation authorities concerned, the decision was finally reached to replace the facades with exactly similar

marble plates, knowing full well that the same disaster will inevitably reoccur within the next fifteen years.

Although the decision to allot some 60 million Finnish marks every fifteen to twenty years to maintain the translucent natural whiteness of the building is an expression of singular public respect for an architect and his work, Finlandia Hall will unavoidably become a serious politi-cal argument against contemporary architecture. With his exceptionally pragmatic attitude and willingness to make alterations and improvisa-tions, Aalto would certainly not have hesitated to replace Italian marble with a more durable material, but not one of the numerous authorities and experts involved had the courage to take this decision. Has the admiration for Alvar Aalto reached such a point that it will eventually turn against his own cause?

Another consequence of this uncritical esteem: the essential dis-tinction has not been made between a great Aalto building and a poor one. Distinguishing between the masterpieces and the run-of-the-mill products of a genius is more important for a sane artistic culture than blind adoration. Considering Aalto's immense production (during his 55 years of professional practice he is estimated to have designed and executed about 500 buildings and urban projects, and the Alvar Aalto Archive contains roughly 200,000 drawings and 20,000 letters), it is self-evident that his tens of masterworks are balanced by hundreds of less exciting projects. This is the human side of any genius.

•

Alvar Aalto's synthetic and inclusive architecture both invites and resists interpretation. His use of historical references, idiosyncratic typologies and geometric complexities, the abundance of formal themes, lighting solutions, detail elaborations, improvisations, and whims, as well as his interplay between context, site and nature, provide ample ground for analysis and interpretation. But even after all the learned scrutiny, his masterpieces seem to maintain their secrets and their poetic freshness. A simultaneous openness to interpretation and inexhaustible layering of content and meaning is, of course, the inherent quality of any great work of art. The abundance of themes and associations in Aalto's archi-tecture appears to be fused through his creative process into chemical compounds that do not expose their true origins. At first sight, his best buildings appear relaxed and effortless, often almost matter of fact, but slowly they begin to hint at layered meanings and mysteries. Aalto's buildings do not reveal their subtleties through photographs; they have to be experienced in person and encountered with one's body in the actuality of their context, scale, and materiality. Irrespective of

the number of visits or the intensity of study, they appear fresh and untouched. Of all the works of the acknowledged masters of modern and contemporary architecture, Aalto's remain unquestionably the most enigmatic. Aalto's secrecy and thematic fusion promises to be both a challenge and an inspiration to successive generations of designers and scholars well into the 21ˢᵗ century.

The enigmatic and idiosyncratic nature of Aalto's architecture has misled many of his critics, as well as his admirers, to regard his work as subjective and irrational. Aalto started off as a rationalist, and he continued, to use his own words, "to deepen rationality by expanding it into the psychological sphere."[4] This subtlety of Aalto's reason, and his intuitive understanding of the role of images in our architectural experience, can provide the most important lessons for today.

•

The architecture of Alvar Aalto is a product of the earth; his buildings echo the soil and the terrain. The philosopher Gaston Bachelard divides forms into two categories; products of 'formal imagination' and 'material imagination.'[5] Aalto's forms are images of matter rather than visual construction or the assemblages of a geometrician. Already in 1924, at the age of 26, he revealed his artistic credo in an article written immediately after his honeymoon in Italy. He praises Andrea Mantegna's fresco *Christ in the Vineyard* in the baptistery of Santa Maria del Eremitani in Padua: "...it contains something we might call a synthetic landscape. This is an architect's vision of the landscape... it is a brilliant analysis of the earth's crust... For me 'the rising town' has become a religion, a disease, a madness, call it what you will: the city of hills, that curving, living, unpredictable line which runs in dimensions unknown to mathematicians, is for me the incarnation of everything that forms a contrast in the modern world between brutal mechanicalness and religious beauty in life."[6]

Throughout his life, Aalto sought to create a synthetic landscape; a man-made microcosm in accordance with Mantegna's painting; his buildings and urban ensembles are architectural still-lifes, complete images of the world. Concerning this idea of architecture as an image of the world, a Paradise, the mature Aalto said in 1957: "Architecture too has an ulterior motive... the idea of creating paradise. That is the only purpose of our buildings. If we did not carry this idea with us all through our lives, our buildings would all be simpler and more trivial, and life would be—well, would there be life at all? Every building, every architectural product that is its symbol, is intended to show that we wish to build a paradise on earth for man."[7]

290 Alvar Aalto's guiding image: the synthetic landscape of an Italian hill town. Andrea Mantegna, *Christ in the Vineyard*, 1460. National Gallery, London.

291 House as an image of a hill town. Alvar Aalto, Maison Carré (House for Louis Carré), Bazoches-sur-Guyonne, France, 1956–59.

In his architecture, Aalto fuses together the terrain and the building through a multitude of means: by mediating terraces and zones of vegetation (the Maison Carré); by the profile of the building echoing the topography of the site (the curved roofscape of the Riola Church repeating the contour of the nearby mountains); by creating an image of a mountain or gigantic rock formation (House of Culture, Helsinki; Church of the Three Crosses, Vuoksenniska; Opera House, Essen); by a horizontal base stratum (the plateau volume of Finlandia Hall in relation to the crowning volume and the planned row of 'Venetian' buildings along the shore of the bay); or by projecting a contrast to the existing landscape (the tower of Church at Seinäjoki; the Neue Vahr Apartment Building, Bremen; the enclosed Pompeian courtyard of his summer house in the uninhabited Finnish lake landscape). He aspires to create a 'hill town' even on flat ground, as in the artificially raised courtyard and terraced hill of the Säynätsalo Town Hall, and the elevated courtyard of the Church at Seinäjoki. Even in dense urban situations, Aalto creates an image of an elevated terrain, as in the skylit court of the Iron House in Helsinki or the roof courtyard of the Cultural Center in Wolfsburg. These devices create a welcome variety to a completely flat landscape, as well as introduce an authoritative experience of an approach through ascension, an up-hill movement.

The Villa Mairea is, perhaps, Aalto's richest and finest architectural miniature, a domestic design which fuses the vertical *staccato* of pines, the clearing cut into the forest with its miniaturized landscaping, and the house itself into a singular image of Paradise.[8] The house is a collage of architectural images gleaned from Modern, timeless vernacular, and traditional Japanese sources.[9]

The master's buildings do not comply with standard categories of architectural typology; Aalto created his own collection of idiosyncratic types (library, concert hall, theatre, urban office block, industrial plant, residential building), which all resonate with a wealth of images from architectural history. Certain formal themes, such as the fan motif, the head-and-tail theme, the sunken floor level and skylights, are used across the categories of type. In fact, throughout an active career lasting more than half a century, Aalto devised a continuously expanding collection of strategies, responses, solutions, forms, materials, details, and even color schemes, which he applied in endless variations with the help of his devoted assistants, sometimes as an uninspired office routine, but always recognizable as his hand.

Aalto's surfaces tend to read as woven instead of assembled or stacked surfaces, and their coherence appears stronger as a consequence. The notion of a woven surface also implies layering, depth,

292 Architecture of earth: building as an echo of the site. Alvar Aalto, Riola Church, Italy, 1966–80.

293 Architecture as the image of a mountain. Alvar Aalto, Church of the Three Crosses, Vuoksenniska, 1955–58.

and tactility. This effect of inner coherence is further strengthened by his characteristic use of a distinct figural outline, profile or boundary, one that gives rise to the reading of a singular *gestalt* instead of an additive surface.

The technique of collage facilitates the combination of disparate elements and images in Aalto's characteristically painterly works. This reading of layered time and tactile intimacy is further strengthened by the lack of any singular system of co-ordinates or reference that would tie the parts into a single system or order. His designs, surface patterns, and textures frequently set out to suggest a systematic modular order, but any reading following the course of simple causality or linear logic is invariably interrupted and confused. The reality of imagery plays against the rational consideration of function and structure.

The settings of Modern architecture usually appear to originate in a single moment of time, and consequently they evoke an image of flattened temporality. Modern architecture, in fact, aspired to an expression of a timeless present and eternal youth. Due to this exclusion of the temporal element, time's revenge has usually hit Modern buildings disastrously. Conversely, Alvar Aalto's mature architecture, after his fervent but short engagement with Functionalism, reflects the presence, depth and density of time. In addition to the echoes of the history of architecture frequently resounded by his buildings, the geological and biomorphic associations of his designs evoke experiences of duration and continuity. Aalto's buildings sit comfortably in the continuum of culture. The Seinäjoki Civic Center, for instance, seems to be composed of individual buildings designed by architects from different eras and stylistic persuasions. The elements of his conglomerate images suggest separate origins and histories, whereas the materials and details present a tactile invitation and a sense of intimacy, and speak of the labor of caressing and skilled hands.

The experience of temporal depth is reinforced by a number of design choices, such as variations in architectural typology, material, shape, texture, and color. Aalto's distinctive device to capture the sense of time is the repeated use of the ruin image.[10] He utilizes images of ruins to evoke a melancholic experience of the past, and to suggest the inevitability of erosion and decay. His images of ruins extend from the explicit imagery of the amphitheatres of Antiquity to 'eroded' corners surfaced in lattices and grids, and the occasional white expanses of marble or plaster against dominant brick surfaces. The brick collage of the courtyard surfaces in the Summer House at Muuratsalo suggests that the entire structure is built on the remains of a past civilization. The ruin motif was, of course, a favored image of the Romantics of the

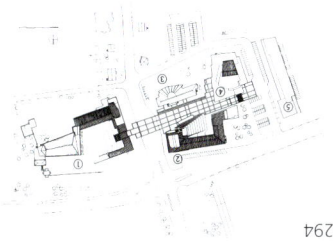

294 Architecture of geology and temporal duration. Alvar Aalto, Civic Center, Seinäjoki 1957–58. 1 Church and parish center, 2 City Hall, 3 Library, 4 Theater, 5 Administration center. The church and the city hall incorporate artificial hill formations constructed on completely flat ground. Each individual building reflects a specific morphology as if constructed by different architects through time. (drawing by Jari Frondelius and Peter B. Mackeith)

295 Wall as a weave, Alvar Aalto, Finnish pavilion, New York World's Fair, 1938–39.

18th century, and its re-emergence in our time is certainly a reaction to the flattening of the temporal experience in contemporary technological environments.

The architectural entities used by Aalto are the result of numerous interacting physical processes rather than of abstract thought. He combines elements deriving from both industrial and craft processes, and thus fuses together two historical modes of production. Although he does not use conventional tectonic logic or syntax, his architecture evokes the labor and skill of fabrication. The overall ambience of his architecture is relaxed and spontaneous; we are not impressed by the designer's willpower and formal control, but delighted by a sense of open-endedness, sanguine sensuality, and spontaneous discovery. This open-endedness also creates a sense of aesthetic tolerance, one that enables alterations, additions, and the incorporation of objects of different visual persuasion. Aalto's furniture and other design products are rare examples of modern aesthetics that also appeal to popular taste.

Instead of appearing as assembled vertical planes, Aalto's facades are skin-like surfaces that wrap themselves around their volumes (in fact, many of his buildings appear to have a single continuous facade circumscribing the entire volume), enhancing an organic cohesion and an animistic feeling. The buildings of his mature period are always some kind of 'architectural creature' instead of abstract compositions. The idea of an architectural creature provides an organizing and ordering device, allowing entirely different imageries than those suggested by the use of Euclidian geometry. The creature-image eliminates the idea of symmetry by implying decisive differences between the back and the stomach, left and right, inside and outside. Such a basis also facilitates imageries of physiognomy, gaze, invitation, protection, and movement. Aalto's architectural creatures often transform into the image of an instrument or a device, as in his innumerable variations of the skylight (the section of the North Jutland Art Museum, for instance).

Usually Aalto's buildings have a rational structural system, but instead of a repetitious modular system, his structure is locally articulated and varied, similar to the skeleton and bone structure of an animal. The independence of spatial configuration, structural reality, and surface treatment allows him great freedom in molding his spaces in accordance with a desired functional configuration or experiential effect, instead of following an abstracted notion of order. Aalto's architecture represents a sensory realism as opposed to a conceptual idealism. As Demetri Porphyrios has shown in his seminal study, Aalto exploits differences rather than similarities.[11] This acceptance of difference leads to different configurations rather than to an aspiration for

296 An image of the ruins of a Mediterranean atrium house in the Finnish lake landscape. Alvar Aalto, Experimental House, Muuratsalo, 1952–53.

297 Wall as the skin of an architectural creature. Alvar Aalto, House of Culture, Helsinki, 1952–58.

unity through similarity (the crescendo fan of the auditoriums in the Cultural Center at Wolfsburg being an obvious example).

Another significant organizational strategy differentiating Aalto from the main lines of the Modern Movement is his manner of compos-ing a building by separate episodes, scenes or acts; among such tactics are the presentation of the building through its silhouette; the inviting gesture of an entrance view or entry court; the lobby space with an ambiance of welcome and coziness; the heightening of anticipation effected by the main staircase; and the memorable image of fulfill-ment in the main spaces. His buildings consist of distinct parts, in the same way as a piece of music is composed of parts or a play of acts. In each of his buildings, one can almost identify the views or sequences in which Aalto was most interested and thus detailed personally, in contrast to the bulk of the building worked out by his assistants on the basis of office precedents. Many of his buildings reveal the joints of these architectural episodes, as well as the backs where all the formally unresolved aspects are hidden (the back facade of the House of Culture is a revealing example of this hidden, unresolved side).

Modern architecture generally aspired to clarity, transparency, and weightlessness. Aalto's entrances are always understated, almost hidden, his buildings are dominated by solid surfaces and closed vol-umes instead of transparent planes, and his structures and details are frequently surprisingly bulky (balanced, however, by skillfully placed strokes of elegance).

•

Modern consciousness and sensory balance have gradually developed towards an unrivaled dominance of the sense of vision. This thought-provoking development has been observed and analyzed recently by a number of philosophers.[12] As a consequence of the hegemony of the eye over the other sensory realms, architecture has turned into an art-form of an instant visual image. The experience of the cold distance of vision is strengthened by a general tendency towards uniformity (of floor lev-els, materials, textures, lighting) causing sensory detachment. Buildings have lost their opacity and depth, weight and authority, mystery and shadow. Curiously, the technologically most advanced buildings of our time, such as hospitals, airports, international hotels, and other struc-tures of transition, are among the most purely visual and, at the same time, sensorially most deprived settings.

However, alongside this dominant retinal architecture, an aspiration for a haptic architecture is emerging. Alvar Aalto's work is a precursor of this haptic orientation, again contrary to the main line of the Modern

298 Architecture of tactility, Alvar Aalto, Armchair 45, 1946–47.
299 Architecture of weak image, Alvar Aalto, Villa Mairea, Noormarkku, 1938–39. The various architectural themes are held together by an archi-tectural atmosphere rather than by tectonic logic.

Movement. The culture of speed and rapid exchange favors an architecture of the eye, whereas haptic architecture promotes slowness; such architecture is appreciated and comprehended gradually, detail by detail, as images of the body and the skin. The haptic sensibility suppresses the dominance of the visual image by enhancing plasticity, tactility, and intimacy. An unconscious element of touch is unavoidably concealed even in the sense of vision; as we look, so the eye touches the object. This hidden tactile experience determines the sensual quality of the object and mediates messages of invitation or rejection, home or hostility.

298

Aalto's architecture is a convincing and stimulating example of tactile architecture; a pleasurable haptic experience is effectively evoked by his use of materials, shapes, and textures. His designs acknowledge that we confront architecture through our entire bodily and sensory existence, not solely through the judgment of the eye; his architecture does not reject Eros. Even Aalto's shaping of light evokes experiences of materiality and tactility: it caresses rounded reflecting surfaces and bounces off textured surfaces. Criticizing the narrow Modernist view of rationality, Aalto analyzed the unpleasant sensory characteristics of tubular steel furniture, and emphasized the importance of the senses of hearing and touch: "A piece of furniture that forms a part of a person's daily habitat should not cause excessive glare from light reflection; ditto, it should not be disadvantageous in terms of sound, sound absorption, etc. A piece that comes into the most intimate contact with man, as a chair does, shouldn't be constructed of materials that are excessively good conductors of heat."[13] An interest in tactile qualities appears to be naturally accompanied by a concern for acoustic qualities, whereas sheer visuality tends to result in aggressive acoustic properties. Acoustic experience is a form of tactile encounter, and Aalto's interiors posses a similar sensitivity.

•

Opposing the Modern tendency towards purity and absoluteness, Aalto's architecture frequently projects images of incompleteness. His episodic architecture suppresses the dominance of a singular visual image. His architecture is not dictated by a single conceptual idea down to the last detail, but rather grows through separate architectural scenes, episodes, and inventions. The entire design is held together by the constancy of an emotional atmosphere, an architectural key as it were, instead of an intellectualized concept.

299

Alvar Aalto's architecture is concerned with real sensory interaction over idealization and conceptual manifestations. He transformed such deep understandings of human sensitivities and the natural world

into the constructed world of architecture and landscape. His architecture obscures the categories of foreground and background, object and context, and evokes a liberated sense of natural duration. In doing so, Aalto's work aspires to fulfill the reconciliatory task of the art of architecture.

300 Aulis Blomstedt´s graphic illustration
of the number 60 and its divisibility.
Undated.

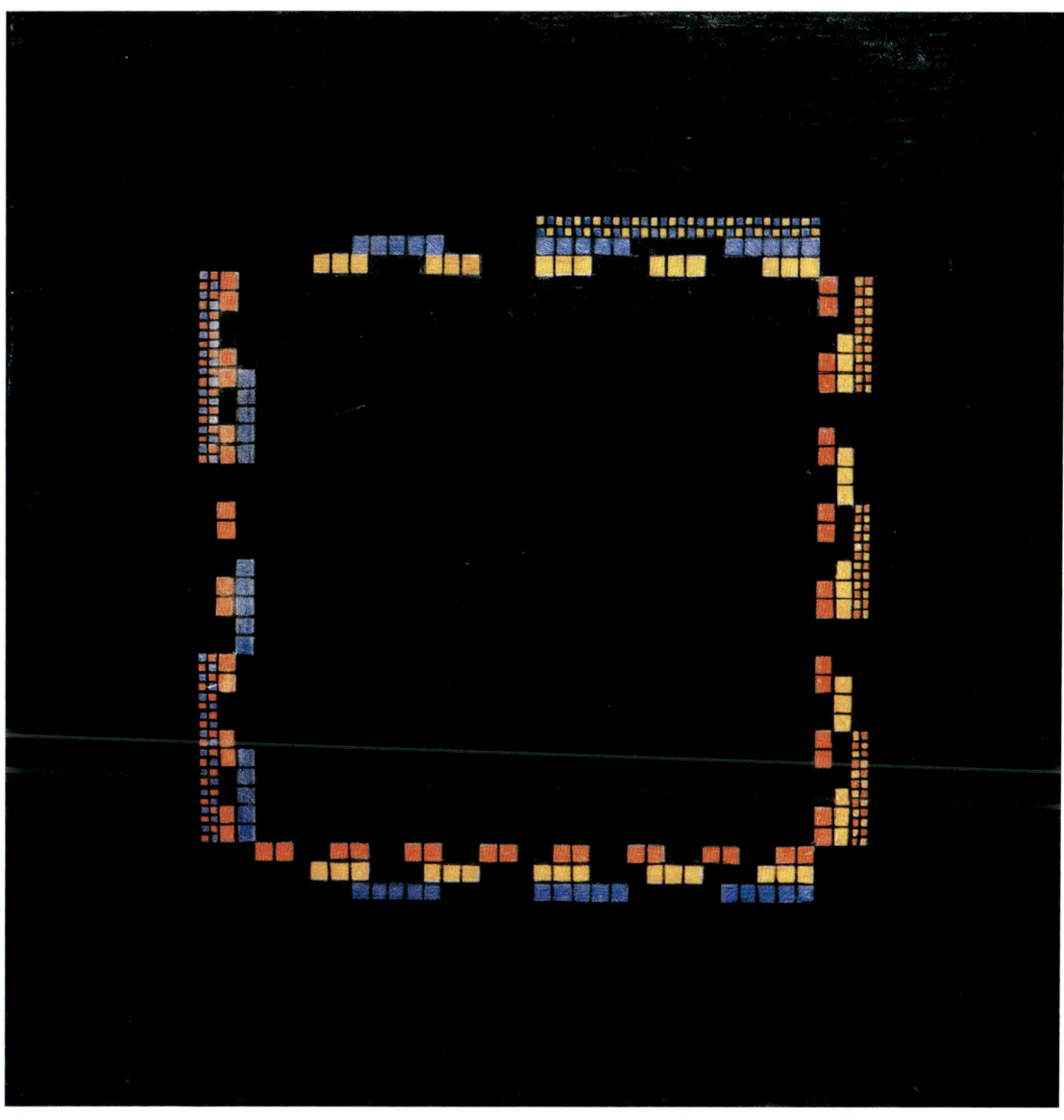

MAN, MEASURE, AND PROPORTION

(1992)

"An architect lives and works in the world of relations, proportions, and measures. The success—or failure—of our work depends on the control we have over this world."[1]

THE ETHICS OF ARCHITECTURE

"If one wishes for something new, one has to seek that which is oldest," the Finnish architect Aulis Blomstedt noted in his journal. In fact the classical, and the eternal and universal principles of architecture, were the predominant themes in his design work and writings. In his architecture Blomstedt sought to diminish subjective and expressive elements, seeking instead a natural and vernacular simplicity.

Indeed, the aphorisms that illuminate Blomstedt's numerous writings and diaries are eloquent in their defense of the value of simplicity in tradition and the assumption of an architectural ethic:

Avoid compulsion—only the natural can be great.
Suspect all that does not appear simple *(Simplex sigillum veri)*.
Style is the outcome of an ethical position and choice.
It is said that art is a way of expressing feelings, but to me architecture is a way of controlling my feelings.

The chief characteristic of Blomstedt's architectural ethic is a respect for nature and landscape: "Make a landscape, an interesting landscape, then you make good architecture." He saw the unchanging and cyclical phenomena of nature—the sun, moon, the seasons, oceans, and winds—as belonging to the quintessence of the classical.

In his ethical and cultural stance, Aulis Blomstedt was an exemplary architect at a time when the Finnish profession was becoming estranged from its traditionally idealistic and politically independent position. His interest in the interaction of architecture with the other branches of art was an important counterbalance to the secularization of Finnish architects into an autonomous discipline and profession.

TWO SCHOOLS

In the late 1950s, Blomstedt became a counterbalance in Finland to the more subjective and expressive view of architecture exemplified by Alvar Aalto. In an article published in 1954, Blomstedt focused his criticism on Aalto's concept of 'elastic standardization': "Enough has been said about elastic standardization. In order that life itself could achieve an elastic freedom, standardization, as its name implies, must be INELASTIC—IN THE RIGHT WAY."[2]

He justified the importance of an architectural theory as follows: "Theoretical contemplation is essential, but let us remember that the Greek verb *theoria* originally meant to examine, not to speculate. It is said that the basis of all brilliant perceptions is an immediate personal observation."

When Aalto, who had earlier prolifically defended theoretical-conceptual analyses in architecture, turned against the whole idea, a rupture occurred in his hitherto close friendship with Blomstedt. This architectural-ideological rift brought about the creation of two, and in many senses, opposing, schools of architectural thought.[3] In fact, Blomstedt's theoretical reflections were long ridiculed within the highly pragmatic Finnish profession, not least due to Aalto's stated position.

In the 1950s, the Finnish CIAM group to which Blomstedt belonged, along with others involved with the Museum of Finnish Architecture, also concerned itself with the theoretical aspects of architecture. *Le Carré Bleu*, the French-language forum for theoretical writings on architecture founded in 1958 was, also profoundly influenced by Blomstedt, particularly during its early years, even down to such matters as its style of presentation.[4] As well, as a professor at the Helsinki University of Technology from 1958 to 1966, Blomstedt was in a position to affect the thinking and attitudes of his students. His philosophy of architecture in particular helped mold the rationalist and constructivist views held by the younger generation of Finnish students and architects during the 1960s.

THE HERITAGE OF THE CLASSICISM OF THE TWENTIES

Within today's prevailing architectural climate, with its superficial radicalism and individualism, buildings designed by Blomstedt are easily overlooked. Numbed by today's architectonic glamor, the observer often fails to notice their refined traditionalism, discreet Classicism, and finely tuned proportions. Behind the Functionalist language of Blomstedt's architecture lies the Nordic Classicism of the 1920s, that particular blend of rustic humility and Classical sensibility with an overall architectural sophistication and elegance.

Aulis Blomstedt's work acquires a universal significance, however, by its research and reliance upon the harmonic measurement and proportion systems of architecture. In this, his ideas are related to the oldest traditions of Western architecture, to the principles of harmonic proportions in architecture that originated in ancient Egypt and Greece.

THE PYTHAGOREAN TRADITION

Blomstedt's concept of harmonic proportions is directly related to the relationship of small whole numbers to the consonances in music, a discovery made by the philosopher Pythagoras in the 6th century BC.

Pythagoras never wrote of his investigations, but his teachings—almost cult mysteries—passed by word of mouth by adherents under strict vows of secrecy until the time of Socrates. While the Egyptians considered mathematics a collection of empirical methods, for Pythagoras it became a subject for theoretical examination.[5]

With the aid of the monochord (a single stringed instrument), it is believed Pythagoras discovered the initial harmonic series:

C   c   g   c¹   e¹   g¹   b¹   c²   d²
1/1:1/2:1/3:1/4:1/5:1/6:1/7:1/8:1/9: and so on.

A note is not made by one vibrating 'pure' tone, but by a blend of the upper partials vibrating simultaneously with the 'fundamental.' According to Pythagoras, concord intervals are those with the simplest relations to frequencies. The starting point of the Pythagorean scale is the pure quint or fifth.

According to the Greek theory of music, the consonances were the octave (1:2), the fifth (2:3) and the fourth (3:4) (in Greek: *diapason*, *diapente* and *diatessaron*), the numerical relationship of whose intervals can be expressed by the smallest whole numbers 1, 2, 3, and 4. Seconds, thirds, sixths and sevenths were still considered dissonances in ancient Greece.[6]

Upon observing mathematical proportions in musical harmony, Pythagoras expounded the idea of world harmony, in the belief that "numbers were the source and origin of all entities."[7]

301 Pythagoras established the relations between number ratios and sound frequencies. The woodcut shows Pythagoras experimenting with bells, water-glasses, stretched cords, and various sized pipes; his Hebrew counterpart, Jubal, uses weighted hammers on an anvil.

Music was thought to illustrate the harmony of the spheres, which even appears as a 'Music of the Spheres,' brought about by the movements of the planets. The idea that world harmony could be expressed by the numbers 1, 2, 3, and 4—something which also appears in Plato's cosmology—led to the predominance of a symbolic and mystical numerology during the next two millennia.[8]

In the 2nd century AD, at the end of Classical Antiquity, the Pythagorean tradition was revived in the form of Neo-Pythagoreanism. Almost 1500 years later, the humanism of the Renaissance again revived interest in Classical Antiquity and a knowledge of Pythagorean concepts became an essential part of a scholar's education. The laws of harmony were again understood in relation to the laws of music. Brunelleschi, for example, studied the classical systems of proportion in music, and Leonardo and Michelangelo, as well, acquired their knowledge of harmonic proportions from the study of music.[9] Palladio (1508–1580) applied the principles of harmonic proportions to his secular buildings. He also extended their use in measuring the relation of individual rooms to the over-all building complex.

Renaissance harmonic studies were continued by the astronomer Johannes Kepler (1571–1630), whom posterity remembers for his three laws concerning the movement of the planets. Yet throughout his life he had one goal in mind—to prove the Pythagorean theory of world harmony.[10] In his work *Harmonia mundi* (1619), Kepler even proved that the same harmonic intervals that appear in music appear in the orbits of planets.

After the Renaissance, harmonic research turned towards mysticism, in particular through the Kabbalah, the secret traditions of the Jews, following its translation into Latin. Scientific rationalism and the Age of Enlightenment deprecated such mystical views. The painter Hogarth, for example, considered it "a strange notion" that there should be any correspondence between beauty as seen by the eye and harmony as heard by the ear. The Scottish philosopher Hume held that 'beauty is in the eye of the beholder' and is entirely subjective. Edmund Burke concurred, "No two things can have less resemblance or analogy than a man, a house or temple."[11]

In our own time, however, the Swiss scholar Hans Kayser (1891–1964) revived the Pythagorean harmonies on the basis of the two-volume opus *Die harmonikale Symbolik des Alterthums* (The Harmonical Symbolism of Classical Antiquity), written by Albert von Thimus in the 19th century.[12] Today the center for harmonical research is at the Hochschule für Musik und Darstellende Kunst (The Academy of Music and the Performing Arts) in Vienna.

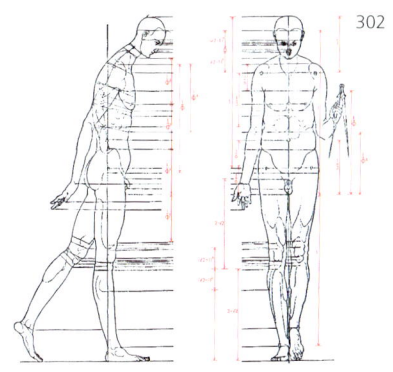

302

302 Albrecht Dürer's human canon, composed of proportions derived from the arithmetic, harmonic, and geometric proportions.
303 Aulis Blomstedt's dimensional and proportional study of the great pyramids of Gizeh, 1965. He observed that when the dimensions of the pyramids are given in ancient Egyptian Royal Cubits, the proportions appear very simple. The Royal Cubit was 52,2 cm, whereas the normal cubit measured only 45 cm.

303

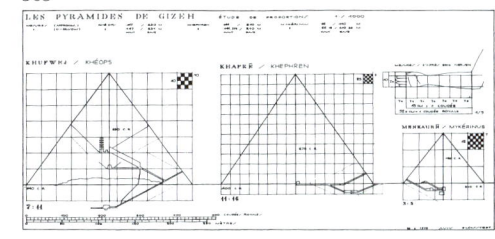

304 Aulis Blomstedt's concept for a modular system of flexible industrialized housing for the competition of summerhouses organized by the Association of Finnish Architects in 1943. Blomstedt's interest in modular coordination clearly dates back to the early 1940s.

In fact, the idea of harmonic proportions based on musical notation can be considered one of the oldest and most persistent Western scientific traditions, even though it has almost completely disappeared from the theory, teaching, and practice of contemporary architecture.

BLOMSTEDT'S MEASURE AND PROPORTION STUDIES

Aulis Blomstedt's interest in the use of modules in architectural design was aroused during the Second World War by Ernst Neufert's lecture in Helsinki on the octameter system based on a 12.5 centimeter module network.[13] "It is becoming increasingly obvious that industrial architecture cannot manage without pre-harmonized measurements," Blomstedt was to write in his journal years later.

In an early work, the Villa Therman in Tolkkis, completed in 1951, Blomstedt still used a 100 centimeter measure in both coordinates without any dimensional and proportional hierarchy. But within the same year, a block of flats for war invalids in Turku is already based on the 60 centimeter measure. The number 60 figured prominently in Blomstedt's harmonic researches during the following decade.

Blomstedt devoted himself energetically to the study of the measurability and divisibility of numerical series, based on the multiples of small whole numbers and their relationships to human measurements and musical proportions. His two starting points were the practical work of the architect, and the demand for harmonic proportions inherited from Classical Antiquity. The concept of the module itself was inherited from these times, because the word originally meant the division into 30 parts of half the diameter of a temple column. The module was thus originally relative, and in proportion, to the size of the building.

In the design and construction of a building, the principles of the module and of harmonic proportions stressed the multiplication of the different measures and units (the distance between columns, window divisions, dimensions of bricks or stones, etc.) by small whole numbers, or the division of larger measurements (the overall size of the building, distance between columns, etc.) into smaller parts by small whole numbers. Blomstedt considered it of practical importance that these calculations should be simple to make and easy to remember.

The selection of a system of measurement for Blomstedt was both a philosophical and a practical question. The philosophical aspect involved the idea of universal harmony inherited from Classical times; the practical side concerned the belief that the use of a harmonic system of measurement related to human measurements would facilitate the work of the architect. "In my studies of the module I have aimed at a more remote and broad goal than has hitherto been seen in my practical work," he wrote, "I have tried to find an invariance (invariances), which would free architects to concentrate on essentials."

THE UNITY OF EYE AND EAR

Blomstedt assumed that the visual harmony conveyed by the eyes originated from the same phenomenalist principles as the aural harmony of music comprehended by the ears.[14] As musical harmony had been studied for 2500 years, the arithmetics of musical harmony were simply the natural, useful basis for a system of measures and proportions in architecture. "What is good enough for music should be good enough for architecture," he wrote in his journal.

In this view of the commonalities of aural and visual phenomena and the theoretical pre-eminence of music compared to architecture, Blomstedt returned to the ideas that had prevailed in art and architecture during the Renaissance. Alberti's *De re aedificatoria libri decem (The Ten Books on Architecture)*, for instance, assumes that harmony is not the result of individual caprice, but of objective reasoning.[15] A uniform system of proportion should be maintained in all parts of a building, one based on the system of musical harmony developed by Pythagoras. In discussing the correspondence of musical intervals and architectural proportions, Alberti stated—with reference to Pythagoras—that "the numbers by means of which the agreement of sounds affects our ears with delight, are the very same which please our eyes and our minds," and continues, "We shall therefore borrow all our rules for harmonic relations from the musicians to whom this kind of numbers is extremely well known."[16]

Rudolf Wittkower's *Architectural Principles in the Age of Humanism* was also a significant reference for Blomstedt throughout his notebooks. According to Wittkower, "There was an unbroken tradition coming down from antiquity according to which arithmetic, the study of numbers, geometry, the study of spatial relationships, astronomy, the study of the motion of celestial bodies, and music, the study of the motions apprehended by the ear, formed the quadrivium of the mathematical 'arts.' By contrast to these the 'liberal arts,' painting, sculpture and architecture were regarded as manual occupations."[17] In order to raise them from the level of the mechanical to that of the liberal arts, Wittkower continues, "they had to be given a firm theoretical, i.e. mathematical foundation," something that was to be found in musical theory.

Blomstedt also greatly admired Hans Kayser's studies and was even in personal contact with the Swiss thinker. Kayser's writings combine the harmony of visual and acoustic phenomena, using such expressions

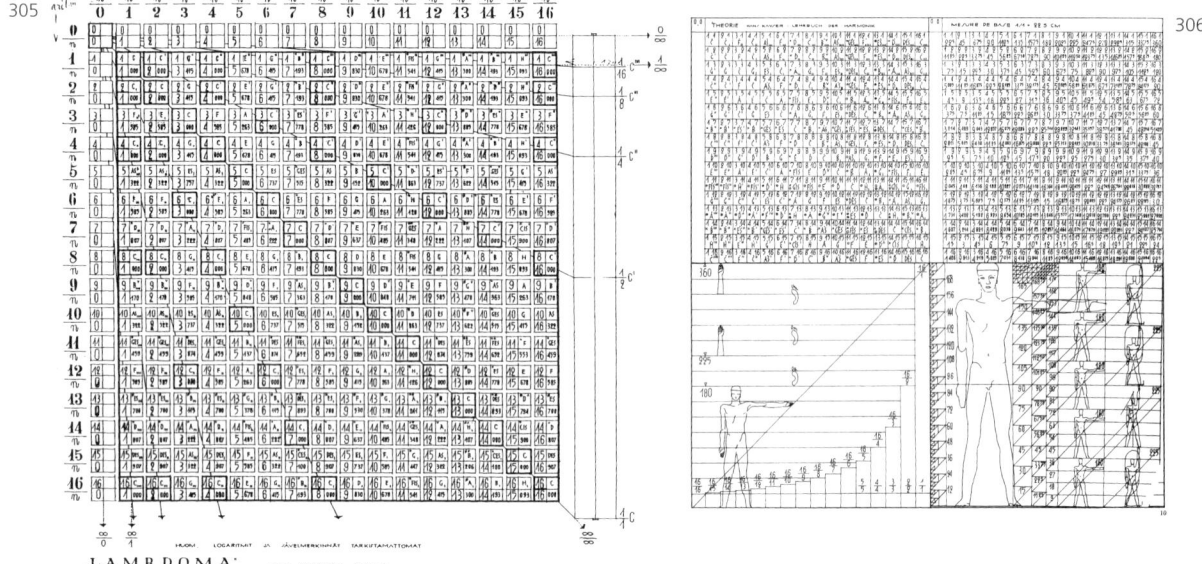

‚LAMBDOMA' HANS KAYSER'IN MUKAAN

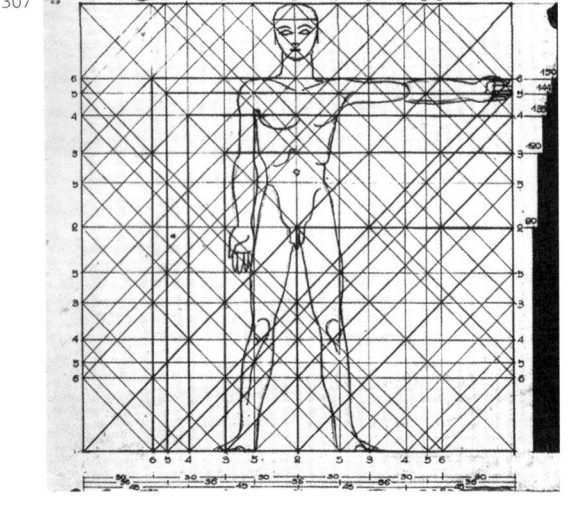

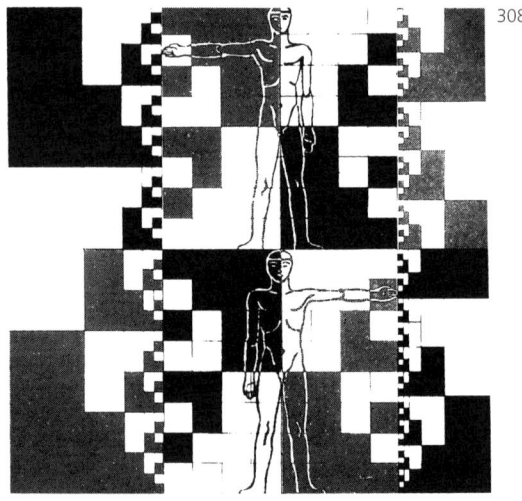

as *Akustische Anschauung* (acoustic seeing), *Audition visuelle* (visual hearing), and a radio term, *Hörbilder* (heard pictures).[18]

MEASURE, PROPORTION AND MAN

Blomstedt studied the harmonic divisions of the human body in countless drawings. In many of them, the artist takes over from the scientist and so the original harmonic intention of the drawings remains unclear. In *Thought and Form*, the 1976 exhibition of his harmonic researches, Blomstedt helped the Museum of Finnish Architecture staff to compose the captions for his drawings. "Once again I have given in to art," he would snort, trying to fathom the harmonic proportions of a drawing made approximately a quarter-of-a-century earlier.[19]

Alongside these metrological and harmonic proportion drawings, Blomstedt continuously made free artistic studies, ones which most often directly tested the visual effects of some module network. Others, such as the numerous sketches he drew with his eyes closed, developed more spontaneous principles of composition.

Although Blomstedt sought a practical, absolute quality for his systems of measures and proportions, he nevertheless considered the aesthetic impression produced by the eye the ultimate criterion.

A human figure, standing with arms outstretched within a square, appears repeatedly in Blomstedt's drawings. This attempt to determine a system of measures and proportions in architecture from human measurements links Blomstedt not only to the Renaissance theoreticians, but to the earliest source of Western architectural thought, the Roman Vitruvius Pollio (84–14 BC). Vitruvius' *De architectura libri decem (The Ten Books on Architecture)*, had collected all that was known about the art of Greek building according to the laws of music.[20]

In his introduction to the third volume of the *Ten Books*, the book dealing with temples, Vitruvius examines the proportions of the human figure, which he considers should also be reflected in the proportions of temples. As proof of the harmony and perfection of the human body, Vitruvius describes how a well-built man, with arms and legs outstretched, fits precisely into the two most perfect of all geometrical figures, the circle and the square. According to Vitruvius, this figure expressed the fundamental truth about man and the world.

The powerful image inspired and engaged numerous Renaissance artists and architects, in the general belief that with this figure it was possible to define the proportions—the common measure, the harmony—of everything in the world. Leonardo himself interpreted Vitruvius's written diagram in his celebrated drawing (at Venice).[21] Leonardo's friend, the mathematician Luca Pacioli, wrote in his book

305 Blomstedt's study of the ancient Pythagorean harmonic division according to Kayser. Pythagoreans associated the series of even numbers 1, 2, 4, 8 with the feminine and the series of odd numbers 1, 3, 9, 27 with the male. The Greeks called these two series the *Lambda*. On the basis of Hans Kayser's *Lambdoma*-series, Aulis Blomstedt conceived a three-dimensional architectural sculpture as the symbol for the exhibition of Finnish architecture at the Moderna Museet in Stockholm, 1961.

306 Aulis Blomstedt: Hans Kayser's Pythagorean harmonics applied to the human figure. Initial conceptions for an issue of the magazine *Le Carré Bleu,* Presumably in 1958, when the magazine was founded.

307 Aulis Blomstedt: Human height 180 cm and its Pythagorean intervals: octave 1/2, quint 2/3, quart 3/4, major third 4/5 and minor third 5/6. Undated.

308 Aulis Blomstedt: Study of Pythagorean intervals applied to the human scale. Undated.

Divina proportione: "First we shall talk of the proportions of man, because from the human body derive all measures and their denominations and in it is to be found all and every ratio and proportion by which God reveals the innermost secrets of nature."[22] Wittkower's commentary is also conclusive on this point: "With the Renaissance revival of the Greek mathematical interpretation of God and the world, and invigorated by the Christian belief that Man as the image of God embodied the harmonies of the Universe, the Vitruvian human figure inscribed in a square and a circle became a symbol of the mathematical sympathy between microcosm and macrocosm."[23]

Renaissance artists adhered to the Pythagorean view that 'All is Number'; by calling on Plato and the Neo-Platonists, and supported by numerous theologians from Augustine onwards, they were convinced of the mathematical and harmonic structure of the universe and all creation. To Pacioli, even the divine functions are of little value if a church had not been built in accordance "with correct proportions."[24]

HARMONICS AND THE GOLDEN SECTION

The school of Pythagoras was particularly fascinated by the dodecahedron—one of the five regular convex solids circumscribed by a sphere—and its relation to the Golden Section. The dodecahedron's twelve regular facets corresponded to the twelve signs of the zodiac and thus was the symbol of the universe. The point of intersection of the diagonals inside each pentagon of the dodecahedron divides each according to the Golden Section. The pentagram and triple triangle formed from the subdivision of the pentagon—a configuration the Pythagorean brotherhood considered the symbol of good health—contained a number of Golden Section ratios. Greek architects and sculptors (such as Phidias) are also assumed to have used the Golden Section.[25]

Leonardo added ratios of the golden section to the proportions diagram inherited from Vitruvius (for instance, the human figure's navel divides the overall measure in proportion to the golden section) and also illustrated Luca Pacioli's 1509 book, a work principally devoted to the Golden Section.[26]

Over the centuries, many scholars have investigated the presence of the Golden Section in the ratios, growth patterns, rhythms and periodicity of both organic and inorganic nature.[27] The Golden Section also appears to be concealed within the harmonic overtones in geometrical constructions.[28]

Le Corbusier's Modulor series of dimensions is also based on the ratios of the Golden Section. Although Blomstedt greatly admired Le Corbusier and the proportionality of the Modulor system, in principle

309 Fra Luca Pacioli, the Renaissance mathematician and teacher of sacred geometry. Hans Kayser has noted that *the Golden Section, the Sectio aurea* or *Divina proportione*, first appears in Luca Pacioli's book.

310 Aulis Blomstedt: Multiplication table of numbers 2, 3, and 5 in a hexagonal grid. Colors indicate the numerical interaction of the three numbers. Undated.

311 Aulis Blomstedt: Modular variations of the 180 cm measure. Published in *Arkkitehti* in 1957.

the Finnish architect could never accept the Golden Section as the basis for a system of measures in architecture, due to its continuing relationship to irrational numbers. Blomstedt had little appreciation for the approximations of numbers in the Modulor and the difficulty of calculating with them in practical design work.[29]

Although he never studied the possible connections between harmonic proportions and the Golden Section, Blomstedt was familiar with the research into harmonic proportions by Alfred Neumann, Ezra D. Ehrenkranz, Matila Ghyka, and Yositika Utida,[30] based either on the Golden Section or Fibonacci's related series.[31] As well, Blomstedt's artist friend Sam Vanni, whose important *Contrapunctus* work adorns the architect's extension to the Helsinki Adult Education Center, has said that these ratios inform his work.

In fact, Blomstedt considered the Golden Section a 'forgery' of the Classical principle of harmony, because of its inexactitudes.[32] His rejection of the Golden Section was based on Hans Kayser's forcefully argued repudiation.[33] Kayser stated that it was unreasonable to assume that the aesthetic system of visual proportions could be based on the irrational Golden Section ratio (0.618…) and that of auditory proportions on precise rational ratios (the equivalents of the Golden Section, the triad 3:5: 8 or the minor sixth), especially when the real differences between the two ratios are so small that the eye cannot perceive them. The ear, on the other hand, differentiates the Golden Section ratios as discords.

Therefore, the triad 3:5:8, or minor sixth 5:8, are not "substitutes" for the Golden Section but the opposite; harmonic proportions are original and the Golden Section is an inexact "substitute" for consonant proportions. According to Kayser, even general efforts to interpret relations of phenomena from only one proportion are biased and primitive. In the theory of harmonic proportions, the minor sixth ec/5:8 (which is close to the Golden Section) only represents one interval, and music is not based only on sixths but on the use of all intervals.

Kayser noted that the Golden Section, the *Sectio aurea* or *Divina proportione*, only first appears in Luca Pacioli's 1509 book and that Alberti, for instance, makes no mention of it. Kayser uses the expression "the specter of the golden section" and believes that the fascinating name for these proportions is one reason for its continued popularity.

MODULE VARIATIONS ON THE 180 CENTIMETER MEASURE

Early on in Blomstedt's research the human height dimension of "module man" within his square stabilized at 180 centimeters (in certain earlier studies this measure had coincided with the module man's eye level).

1. The numbers of the triangle 75,
100, 125 in rapport with human
scale. According to Blomstedt's own
acknowledgement this illustration
was added to the Canon 60 scheme
at the suggestion of Reima Pietilä
to show its relation to the human
figure.
2. In the center is a right-angled
triangle 75, 100, 125 (3, 4, 5). On
either side is a smaller triangle,
composed of parts of the former. The
segments of the three triangles are
expressed by 10 different numbers.
3. The numbers of the triangles
on the left arranged in a pattern
according to their arithmetic properties, with indication of their musical
values provided the center digit 60 is
assumed as C.

In 1954, in *Arkkitehti: the Finnish Architectural Review*, Blomstedt described an industrial system originally devised for the Finnish Association of Architects' summer house competition in 1942 and then further developed between 1946 and 1948. At that time the system appeared extremely radical and far-reaching. In his article, he assumed that the series of numbers brought about by continuous bisections "would appear to have some of the criteria for a general series of meas-ures for architecture," suggesting, for instance, the progressive series: 1, 2, 4, 8, 16, 32, 64 centimeters, and so forth.[34]

In 1957, Blomstedt published the intermediate findings of his study *Module Variations on a 180 Centimeter Measure*, characterizing as a "private experiment for a module system."[35] The basic measure repre-sented by the height of a man was divided into 60 parts, because 60 was the lowest common denominator of the whole numbers that form the five main harmonic intervals (the octave 1:2, the fifth 2:3, fourth 3:4, major third 4:5, and minor third 5:6). In his brief description, Blomstedt recalls that during the Renaissance, proportions in architecture and music were considered adaptations of the same universal harmonies (he also makes the assumption that the adaptation of the metric system during the French Revolution led to the partial demise of traditional crafts). Due to its arithmetical basis, Blomstedt considered his module study related to Hans Kayser's harmonic researches and a rational development of Le Corbusier's Modulor.

CANON 60

Blomstedt's harmonic studies came to a conclusion around 1960 with the completion of Canon 60, a system of measures and proportions based on the number 60 harmonic division.[36] The number 60 had already frequently appeared in his earlier studies of numerical divisions, as well as in the module system based on the 180 centimeter measure.

Canon 60 is a system of measurement and proportion that fulfills, to an amazing degree, all the numerical subdivision, human scale, and musical harmonic requirements Blomstedt set out for a system of dimensioning in architecture. The set of ten numbers appears, however, to have been the almost accidental result of tireless experimentation. After more than a decade of continuous study, the result appeared so final to Blomstedt that he discontinued his work on measurement and harmonic proportions thereafter, even though in his 1962 exhibition he admitted with characteristic modesty that his experiments did not attempt to offer anything conclusive.

In his own practice Blomstedt had used the harmonic proportions of music and Canon 60 numbers long before he identified Canon 60 as

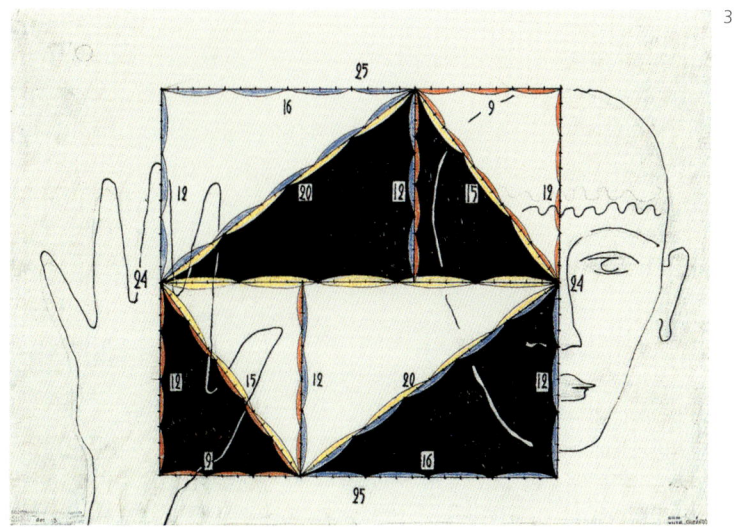

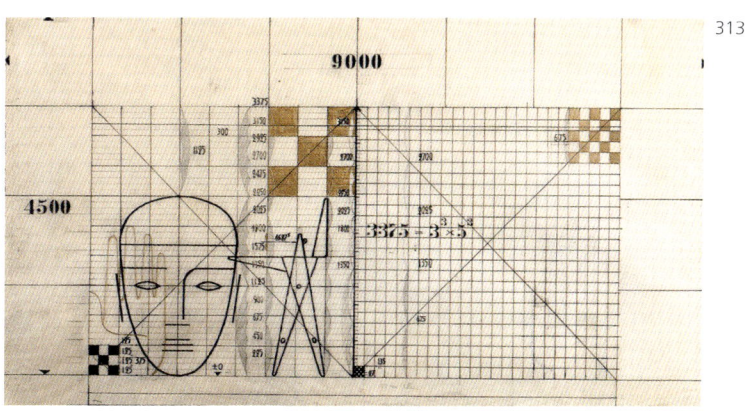

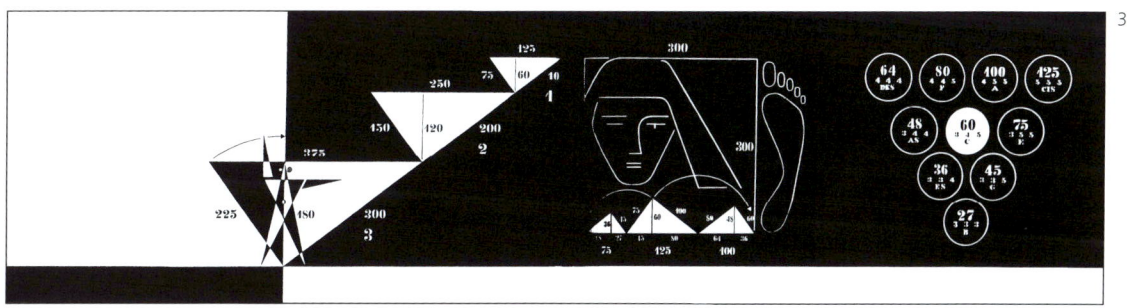

a formal system. His discovery of a system of harmonic proportions did not change the nature of a practice formed during the late 1940s and early 1950s. Canon 60 merely encapsulated the proportional aims of Blomstedt's post-war architecture and research into a complete entity.

THE CONSTRUCTION AND HARMONIC CONTENT OF CANON 60

The basis of Canon 60 is a simple arithmetic-geometric operation and its application to the human scale in the metric system.

For the basic module of Canon 60, Blomstedt chose the numbers 75, 100, and 125 millimeters, which he knew had been elsewhere suggested as the basic measures of a universal module system. To Blomstedt this was specifically a question of numbers which could provide in practice any metric content whatever—75 millimeters, 75 centimeters, 75 meters. In the Pythagorean right-angled triangle formed by these numbers, he drew a perpendicular against the hypotenuse and others in the small resultant triangles. The lengths of the ten segments thus created were all expressible in whole numbers.

These ten whole numbers Blomstedt placed in a triangular configuration, a construction the Pythagoreans had called the tetractus. The tetractus was the basic diagram of Pythagorean mystical numerology; all the numbers required to describe the world were assumed to be given by this numerology.

In Blomstedt's tetractus the number 60 is in the center of the triangle and the other nine numbers are logically arranged according to their prime factors. The ten numbers of the Canon are: 27, 36, 45, 48, 60, 64, 75, 80, 100, and 125; the numbers have their exact musical equivalents, and triple musical chords are contained within the nine symmetrical triangles in the tetractus diagram.

Canon 60 is thus a harmonic series, whose numbers can be given different metrical meanings. Nothing prevents the numbers from also being used as inches. Furthermore, the numbers can be divided and multiplied by whole numbers without disturbing their harmonic proportion, as it is a simple matter of moving from one octave to the next (e.g. 7 x 100 = 700 or 3 x 75 = 225, and so forth). The extra drawing included in the graphic representation of Canon 60 connects the number series with the 180 centimeter human height dimension and means the multiplication by three of the original series of numbers, or a two-octave transfer.

Due to this octave transfer, Blomstedt's harmonic system of numbers is highly flexible. For example, near the base number 60 it is possible to choose the numbers 62.5 (125/2) and 64, and near the number 120, the numbers 125 (5x25), 126 (7x18), 128 (2^7) and 117 (13x9). "The purpose of standardization cannot be the vulgarization of measure-

244

ments, but their systematization, and that's two quite different things," Blomstedt noted in his journal.

THE SYSTEMS OF MEASURES AND PROPORTIONS IN DESIGN WORK

To facilitate the choice of measures required in the design work in Blomstedt's office, a visual presentation of the multiplication tables of the small whole numbers was drawn up. Color was used to highlight the interaction of basic numbers. These aids for the office assistants thus contained "preharmonized" numbers, the use of which guaranteed an overall musical harmony.

During the preliminary stage of a project, a considerable amount of time was spent searching for a system that would suit all the measurable characteristics of the site and room program. Office assistants at this stage might well spend weeks on end plotting different harmonic grids on board or tracing paper, as the basis for the actual design work later on. For each specific design project, Blomstedt sought the basic measure, the "kernel," that lay behind the innumerable measurements in each task and would provide the basis for developing the dimensioning system. He created a specific "metrology" for each different project and whether the dimensioning concerned a golden ceremonial knife for Princess Takamatsu of Japan (1967), a building project, or a town planning scheme, the metrology was equally specific and important.

Only after discovering the specific system, a kind of upper chromatic scale, did Blomstedt attempt to solve the functional or technical aspects of the task.

For certain design jobs Blomstedt made a scale stick containing the harmonical measures extracted from the different factors that appeared in the particular design task. He also used a measuring rod that contained only harmonic measurements, which was to be used instead of the conventional unharmonic metric ruler.

THE APPLICATION OF CANON 60 IN DESIGN WORK

Throughout various projects, over twenty years, Blomstedt utilized the following basic numbers:

Block of flats, Turku, 1951	60
Terrace House, Tapiola, 1954	80
Concert hall, Oslo (competition entry), 1957	60
Block of flats, Tapiola, 1961	36
Terrace House, Tapiola, 1964	75
Parish Center, Helsinki (design), 1967	80
Pompidou Center, Paris (competition entry), 1971	27

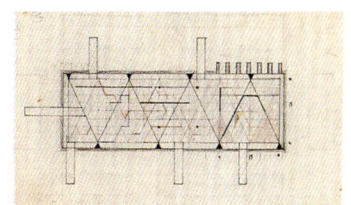
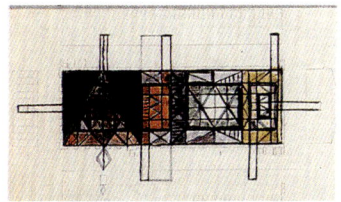

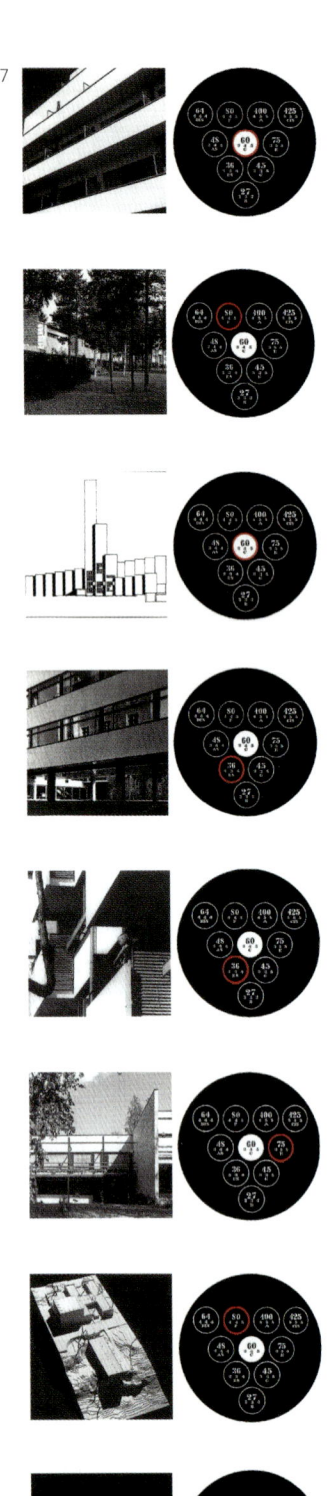

Here we can see that the numbers used as the bases for the dimensioning and harmonization of these designs are those included in the Canon 60, even before this harmonic system of numbers finally took shape.

The most extensive and complex of all of Aulis Blomstedt's completed designs is the extension to the City of Helsinki's Finnish-language Adult Education Center. The constricted area and difficult terrain of the site, Gunnar Taucher's original building from 1927, plus the rather complex room requirements, all combined to problematize the choice of a dimensioning system. The annex was ready in 1959—before Blomstedt had completed his research culminating in the creation of Canon 60. Even so, throughout this building the principles of musical harmony and the numbers of Canon 60 have been applied.[37]

The base number for the Center's extension is 36 and the chief module is 360 centimeters (10 x 36). All sides, according to Blomstedt, were formed from 360 centimeter sized "invisible cubes." Undoubtedly the chief module derives from the measurements of the old building, but it is also twice the size of Blomstedt's human scale module. The subdivision of the chief module is 90 centimeters (360 : 4 = 90) lengthwise, 72 centimeters (360 : 5 = 72) vertically and 60 centimeters (360 : 6 = 60) in width. Thus the module cube of the building subdivides into a 4 x 5 x 6 = 120 right-angled prism—this is the 'kernel'—the sides of which are 90, 72, and 60 centimeters.

When even smaller measurements are required, the basic ones can be further subdivided by two—a change of one octave in musical terms—at which point the measurements become 45, 36, and 30 centimeters. The variation in module measurements on the different coordinates is connected to the relativity of the original Greek concept of the module; in other words, a module is building and situation-related and is not a regularly divided, non-hierarchical grid spreading in all directions, as in its technologically accentuated use today.

Blomstedt considered that the vertical and horizontal measurements possessed different significances, the former being ten times more sensitive in design work; that is, when one meter was the significant horizontal measure, the equivalent exactitude in the vertical direction was, perhaps, ten centimeters.

"The choice of module implies the fixing of the scale," as Blomstedt noted in his journal.

THE MUSICAL SIGNIFICANCE OF THE DIMENSIONS OF THE ADULT EDUCATION CENTER

The 60, 72, and 90 basic measurements of the x, y and z co-ordinates of the building are in harmonic proportion to each other, i.e., 10:12:15.

The ratio of the numbers is one of the Pythagorean divisions (arithmetical b - a = c - b, geometrical a : b = b : c, and harmonical b - a : a = c - b : e), which are central to the Renaissance theory of ratios and which Palladio, for example, recommended as the ratio for the height, width and length of room spaces.

The 'kernel' ratios of the Center building can be musically interpreted such that the ratio of width to length (10:15 = 2:3) forms a fifth, width to height (10 : 12 = 5 : 6) the minor third, and height to length (12 : 15 = 4 : 5) the major third.

The more important outer and inner spatial ratios are easily revealed as whole numbers and their equivalent musical consonances. Harmonic ratios also appear in the division of the façades. The height of the lower part of the façade of the long building mass is configured by the consecutive numbers 72, 108, 180, and 288, which constitute the beginning of the Fibonacci Series (2 : 3 : 5 : 8), even though Blomstedt did not otherwise associate the principle of harmonies with the Golden Section.

HARMONICS AND THE INDUSTRIALIZATION OF BUILDING

Aulis Blomstedt developed his architectural dimensioning system from the Classical principles of harmonics prior to the widespread application of industrial methods to building in the 1960s. Throughout the preceding decade, he had tested the validity of his system of harmonics in his own architectural practice. Due to their healthy modesty and finely proportioned beauty, many of his buildings belong to the more responsible tradition of our new architecture.

In spite of the publication of Canon 60, and after having surpassed the world record in the percentage of industrialized building, the Finnish building industry standardized without the philosophical and harmonic objectives that Blomstedt considered so essential. The 3M module grid used extensively in industrialized building in the 1960s was a standardization achieved without any appreciation of history or sense of beauty, whose sole consideration was the rationalization of production. But the brutal standardization was also the outcome of a tragic amnesia in the 2500-year-old tradition of harmonic proportions, a tradition whose purpose was to link man to his built world, to creation, and the universe.

Aulis Blomstedt's words, written in 1971, are as germane today as in the early years of industrialized construction:

It is probably superfluous to say that the Classical requirement of proportional beauty has been completely removed from our present

317 Examples of Aulis Blomstedt's application of his Canon 60 on various architectural projects. For each project the modular base number is indicated by a red circle in the Canon 60 number pattern. Blomstedt conceived the Canon 60 around 1960, but the examples show that his use of the harmonic division had already earlier led him to use numbers of his later Canon.

1. Blocks of flats, Turku, 1951.
2. "Chain"-houses, Tapiola, 1954.
3. Concert Hall, competition project, Oslo, 1957.
4. Workers' Institute, annex, Helsinki, 1959.
5. Blocks of flats, Tapiola, 1961.
6. Terrace houses, Tapiola, 1964.
7. Parish center, competition project, Helsinki, 1967.
8. Beaubourg Center, competition project, Paris, 1971.

318 Aulis Blomstedt: Golden ceremonial knife for Princess Takamatsu of Japan for the symbolic cutting of a silk ribbon at the inauguration of an exhibition of Finnish architecture in Tokyo in 1967. According to Blomstedt´s own account the dimensions are based on a harmonic division of the ancient Egyptian Royal Cubit.

idea of the module. It is my opinion that it should be returned to present-day architecture. We have already suffered enough from the visual pollution that a constant stream of system building has forced upon our landscape ... In itself, system building is an integral, positive feature of industrialism. We are living through its infancy, and I am convinced that the situation will improve once we start to give the matter sufficient attention.[38]

318

ARCHITECTURE AND THE REALITY OF CULTURE

The Feasibility of Architecture in a Post-Modern Society

(1987)

PROLOGUE: ARCHITECTURE AND PHILOSOPHY

In a fictitious dialogue with Siegfried Giedion (to which Socrates also contributes a comment), published in *Arkkitehti: The Finnish Architectural Review* in 1958, Alvar Aalto canonized the pragmatic, anti-theoretical attitude prevalent among Finnish architects. "God created paper for architecture to be drawn on. Everything else is—at least for me—a misuse of paper. *Torheit* (Madness), as Zarathustra would say," Aalto says to his friend Giedion.[1]

Such arguments, hostile to theory and speculation, can be heard and read in the profession even today. Fortunately for us, Aalto did not always practice what he preached in his last years—many creative people are thus split into two mutually exclusive personalities—and wrote an exceptional amount of significant material that can be defined as architectural philosophy. I do not wish to claim that a consciously fabricated theoretical-philosophical framework is essential for the creation of architecture or to ensure its quality. Actually, I see conceptual dissection and creative action in architecture as two complete opposites. Analysis demands a certain psychological distance from the object, whereas eliminating this very distance, that is, identifying with the object, is vital for artistic synthesis. An architect who attempts to both design and write about design has to develop a sort of dual personality for himself. Without this dualism, his intellectual appraisal will prematurely arrest the vulnerable, emotionally motivated design process. Although creation does not, therefore, proceed from philosophy, all that has been said and written forms a foundation for the consciousness from which creative conceptualization springs. For example, my conception of city planning changed forever after hearing an aphorism expressed by Sverre Fehn at a symposium in Venice: "A city planner should also think of the shoe waiting to be purchased in the shoe shop window."[2] This startling image of a personified object completely revolutionized my view of a city.

Henry Moore, one of the greatest sculptors of this century, advised the artist not to speak of his art too often, as this releases the tensions vital for his work. However, Moore made a significant addendum, which also crystallizes the value of philosophical scrutiny in architecture: "The artist works with a concentration of his whole personality, and the conscious part of it resolves conflicts, organizes memories, and prevents him from trying to walk in two directions at the same time."[3]

In Aalto's fictitious dialogue, he presents a prognosis of architecture as he foresaw it in the 1950s: "The horoscope of architecture today is one in which the words are negative—it does not make nice reading." I, too, intend to read the horoscope of late 20th century architecture from my own cultural and philosophical point of view. The picture I present of our time will probably not please everyone, but it coincides with the pronouncements of many cultural philosophers; thus, I am not alone in the drifting sands of speculation. For those who perhaps recognize themes from previous articles of mine in this one, I can say in defense that most of us have but one thing to say in life—we are continually building a house in our own image.

A BREAK IN CULTURE, A CHANGE IN CONSCIOUSNESS

In the past few decades, the standard conceptions of Modern architecture have had a rough time.

The technological optimism of the Modern Movement has been transmuted into an indifference about building technology or even into an anti-technology stance. Whereas the Modern Movement obsessively avoided symmetry, ornament, Classical motifs, and allusive references in general, these vices have unexpectedly returned to the pages of current architectural journals. The flowing spatial continuum of Modern architecture has halted and sub-divided itself once more into compartments. Motion is replaced by stasis; weightlessness by gravity and earth.

What is the meaning of this sudden about-face in the last fifteen years?

The schism occurring now speaks clearly above all of the twilight of industrial Utopia and the transformation of architecture's innocent idealism into disillusioned doubt or straightforward cynicism. After optimistically representing industrial man's Utopia for a full century, technology has been suddenly transfigured into the manifestation of all the negative and destructive characteristics of cultural development. Technology is no longer a liberator, but the herald of an impending holocaust. Industrialized building has become for many a reflection of spiritual frustration, betrayal, and hostility.

But the change goes even deeper than that: within twenty years we have reached a new level of consciousness that has imperceptibly but drastically changed our values. This change of consciousness is also changing our concepts of time and history, our ideas about knowledge and morals and, fundamentally, our self-image. The new art and architecture are the clearest expressions of these changes.

POST-MODERN CULTURE

Many labels have been attached to the new cultural phase in which we live: the consumer society, the media society, the information society, post-industrial or high-tech society, and the society of affluence. Architectural debate has talked of 'Post-Modernism' *ad nauseam*. What is interesting, however, is to note that many cultural philosophers—Habermas, Jameson, Eco, and Skolimowski, to name a few—have come to their conclusions by examining changes in architecture. All the labels mentioned above describe something of our age, but none of them is inclusive. The term 'Post-Modern' seems aggravatingly manipulative—as if the world were attempting to influence the course of history—and moreover, the concept is debatable. Habermas, for instance, speaks of "the unfinished project of Modernism."

Thus, although our new age does not yet have a name, we can already distinguish some of its characteristics. The phase we have moved into is characterized by a new consciousness that is imperceptibly displacing our earlier view of the world and with it our way of experiencing things. This new consciousness, this new reality of life, is disillusioned and without idols, atomized and fragmented, disruptive of values and ethical principles, devoid of history and stylistic coherence, and generally a random collage of consciousness and life horizons. Fredric Jameson offers the following definitions about our age: political and aesthetic populism, materialism and the fetishism of products, the collapse of temporality and the colonization of the present, the ebbing of affections, the splintering of subject, and the end of unique, personal style.[4] Jean-Francois Lyotard, on the other hand, uses the concept 'laxing' in speaking of the present,[5] and Jurgen Habermas speaks of "the new insummarizability" (*die neue Unübersichtlichkeit*, a disappearance of horizon).[6]

Jameson divides the development of recent history into three periods: Realism, Modernism, and Post-Modernism. Benjamin and

Adorno, for instance, identify the beginning of Modernism with the poet Baudelaire, but for Habermas (as with many historians of modern architecture, such as Joseph Rykwert) the 'project of Modernism' begins a century earlier.[7] The shift from Modernism into a new phase is seen to have begun in the late 1950s. According to Jameson, the three periods of culture correspond to the three periods of capitalism described by Ernest Mandel in his book *Late Capitalism: Market Capitalism and Multinational Capital*. Many see the dominant status of multinational capital as the prime reason for the phenomena of our age.[8]

The Post-Modern phase is a kind of "imperialism of lifestyle" which works its way everywhere.[9] Therefore, we architects should cease puzzling over and frowning on the products of Post-Modernism and turn our attention to the more productive analysis of the reasons behind the phenomenon. Art—including architecture—is inseparably bound to its cultural background, and we have to live in this Post-Modern cultural reality whether we like it or not, whatever we choose to call it. The Modernists' belief that architecture could be separated from its cultural context and resurrected as society's savior has, during this century, proven to be unfounded idealism.

THE TESTIMONY OF A PAIR OF SHOES

In his article "Postmodernism, or the Cultural Logic of Late Capitalism," Fredric Jameson demonstrates the difference between the Modern and Post-Modern cultural consciousness by juxtaposing two paintings.[10] As I have already used one shoe metaphor in a previous essay, I may be allowed to expand on the theme using Jameson's comparison. He uses a Vincent van Gogh painting of a farmer's old pair of shoes as an example of Modern consciousness; the Post-Modern is represented by Andy Warhol's painting *Diamond Dust Shoes*. Typically, a Modernist work of art represents something larger, broader and more idealistic than itself. Realism required the subject to fill the whole canvas, but in Modernism even the fragment, the part, or the montage was invested with the ability to tell the whole story.

Van Gogh's pair of shoes turns into an epic before our very eyes, the legend of a Dutch farmer. This insignificant footwear represents an entire way of life, reflected in the worn-out shoes. In his essay "The Origin of the Work of Art," Martin Heidegger provides an excellent analysis of the effect of van Gogh's painting. Heidegger eloquently and touchingly writes:

From the dark opening of the worn insides of the shoes the toilsome tread of the worker stares forth. In the stiffly rugged heaviness of

THE EPIC OF SHOES

320 Vincent van Gogh, *Still life with shoes*, 1886. Amsterdam, Rijksmuseum Vincent van Gogh, Fondation Vincent van Gogh.
321 Andy Warhol, *Diamond Dust Shoes*, 1980. Private collection.

320

321

the shoes there is the accumulated tenacity of her slow trudge through the far-spreading and ever-uniform furrows of the field swept by raw wind. On the leather lie the dampness and richness of the soil. Under the soles slides the loneliness of the field-path as evening falls. In the shoes vibrates the silent call of the earth, its quiet gift of the ripening grain and its unexplained self-refusal in the fallow desolation of the wintry field. This equipment is pervaded by uncomplaining worry as to the certainty of bread, the wordless joy of having once more withstood want, the trembling before the impending childbed and shivering at the surrounding menace of death.[11]

When we turn to Andy Warhol's Post-Modern shoes, we are startled to find the image deflated into a mere image, a fetish. The picture no longer has a message; it no longer represents an association of experiences. It has lost its depth and resonance, its human message. The image has fallen flat and been converted into an item on the art market. However, the whole point of Warhol's Post-Modern art is materialism and the fetishism of products. In his paintings even people have become goods, transformed into their own images, their own trademarks. We can no longer see inside the sign and the symbol; we cannot feel the living breath of the picture.

While the Modernist picture exuded a capacity for sympathy and sharing, the Post-Modern picture conveys an impression of narcissistic self-centeredness and the death of empathy.

I wish to add a third pair of shoes to Jameson's shoe simile. The Late Modern shoes of the Czech-born Jiří Kolář, covered with the shreds of old banknotes, are a purely poetic image, a nostalgic and melancholy reference to a lost world. Whereas van Gogh's early Modernist shoe vivifies the present, Kolář's shoe provokes simultaneously pleasant and poignant emotions from the past. This third shoe operates with cultural memory and carries with it the entire spiritual depth of the Central European cultural heritage. It is vibrant with subtle emotional fluctuations and delicate sensuality, whereas Warhol's shoe is frozen to death and disconnected from reality. These shoes exist at the very center of the cultural change we now witness. I may well say now that in my view these last shoes represent a positive chance for art in our Post-Modern age. But I will now proceed from shoes to architecture.

THE DEATH OF ARCHITECTURE

Victor Hugo appended an enigmatic paragraph to the eighth edition of *Notre Dame de Paris* entitled "*ceci tuera cela* (this will kill that)," pronouncing the death sentence of architecture: "In the 15th century the human mind thought up a way to immortalize itself that is more durable and resistant, simpler and easier than architecture. After the stone letters of Orpheus come the lead letters of Gutenberg."[12]

Hugo further examines this thought, which he placed in the mouth of the Archdeacon of Notre Dame: "The statement revealed a premonition that in changing shape the human idea would also change its form of expression, that the leading idea of each generation would be no longer recorded with the same substance and in the same form, that the firm and lasting book of stone would give way to an even firmer and more lasting printed book."[13]

Although Hugo's prophecy has been quoted time and again, its meaning for the course of history has not, I think, been correctly interpreted. Hugo's prediction that architecture would lose its status to newer media as the most important cultural medium has undoubtedly come true. But the new media have not ousted architecture because of their greater strength and durability, as Hugo said, but for exactly the opposite reasons: because they are fast, fleeting, and dispensable. When even styles have become articles of consumption in a consumer society, architecture has proved to be a hopelessly cumbersome medium among these disposable mass media. The fundamental meaning of architecture is integration and stability, and these qualities are in open conflict with the ideology of consumption; the strategy of consumerism requires ephemerality, alienation, and the splintering of consciousness. A coherent view of the world would reveal the insanity of obsessive consumption.

In all areas of communication and artistic expression, our culture favors the quick, the forceful, and the overwhelming rather than the slow, low-efficiency communication of architecture. In all forms of artistic expression, nuances and subtleties have been brushed aside by an increasing force of effect. Even within architecture, a commercially oriented image effect, a sort of image shock, has gained popularity in the competition for the attention of the citizens of 'Plentiville.' Today's architecture is increasingly the product of conscious commercialism, sensationalism and image formation, "the tendency to let image determine form rather than vice versa."[14] In our culture of advertisement, architecture is itself imperceptibly taking on the function of an advertisement. But when image effect supercedes artistic quality and cultural symbolism, anything with image value can be used. Images of decadence and decline are notoriously popular today … the favorite assignments at architectural schools around the world have recently been crematoriums and cemeteries. This interest reveals, apart from the weakening of affections, our culture's fascination with death.

Until now, architecture was an art-form devoid of humor. There is, in fact, an evident conflict between the permanence of architecture and the transient and situation-bound character of humor. The demand that architecture should be fun and humorous shows the warped conception of reality and art prevalent today. Surely it would not occur to us to accuse Michelangelo's architecture, for instance, of lack of humor. The way that Post-Modernism calculatingly exploits the values of fashion and styles previously practically unknown in architecture, such as humor, parody, irony, and satire, has to be interpreted as an attempt on the part of architecture to dramatize its language of expression in order to regain its status in the public consciousness.

Before long, the architectural avant-garde of Plentiville will no doubt unveil buildings that have totally forsaken the prime function of a building to act as protection for man and his institutions, becoming instead instruments of torture, threat, and termination. Our sensationalist culture will probably even produce buildings designed to collapse and crush. The ritualized cruelty of comic books and music videos is a premonition of this possibility.

REALITY AND DREAM—THE EMPTY IMAGE

In a society dedicated to the mass manipulation of the human mind, reality and dream have become interchangeable. As Umberto Eco has assumed, the hyper-reality we have created, with its forgeries of time and history, will become the new standard of reality.[15] Consequently, the creative mind must reconquer the real, authentic world, and the creative artist's task undergoes a strange inversion: it has changed from broadening the realm of the imagination, the possibilities of being human, to defining and confirming our standing in reality. Here I see the crucial ethical task for art and architecture in the cultural phase which has now begun: art must be a fortress shielding the individual's uniqueness and authenticity of experience in a culture that is rapidly becoming a worldwide waxworks show.

The artificial reality characteristic of our culture is, according to Plato's definition, a simulacrum: an authentic copy of an original that has never existed. Instead of creating tension—that is, dialogue— between past and present, our present is devouring the past. We have lost our ability to "speak with the dead," the ability T. S. Eliot regards as the nucleus of a living tradition.[16] Our environment now changes into an ahistorical portrait of itself, precisely similar to Warhol's dancing shoes. The new hyper-reality is symptomatic of our inability to dream. Even if the much-abused Modern architecture has not necessarily lost its communication capacity, perhaps we have become incapable of projecting meanings into it. A Disneyworld world is the refuge of a culture that has lost its capacity for spontaneous dreaming and imagination. The seemingly perfect illusion of hyper-reality has in fact lost its plasticity, its depth, its three-dimensionality. Hyper-realism is the mirror of a culture that has lost its sense of depth.

In his hilarious essay "What are you doing after the orgy?," Jean Baudrillard describes a hyper-realist exhibition at the Pompidou Center thus:

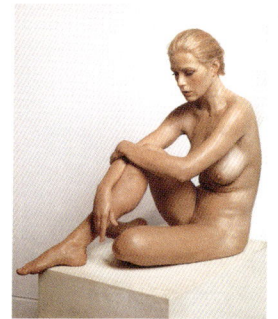

322

> There they are, statues, not exactly sculptures, more like dummies, completely realistic, flesh-colored, absolutely naked and in a position that is neither provocative nor pornographic; unequivocal, banal … People's reactions were interesting: they bent forward to see something, the grain of the skin, the pubic hair, everything, but there was nothing to see. Some of them even wanted to touch the bodies, to test their reality, but of course that did not work because everything was already there. Not even the eye was deceived. If the eye is deceived, then your judgment has to try and guess how it was deceived, and when no one is seeking to deceive you, there is always a kind of guesswork in the aesthetic and tangible pleasure that a form arouses in you. They bent themselves nearer to discover the amazing fact: an image where there is nothing to see. The obscenity lies in the fact that there is nothing to see.[17]

323

I have on many occasions been equally bewildered by the products of hyper-realistic architecture—shopping centers, hotel foyers, restaurant decors—and come to the same conclusion: their obscenity is that there is nothing to see. Have you ever tried to concentrate on listening to Muzak? It is distressing because there is nothing to hear.

In the same essay, Baudrillard brings up another characteristic of image culture. He shrewdly observes that today we prefer looking at the photograph of a detail of a painting rather than the painting itself. Similarly, we would much rather examine the photograph of a detail of the building than the building itself. The image has become a fetish. Similarly, anyone can find himself in a foreign country looking at architectural sights or landscapes as pictures that have lost their plasticity and uniqueness, as if they were on a page of a glossy magazine or in a travel film on television. Our reality is very nearly hermetically sealed and lined with reproduced images.

The seeming richness of ideas and innovation in commercialized architecture should not mislead us: instead of stimulating independent and spontaneous images, this architecture offers a conditioned and

REALISM BEYOND REALITY

322 John de Andrea, *Seated Blond Figure with Crossed Arms*, 1982. Collection of the Virlaine Foundation, New Orleans.

323 Duane Hansson, *Hard hat, construction worker*, 1970. Private collection.

superficial ersatz. The bays and protrusions, arches and contours, cornices and corners of today's architecture no longer delineate the world; they are merely autonomous images pasted together with florid cosmological explanations extolling the intelligence of the borrowings.

The emergence of disposable architecture in restaurant and shop decors is a manifestation of the accelerating consumption of architecture. Disposable architecture exploits the fashionable. Based on the idea of immediate satisfaction and almost as immediate disposal, such architecture enables a quick shift to the next cycle of image consumption. Built-in obsolescence, then, is even a characteristic of architectural style today. The consumer culture will turn architecture into harmless environmental Muzak and promote the dreamlike and nonchalant consumption of man's existence.

USURPING USABILITY

In 'Necessityville,' the artistic expression of buildings and things usually stemmed from the utility of the artifact, but in Plentiville, architecture and artifacts are isolated from their functions and changed into signs, autonomic social fetishes whose real utility has become an imaginary cultural currency. "All values turn into sign values, and they are thus indifferently interchangeable," Baudrillard has said.[18]

A culture obsessed with production has to transfer that production to the allegorical and imaginary when the market for real needs or shortages is saturated. This is the very foundation of the aesthetics of capitalism's last phase. The aesthetic production of Post-Modernism coincides exactly with goods production, as Jameson has said. The transformation of clothing from wearable and protective garments into pure *objects d'art* with none of the original function left, or much contemporary design, which foregoes the ergonomic demands of the object, are examples of this eroding functionality. In fact, the image value of today's design objects is frequently based on a questioning or a parody of functionality. Post-Modern culture is therefore deliberately undermining Functionalist ideology.

I wish to point out that I do not underestimate the artistic value of new textile art, for instance. Nor do I offer value judgments on Warhol's work, but rather of the view of the world behind it. I am attempting to demonstrate with these examples the shift from functional value to symbolic or sign value that is so crucial to the development of the consumer society, and consequently the separation of functional art from its traditional utilitarian basis. It so happens that the same development is irrevocably occurring in architecture, too.

THE SECOND REALITY DISAPPEARS

Our culture has become "one-dimensional" exactly as predicted by Herbert Marcuse and Erich Fromm. Guardianville tries to remove all conflict and tension, and in doing so flattens our existence into harmless consumption—we become consumers of our own lives.

Herbert Marcuse has suggested that the mind of an industrial person becomes one-dimensional when the 'second reality' and the tension between the ideal world and the real, everyday world disappear.[19] Our culture identifies the world of ideals and the everyday, and thus nullifies the function of art as a mediator between the two. In this materialistic and secular culture, art is harnessed to producing alternative secular realities, rather than to stirring a consciousness of a metaphysical dimension superceding the everyday. In *One Dimensional Man*, Marcuse writes: "Today's novel feature is the flattening out of the antagonism between culture and social reality through the obliteration of the oppositional, alien, and transcendent elements in the higher culture by virtue of which it constituted *another dimension* of reality. This liquidation of *two-dimensional* culture takes place not through the denial and rejection of the 'cultural values,' but through their wholesale incorporation into the established order, through their reproduction and display on a massive scale (italics by Marcuse)."[20]

This disappearance of hierarchy, the equalization of everything—the sacred and the secular, the here and the hereafter, and the equality and interchangeability of the spiritual and the material—drains architecture of its message. Architecture becomes visually witty, but spiritually or existentially empty. Our buildings will suffer the fate of all logical clauses according to Wittgenstein: they will all say the same thing—nothing. Now that God is dead, as the Polish-American eco-philosopher Henryk Skolimowski has said, we must remake the world in our image.[21] The question is: what is man's image in the next millennium?

THE DISAPPEARANCE OF IDEALS

Early Modern buildings affect us because they stem from an ideal, a Utopia. Hope is the patron saint of architecture, as I have said many times. But the innocent optimism and ideals of those early pioneers is lost to us. Our buildings can only be astonishing or virtuoso, witty or dramatic, but without the ideal dimension they rarely affect the soul.

A few comparisons continue my dialogue of the shoes. Le Corbusier's drawing of his *jardin suspendue* project speaks touchingly of a new form of life, new ideals, and human relations. This architecture has plasticity and empathy; it is architecture meant for life.

324 Le Corbusier, Jardin suspendue, project, 1928–29. Architecture designed for real situations of life.
325 Peter Eisenman, House IV (Frank House), Cornwall, Connecticut, 1972–73. Architecture as a formal exercise devoid of life.

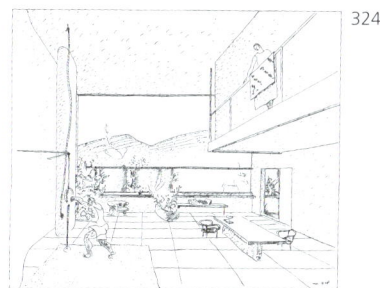

324

325

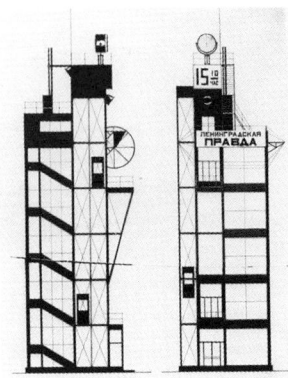

326

327

Richard Meier's Douglas House (1971–73) in Harbor Springs, Michigan, which follows Le Corbusier stylistically, strangely lacks the feeling of life. I do not mean simply that there are no people in the photograph, but that the architecture is so artful that it makes old Corbu seem like an amateur, but still the design lacks content.[22] Here, architecture has become a cultural sign, an artful but empty image.

In my second comparison, the Leningradskaya Pravda tower by the Vesnin brothers exudes an optimism and faith in the future; it offers technology as an object for innocent wonder and a promise of a better tomorrow, but also subjugated to the poetry of the architecture.

Norman Foster's Hong Kong and Shanghai Bank and the Lloyd's building by Richard Rogers in London are triumphs of high-tech architecture. Here, however, technology has gotten out of hand and become self-centered juggling tricks and artful structural utility out of touch with life. Utopia and faith, innocence and idealism have been lost; such buildings stand icily in their one-dimensional 'now.'

The spiritual message of architecture and architectural quality do not grow out of a perfect mastery of the functional, technical and economic requirements of a commission. Born of the same spiritual dimension traversing the everyday as poetry and music, painting and drama, architecture is always something more than the tangible building. The task of architecture is not to beautify or 'humanize' the world of everyday fact, but to open a view into the second dimension of our consciousness, the reality of dreams, images and memories.

A lack of ideals also precludes radicalism. If no social Utopia is visible or imaginable, there are no grounds for revolution. Aimless discontent and angst lead to absurd and nihilist acts—this is one of the causes of terrorism.

"Everything in our time seems to embody its own opposite...It seems the achievements of art are bought at the expense of loss of moral quality," wrote Karl Marx in 1856.[23] In its time this statement indicated a conservative view of the arts, but its perspective seems to have been vindicated 130 years later.

THE EUTROPHICATION OF CULTURE

In Plentiville, the central problem is *muchness*: too much of everything is produced, both material and cultural. When everything becomes sexual, political, and social, when categories become subject to cancerous overgrowth and sprawl everywhere, they also lose their significance. The result is a slump into inactivity, indecision, and insanity, as Baudrillard's grim prophecy has it.[24] "Culture permeates all of social reality, and eventually everything becomes culture," is Jameson's opinion.[25] This overgrowth, this eutrophication of culture and overproduction, will produce a kind of spiritual anoxia, a cultural Sargasso Sea.

The broadening of the cultural field *ad absurdum* creates a new set of moral values for art. In an over-productive society, art should not make more but make less. After the Post-Modern bacchanal, the time has again come for neo-minimalism, neo-asceticism, neo-denial and sublime poverty. Quality, the dimension of spiritual depth, is reinstated as the only criterion of art.

There is no doubt that the disappearance of the spiritual quality of architecture from our environment is due to the disappearance of the collective intellectual 'soil' that produces architecture. Consequently, this makes the society of welfare, plenty, and guardianship a very dubious patron of architecture.

The growth of the consumer society—hardly able anymore to conceal its quasi-democratic character—raises serious questions about the function of architecture, the validity of social convention as a goal for design and, ultimately, the survival of architecture in the society to come.

What will the architecture of the ultimate consumer society look like? The answer is inevitable: there is no architecture. When architecture disassociates itself from its metaphysical and existential basis, it becomes entertainment, amusement, and architectural Muzak. The architecture that brought the existential questions of life into our consciousness will be replaced by a way of building that, paradoxical to its own nature, buries all significant questions under the paralyzing poultice of comfort and pleasure. This form of culture will construct a universal old folks' home.

There are signs of a split in our profession: on the one hand, there is design that executes consumer conventions and commands without protests, and on the other hand, there is a serious architecture whose function, following the essence of art, is to fathom the fundamental essence of our existence. This division of a whole field of art into an entertainment branch catering to cultural consumption on the one hand, and a branch offering serious art on the other has already taken place in music, literature, and film.

Many young architects have drawn their conclusions: in a consumer society, architecture can exist only by resigning its social brief and withdrawing into the world of autonomous art and cultural anarchy. Serious architecture is approaching cultural anarchy in consumer society, acting against the social norms instead of reinforcing them.

Frank Gehry's eloquent buildings, for instance, have a generous helping of anarchy—they lash out at the blunted materialism of high-living standards and the dictatorship of money. Where a Warhol painting genuflects to money, Gehry's house thumbs its nose or, rather, shows its arse, to the financial god of our time.

In a society devoted to efficiency and lacking the spiritual dimension of life, authentic architecture is severed from its utilitarian foundation. To preserve its spiritual dimension, architecture must come into conflict with its own essence, which is tied to social reality. Ergo, to ensure its existence, architecture must deny itself.

The major aesthetic question today is not "What is beautiful?" but "What is art?," as Thierry de Duve has so appropriately said.[26] The development of our culture has brought the ethical content of art into the spotlight again. In this regard, the respected Finnish philosopher Georg Henrik von Wright has adopted an anarchistic view in his field. Quoting Nietzsche, von Wright states that when the basic values of culture weaken and become false, the task of a philosopher is to "philosophize with a sledgehammer." "A philosopher must preach a kind of anarchy as the prerequisite of a healthy society," says von Wright.[27]

EPILOGUE

This might seem a very pessimistic view of the future. The amount of pessimism, however, is in direct proportion to one's expectations. I hope that architects could perceive our cultural reality as clearly as possible so that we can define the territory and ethical basis of our art. The dream of world improvement dating from the fervent early days of the Modern Movement must today be replaced with a more realistic view. I call this view 'the strategy of cultural resistance.' The task of creative culture remains to struggle against the mainstream of prevailing convention—since otherwise it would not be creative at all—and once we see which way the stream is flowing we will know how architecture must orient itself. Considering the views I have presented, one logically and ethically motivated orientation is to further explore 'Modernism's unfinished project.'

In conclusion, I would like to freely quote Frank Gehry in an interview with *Arkkitehti* in May, 1986: "I remember when I was younger," Gehry mused, "I was also optimistic... When you get older you become very cynical sometimes... but younger people say: 'Don't worry, pa, we'll take care of it.'"[28]

TRADITION AND MODERNITY

The Feasibility of Regional Architecture in
Post-Modern Society
(1988)

TECHNO-UTOPIA AND IDENTITY

The Modern Movement enthusiastically aspired to create a universal culture. The new "machines for living in," set in "space, light and greenery," were to emancipate their inhabitants from their bonds with the past, and to cultivate a New Universal Man.[1]

Half a century later, however, the techno-rationally biased and economy-obsessed buildings that have become only too familiar everywhere impair our sense of locality and identity. Today's standardized building accelerates estrangement and alienation, instead of integrating our world-view and sense of self. Simply, we have lost our faith in Utopia.

Meanwhile, we have learned to admire unique and authentic forms of indigenous and vernacular traditions that were earlier hardly considered part of the realm of architecture. We admire the tangible integration of natural and material conditions, patterns of life and forms of building in traditional societies, and this gives us a strengthened sense of causality and existence.

The diversity of building in traditional societies is brought about by the influence of local conditions and the specificity of culture. In our own culture, the sheer force of industrial technology, combined with mobility, mass-communication, and uniformity of life-style, is causing a cultural entropy that minimalizes diversity. What is the feasibility of regional culture and architecture in a world in which two billion people simultaneously gather around television sets to watch the same football match? Are we not gradually becoming detached from our foothold in geographic and cultural soil? Are we not coming to inhabit a fictitious and fabricated culture, "the culture of simulacra," of which Umberto Eco has written?[2] Are we not moving towards a worldwide consumerist folklore, a mosaic of impressions and information detached from their origin? Is our culture doomed to lose its authenticity and become instead a planetary waxworks show?

DIVERSIFICATION VERSUS UNIFICATION

The gradual disappearance of a sense of locality and of human message from our buildings is doubtless the result of cultural factors underlying the act of building—the values and ways of thinking and acting that govern our civilization.

Is it possible to alter the course of our culture? Is the resuscitation of regional architecture in post-industrial and Post-Modern society feasible? Indeed, can authentic architecture exist at all in the materialism in which we live?

Clearly a universally standardized and abstracted environment cannot support our identity and mental well-being. Cultural anthropology has revealed that we do not live in separate physical and mental worlds. The two realms are entirely fused and consequently, the organization of our physical world is a projection of the mental one and vice versa.

An architecture capable of supporting our identity must be situationally, culturally, and symbolically articulated. I am disturbed by the notion of regionalism because of its geographic and ethnological connotations and would rather speak of situational or culture-specific architecture.

The fundamental question of architecture is existential: how does a human being experience his or her existence in this world? The task of architecture is to make us experience our existence with deeper significance and purpose; architecture assists us to know and remember our identity. In the words of Aldo van Eyck: "Architecture need do no more, nor should it ever do less, than assist man's homecoming."[3]

THE CONSTITUENTS OF LOCALITY

What constitutes a sense of specific locality? The constituent elements are, of course, reflections of natural, physical, and social realities. They are expressions and experiences of specific nature, geography, landscape, local materials, skills, and cultural patterns. However, the qualities of culturally adapted architecture are not detached; they are inseparably integrated into tradition. Without the continuity of an authentic tradition, even a well-intentioned use of surface elements of a regional character is doomed to sentimental scenography, to be a naively shallow architectural souvenir.

Culture is not composed of elements that can be disassembled and re-composed; culture has to be lived. Cultures mature and sedi-

329

330

DISAPPEARANCE OF SITUATIONAL CHARACTER

329 Huvilakatu (Villa Street), Helsinki. A street front composed by predominantly lesser known designers in the early 1900s.
330 Apartment blocks, Gladsaxe, 1960s, Denmark.

ment slowly as they became fused into the context and continuity of tradition. Culture is an entity of facts and beliefs, history and the present, material realities and mental conditions. Culture proceeds unconsciously and cannot be manipulated from the outside. Hence, an authentic, culturally differentiated architecture can only be born from differentiated patterns of culture, not from fashionable ideals in design. Do such conditions really exist in our time?

The profound Mexican architecture of Luis Barragán, for instance, echoes distinct deep-structure features of Mexican culture and life—particularly the presence of death as an accepted dimension of life—and turns these cultural ingredients simultaneously into a unique metaphysical and surreal art, one traditional and individual, timeless and radical.

The architecture of Alvaro Siza is an abstraction and condensation of the social and building traditions of Oporto. His architecture is abstracted to the degree that one can hardly identify this tradition but its presence is felt in the authoritative quality of his work.

The regionalist architecture of the Hungarian Imre Makovecz is more explicitly generated from images of Hungarian mythology and folklore. There is a feeling of cultural scenography in Makovecz' work that suggests archaic rites; one expects people to appear on the scene dressed in medieval tunics.

Regional identity, it seems, is possible today only on the fringes of culture that have not yet been conquered by consumer society.

THE HIDDEN DIMENSIONS OF CULTURE

As structural anthropology has taught us, the relations of man, artifacts and culture are very complex. The difficulties of rationally conceiving these relations arise mainly because their decisive interaction takes place on an unconscious bio-cultural level. The anthropologist Edward T. Hall, whose books on unconscious and culturally conditioned uses of space are invaluable to an architect, has brilliantly observed these hidden dimensions. To deny these differences is now pure ignorance; this knowledge of the cultural conditioning of our behavior in space and place is rapidly increasing. Recent studies on the spatial geometry concealed in language, for instance, demonstrate that even language conditions man's spatial behavior in a way specific to that particular language.[4]

The psycho-linguistic studies of Professor Frode Strømnes, the Norwegian-born Finn, have revealed astonishing differences in the spatial imagery and the use of space between Finnish and Swedish speaking people, for instance; these differences are no doubt reflected in Finnish and Swedish architecture.[5] What constitutes Swedishness or Finnishness in architecture is difficult to analyze, yet the difference can be perceived at a glance. Language itself can be used to generate architecture. In addition to his morphological studies of Finnish landscapes, Reima Pietilä has deliberately attempted to project the rhythms, complexities, and topological nature of Finnish language through his architecture.

We Finns tend to organize space topologically, on the basis of an amorphous 'forest geometry,' as opposed to the 'town geometry' that guides European thinking. The geometry of the forest is most clearly expressed in Alvar Aalto's work, evidenced especially in the elaborate use of the forest imagery and metaphor at the Villa Mairea and the 1939 New York World's Fair Pavilion. This kind of distinctive assumption is not at all surprising given Hall's observations on the radial pattern of spatial thinking among the French or the gridded spatial thinking of the Americans.

Certain deep-structure properties specific to a local culture vigorously resist change. For instance, the tone of speech characteristic to a region has been observed to persist through many successive generations even after a family has moved from the region. The persistence of a gestural and body language characteristic of a given culture is equally astonishing. One could identify a French or an Italian by his gesturing, or an American by his way of walking, or recognize an American in the European context by his higher level of voice.

The body and its muscle system are strongly connected with cultural identity. An authentic building tradition evidently must be related to such unconscious factors. Mud-building traditions, in West Africa for instance, seem more related to man's tactile sense than to the visual sense. Culturally there is nowadays a disturbing tendency to develop away from the tactile towards the visual. Yet we always return to the tactile mode in certain emotional states, for instance in caressing those dear to us.

Consequently, a culturally adapted architecture is not merely a matter of visual style, but of the integration of culture, behavior, and environment. To deny cultural differentiation is foolish, but equally, a culturally-specific character or style cannot be consciously learned and layered onto the surface of design. A culturally-specific design is a result of profound subjection within a specific pattern of culture, and of the creative synthesis fusing conscious intentions, unconscious conditioning, memories, and experiences, in a dialogue between the individual and the collective.

All artists elaborate their self-image in their art, and a differentiated building tradition supports the collective self-image of an entire

331 Cohesion of local oral culture.
332 Two billion people may watch a
world championship game in soccer.

331

332

culture. This even applies to the apparently traditionless architecture of the United States—in 'the Strip' architecture, for instance.

INDIVIDUAL AND TRADITION

The creative artist's relation to history is equally complex. Authentic artists are usually more concerned with a general feeling for time and history than any factual history or its products. In his 1919 essay "Tradition and the Individual Talent," T. S. Eliot perceptively describes this "historical sense" and a poet's position in the challenge of tradition:

> Tradition is a matter of much wider significance. It cannot be inherited, and if you want it you must obtain it by great labor. It involves, in the first place, the historical sense … and the historical sense involves a perception, not only of the pastness of the past, but of its presence; the historical sense compels a man to write not merely with his own generation in his bones, but with a feeling that the whole of the literature … has a simultaneous existence and composes a simultaneous order. This historical sense, which is a sense of the timeless as well as of the temporal and of the timeless and of the temporal together, is what makes a writer traditional and it is at the same time what makes a writer most acutely conscious of his place in time, of his own contemporaneity.
>
> No poet, no artist of any art, has his complete meaning alone. His significance, his appreciation is the appreciation of his relation to the dead poets and artists. You cannot value him alone; you must set him, for contrast and comparison, among the dead.[6]

Today's fashionable attempts to recreate a sense of place and rootedness in history through the application of historical and regional motifs usually fail, due to the one-dimensional, literal use of reference and a superficial manipulation of the motifs.

Instead of being born from an integrity of cultural forces—"the inner necessity," as Kandinsky named it—the historicism of today is a form of intellectual manipulation. Culture is taken as an objectified, external, and given reality that can be consciously applied and expressed in design. The past is taken as a source from which to select instead of being the continuum and context of creative work. Instead of being accepted as an autonomous process, culture has become an object of deliberate fabrication.

The present concern with regionalism has the evident danger of becoming a sentimental provincialism, whereas the vital works of art in our specialized culture are always born from an open confrontation

TRADITION IN MODERNITY

333 Luis Barragán, San Cristobal Ranch, Mexico City, 1967–68.
334 Imre Macovecz, Visegrad camping site, Hungary, 1978.

between the universal and the unique, the individual and the collective, the traditional and the revolutionary.

Eliot identifies such mental provincialism in his essay "What is a Classic": "...a provincialism, not of space, but of time: one for which history is merely the chronicle of human devices which have served their turn and been scrapped, one for which the world is the property solely of the living, a property in which the dead hold no shares."[7]

ALVAR AALTO'S REGIONALIST STRATEGIES

The most outspoken advocate of situationally adapted Modern architecture in the Nordic countries, as well as within the Modern Movement as a whole was, of course, Alvar Aalto.

After his brief enthusiasm for the mainstream dictates of the Modern Movement and its universalist ideals, Aalto emphatically expressed his suspicion of universal and techno-utopian ideology. In Aalto's thinking, the task of architecture was to mediate between man and technology and to support man's social and cultural integration.

Aalto's designs possess an inexplicable sense of rootedness and Finnishness. His architecture works to activate certain deep responses in the observer; bio-morphisms suggest subconscious associations with the organic world and layered compositions give an impression of environments formed by tradition and history. Aalto's imagery activates subconscious associations: metaphorically condensed images of town and landscape, for instance, reminiscent of medieval paintings. In one of his early essays—presumably an introduction to a planned book which never progressed beyond the initial essay—Aalto praises Andrea Mantegna's painting *Christ in the Vineyard* as a magnificent representation of "an architectural vision of the setting" and as a "synthetic landscape."[8] The desire to create a 'synthetic landscape' seems to have persisted in his own work throughout his life, and it clearly contributes to the adaptive character of his architecture. Aalto synthesized not only the Finnish landscape in his architecture but also the Finnish temperament.

In his compositions Aalto tended to understate significant compositional elements, such as the entrance, and guided one's attention elsewhere. This understatement is reminiscent of Pieter Brueghel's paintings in which the mythical event is hidden in the middle of everyday life. There is a relaxed vernacular feeling to Aalto's work, an air of invitation and curiosity, rather than an attempt to impose authority and silence participation.

Aalto's architecture is connected with a general sense of time and place, rather than with any specific style or place. His work simultaneously hints at archaic history, antiquity, vernacular Mediterranean building, and anonymous Finnish peasant tradition. His work did not aim at the absoluteness typical of the Modern Movement's main line. As a result, Aalto could use motifs of history and vernacular tradition, combined with a Modern language, and create architecture remarkably rooted in place and time.

Vernacular style is usually an unorthodox mixture of influences and motifs that have lost much of their original meaning and intactness. In a similar manner, Aalto used the Modernist vocabulary in shamelessly unorthodox combinations with romantic, historicist and folk motifs. But Aalto's motifs are not borrowed; they are re-creations and merely hint at a possible origin elsewhere. The use of vernacular motifs gives Aalto's buildings a relaxed and unpretentious atmosphere and certainly has facilitated public acceptance of his designs. His furniture designs, equally accepted by the general public, represent some of the very few examples of a Modern vernacular. The innumerable variations and modifications by other designers of Aalto's design work are a clear indication of the acceptance of his design in this way.

An interaction between the self-conscious high style of the academic discipline of architecture and an unself-conscious vernacular application is an essential aspect of the evolution of architectural form. A style becomes socially significant as it generates a tradition of anonymous application. One of the shortcomings of the Modern Movement at large has been its inability to produce a positive vernacular.

Culturally adapted architecture reverberates with tradition, fusing and reflecting the timeless vernacular idiom; consequently, an authentic culture-specific architecture cannot be invented. It has to rediscover and revitalize aspects of tradition, by either the explicit characteristics of style or, more convincingly, by the hidden dimensions of culture.

UNITING OPPOSITES

The architectures of Alvar Aalto and Luis Barragán reveal that the culture-specific character of architecture is not a matter of a simple manipulation of recognizable elements. Cultural isolationism and protectionism do not offer any guarantee of unique architecture.

Regional character may be achieved—and usually is achieved—from totally contradictory ingredients. Frank Lloyd Wright's American architecture synthesized themes from North American and Mexican Indian cultures, and from European architectural history as well as traditional Japanese architecture. The overall impact of traditional Japanese art on twentieth-century Western aesthetic ideals is a more general example of the incredibly composite nature of culture. On the other hand, Le Corbusier's architecture, so strongly influenced by the Mediterranean vernacular tradition, has given rise to one of the strongest contemporary traditions in Japan and India. This influence in turn is again reflected back into Europe and other parts of the world through the work of Tadao Ando, Charles Correa, and many others. The journey of Louis Kahn's architecture, from his native Estonian island of Saarenmaa, via Philadelphia and elsewhere in the United States, and then ultimately to Bangladesh (where his geometric architecture has created a strong school) is equally astonishing. The most outspoken regionalist group in Finland today, the northern Oulu School, has been most strongly influenced by Charles Moore, whereas today's vibrant Estonian avant-garde is a curious fusion of Russian Constructivism and American Post-Modernism, an artistic marriage of Leonidov and Michael Graves.

A colleague recently made a comment that regional architecture today looks the same in all parts of the world. Yet all great art tends to be regional, for the simple reason that it is open to interpretation and consequently can echo any cultural conditions. All great art is the common property and heritage of mankind.

But these crusades of inspirations and impulses in the development of culturally adapted architecture are not just products of our communication age. Peasant churches in Finland, usually considered to be genuine products of an indigenous tradition, are clearly echoes of continental high styles. Similarly, the architectural identity of the Grand Duchy of autonomous Finland was created in the Neo-Hellenic spirit, which was, of course, totally alien for the underdeveloped forestland of the time. The Finnish National Romanticism of the turn of the century, which deliberately aimed to create a national style and overtly sought its inspiration from indigenous mythology and tradition, was in fact closer to contemporary examples in Germany and Scotland, or even to work on the other side of the Atlantic in the American Midwest. The Nordic Classicism of the 1920s found its inspiration in the Classical vernacular of northern Italy. Half a century later the universal ideals of the International Style became a humane and somewhat romantic version of post-war Modernism in the Nordic countries.

One of the most convincing achievements of Western architecture in a foreign cultural context is Henning Larsen's Saudi Arabian Foreign Ministry in Riyadh, a building which clearly shows the Nordic sensibility towards cultural assimilation. This building is an exceptionally successful example of architectural diplomacy. Psychologists speak of the 'situational personality,' referring to the fact that the behavior of a single individual varies more under different environmental conditions than

335 Le Corbusier, Maison Cook,
    Boulogne-sur-Seine, 1926.
336 Frank O. Gehry, House in Santa
    Monica, California, 1978.

the behavior of different individuals under the same circumstances. We should perhaps credit a designer's exceptional cultural adaptability to a particularly adaptable situational personality.

One more note in this overlay of regionalisms: in 1921, as Eliel Saarinen drew the prototype of the American skyscraper, the Chicago Tribune Tower, in the woods of southern Finland, his painter friend Gallen-Kallela, the greatest painter of the period of National Romanticism in Finland, began his own illustrations of the Greater Kalevala, the Finnish folk epic, in Chicago. "…(O)nly in the desert of Chicago did the work [the Kalevala illustrations] burst into a miraculous bloom," wrote the painter's daughter.[9]

CONSTITUENTS OF STYLE

Architecture is not an expression of knowledge and certainty, but of existence and faith; it is a perpetual search for reconciliation.

An architectural style is defined, both on individual and collective levels, by a combination of certain mental orientations. Stylistic evolution seems to move like a pendulum as priorities shift from one polarity to the other. A series of opposite notions begin to exemplify the range of orientations:

universal	situational
collective	individual
standardized	unique
conscious	subconscious
future-oriented	history-oriented
idealistic	realistic
structure-oriented	form-oriented
rational	emotional
absolutist	relativist
theoretical, orthodox	pragmatic
exclusive	inclusive

The first column of the listed orientations clustered together in the main stream of International Style, whereas the second set of orientations have characterized Nordic architecture through the century. Today there seems to be a rather general shift towards the latter orientations, away from the mental constructions of the International Style. Consequently, a culture-specific attitude is gaining strength universally and a renewed interest in Nordic architecture is foreseeable in the near future.

Without wanting to expand the vague terminology of architectural debate, I would argue that Modern architecture has progressed to a new phase during the past two decades. I would like to speak of a 'First' and a 'Second' Modernism. This implies a change in external stylistic features, but above all, a shift in mental factors and a new understanding of culture.

Milan Kundera's thought-provoking book, *The Art of the Novel*, declares that Modernism has transformed into kitsch: "The aesthetics of mass media are by necessity the aesthetics of kitsch; as the mass media gradually extend and penetrate into every aspect of our life, kitsch becomes our everyday aesthetics and morality. Only some time ago Modernism implied a non-conformist rebellion against received thought and kitsch. Nowadays Modernity blends into the immense vitality of mass media and to be Modern means a fierce attempt to keep up with time and adapt, to be even more adaptive than the most adaptive. Modernity has pulled the robe of kitsch on its shoulders."[10]

Kundera's severe verdict is undeniable, but only the Modernist dialectical relation to history, culture, and society can re-emancipate architecture from kitsch. I am convinced that the new Modernism now taking shape is again shaking the robe of kitsch off its shoulders.

THE TWO MODERNISMS

The First Modern architecture was a utopian, idealistic, purist and demagogic movement, which drew its artistic strength from an innocent faith in a future to be brought about by new architecture and art. A fighting movement with momentum and a polemical dynamic, this First Modern architecture believed in the possibility of cultural expansion and radical change—change that could quickly lead to a humane, healthy, and sane world.

The Second Modern architecture is premised on a realistic view of culture unblinded by illusions. Having lost any innocent faith in an immediate victory of humanism, its potential is merely as a strategy of cultural resistance, in slowing down undesirable and inhumane development. Instead of dreaming of an emancipated world, this Second Modern architecture aspires to set individual examples of cultural will and resistance.

Stylistic change has been equally multi-faceted. The First Modern architecture aspired to immaterial and weightless dynamism, whereas the Second frequently expresses gravity and stability, and a sense of materiality and earth. The return of earth and gravity as expressive means of architecture has more than metaphoric meaning; after its arrogant and overly-ambitious Utopian journey, architecture has returned to the safety of Mother Earth, back to the source of rebirth and creativity.

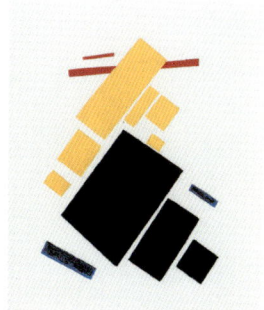

337

338

WEIGHTLESSNESS AND EARTH

337 Kasimir Malevich, Suprematist composition, *Aeroplane flying*, 1914.
338 Robert Smithson, *Spiral Jetty*, Rozel Point, Great Salt Lake, Utah, April 1970. DIA Center for the Arts, New York.

In its aspiration for pure plastic expression, the First Modernism avoided symbolism, allusion, and metaphor, qualities that have become essential parts of the expression of the Second. As the first phase aimed at an impression of timelessness, the new Modernism now seeks an experience of time through material, memory, and metaphor. The First Modernism admired perfection and finiteness, while incompleteness, process, and imperfection are part of the new expression. The First Modernism aimed at perpetual innovation, the Second consciously uses stylistic borrowings. However, the contemporary use of quotation takes place in two directions in history, giving the past a new meaning, as opposed to the one-directional appropriation tactics of eclecticism. Such eclectic art always possesses an air of necrophilia—because of its inability to resurrect the dead.

MOTIVES OF CHANGE

The motivating forces behind this shift are to be found in the alterations in consciousness that have taken place during the past two decades, alterations more radical than most of us are willing to accept. The emergence of the Third World, the energy crisis, the university revolutions, and the development of mass-communication and information technology are all part of the mosaic of change alongside the Post-Modern debate. An awareness of the dangers implied by extreme technological development, and a disappointment with the achievements of Western democracy, also underlies the Second Modernism.

This transformation of Modernism did not happen at once. Even in its early phases, expressionist, organic and regionalist tendencies existed within the Modern Movement. The momentum of the First Modernism began to expire in the 1950s; the emerging change was revealed in the CIAM discussions of the decade. Louis Kahn and Aldo van Eyck appeared as the most outspoken heralds of change in architecture: Kahn restored architecture's archaic and metaphysical dimensions and van Eyck introduced an anthropological and structuralist view.

My view of the continuity of Modern architecture is based on a more explanatory and hopeful dialectics of evolution than the popular conception of a bankrupt design culture. Fundamentally, I see Modernism as a dialectical view of culture that perpetually challenges and re-integrates the past.

THE NEW TRADITION

The touching and optimistic vitality of the early Modern Movement arose from its origins at the point of confrontation between tradition and reform. Modern architecture lost its spiritual depth through a succession of generations who accepted the style as a ready-made aesthetic, neglecting both its cultural background and the necessary continuity of tradition.

The interdependence of architecture and culture has not been sufficiently recognized. Today's international consumerist architectural journalism violently detaches buildings from their cultural context and presents them in an arena of individual architectural showmanship.

The Second Modern architecture must relearn a way of seeing architecture as part of a cultural tradition, at the same time as it analyzes its timeless essence. Significantly, the creators of First Modernism were themselves artists or collaborated closely with artists. The spiritual withering of Modern architecture can be associated with the post-war generations, who, through prevailing educational practice and shallow professionalism, alienated themselves from the fine arts. The renewed architecture of today again seeks inspiration from the fertile ground of the arts.

POPULISM

The assumed failure of the mythical hero-architect has given rise to a form of populism in design, and a reverence for consensus, or popular taste, as the sole authority of design. This view denies the essential dynamism of cultural development, the dialogue and opposition between the creative individual and popular convention.

I have previously referred to Umberto Eco's belief that significant literature can only result from a writer who constructs an ideal reader.[11] Only an architect who mentally constructs an ideal client, and ultimately an ideal society as he designs, can create memorable architecture. This view does not imply empty Utopianism or a belief in a messianic mission for architecture. Touching art is simply born from the reality of hope and idealization, from a belief in a better future. The art of architecture turns into the production of commodities for the consumer society when it loses its poetic and metaphysical content and sees as its sole duty the mere fulfillment of popular desire. "To caress a cat to death," is the wise warning of a Polish proverb.

Architecture, as with all art, is simultaneously autonomous and culture-bound: culture-bound in the sense that tradition, the cultural context, provides the basis for individual creativity, and autonomous in the sense that an authentic artistic expression is never an answer to prescribed expectation or definition. The fundamental existential mystery stands at the core of architecture and the confrontation with this mystery is always unique and autonomous, totally independent of the specifications of the 'social commission.' A church and a cellulose factory do not differ at all as commissions for an architect.

343

344

The human task of architecture is neither to beautify nor to humanize the world of everyday facts, but rather to open up a view into the deeper dimensions of our consciousness, the second reality of images, memories, and dreams.

QUASI-INTELLECTUALIZATION

In today's neurotic architectural climate, the intellectual construction supporting a design often seems to be more important and more central than a sensory and emotional encounter with the architectural work. This fierce quasi-theorizing and intellectualization only accelerates architecture's alienation and separation from social reality, instead of supporting the integration of architecture and culture, artifact and mankind.

A number of architects today seem to attempt to be more clever and more wise than their work. Milan Kundera speaks of "the wisdom of the novel" and states that all authentic writers listen to this supra-individual wisdom: all great novels are always more intelligent than their authors. Writers who are more intelligent than their works ought to change their profession, says Kundera.[12] In my view, Kundera's argument also holds in our profession—there is, as well, "the wisdom of architecture."

I believe that there is a "natural philosophy of architecture" that ties together theory, practice, and experience. I believe that such a natural philosophy is the silent message of the Nordic tradition. Is there a shared Nordic consciousness that could have given rise to a shared Nordic tradition in architecture?

Particular geographic, climatic, as well as political and cultural circumstances, have all certainly molded an identifiable Nordic mentality regardless of national differences. Nordic culture is a combination of agrarian and small-town world-views sharing a distinct sense of scale, and an appreciation of understatement and smallness, compared to the desire for monumentality and grandeur in many other cultures.

The Nordic mentality is characterized by a strong sense of causality and contextuality, combined with a rather pragmatic and non-doctrinaire attitude to life. This is united with a strong sense of social cohesion and solidarity based on a shared cultural and social horizon.

Common, as well, is the avoidance of polarization, both in thinking and in the social scene. Consequently, it has been characteristic of Nordic architecture that extreme or purist attitudes have generally been avoided. Architecture has developed as a process of gradual assimilation that has fused influences and inspirations from various sources. Juha Leiviskä's contemporary work is an example of this sensibility:

OBJECTS OF NECESSITY AND OF ABUNDANCE—THE SIGNIFICANCE OF CONSTRAINTS

345 Finnish peasant chair, late nineteenth century.
346 Post-modern furniture. Alchimia, Cupboard from the "Mobile infinito" project, 1981.

the assimilation of De Stijl planar aesthetics, a Gustavian Rococo delicacy, the rich articulation of light of the Bavarian Baroque, and an Aaltoesque modern imagery are all to be found in his architecture. Kristian Gullichsen's recent church in Kauniainen is another example of this assimilation, fusing motifs from Finnish Medieval churches, direct quotes from Le Corbusier (the entrance structure is from page 123 of Le Corbusier and Jeanneret, *Oeuvre compléte 1910–1921*, according to the author), a Danish sense of scale and, again, Aalto's sense of materials.

The fusion of the polarities of Romanticism and rationality is a specific characteristic of Nordic art and culture. This, I think, is the essence of *Northern Light* and *Dreams of the Summer Night*, to paraphrase the titles of two recent international exhibitions on turn-of-the-century Nordic painting. This sensible *petit-bourgeois* attitude is well illustrated in the idyllic scenes of Carl Larsson.

An innate sensitivity to nature, with mystical and pantheistic overtones, and the impact of a peasant background has further softened didactic intellectual aspirations. A rational and constructive tradition has been surprisingly strong in Finnish visual arts. The ideal of simplicity and asceticism related to peasant life seems to motivate Nordic Constructivism and Purism more than Cartesian ideals.

Nordic architecture and everyday aesthetics have developed remarkably organically, from ageless peasant traditions through various Classicist phases and then Functionalism to the present day. The transformation of Nordic Classicism in the 1920s to Functionalism, for instance, is a rare example of a decisive cultural transformation without confrontation. Although there is an overt conflict between Classicist and Modernist ideals, the shift in the Nordic countries was surprisingly smooth. The aesthetic asceticism and spirituality of Nordic Classicism paved the way for Modernism. The ideals of social empathy and responsibility, so characteristic of Nordic architecture, were already planted during the era of Nordic Classicism.

The most significant feature of Nordic architecture, however, is the integration of architecture and society. The degree to which the philosophy and aesthetics of Modernism have become part of the Nordic social reality is unique. Modernism is the self-evident architectural condition of the Nordic democracies and it is impossible to imagine a wider eclectic or historicist revival in Nordic culture.

In our obsessively consumerist culture, gradually detaching objects and buildings from their use value, converting everything into marketable signs, the traditional Nordic morality, restraint, and asceticism acquire a wider cultural value. In a culture steering into a Sargasso Sea of too many goods, too much information, too many ideologies, too

347 Kristian Gullichsen, Kauniainen Church, Espoo, 1983. The entrance structure is deliberately derived from a design by Le Corbusier.

348 Juha Leiviskä, Myyrmäki Church, Vantaa, 1984. The design echoes De Stijl aesthetics.

347

348

much of everything, the ideal and aesthetics of a 'noble poverty' have a new moral value. As our materialist culture hysterically produces new marketable images and transforms even crime, violence, and decadence into profit, the Nordic tradition represents a philosophy of common sense and a poetry of the commonplace.

Regionalism in the industrial world can no longer be founded on a set of isolated and perfectly integrated conditions. Perhaps the most meaningful form of cultural survival that remains is a regionalism of the mind, a strategy of resistance, a quiet, tough, specific culture that believes in and searches for authenticity, not authenticity on ethnographic grounds, but on the foundation of human experience and interaction.

The mission of Nordic architecture lies in the continuous development of the tradition of socially concerned, responsive, and assimilative Modernism.

THE LIMITS OF ARCHITECTURE

Toward an Architecture of Silence
(1990)

IS THE STAGE-LIKE HISTORICISM OF
TODAY'S ARCHITECTURE AN OMEN OF
THE END OF REAL HISTORY?

350 Charles W. Moore, Piazza d'Italia,
New Orleans, Louisiana, 1974–78.
351 Ricardo Bofill and Taller de
Arquitectura, Les Espaces d'Abraxas,
Marne-la-Vallee, near Paris, 1978–82.

"May he live in an interesting period," was an oft-quoted hex used among the ancient Chinese.[1]

Without doubt, our entire generation has fallen under this ancient Chinese curse. The old world changes so quickly, startlingly, and radically that the true avant-garde of today's culture seems to appear on the political stage instead of the artistic one. But alongside these apparently dynamic and optimistic development prospects there are other images: the American Francis Fukuyama, for example, claims that we are now living at "the end of history."[2]

The idea of the end of history is by no means Fukuyama's alone, however, for Karl Marx himself believed that the interplay of material and economic forces would culminate with the establishment of a Communist Utopia. Yet Marx, too, borrowed from Hegel the concept of history as a dialectical process with a beginning, a middle, and an end. Hegel proclaimed history to have concluded in 1806 with the victory at the Battle of Jena of the ideals of the French Revolution–and the attendant birth of the universal homogenous state.

Thus the process of history has received almost two centuries of extra time.

By "the end of history," Fukuyama means the culmination of the great historical narrative, the battle of ideologies, and its replacement by a kind of historical vacuum, a continuous present experienced through uniform, worldwide liberalism. Fukuyama's sobering estimate of the post-historical condition struggles for a means of optimism: "The end of history will be a very sad time. The struggle for recognition, the willingness to risk one's life for a purely abstract goal, the worldwide ideological struggle that called forth daring, courage, imagination, and idealism, will be replaced by economic calculation, the endless solving of technical problems, of environmental concerns, and the satisfaction of sophisticated consumer demands. In the post-historical period there will be neither art nor philosophy, just the perpetual caretaking of the museum of human history…Perhaps this very prospect of centuries of boredom at the end of history will serve to get history started once again."[3]

Architecture, as well, has been thought to develop according to the logic of a progressive narrative, but perhaps the great story of architecture, too, is coming to an end. Shall we henceforth know only random mutations? With the declaration of "the end of history" are we perhaps also coming to "the end of architecture"? Does the fragmentation and lifeless eclecticism of present-day architecture signal the proximity of the end of history? Does the universal disenchantment with technology and reason, and with the related architectural styles, indicate the conclusion of the dialectical process in culture? Or does the polymorphology of today's architectural flora presage its cultivation in another more fertile ground of creativity?

TOWARDS A NEW MIDDLE AGES

The contemporary articulation of history's end is supported by certain Italian writings beginning in the 1960s, advancing the idea that our culture is drifting towards a new Middle Ages.

Roberto Vacca's Neo-medievalist perspective, for example, forecasts the inevitable disintegration of the great systems of our technological era. Too extensive and complex to be coordinated by central authorities or even the more efficient corporate-based managerial systems, these infrastructures are doomed to extinction and will cause the retardation of the whole of industrial civilization.[4] Based on this view, Vacca has created an apocalyptic vision of the future, a new Middle Ages, similar to the apocalypse and salvation writings of the Finn Pentti Linkola.

Umberto Eco offers an interesting extension to this theme, from the perspective of both a medievalist and an analyst of such curious contemporary phenomena as the semiotics of Disneyland and waxwork museums.[5] To Eco, nothing is closer to medieval intellectualism than contemporary structuralist logic, logical formalism, or the modern sciences of physics and mathematics. "What is required to make a good Middle Ages?" he asks. "First of all, a great peace that is breaking down, a great international power that has unified the world in language, customs, ideologies, religions, art, and technology, and then at a certain point, thanks to its own ungovernable complexity, collapses.

MEDIEVAL IMAGES

352 A medieval war machine.
353 Morphosis, Kate Mantilini Restaurant, Beverly Hills, Los Angeles, 1987.

It collapses because the 'barbarians' are pressing at its borders; these barbarians are not necessarily uncultivated, but they are bringing new customs, new views of the world."[6]

Is the present breakdown of the Soviet Communist empire simply Eco's predicted attack of the barbarians beyond the gates? Are we perhaps living on the threshold of a new Great Migration and an intermingling of cultures?

Although my subject here is not to discuss the history of culture, permit me to introduce Eco's views of the similarity between art in the Middle Ages and art in our own time. Both periods, for example, have tried to eradicate the gap between the educated and the common people, particularly through visual methods of communication. "Cathedrals in the Middle Ages were great books of stone, posters, screens, mystical cartoons, whose function was to explain all to the people...," Eco writes.[7] "Briefly speaking," he continues, "modern Western man matured (in the Middle Ages), and here the example of the Middle Ages may be of benefit to us if we wish to understand what is happening in our day and age..."[8]

THE NEW ALCHEMY

I am not academically qualified to develop further the theme of the medievalization of our culture, other than to add to Eco's views my own observation of a form of new alchemy within artistic and architectural circles. The alchemy appears as an endeavor to discover the philosopher's stone, sometimes in old, sometimes in new, fields of knowledge, to breathe life into material, to bestow the halo of sanctity on the banal, trivial, worthless, and rejected. Many recent architectural projects and writings express an intention to return, or even depict an actual return, to medieval mystery and superstition. Objects and houses in our day have been restored to life after being given the kiss of death by positivist thinking.

Surprisingly, the designs of the architectural avant-garde of today often appear as metaphorical mechanical devices devoid of any purpose. At the same time as these devices represent a defensive return to the natural world of the senses, away from the electronic unfeelingness of our age, they also express a fascination for medievalism.

A secret interest in medieval thinking and art has been apparent in many architectural schools in recent years. In building the 'architectural reading machine' (based on a medieval reading device), one of three 'machines' which won the Gold Lion at the 1985 Venice Biennial, Daniel Libeskind's students dressed, lived, and worked as medieval monks.

A TIME OF FREEDOM AND FRUSTRATION

I have addressed these ideas of "the end of history," and a "new Middle Ages," as a prologue to my stated themes of the relationship between current architecture and reality. Alongside the crumbling of walls and the integration of Europe, perhaps even more profound transformations are taking place; I hope my observations are both suggestive and relevant.

Architecture, similar to the other arts, is a product of the conflict of pressures in cultural reality and the inherent struggle for autonomy in art. Art simultaneously reflects reality and initiates changes in consciousness: it is both cause and consequence. "Reality is the opposite of the obvious," writes Viktor von Weizsäcker.[9] There is nothing axiomatic or revealed about 'reality'; it is thematicized and made perceptible in a significant way by art. The close intermingling of reality and art makes its analysis so difficult.

We live simultaneously in a time of frustration and a time of freedom, a time of frustration for those who believe that the Old Order can still reassemble the fragments of our world outlook, a time of freedom for those who see in the surging mosaic of our consciousness—as yet unfocussed—a new, more exciting, more dynamic, and altogether higher system, the possibility of a system born out of chaos. Many recent architectural projects express a clear transition from the classical Euclidean geometries and forms to the aesthetics of the laws of chaos and chance.

THE END OF UTOPIA

Above all, today's architecture expresses the end of the Great Utopia. The struggle to bring a clear and progressive order to the world has failed. The great world outlook, so near to assembly, has been shattered into fragments whose origins are no longer recognizable.

With the scrapping of Utopia, our culture has perhaps finally lost its innocence. A culture that has lost its innocence is, however, no longer capable of curiosity, of the joy of invention and discovery, or of the ecstasy of idealism, because the knowledge of the limits to knowledge has secularized our thinking. The time of the great discoveries is over; even the exploration of space has become a routine *(editor's note: recent tragedies have, however, brought the programs to a temporary halt)*. With the end to the age of real inventions, all that remains is to counterfeit new forms. Ideology, idealism, and enlightenment have been replaced by cynicism, narcissism, and the transient, a thirst to achieve lasting reputation through a fleeting moment of glory.

When all serious efforts to improve the world have failed, life transforms into a collection of diversions and pastimes. If matters can

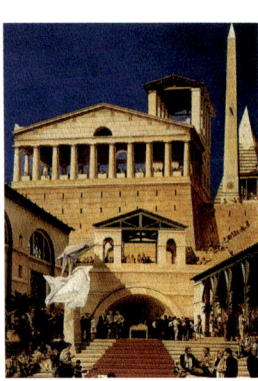

no longer be controlled or understood, it is not even necessary to try. As Fredric Jameson pessimistically notes, to the Post-Modernist, truth simply does not exist. [10]

Today's architecture expresses this superficiality and lack of belief. Architecture is just one game among many, lacking existential seriousness, that "inner necessity" required of art by Kandinsky.

THE POSSIBILITY OF UTOPIA AND AVANT-GARDE

The central question in our culture is: is Utopia possible? To my way of thinking, the end of the era of the great narratives has also rendered the Utopian story impossible. In Jameson's opinion, the disappearance of this Utopianism also means the disappearance of dignity, of sincere alternatives in life. Utopia has been replaced by science fiction, the scientific fairy tale, in which it is not necessary to believe, let alone sacrifice one's life for its fulfillment. In an age without Utopian basis, only apocalyptic anti-Utopias appear possible and, in fact, these are now cultivated in all fields of art.

The impossibility of Utopia promotes the question of the possibility of an avant-garde. Can the avant-garde of our time achieve sufficient distance and resistance in its relationship with convention before succumbing to the all-approving and salutary embrace of a media-consumer culture? Will the motto of the Futurists—"Down with the moon!"—remain but a phrase on the lips of artist-actors playing their avant-gardist roles? Will art ever again be able to upset the applecart of our everyday emotions, or is it, even at its most radical, mere titillation? Will art ever again be able to add something genuine to the hyperbole of everyday reality flooding into our consciousness from the media?

THE SOCIAL CONTENT OF ARCHITECTURE

Modern architecture received its lyrical quality from its social content and optimism. The Modernist avant-garde was socially motivated and its art was inspired by a social vision, a view of a better future; even the Surrealist and Dadaist art that questioned the basis of the real world aimed at social emancipation. This collective motivation and social idealization—the very essence of the ethical dimension of art—appears to have weakened in the works of today's avant-garde. In many respects this collective vision has become a language of form, a role-play, or an intellectual deconstruction and decoding of meanings and history.

The challenge of Modern architecture was to address real social problems, whereas in an existentialist sense the welfare-state architecture of our time has only ostensible problems to solve. The goals of architecture today often concern the appearance of things, rather than the essence of

THE GREAT QUESTIONING

354 Radical questioning. Coop Himmelblau, Roof conversion for an office, Vienna, 1988.

355 Fundamentalist questioning of contemporary architecture. Leon Krier, The Atlantis Project, Tenerife, 1987.

things. Avant-garde motivations today are, sadly, often only a need to be noticed or the relief of boredom, rather than a social vision.

"Without a clear understanding of its social influence and external importance the narcissism that inspires art becomes sick," the American art critic Donald B. Kuspit writes.[11]

It is not difficult to anticipate that in the future, the greatest reformer of architecture will be a new, inevitably ecological way of life that will restore the ethics of necessity to architecture. "Strength is born out of opposition and dies in freedom," as Leonardo da Vinci perceived.[12]

ARCHITECTURE AS IMAGES

Architecture creates images. The most powerful images become myths structuring the entirety of culture.

The important architectural works of Modernist history are images of a living reality and a new, emancipated way of life; those of our own time are pictures of architecture itself, discourses within the discipline that do not reflect any authentic way of life. In this respect these works are empty images. Many of them convey an unintentional necrophilic ambience.

Following the ascetic tenets of their beliefs, the Shakers dispensed with all sensual pleasures and comforts. Yet in spite of this asceticism, their buildings are pictures of spirituality and sublimity, especially when compared to the exuberant but empty settings of our time. Peter Eisenman's intellectual and witty projects are examples of this kind of architectural autism, one that appears to have completely lost its connection with life. I can only estimate that this rejection of life is quite intentional in Eisenman's method of alienation. Does he draw the right conclusions concerning the precepts of our culture? Are those yearning after an architecture with a human face exposed as deluded romantics?

THE AVANT-GARDE OF THE GREAT RETREAT

Jürgen Habermas has characterized our time as the "Avant-garde of the Great Retreat."[13] This is represented by the forward march of populist culture, playing on the disillusionment of the masses. This aesthetic fundamentalism is undoubtedly motivated by a genuine disappointment in contemporary architecture. But these attitudes are naively unaware of cultural development, of the dialectic of the individual and the collective, of the avant-garde and convention. The same, too, must be said for the idea proposed by many a learned voice in our press that the *Vox populi* should become the client and arbiter of quality in architecture. The negative feelings aroused by the architecture of the

THE ARCHITECTURE OF CONSUMERISM

356 Barbara Kruger, *Unnamed (I shop, therefore I am)*, 1987. Thomas Amman, Zurich.

357 Venturi, Rauch, and Scott Brown, House, Stony Creek, Connecticut, 1984.

past decades is a sad condition, but the acceptance of the idea that the direct satisfaction of the people's tastes and expectations is the goal of architecture means the triumph of populist culture. This people's souvenir architecture has been seen enough in today's homes and restaurant interiors!

In calling Sir Christopher Wren as a witness in defense of tradition, Britain's Prince Valiant forgot his architectural history. When building St. Paul's Cathedral, Wren had a five-meter wall erected around the site so work could proceed in peace from his Royal critics! A five meter wall—in spite of the fact that Wren carried out a rather mild design, artistically and structurally, compared to his earlier ones rejected in the name of convention![14]

TWO REALITIES

Let us not naively search for the reason for the current aesthetic catastrophe in the environment in the contradiction between architects and "the people." The reason is not that architects today have become estranged from the people's reality; on the contrary, it is that architects have not been able to take a sufficiently critical and oppositional distance from the structural inhumanity of our culture, distorting as it does the values of both the people and the architects. The fault of the new architecture lies not in its extreme radicalism, but in its lack of a radicalism capable of questioning cultural reality.

In previous lectures and essays, I have referred to Herbert Marcuse's view of the one dimensionalization of thought when "the other level of reality," the tension between the world of ideals and everyday reality, disappears. Our culture now integrates ideals and everyday life, and thus invalidates the central function of art as the mediator between these two worlds. In eliminating the antagonistic, alienating, and transcendental elements of higher culture, the interaction between culture and everyday reality disappears, as Marcuse has shown.[15]

KITSCH—A NEW FOLKLORE

The only folk tradition in our form of culture is undoubtedly that of kitsch, a tradition that can be justifiably claimed as the first universal style in the history of the world. A culture without the influence of a guiding tradition resorts to plagiarizing avant-garde products and produces kitsch. According to the art critic Clement Greenberg, when the avant-garde itself imitates artistic processes, kitsch copies the influence of this imitation.[16] "Everything which remains outside of tradition is plagiarism," Igor Stravinsky writes both paradoxically and wisely in *The Poetics of Music*.[17]

The interaction between elite and popular culture has always been the mechanism for the development and dissemination of stylistic ideals. Perhaps now, more than at any other time, kitsch, programmatic amateurism, and bad taste have been accepted as the stylistic devices of the avant-garde. The American cowboy classicism of Robert Venturi, Robert A. M. Stern, and Stanley Tigerman is an example of the kitsch accepted by the avant-garde. This acceptance constitutes a conscious revolt against Paul Valéry's "tyranny of beauty." This explicit American aesthetic chauvinism possesses a clearly subconscious jealousy of the cultural tradition of Europe, one that has turned to mockery.

The stamp of kitsch is seen equally in the architecture that imitates the language of Modernism. Even the buildings of such a skilled architect as Richard Meier contain either a strong element of Modernist eclecticism, or avant-garde kitsch.

THE POSSIBILITY OF TRADITION

But is tradition at all possible in our time? A genuine tradition is the sum of a way of life, in which architectural forms are determined by the effect of many known and unknown factors, and ultimately very little as a direct consequence of aesthetic choice. Is there such a basis for a common way of life in our culture today?

For example, is Hungarian regional architecture, with its air of folklore, a genuine tradition? Not in my opinion, simply because Imre Makovecz and his school have thematicized tradition and use these themes to generate architectural form. Tradition has become a set of subjects and motifs, arousing only nostalgia for a lost tradition. It is precisely this longing that has such a powerful political meaning in reinforcing national identity. My observation in no way diminishes the undoubted artistic merit of Makovecz's work. But it is important to realize that in speaking of the tradition of our own time, we clearly mean something quite different from the building traditions of established societies.

The Modern tradition does not reside in specific forms or styles of architecture, but in a questioning and dialectical attitude. Even Modern architecture lapses into kitsch when it ceases its questioning stance and stagnates into an unquestioned set of stylistic directives.

Clement Greenberg considers the inner critical quality of art, "the immanent Kantian critique," to be the essence of Modernism and the very basis of art. "The essence of Modernism, in my view, is that the characteristic methods of a branch of science are used for the criticism of that branch, not to overthrow it, but to strengthen it within its own field," he writes.[18]

358 Luis Barragán, Francisco Gilardi House, Tacubaya, Mexico City, 1978.
359 Daniel Libeskind, *Leakage*, drawing from the Micromega series, 1979. Detail.

358

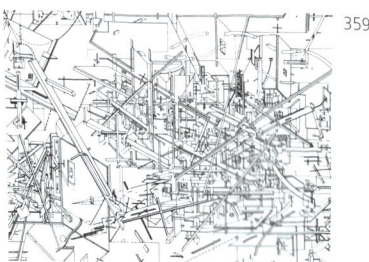

359

THE GREAT QUESTIONING

The last two decades have perhaps witnessed the most poignant questioning in architecture since the beginning of the century, directed not only at the established style of architecture, but also at the bases of architectural experience: gravity, verticality and horizontality, stability and structural logic, order and consistency, usefulness and practicality. The 'Avant-garde of the Great Retreat' in turn has questioned both the century-long Modern Movement and the overall possibility of progress—often demanding, as Leon Krier has, a complete return to pre-industrial times. Krier's aesthetic retreat has its parallel within ecological circles, as well.

Within the space of barely two decades, an atomic explosion has occurred in the form language of architecture, an explosion that equals Cubism in its radicalism. Orthogonal order has been replaced by disorder, oblique angles and overlapping coordinates. The principle of a dominating theme has been replaced by multi-thematics and lack of hierarchy. Deliberate disorder, imperfection, and incompleteness have replaced the enclosed, complete, and perfect forms of Modern architecture.

To quote Baudelaire's criticism of Ingres's portraits in the 19th century, this explosion can be seen as a reaction to the "despotic perfection" of the classical art tradition.

THE CULTURE OF COLLAGE AND COMPILATION

What is most striking after the puritanism of Modernism is the 'impurity' of today's architecture, the permissive joining together of the logical and illogical, the structural and unstructured, functional and non-functional elements. Alvar Aalto, in fact, pioneered this kind of 'hybrid' architecture, one which encourages multiple readings.

The main methods of art in our time, as well as its messages, are discontinuity, fragmentation, and a collage of unrelated elements. These methods well illustrate the new information-reality's mosaic, the flow of consciousness without any fixed point or hierarchy, whose familiar expression is a stream of images, dreamlike, without the logic and significance of everyday reality.

This predilection for combining unrelated elements and images has associations with Eco's view of the medievalization of our time. Eco indicates that the similarity between our time and the Middle Ages lies in the collection, inventory, and use of remnants of past cultures through recomposition and collage: "The art of our time, as also medieval art, is not systematic, but additive and composite. Sophisticated elite experiment lives alongside the great efforts of the people, and between them exists a continuous interaction of exchange and borrow-

...which is due to the need to dismantle and revalue the remnants of the preceding world..."[19]

In *Travels in Hyper-Reality*, Eco enumerates the contents of the treasure chamber of Charles IV of Bohemia: St. Adalbert's skull, St. Stefanus's sword, a thorn from Christ's crown, pieces of the Cross, a piece of one of St. Vitalisis' bones, a rib from St. Sofia, the jaw of St. Eobanus, a whale's rib, an elephant's tusk, Moses's staff, the Virgin's garments, among many fragments.[20] Does not this collection of curiosities equally resemble the typical compilation art of our times, the works of Joseph Cornell, Arman, Daniel Spoerri, Robert Rauschenberg, or Josef Beuys, for example? The sanctification of worthless relics also belongs to our culture; what else could be said of the Smithsonian Institute's recent acquisition of the rocking chair used by the character Archie Bunker in the well-known American television series *All in the Family*? Summaries, quotations, and borrowings are as much a part of the methods of modern architecture, and many current designs recall those medieval collections of relics and curiosities, gathering together the bones of St. Corbu, St. Alvar, or some other holy man of architecture.

Today, the myth of Modernism's originality appears questionable. As William Faulkner has said, "The artist is a creature driven by demons...He is completely amoral in that he robs, borrows, begs and steals from anybody and everybody in order to complete his work."[21]

USE-VALUE VERSES IMAGE-VALUE

One aspect of contemporary design is its skepticism of functionality, another is its disregard for ergonomic demands in design. Both are apparent reactions to strict Functionalist determinism in form, but these aspects also illustrate the inevitable departure from the demands of usefulness and practicality in the latter stages of consumerism. Functionalism represented the moralistic aesthetics of scarcity and necessity, whereas Post-Modernism produces the narcissistic aesthetics of abundance. When even a chair has sunk to the level of a social status symbol or a role-playing object, there is no need to fulfill the demand for comfort. The chair is no longer a chair, only its image. Design and art objects, even houses, became signs, or lines of dialogue appealing to the imagination, but with a non-existent use-value. In our contemporary culture, utility articles only look useful; houses only look like houses.

In fact, the art product is not the essential factor in creating image-value: it is the product's creator. The artist is selling his personality, his myth, and perhaps ultimately that enviable freedom, his independence from convention. As Roland Barthes describes, "Thus in an artist's work

361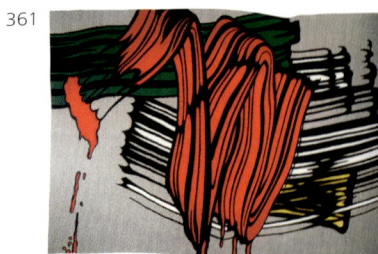

it is his body that is purchased: an exchange in which we are compelled to recognize all the signs of prostitution."[22]

In this, architecture no longer differs from the so-called "free arts." Architecture has also become a product, a packaged image, whose social charisma can be bought and sold. I have actually met a collector of architecture who owned a 'Frank Lloyd Wright' and a 'Mies van der Rohe,' and had just acquired for his collection a valuable 'Le Corbusier.' Collecting architecture is especially popular in Japan, and those who pass into the limelight of the international architectural press can expect prompt commissions from this source.

DENIAL AND NEGATION

The close of the millennium has brought with it a passionate reappraisal of the domains of art. This is an apparent "self-defense of art," against the exploitive, materialist character of our culture. Through continuous self-examination and self-determination, art now flees from the approval that threatens its existence, and yet seeks popularity for its new role. This internal denial is concealed as a paradoxical consciousness of tradition in emerging art and architecture—tradition is intensively present in the negation of the artistic inner tradition. The most influential art of our time always works in the context of tradition and acquires its significance by incorporating history and tradition. Great art in this way endeavors to restore to life the history of art—"to talk with the dead," as T.S. Eliot described in his erudite essay "Tradition and the Individual Talent."[23]

THE DOMAINS OF ART

In abandoning the criteria of usefulness and even structural credibility, architecture has moved into the fields of expression typically reserved for sculpture, conceptual art, theatre, performance, and drawing. Sculpture in turn has, generally speaking, rejected traditional plastic representation and gone on, for instance, to address issues of landscape and architecture.

The definition of place, originally the basic task of architecture, has even become the central task of contemporary sculpture. Instead of plastic representation, sculpture now aims at the poeticization or ritualization of place.

The new sculpture's aims are represented by a remarkable variety of works: a gallery half filled with earth (Walter de Maria), live horses in the exhibition area (Jannis Kounellis), a field of lightning-conducting steel rods in the desert (Walter de Maria), a pile of rocks on the slope of a mountain (Richard Long), a photograph of a landscape of variously

THE DISAPPEARANCE OF INTIMACY

360 Giorgio Morandi, *Still life*, 1958. Private collection, Como.

361 Roy Lichtenstein, *Big Painting VI*, 1960. Kunstsammlung Nordrhein-Westfalen, Düsseldorf.

positioned mirrors (Robert Smithson), the Pont Neuf bridge of Paris wrapped in cloth (Christo), or a map of the route of a walking tour (Richard Long). To this list can be added the functionless architecture of Per Kirkeby, Björn Nørgaard, Nancy Holt, and Allan Wood, as well as Gordon Matta-Clark's dismembered houses.

THE ONTOLOGICAL ABSENCE

As Rosalind Krauss describes, sculpture has thus transformed into a kind of ontological absence, a combination of exclusion. She even defines current sculpture by such concepts as externally limited "non-architecture" and "non-landscape."[24]

At the present moment, too, architecture is defined through absence or exclusion, and perhaps the present field of architecture should be limited in the same way, using the exclusionary concepts of "non-natural," "non- sculptural," and "non-painting." In any case, the definition of architecture as being solely bound to functionality and usefulness has become unsatisfactory.

Probably the most significant development in current architecture is occurring in the fields of painting, film, and poetry. By this I mean that these branches of art, perhaps more independently than architecture itself, are delineating architecture on an experiential, phenomenological basis. The films of Andrey Tarkovsky exemplify this development, offering a harrowing poetic experience of an architecture of space, light, and silence of a kind that has not yet been built from stone.

THE UNITY OF ART

The examination of other artistic works from other genres probes the limits of architecture, and assists in the generation of architectural form. The creation of architectural form through the structures of another branch of art is diametrically opposed to the holy alliance of form and function central to Functionalism. Architectural expression does not, perhaps, grow out of the definition of function or even a social commission, but from a ground common to all the arts. A kind of structural similarity exists between the arts, an energy that we can use in creative work. Aalto referred to this, for instance, when he spoke of the common roots of the three arts.[25] This common ground is poetry, the capturing of life in emotionally charged images.

The production of architecture using this kind of interpretive method has proved equally acceptable through *Finnegan's Wake*, *Moby Dick* and *Grimm's Fairy Tales*, Bach and Meredith Monk, Renaissance paintings and Cubist collages. Dan Hoffman's students at the Cranbook Academy of Art produced architecture with the aid of the force of grav-

363

EXTENDING THE NOTION OF SCULPTURE TO THE LANDSCAPE

362 Richard Long, *Rocks in Nepal*, 1975.
363 Hamish Fulton, *Bird Rock, a twelve and half day walk on Baffin Island*, Arctic Canada, summer 1988.

ity and their own bodies. Their endeavors can be understood as a kind of architectural automatism.

As architecture aims for a connection with the world of myths and rituals, it approaches the worlds of theatre and dance. Above all, architecture is returning from a world dominated by the eye to the sphere of the corporeal, of all the senses.

THE AUTONOMY OF ARCHITECTURE

In 1975, at the 25th anniversary of the Museum of Finnish Architecture, Aulis Blomstedt delivered a lecture entitled "The Autonomy of Architecture." In the socially committed atmosphere of that time, the lecture was considered reactionary in both subject and outlook. However the question of the autonomy of art and the methods for its achievement is fundamental and even revolutionary. Trotsky addressed the revolutionary nature of an autonomous art in 1938 explaining that, "Art, like science, does not merely stop looking for orders, rather its nature cannot tolerate them ... Art may form a close union with the revolution only if it is able to remain faithful to itself."[26]

As a result of its own internal critique, painting has given up the search by which to represent any external reality and instead concentrated on problems which concern the nature and instruments of painting itself. Painting has guaranteed its autonomy by rigidly defining its limits, by concentrating solely on its own instrument: color on a two-dimensional surface. For its part, poetry has turned inwards to language and the images concealed therein.

At the time Functionalism was born there was no overt call for architectural autonomy. On the contrary, architecture succumbed with pristine enthusiasm to being an instrument of social reform. In fact, the artistic independence of architecture was ensured by its social innocence and an incredibly regenerative energy.

THE SOCIAL COMMISSION OF ARCHITECTURE

The situation today, however, is quite another: architecture has become instrumentalized, bound so tightly to our techno-economic system that its poetic and critical expression is threatened. Architecture is not allowed to exist as an autonomous branch of art, but is instead harnessed to the demands of utilitarian materialism. Consumer ideology in turn has amputated the metaphysical functions of architecture by turning it into an entertainment, a luxury.

Architecture as an art, however, does not necessarily have much to do with feelings of comfort or pleasure; more often, it arouses feelings of estrangement. Architecture is no more a direct reflection of everyday reality than any other art form; it illustrates critical concepts of reality, clarified by idealizations.

In order to survive as a branch of art, architecture must guarantee its independence from the 'social commission,' and win back its artistic autonomy. Here my view varies sharply from those who wish to bind architecture to public expectations and see in this hope-fulfilling architecture the framework for a happy and peaceful life.

THE ARCHITECTURAL REFORMATION

One way for architecture to achieve autonomy and 'purification' is, paradoxically, to question its usefulness and practicality. A second method is to return to first principles, to outline the experiential basis of architecture; a third is to return its language of expression to a pure architectural language, to the characteristic images of architecture. A fourth way, finally, is for architecture to extricate itself from the superficial, topical, and fashionable, from the myth of originality, and concentrate on ordinary poetry, that 'other reality' behind the quotidian.

One of the most important architects of today is Tadao Ando, simply because he has reduced his expression to its most fundamental, to the purest language of architecture. His architecture similarly defines the boundaries of "useful" and "useless." Ando's work represents the poetry of ascetics, of concentration and reduction, which today is an important counter to the architecture of abundance and irresponsible 'freedom.'

TWO ARCHITECTURES

Nowadays it is possible to identify two different types of architecture: the architecture of essence and the architecture of form. The architecture of essence perceives the metaphysical and existential problem of being a human and tries to reinforce man's foothold on earth. The architecture of form aims at capturing the viewer's attention and approval through its voluble language of expression or through an appeal to indolence. The first type of architecture questions, arouses and stops, whereas the second conceals the problems of life by dulling the senses with pleasure.

Donald B. Kuspit criticized the art of the 1980s for its extreme theatricality. This attitude, he assumes, was due to the important contribution of performance art, which, in his opinion, has influenced traditional art forms such as painting, sculpture, and architecture. "Because a canvas could be thought of as an intimate area," he writes, "it changed into a colossal stage designed to attack us, and force us to believe in its rhetoric."[27]

364

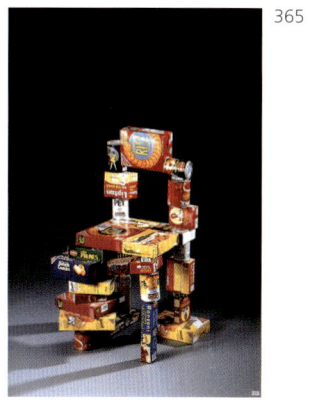

365

USE-VALUE VERSUS IMAGE-VALUE

364 Arne Jacobsen, chair, 1955.
365 Sylvia Netzer, kitchen chair, 1986.

In Kuspit's opinion, nearly all the major artists of the 1980s behaved operatically and are thus Wagnerians.[28] The same loss of intimacy and the forward march of Wagnerianism can be seen as major trends in the architecture of the same decade. Architectural journals have been flooded with the aggressive products of this 'spirit' that so pompously controls our emotions.

TOWARDS AN ARCHITECTURE OF SILENCE

But Kuspit remains hopeful, as well, proclaiming that, "A new inner need, a new vigor may be in the process of being born: an art that is not interested in direct communication, or any attempt to bring about an immediately observable significance. If the time of opera is on the wane, then the time of chamber music may be waxing. Where Opera externalizes, chamber music internalizes. Where the former appeals to the crowds, the latter appeals to the individual, offers only one experience, a feeling of being oneself."[29]

In architecture today we yearn for a similar expression that aims at silence, at the spontaneity and authenticity of the individual experience. We need today an ascetic, concentrative, and contemplative architecture. We yearn for an architecture that rejects noise, efficiency, and fashion. We need an architecture that does not aspire after the dramatic, but rather aims at lyricizing the real things of everyday life. We yearn for radical ordinariness and everydayness, a natural architecture, of the type that fills our mind with good feelings, as when we enter a peasant cottage or sit upon a Shaker chair. Alongside an architecture that breaks through its boundaries and redefines itself, we need today an architecture of silence.

BACK TO AN ARCHITECTURE OF SILENCE

366 Charles Jencks, Living Room in the Thematic House (Jencks' own house), 1978–80. Meaningless architectural noise.

367 Upstairs hallway, meeting house, Sabbathday Lake.

368 The *sawatari-ishi*, "steps across the marsh," in the garden of the Heian Shrine in Kyoto.

SIX THEMES FOR THE NEXT MILLENNIUM

(1994)

"There is a widely shared sense that Western ways of seeing, knowing and representing have irreversibly altered in recent times; but there is little consensus over what this might mean or what direction Western culture is now taking," writes Jon R. Snyder in his introduction to Gianni Vattimo's seminal philosophical investigation of our age, *The End of Modernity*.[1] The emerging new horizon of Western culture, or perhaps more correctly, the disappearance of such a horizon altogether, seems to annihilate the ground of the ideals and aspirations of Modernity. The view of the world and of the mission of architecture—as belief structures unquestionably grounded in concepts of truth and ethics as well as in a social vision and commitment—has shattered, and the cultural sense of purpose and order has faded away. The architectural avant-garde of today has all but abandoned the central challenges of the Modern Movement: the issues of planning, housing, mass production, and industrialization.

Why is it that contemporary architecture turns away from social reality and becomes self-referential and self-motivated? Why are narcissism and self-indulgence in our work replacing empathy and social conscience?

The idea of totality, so central for the conception of Modernity, and the accompanying notions of a discrete historical era and of cultural progress have lost their validity; it is no longer possible to understand reality through a single conceptual construction or representation. At the end of this millennium, the concept of a universal history has become impossible, disintegrating into a multitude of alternative heterogeneous histories; simultaneously, the perspective of redemption has vanished. The great prospect of redemption underlying Modern architecture, as narrated by Siegfried Giedeon and others, has also lost its credibility; as a consequence, a multitude of suppressed alternative histories are being unveiled from the shadow of the pathetic story of the emancipation of architecture.

"For some time now there has been an extraordinary receptiveness to theory, more especially to philosophy, in the architectural community," writes Karsten Harries, and continues, "That fact invites thoughtful consideration...One thing the widespread interest in philosophy that has become so much part of the post-modern architectural scheme suggests is that architecture has become uncertain of its way."[2] The bewildering interest in theorizing and the verbal explanation of architectural meanings and intentions today reveals an uncertainty of the role and essence of architecture. Architecture is nervously seeking its self-definition and autonomy in the embrace of the culture of consumption, a culture which otherwise will transform architecture into a commodity and an entertainment.

Today, truly disturbing buildings barely conceal their attachment to nihilism and mental violence, and are viewed and accepted as manifestations of a new aesthetic sensibility. The unprincipled ideology of consumption immediately accepts and exploits any aesthetic or moral diversion, well before it can create a sufficient critical distance to function as an authentic opposition. The post-historical condition has eliminated the possibility of a true avant-garde.

The growing entanglement of the arts and their philosophical foundations has been apparent since the 1960s. This development is also reflected in the current tendency of architecture to increasingly seek identification with its own theory and rationalization. Art has turned away from the task of representing reality to the surveillance of the problem of representation itself, and to the essence of its particular medium. The disappearance of a stable conceptual ground has forced art at large into critical negativity, into attempts to define its territory through negation and denial. The logocentrism of today's architecture also reflects a similar loss of innocence; the tacit practice of architecture within the continuum of architectural culture has become a conscious intellectual fabrication. Moreover, the obsession for architectural originality has eliminated the possibility of acquiring and retaining a cumulative knowledge of the art.

The current uncertainties of architecture can be understood more clearly by examining the cultural condition that we inhabit at the end of our millennium. This examination could enable us to grasp why "the horoscope of architecture" does not look good, as Alvar Aalto prophesied as early as 1958.

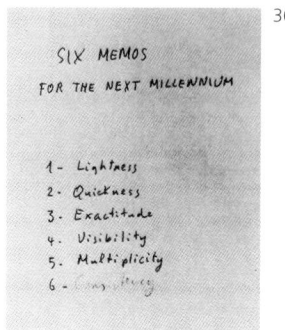

369

369 Six Memos for the Next Millennium: Italo Calvino's titles for his six Charles Eliot Norton lectures, scheduled for Harvard in 1985–86.

A central theme in Modernist architectural theory was the representation of the space-time continuum. Architecture was seen as a representation of the cultural world view, and as an expression of the space-time structure of physical and experiential reality. Of course, the space-time dimension is central to all ideas and activities of mankind, from the hidden geometries of language to the forms of production and politics. An analysis of the contemporary, post-historical space-time experience brings us to the core of current frustrations in architectural representation.

In *The Condition of Postmodernity*, David Harvey uses the notion "time-space compression" to describe the fundamental changes in the qualities of space and time contemporary culture is undergoing. He argues that we are consequently forced to alter radically our representation of the world.[3] In Harvey's view, "the experience of time-space compression is challenging, exciting, stressful and sometimes deeply troubling, capable of sparking, therefore, a diversity of social, cultural, and political responses. We have been experiencing, these last two decades, an intense phase of time-space compression that has had a disorienting and disruptive impact upon political-economic practices, the balance of class power, as well as upon cultural and social life."[4]

The implication is clear: man used to seek eternal life through overcoming the limitations of time, whereas today we seek salvation through overcoming the limitations of space. The "time-space compression" and the consequent flatness of experience have caused a curious fusion of these two dimensions: the spatialization of time and the temporalization of space. Instantaneity and the collapse of discrete time horizons have reduced our experience to a series of unrelated presents. Furthermore, the commodity production cycle emphasizes instantaneity and disposability, novelty and fashion, and this development has expanded to the realm of values, lifestyles, cultural products and architecture.

Architecture's reversion to images of a lost, inaccessible, or romanticized past is grounded in the very strategy of capitalist economy; the whole of history becomes a market place, in which local and ethnic traditions, and historical settings, are fabricated under the disguise of a search for tradition and stability. Thematization is but the newest strategy of persuasion, of directing and controlling emotional response by detaching imagery from its autonomous spontaneity; the image is not allowed to arise from within our perception and experience, but is forced upon us by a preconceived interpretation.

"Everything tends to flatten out at the level of contemporaneity and simultaneity, thus producing a de-historisation of experience," asserts Fredric Jameson.[5] The loss of temporality is accompanied by loss of depth. Jameson has emphasized the 'depthlessness' of contemporary cultural production and its fixation with appearances, surfaces, and instant impacts. By extension, he describes post-modem architecture by the notion of "contrived depthlessness."[6]

"It is hardly surprising that the artist's relation to history...has shifted," writes Harvey, "that in the era of mass television there has emerged an attachment to surfaces rather than roots, to collage rather than in-depth work, to superimposed quoted images rather than worked surfaces, to a collapsed sense of time and space rather than solidly achieved cultural artifact."[7]

In the post-historical experience, truth becomes replaced by the aesthetic and rhetorical experience. Every aspect of cultural activity and production of daily life turns into pure aesthetics: technology, economics, politics, love, and war.

The surprising success of high-tech architecture in our eclectic and revisionist age can be understood through such architecture's capacity to determine its own criteria of quality and goals. Within its self-defined realm, high-tech architecture succeeds by replacing the issues of representation with the inner logic of technological rationality.

The criteria of performance that high-tech architecture promotes appear to have objective ground; all metaphysical questions of architecture have been answered by and transformed into the logic of technology. In Heidegger's view, "twentieth-century technology is historically the most advanced form of Western metaphysics," for technology has brought the objectivization of thought to its conclusive historical extreme.[8]

THE DEFENSE OF LITERARY QUALITY

In his literary testament entitled *Six Memos for the Next Millennium*, Italo Calvino, the author of *Invisible Cities*, acknowledges the confusion and superficiality of our time, but simultaneously expresses an emphatic confidence in literature: "My confidence in the future of literature consists in the knowledge that there are things that only literature can give us, by means specific to it," he writes.[9]

Calvino gave the manuscripts for his Charles Eliot Norton lectures at Harvard University the following six stimulating titles: 1. Lightness, 2. Quickness, 3. Exactitude, 4. Visibility, 5. Multiplicity, 6. Consistency.

Sadly, due to Calvino's sudden death in 1985, the lectures were never delivered. Although, in fact, no manuscript for the sixth lecture has been found, Calvino did leave on his work table five poetic and wise essays on the feasibility of literary art in the post-modern condition. The essays present essential criteria for literary quality, with the

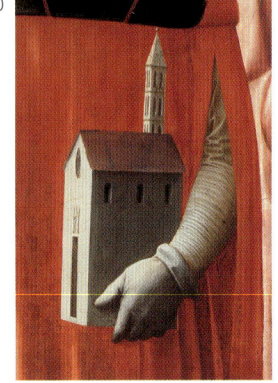

370

371

372

373

intention to strengthen the self-defense of literature against the reductive force of post-historical culture. "In each of my lectures," he writes, "I have set myself the task of recommending to the next millennium a particular value close to my heart. The value I want to recommend today is precisely this: In an age when other fantastically speedy, widespread media are triumphing, and running the risk of flattening all communication onto a single, homogenous surface, the function of literature is communication between things that are different simply because they are different, not blunting but even sharpening differences between them, following the true bent of written language."[10]

"Only if poets and writers set themselves tasks that no one else dares imagine will literature continue to have a function," he continues, and concludes, "the grand challenge for literature is to be capable of weaving together the various branches of knowledge, the various 'codes' into a manyfold and multifaceted vision of the world."[11]

Confidence in the future of architecture can, in my view, be based on the very same knowledge; existential meanings of truly inhabiting space can be wrought by the art of architecture alone. Architecture continues to have an essential human task: to mediate between the world and ourselves, and to provide a horizon by which to comprehend our existential condition.

THE DEFENSE OF ARCHITECTURAL QUALITY

The current cultural condition renders the emergence of profound architecture as difficult as that of profound literature. The post-historical condition tends to erase the very foundations of any valid architectural manifestation by uprooting ideas and experiments before they have had time to take root in societal soil. Such attempts are quickly transformed into instantaneous commodities in the market of images, into harmless entertainments devoid of existential sincerity.

Essential questions face the architectural profession today: can architecture define a credible social and cultural goal for itself? Can architecture be rooted in culture in order to create an experience of locality, place, and identity? Can architecture re-create a tradition, a shared ground, that provides a basis for the cultivation of authenticity and quality?

In response to these prevailing questions, and following Calvino's scheme, I wish to suggest six themes for the re-enchantment of architecture at the turn of the millennium. I firmly believe in the continued human mission of architecture and in its possibility of grounding us in the continuum of time and in the specificity of place. The six themes that I regard essential for the strengthening of architecture's position in the post-historical reality are: 1. Slowness, 2. Plasticity, 3. Sensuousness, 4. Authenticity, 5. Idealization, 6. Silence.

Each theme has the potential for a separate essay, but here I shall simply sketch short suggestive notes on each, with the intention of stimulating further thinking by the reader.

1. SLOWNESS

"Architecture is not only about domesticating space," writes Karsten Harries, "it is also a deep defense against the terror of time. The language of beauty is essentially the language of timeless reality."[12] This may be so, but the contemporary cultural condition prevents us from grasping this dimension of time, as Italo Calvino describes: "long novels written today are perhaps a contradiction: the dimension of time has been shattered, we cannot live or think except in fragments of time each of which goes off along its own trajectory and immediately disappears. We can rediscover the continuity of time only in the novels of that period when time no longer seemed stopped and did not yet seem to have exploded, a period that lasted no more than a hundred years."[13]

Indeed, today we experience the slow progression of time in the great nineteenth-century Russian, German, and French novels with the same pleasurable nostalgia and fascination with which we regard the architectural remains of the glorious civilizations of the past. But architectural works also are museums of time, with the capacity of suspending time. Great architecture petrifies time; even today we can experience the slow time of the Middle Ages in the voids of the great Gothic cathedrals.

There is a tacit wisdom of architecture that has accumulated in tradition and history; this wisdom luminously reveals the mental essence of the art of architecture. However, architecture needs slowness to re-connect itself with this source of silent knowledge. Architecture requires slowness in order to develop again a cumulative knowledge, to accumulate a sense of continuity, and to become enrooted in culture.

We need an architecture that rejects momentariness, speed, and fashion, instead of accelerating change and a sense of uncertainty, architecture must slow down our experience of reality in order to create an experiential background for grasping and understanding change. Instead of the current obsession with novelty, architecture must acknowledge and respond to the archaic, bio-cultural dimensions of the human psyche.

2. PLASTICITY

Architecture has become an art of the printed image. As buildings lose their plasticity and their connection with the language of the body, they

374

375

376

377

A WORK WITH ONLY ONE PROPERTY.

become isolated in the distant and cool realm of vision. The dominant role of the photographed image in today's architectural culture, as well as new graphic means of generating architectural images, have contributed to the flatness and sheerly retinal quality of architecture. With the loss of tactility, and the measures and details crafted for the human body and hand, architecture becomes repulsively flat, sharp-edged, immaterial, and unreal.

Flatness, the lack of three-dimensionality, is also due partly to the techno-economic requirements for thinness, lightness, and temporality; buildings are constructed merely as virtual visual images, and their surfaces become ever thinner and more weightless. Our capacity for plastic imagination is weakening; buildings tend to be a combination of the two-dimensional projections of plan and section, instead of conceived and constructed through a sensory and spatial imagination. The architectural profession at large has turned into a paper profession, one that thinks and communicates through lines on paper rather than through a bodily and physical participation. The sense of flatness is reinforced by the diminishing role of craft in construction, by atectonic construction, and by the extensive use of synthetic materials, whose technically perfect surfaces are impenetrable to our vision.

Architecture must again learn to speak of materiality, gravity, and the tectonic logic of its own making. Architecture must become a plastic art and engage our full, bodily participation.

3. SENSUOUSNESS

Architecture is inherently an art form of the body and of all the senses. But the constant "rainfall of images,"[14] as Calvino labels the incessant totality of ephemeral, momentary cultural flickers, has detached architecture from other sensory realms and turned it solely into an art of the eye. However, even vision implies an unconscious ingredient of touch: with our eyes we stroke the edges, surfaces, and details of buildings.

We live in an era with a frustrating discrepancy and distance between the sensory experience of the world and the consciousness created by it on the one hand, and the bio-cultural responses accumulated over the course of human evolution, in our unconscious reactions, on the other. Our relation to experienced, physical reality keeps weakening—we live increasingly in a virtual world, in a stream of unrelated superficial sensory impressions.

Architecture mediates between these outer and inner realities that would otherwise tend to separate from each other. Architecture's task is to provide the stable and reliable ground for the perception of the world, for the ground of homecoming into the world. Such a homecoming cannot be grounded in a sentimental return to the past; it has to be created through a profound understanding of the phenomenological essence of the art of architecture, and of the current human condition, and through means that are radical enough to resist the cultural forces of conditioned desire.

In *The Notebooks of Malte Laurids Brigge*, Rainer Maria Rilke describes the traces of lives lived in a demolished house, traces left on the wall of the adjacent building: "There were the midday meals and the sicknesses and the exhalations and the smoke of years, and the stale breath of mouths, and the oily odor of perspiring feet. There were the pungent tang of urine and the stench of burning soot and the grey reek of potatoes, and the heavy, sickly fumes of rancid grease. The sweetish, lingering smell of neglected infants was there, and the smell of frightened children who go to school, and the stuffiness of the beds of nubile youths."[15]

Here is an astonishing document of a poet's empathetic capacity and the epic resonance of his work.

Our architecture is certainly sterile and schematic in comparison to the poet's sensibility. The spectrum of emotions conveyed by today's architecture is confined to the narrow range of the visual aesthetic experience, and it lacks melancholic and tragic, as well as ecstatic, polarities. Great architecture is not about aesthetic style, but about embodied images of an authentic life, with all its contradictions and irreconcilabilities. Authentic architecture communicates its existential significance through our entire bodily and mental constitution. Architecture provides us the ground by which to perceive and understand the world as a continuum of time and culture.

4. AUTHENTICITY

I am aware of the philosophical difficulties of distinguishing between 'essence' and 'appearance,' and the consequent ambiguity of the notion of authenticity. Regardless of that, and the somewhat fashionable tone of the term itself, I want to argue for the possibility and significance of authenticity in architecture. Authenticity is frequently identified with the ideas of artistic autonomy and originality. I understand authenticity more as the quality of deep rootedness in the stratifications of culture.

In the consumerist world, emotions and reactions are increasingly conditioned. We need works of art and architecture to defend the autonomy of emotional response. In a world of inauthenticity and simulation, we need islands of artistic authenticity that will let our reactions grow autonomously and allow us to identify with our own emotions.

378

379

IDEALIZATION

380 Pierre Chareau and Bernard Bijvoet,
The Glass House (*Maison de Verre*),
Paris, 1929.
381 Tadao Ando, Kidosaki House,
Setagaya, Tokyo, 1982–86.

In Calvino's 'rainfall' of placeless and timeless information, our existential experience loses its coherence; we become detached from traditional sources of identity. Architecture provides a horizon on which to measure and understand ourselves. Authentic architecture builds confidence in our comprehension of time's duration and human nature; it provides the ground for individual identity.

Architecture is a conservative art in the sense that it materializes and preserves the history of culture. Buildings and cities trace the continuum of culture in which we place ourselves and by which we can recognize our identities. Architecture's conservatism does not exclude radicalism; on the contrary, architecture must reinforce our existential experience in a radical manner against the forces of alienation and detachment. Architecture, as all art, makes us experience our own being with extraordinary weight and intensity. This dense authenticity enables us to dwell with dignity.

5. IDEALIZATION

In our troubled time, we cannot expect to build an Arcadia through architecture. But we can create works of architectural art that confirm human value, reveal the poetic dimensions of everyday life and, consequently, serve as cores of hope in a world that seems to have lost its coherence and meaning. As the continuity of architectural culture is lost, the world of architecture becomes fragmented into detached and isolated works, an archipelago of architecture. As I have said many times: the patron saint of the archipelago of architecture is Hope.

My acknowledgement of a conflict between architecture and the current cultural condition could, perhaps, be interpreted as a support to the view that the architect should faithfully fulfill the explicit desires of the client. I do not believe in such a populist view. The uncritical acceptance of the *vox populi* or the client's brief only leads to sentimental kitsch; the architect's responsibility is to penetrate the surface of commercially, socially, and momentarily conditioned desire.

The authentic artist and architect must engage in an ideal world; architecture reifies an ideal view of life. Architecture is lost at the point at which this vision and this aspiration for an ideal is abandoned.

Only the architect who projects an ideal client, and an ideal society, as he designs, can create buildings that give mankind hope and direction. Without the masterpieces of Modern architecture, our understanding of contemporary life, and of ourselves, would be decisively weaker than now: these works materialize idealized possibilities of human thought and existence.

380

381

Architecture can either tolerate and encourage individualization, or stifle and reject it. We can make a distinction between an architecture of accommodation and an architecture of rejection. The first one facilitates reconciliation, the second attempts to impose a preconceived order through its arrogant forms and gestures. The first is based on images that are rooted in our common memory, that is, in the phenomenologically authentic ground of architecture. The second manipulates images—striking and fashionable, perhaps—but ones that do not incorporate our identities, memories, and dreams. This approach likely creates more imposing buildings suitable for fashionable publication, but the first attitude provides the condition of homecoming.

Today we need an architecture that does not seek bombast, effect, or adoration. We need an architecture of empathy and humility.

6. SILENCE

I have earlier written extensively about an architecture of silence, but I shall, however, add a few concluding notes on my last stated theme.[16]

"Nothing has changed man's nature so much as the loss of silence," writes the Swiss philosopher Max Picard in his thought-provoking book *The World of Silence*.[17] "Poetry comes out of silence and yearns for silence."[18] Picard concludes his thoughts with Kierkegaard's instruction: "Create silence."[19]

All great art is engaged in silence. The silence of art is not the mere absence of sound, but an independent sensory and mental state, an observing, listening, and knowing silence, a silence that evokes a sense of melancholy and a yearning for the absent ideal. Great architecture also evokes silence. Experiencing a building is not only a matter of looking at its spaces, forms and surfaces—it is also a matter of listening to its characteristic, unique silence.

A powerful architectural experience eliminates external noise and turns my consciousness inwards, to myself. I hear only my own heartbeat. The innate silence of an experience of architecture results, it seems, from the fact that it turns our attention to our own existence—I find myself listening to my own being.

The task of architecture is to create, maintain, and protect silence. Great architecture is silence turned into matter; it is petrified silence. As the thunder and clatter of construction fades, as the shouting of workers cease, the great building turns into a timeless monument of silence. What faithfulness and patience can be felt in the great works of architecture!

382

383

SILENCE

382 Vilhelm Hammershoj, *Dust Motes Dancing in Sunlight*, 1900. Private collection, Copenhagen.
383 Walker Evans, *Farmer's Kitchen, Hale Country, Alabama*, 1936. Silence is an independent sensory and mental state.

384 A ruin in southern Spain, north of the town of San Pedro.

MELANCHOLY AND TIME

(1995)

"It is as though space, cognizant . . . of its inferiority to time, answers it with the only property time doesn't possess: with beauty."[1]

Joseph Brodsky

THE FEAR OF TIME

We do not live in an objective material world: we live in mental worlds in which the experienced, remembered, and dreamed, as well as the present, past, and future, constantly fuse into each other. Our mind's capacity to transcend the actuality of time creates the imagination. Our culture's imagination and our experience of time were initiated after the loss of Paradise—through the longing for the lost unity. We transform time and space through our imagination and our dreaming into the specific human mode of existence: the world of possibilities. The self and the world mutually define each other in a perpetual intertwining process.

Time is the most frightening dimension of human experience because of its seemingly absolute power over us. Once the human grasp of time lost its primordial cyclical nature, time was transformed into a line, with an irrevocable beginning and end. We feel helpless in relation to time, and find ourselves at its mercy. We can shape matter and structure space, but we cannot throw time off its predestined course. Man's greatest desire, therefore, is to halt, suspend, and reverse the flow of time.

"What the past and the future have in common is our imagination, which conjures them," writes Joseph Brodsky, and continues, ". . . our

imagination is rooted in our eschatological dread; the dread of thinking that we are without precedence or consequence. The stronger that
dread, the more detailed our notion of antiquity or of Utopia."[2]

Our era has an especially frustrated relation to time. Modern man
suffers from *khronophobia*, the fear of time. This anxiety originates in
an obsessive rejection of aging, decay, and death. "The anxiety towards
death is 'ontological'," writes Roger Scruton, "it spreads over the face of
existence itself, and undermines the 'ground of being.'"[3] Unconsciously,
we attempt to halt time in its present tense in order to maintain a
permanent youth. The unavoidable aging of buildings and objects, as
well as people, is censored. The elderly are pushed to the periphery of
public consciousness, buildings are designed for a timeless present, and
objects are replaced before they have acquired any trace of use and age.
Time has become instrumentalized and commodified; today, it is sold
and purchased like any material commodity. The aspiration for novelty
in the arts and architecture reflects the same irrationality in our relation
to time. The other side of this fear is the fear of life, a necrophilia that
one can often sense in the images of contemporary architecture.

The weakening of the experience of time in contemporary life has
devastating mental effects. As time loses its depth and resonance in
the archaic past, man loses his sense of self as a historical being, and
is threatened by time's revenge. In the words of the American therapist
Gotthard Booth, "The natural satisfaction of life lies in vital participation in forms of life that extend beyond the boundaries of individual
existence."[4] We have a mental need to experience that we are rooted
in the continuity of time. We do not only inhabit space, we also dwell
in time.

THE SIGNIFICANCE OF TIME

Humankind has devised an instrument, a magical invention, to deceive
time and lead it astray: art. We can traverse across time through the
power of imagination and dreams, and objects of art fix these fleeting
images for others to enter at completely different moments.

The dimension of time, essential in all artistic manifestations,
exists not as an actual duration, however, but as a psychic dimension.
An encounter with an object of art leads us back to the world of the
child and the primitive, a world which is not categorized and which
reappears as an undifferentiated experience of existence. "Literature is
made at the borderline between the self and the world," writes Salman
Rushdie, "and during the creative act, this boundary softens, becomes
penetrable and allows the world to flow into the artist and the artist to
flow into the world."[5]

We expand our temporal boundaries by making art. Art seeks to prolong life through metaphors of timeless existence. "Form is nothing else but a concentrated wish for everlasting life on earth," the young Alvar Aalto wrote.[6] Equally, the celebrated theater director Heiner Müller asserted similar beliefs in an interview shortly before his death: "Making art has only one purpose for me; art prolongs the distance between myself and Death."[7]

Art relativizes time, transforming it into a malleable dimension that can be contracted and suspended; through art, we are able to tame and domesticate time. An artistic image may sink into oblivion for centuries, and be reborn in full vigor to again touch human hearts and minds. The persistence of artistic images is one of the great mysteries of culture. Why are powerful artistic images independent of the sedimentation of time? Why are stone-age images able to touch our emotions so forcefully? How do objects of foreign cultures find their echo in our soul? How does art communicate across the abyss of centuries, although we have no possibility of reconstructing the artist's feelings, intentions, and meanings?

I believe this miracle of art—to overcome the distancing and separating impact of time—is possible because objects or acts of art confront us with our own existential experience; works of art are mirrors held against our self-image. In the same way that a four-thousand-year-old polished Egyptian bronze mirror reflects *my* physical image through its utilitarian quality, through its essence as a work of art, it enables me to confront *my own* existence. The artistic image focuses my consciousness on my very being. I am not experiencing something distant in space and time; I am listening to myself, confronted with the timeless experience of being human. I intensify my own existential experience through the ancient image; art brings me to the threshold of my own being. The most ancient, and the most novel, artistic images accompany us to the very same threshold.

Architectural constructions are a defense against the anxiety of death, disappearance, insignificance, and non-existence. As a consequence of consciousness, humankind became conscious of death, and began to aspire for eternal life. The imposing constructions of past cultures are instruments for overcoming time and death. From a defense against threats in the natural surroundings, our domiciles were transformed into protection against the metaphysical fears staged by the mind itself. Architecture protects us from the elements, but equally important, it protects us from our inner fears. Architecture organizes our inner world as much as our external world.

TIME SCALES

We are suspended between two time scales: as biological beings, we are genetically attached to the slow time of evolution, but at the same time, we live in the ever-accelerating time of culture. Our environmental behavior and reactions continue to be largely genetically and unconsciously conditioned, but on the other hand, we are manipulated by the exceedingly rapid mechanisms of culture.

The conflict of the two time scales is tragically exemplified in a piece of news that I read some time ago. In the most radioactively affected areas of Chernobyl, there are mutant moles whose evolution would have required ten million years under natural conditions, while the technologically accelerated time of our contemporary culture made them appear in a split-second. Should we expect the humans of this "Brave New World" to be free of all biologically determined reactions to space and time? I do not believe so; the cave man still resides in my body and continues to make his justified demands.

I believe it is the task of architecture to mediate between the two polarities of time. Architecture must echo primordial levels of being at the same time that it frames our existence in the technological present.

THE ART OF PERMANENCE

Architecture domesticates space, structures the lived world, and provides a horizon of behavior and understanding. It provides stability and a sense of continuity for human existence, as well as a ground for symbolization and meaning. More than any other art form, the art of building is an instrument by which to slow and halt time. Architecture builds dams to hold back the flow of time. Buildings and cities of history form ponds of stilled time that enable us to return to the past. Architecture is the art of permanence.

Periodically, an idea of emancipating architecture from its roots in the earth emerges: the thought-provoking revolving house, 'Il Girasole,' for example, designed by Angelo Invernizzi and Ettore Fagiuoli near Verona in 1935, is an impressive but a mentally disturbing building. The idea uproots architecture from its connection to the earth and landscape and turns the house into a vehicle; the ground of reference, the mental horizon, provided by architecture is lost. Similarly, 'Walking City,' the well-known Archigram utopia designed by Ron Herron, is an ocean liner on legs, without the organizing power and authority of an authentic city.

Architecture both concretizes time and transcends it; the materiality of time is traversed in both directions. The gigantic columns of the Peristyle of Karnak concretizes the abyss of three thousand years of time, but they also transfer us back to the time of the Pharaohs and enable us to imagine their distant life; these columns touch our senses through their shocking power to unite time, space, and matter into a single elemental experience, an experiential singularity.

Buildings and cities are museums of time. They emancipate us from the hurried time of the present, and help us to experience the slow, healing time of the past. Architecture enables us to see and understand the slow processes of history, and to participate in time cycles that surpass the scope of an individual life. Architecture connects us with the dead; we are able to imagine the bustle of the medieval street, and to picture a solemn procession approaching the cathedral. The time of architecture is a detained time; in the greatest of buildings, time stands firmly still. Time in the Pantheon has petrified into a motionless present in which the elements are eternally fused into each other.

In the same way, the great works of Modern architecture preserve a utopian time of optimism and hope; even after decades of trying faith they radiate an air of spring and promise. Today, the Villa Mairea is heartbreaking in its radiant belief in a humane future, in the reconciliation between nature and construction, and in the societal mission of architecture. The Villa Savoye still makes us believe in the union of reason and beauty, ethics and aesthetics. The Maison de Verre continues to promise a technological world of poetic mystery and humane warmth. Throughout decades of tragic social and political change, the Melnikov House continues to stand as a silent witness of the will and faith that once conceived it. These works do not symbolize optimism and faith; they actually awaken the seed of hope within us.

The incredible acceleration of speed in our time, however, is collapsing time into the flat screen of the present, upon which the simultaneous kaleidoscope of the world is projected. Buildings as well as objects lose their temporal essence and turn into instantaneous commodities, objects of fashionable image and desire. "Modern commodities threaten the stability of the world," writes Charles Taylor in his book *The Ethics of Authenticity*.[8]

THE VERTIGO OF NOWNESS

In Paul Virilio's view, Western culture began a massive acceleration of speed in the mid-19th century.[9] Whoever possesses the greatest speed, possesses power in both circumstances of war and peace—and both circumstances, in fact, have lost their difference due to speed, he states. The acceleration of speed is obvious also in the current circulation of architectural imagery; new stylistic fashions travel across the globe in a matter of weeks. Whereas the construction of the human habitat used to be a slow local accumulation, it has become a global mosaic, and architecture has lost its role as the prime source of the permanence, stability, and security of the existential experience. Architecture provided the frame of identity in previous eras, but identity is now sought through momentary consumption.

Michel Serres speaks of an "inflation of time" that causes the shattering of history and a sense of lawlessness.[10] This post-historical condition seems to arise from an acceleration of social and cultural change beyond our capacity to conceive of change as a pattern; the dialectic of permanence and change is lost.

In *Unexpressionism—Art Beyond the Contemporary*, Germano Celant uses such notions as 'contemporaryism,' 'hyper-contemporary,' 'terror of the contemporary,' and 'vertigo of nowness,' in referring to "a pathological and conformist anxiety that...turns the present into an absolute frame of reference, an indisputable truth."[11] Remo Bodei suggests that "our temporal relations have gone through an inversion; we regard the flow of time as something that runs from the future to the present and the past, and not as it does traditionally, from the past to the future."[12]

The Modernists regarded the future as a deliberate subject of planning, but the reversal of the flow of time has made the future independent of the present and of our actions; we are left at the mercy of the future. Whereas the generation of the previous *fin de siècle* awaited the promises of the new century with excitement, our horizon to the twenty-first century is curiously closed and filled with uncertainty and anxiety.

TIME-SPACE COMPRESSION

The central theme of Modern architectural theory is the representation of the space-time complex. Architecture is seen as the representation of the contemporary world view, and as an expression of the space-time structure of physical and experiential reality. Architecture articulates man's being in space and time; an analysis of the current post-historical time-space experience is likely to inform us of the causes of the current frustrations in architectural representation. Today's exploded architectural scene is reflected in a panic of representation.

In *The Condition of Postmodernity*, David Harvey uses the idea of 'time-space compression' to refer to the fundamental changes in the qualities of space and time, and argues that we are forced to alter our representation of the world in radical ways.[13]

In Daniel Bell's view, the structuring of space has "become the primary aesthetic problem of mid-20th century culture as the problem of time (in Bergson, Proust and Joyce) was the primary aesthetic problem of the first decades of this century."[14] Indeed, throughout history, humankind has sought eternal life by overcoming the limitations of time, whereas today we seek salvation by overcoming the limitations of space. Instead of attempting to expand the duration of our earthly existence in time, we seek to expand boundaries of our existence in space. Witness our desire to expand the boundaries of outer and inner space, as well as the obsessive efforts to universalize cultural space, life style, and thought.

The compression of time and space and the consequent flatness of experience has caused a curious fusion of these two dimensions: the spatialization of time and the temporalization of space. Time is measured in spatial terms, space through units of time. Instantaneity and the collapsed time horizon reduce experience to a mosaic of unrelated presents. The obsessive production of commodities places further emphasis on instantaneity and disposability, novelty and fashion, and this development expands to the realms of values, cultural products, and architecture. The guiding narratives of history and progress, as well as the perspective of redemption, that together provided an experience of continuity and purpose have also evaporated as sources of the sense of permanence.

PERMANENCE IN TRANSIENCE

Human experience confronts dramatically differing scales of time: cosmic time, geological time, biological time, cultural time, and the time scale of family and individual life. Historically, architecture has adapted the formal language of geological time—crystallization, sedimentation, layering, fissure—and not the time language of the biological world. Architecture is engaged with 'material imagination' rather than 'formal imagination,' to use Gaston Bachelard's notions for two processes of form.[15] Geological processes challenge the progression of time because of their innate slowness. A rock polished by the weight of glacial ice is reassuring, and a smooth stone on the palm is soothing; they both speak of the patient processes of their formation. Architecture traditionally seeks permanence through the process of man-made petrification expressed in architecture.

The confrontation of distant time scales creates extraordinary poetry: the waver of a shadow, the rustle of leaves, and the patter of rain emphasize the solidity and permanence of the stone wall.

The acceptance of death projects a new depth into our awareness of the fragility of life. Our non-existence in death becomes mentally bearable through the acknowledgement of our non-existence before birth. Ruins make us experience this fragility and depth of time even more vividly than buildings that we use, having lost their mask of utility and become pure metaphysical devices. Its vulnerability revealed, a ruin has lost the illusion of its permanence. The sole task of a ruin is to accompany time without resistance: vulnerability meets endurance.

The experience of permanence does not necessarily rely solely on material durability. Architecture has also sought union with the Cosmos and with eternity by means of geometry, mathematics, proportional harmony, cosmology, astronomy, archetype, myth, and ritual. The two thousand year history of Pythagorean harmonics and the persistence of the Golden Section exemplify our aspiration for Cosmic harmony. We have often sought the source of eternal life through "the Harmony of the Spheres."

In the Shinto temple, reconstructed every twenty years, permanence is believed to reside in the form, the immaterial idea, not in the matter, or the actual physical manifestation. The concept of permanence for a practitioner of Zen is entirely different from the Western one-dimensional understanding of endurance.

Nomads reconstruct their world every night. At the end of each day, the women of the Rendile tribe in Kenya erect the tribe's circular houses (transported from one domicile to the next on camelback), in a circular configuration that has an opening towards the rising sun, and opposite to the chief's house. Each reconstruction of the settlement reenacts their beginning, reorganizes the world, puts humans in relation to the Cosmos, and establishes social order. The activities and objects of every individual hut are equally strictly ordered to maintain comprehensible order. The order of the nomad's world is preserved in the memory of the tribe. The material permanence of the architectural structures of Western societies is here replaced by the cyclical repetition of a ritual, one that connects its adherents with both the past and the future. Such ritual cycles have their echo in the repetitive rhythms of architecture; repetition is thus a fundamental aspect of architecture.

Alongside the desire for objective and material permanence in our culture, a new sensibility towards a subjective and private transience is emerging in recent artistic aspirations, in the works of Richard Long, Hamish Fulton, Andy Goldsworthy and Nils-Udo, for example. Whereas the works of Richard Serra strengthen our experience of earth and gravity, James Turrell's works bring us to the mystical threshold between physical and perceptual realities. Current developments in art suggest a renewed interest in essences, and the emergence of a new nomadic sensibility. The emerging ecological perspective also suggests a new understanding of permanence, and, consequently, new ideals of form and beauty. In today's architecture, Glenn Murcutt's maxim—'touch the earth lightly'—deriving from Australian aboriginal wisdom, expresses this new ethical and aesthetic sensibility. The focus now seems to shift from the permanence of cultural artifacts to the sustenance of natural systems. This paradigm shift may well be the most important one in the history of Western civilization.

MELANCHOLY

Experiencing a work of art is a private dialogue between the work and the viewer, one that excludes other interactions. "Art is made by the alone for the alone," writes Cyril Connolly in *The Unquiet Grave*; significantly, Luis Barragan underlined this sentence in his copy of the book.[16]

A sense of melancholy seems to reside beneath moving experiences of art; the sorrow of the intangibility and fragility of beauty. Art projects an ideal unattainable in life—the ideal of beauty that momentarily touches the eternal. Julia Kristeva writes about "melancholic imagination"; for her, all imagination is an expression of manifest or secret melancholy. Imagination originates in the recognition of distance, absence, and loss. She considers melancholy as the other side of Eros: "Melancholy is amorous passion's somber lining."[17]

Melancholy is meditation on time, transitoriness, and distance the experience of the depth and opacity of time unavoidably eroding memory and beauty. Melancholy is the recognition of the tragic dimension within the moment of bliss. This mental state combines happiness and sadness, possession and loss, understanding and bewilderment, into a heightened experience of being. Melancholy is the sorrow accompanying the comprehension of limits.

WATER AND TIME

In *Watermarks*, his poetic book on Venice, Joseph Brodsky repeatedly equates time and water, stating, "I simply think that water is the image of time."[18] The poet is right. Water has the liquidity of time and also its alternating transparency and opacity. Water flows rapidly or slowly, and its final destination is unavoidable; both time and water approach death, a final equilibrium in immobility. No wonder water, the double of time and beauty, is so important for architecture. Water amplifies the experience of permanence in architecture. "The hesitancy of water reveals architectural immobility," as Adrian Stokes writes.[19]

Carlo Scarpa's Brion Vega Cemetery serves as a consummate (Venetian) example: the architecture extends under water: the surface of the pool surrounding the chapel is a mirror between life and death.

The realization that architecture mediates between these two realms is soothing, but, at the same time, the presence of death evokes a sense of melancholy. This is the calming melancholy of the cemetery of the miniaturized architecture of the Cities of the Dead. In many cities, graveyards are the most impressive architectural settings. Alvar Aalto's unexecuted crematorium project in Lyngby, Denmark, still radiates a calm and beautiful sense of time and melancholy. Architecture gives dignity to Death.

Given our culture's rejection of time, contemporary architecture, however, is rarely capable of evoking an experience of *melancholia*.

THE TEMPTATION OF BEAUTY

Contemporary architecture today is also obsessed with form and novelty. Any art, however, that engages itself too explicitly with form turns into formalism, any art that searches for novelty loses its roots, and any art that obsessively grasps for beauty becomes sentimental.

Architectural fashions today aim too directly at explicit architectural statements, and even attempt to detach architecture from life altogether, as if the realities of life would contaminate architecture's pure beauty. As a result, architecture becomes autistic and self-referential. In many schools of architecture today, there is an unfortunate and misguided attitude that the art of architecture should necessarily imply something strange and shocking. The true aim is quite the contrary: by engaging in the realities of life and construction, architecture can reveal the eternal mystery of all things; architecture can reveal the poetry and magic of the commonplace and the unavoidable. Instead of being the object of experience itself, architecture must direct our attention to other things. The significance of architecture is not in its form, but in its capacity to reveal deeper layers of existence. Here, we must make a distinction between an architecture of form and an architecture of essence.

Great artists usually speak of practical difficulties in their work and life instead of explicit intellectual or metaphysical aspirations. Joseph Brodsky's critique of Ezra Pound's *Cantos*—"…he hadn't realized that beauty can't be targeted, that it is always a by-product of other, often very ordinary pursuits"—is a constant reminder of this difficulty.[20] Pentti Saarikoski, a seminal contemporary Finnish poet, used to work at his kitchen table. After he had published his astonishing translations of Greek poetry in the late 1950s, I asked him how he managed to transpose the Greek verse into the very different rhythms of the Finnish language. "By measuring the length of the verses by the kitchen knife," the poet answered dryly and truthfully.

Beauty is not the conscious aim of true art. The consequence of other aspirations and engagements—precision, propriety, sincerity, utility, and perfection—beauty arises from a passion for life: it is the way things are, not a separate ontological category. Beauty is achieved when the necessary is done right. "Beauty is not the opposite of the ugly, but of the false," as Erich Fromm writes.[21]

Artistic impact should not be attached to the notion of symbolization. Works of art may contain conscious symbolizations, but symbols are meaningless for artistic quality. Art is not symbolic presentation: it is distilled existence, a concentrate of existential experience.

"Tintotetto did not choose that yellow rift in the sky above Golgotha to *signify* anguish or to *provoke* it," as Jean-Paul Sartre writes, "It is anguish and yellow sky at the same time. Not sky of anguish or anguished sky; it is anguish become thing, an anguish which has turned into yellow rift of sky, and which thereby is submerged and impacted by the proper qualities of things, by their impermeability, their extension, their blind permanence, their externality, and that infinity of relations which they maintain with other things. That is, it is no longer *readable* ... there will remain only things haunted by a mysterious soul. One does not paint significations; one does not put them to music."[22]

In the same way, Michelangelo's buildings do not symbolize melancholy, they actually mourn, and Louis Kahn's buildings are not symbols of metaphysical concerns, they are metaphysics. Or to be more precise, we lend these buildings our own sense of sadness and seriousness; we meet our own emotions through the specific medium of architecture.

THE VIRTUE OF TRADITION

One of tragedies of modern culture is the rejection of tradition. The breaking of tradition has resulted in a benumbing uniformity of architecture, on the one hand, and in a rootless architectural anarchy, on the other. Many of today's celebrated buildings appear as mere stylistic inventions, arrogant fabrications of an architectural language not rooted in our experience of reality. Architecture, as any form of art or language, can develop only on the basis of a cumulative tradition that balances the inventive and conservative elements of culture. Our troubled relation to tradition also contains an obsessed relation with the concept of freedom. The aspiration for freedom and autonomy has turned into an irrational inherent value that rejects and excludes tradition.

As T.S. Eliot states, an authentic writer writes with the entire history of literature in his bones. Eliot speaks of a "sense of history" as the poet's mental position.[23] In the same way, a real architect is aware of his position in the continuum of architectural culture, not in terms of attempting to exploit his heritage, but placing himself in the framework of architectural culture with proud humility.

Architecture is engaged with the most fundamental and deepest existential issues. It is not a formal play, but a perpetual re-encounter with, and re-articulation of, certain fundamental existential positions: inside and outside, entering and departing, transparency and opacity, darkness and light, separation and integration, participation and withdrawal, departure and return, silence and solitude. Being active confrontations and encounters, all basic architectural events have a *verb-form* rather than *noun-form*. Architecture is fundamentally an art of actions, not forms.

Statements by today's avant-garde to the effect that architecture does not need to symbolize its sheltering function are absurd. The primary task of architecture has never been the physical sheltering function anyway. Throughout all time, architecture has been fundamentally concerned with the metaphysical domestication of space and time, sheltering the mind against the immensity of the world, and carving a refuge for man amidst the overpowering deluge of time. Even today, architecture continues to domesticate reality, to make it mentally comprehensible, and thus, bearable.

There is a tacit wisdom of architecture accumulated in history and tradition. But in today's panicked rush for the new, we rarely stop to listen to this wisdom. Architecture needs slowness to re-connect itself with this source of silent knowledge. Architecture requires slowness in order to develop a cumulative tradition again, to accumulate a sense of continuity, and to become re-rooted in culture.

In order to create an experiential background for grasping and understanding the dialectics of permanence and change, I believe that we need an architecture that rejects ephemerality, speed, and fashion; we need an architecture that slows our experience of reality.

HAPTICITY AND TIME

Notes on Fragile Architecture
(2000)

386 Fragile architecture: Carlo Scarpa's
    entrance to the Architectural Faculty
    of the University of Venice 1966,
    1972, 1985 (in collaboration with
    S. Los).
387 Pathology of the eye: a still from *The
    Andalucian Dog* (Le chien Andalou)
    by Luis Buñuel and Salvador Dali,
    1928.

THE HEGEMONY OF VISION AND RETINAL ARCHITECTURE

Modern consciousness and sensory reality have gradually developed towards the unrivalled dominance of the sense of vision. This thought-provoking development has been observed and analyzed by a number of philosophers in recent years.[1] David Michael Levin, one of today's thinkers concerned with the hegemony of vision, motivates the philosophical critique of the visual bias in the following words: "I think it is appropriate to challenge the hegemony of vision in the ocularcentrism of our culture. And I think we need to examine very critically the character of vision that predominates today in our world. We urgently need a diagnosis of the psychosocial pathology of everyday seeing—and a critical understanding of ourselves, as visionary beings."[2]

386

I believe likewise that many aspects of the pathology of today's architecture can also be understood through a critique of the ocular bias of our culture. As a consequence of the power of the eye over the other sensory realms, architecture has been transformed into an art form of the instant visual image. Instead of creating existential microcosms, embodied representations of the world, contemporary architecture projects retinal images for the purpose of immediate persuasion. The flatness of surfaces and materials, the uniformity of illumination, as well as the elimination of micro-climatic differences, further reinforces the tiresome and soporific uniformity of experience. All in all, the tendency of technological culture to standardize environmental conditions and make the environment entirely predictable is causing a serious sensory impoverishment. Our buildings have lost their opacity and depth, sensory invitation and discovery, mystery and shadow.

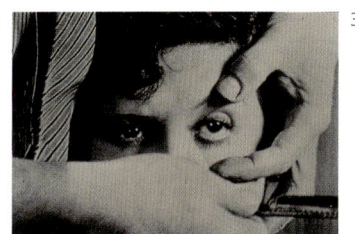

387

MULTI-SENSORY EXPERIENCE: THE SIGNIFICANCE OF TOUCH

Every significant experience of architecture is multi-sensory; qualities of matter, space, and scale are measured by the eye, ear, nose, skin, tongue, skeleton, and muscle. Maurice Merleau-Ponty emphasizes this simultaneity of experience and sensory interaction as follows: "My perception is (therefore) not a sum of visual, tactile, and audible givens: I perceive in a total way with my whole being: I grasp a unique structure of the thing, a unique way of being, which speaks to all my senses at once." [3]

Even the eye collaborates with the other senses. All the senses, including vision, are extensions of the sense of touch: the senses are specializations of the skin, and all sensory experiences are related to tactility. The anthropologist Ashley Montagu confirms the primacy of the tactile realm based on medical evidence: "[The skin] is the oldest and the most sensitive of our organs, our first medium of communication, and our most efficient protector...Even the transparent cornea of the eye is overlain by a layer of modified skin...Touch is the parent of our eyes, ears, nose, and mouth. It is the sense that became differentiated into the others, a fact that seems to be recognized in the age-old evaluation of touch as 'the mother of the senses'." [4] Touch is the sensory mode that integrates our experience of the world and of ourselves. Even visual perceptions are united and integrated into the haptic continuity of the self; my body remembers who I am and where I am placed in the world. In the opening chapter of *Combray*, Marcel Proust describes how the protagonist wakes up in his bed and gradually reconstructs his world on the basis of "the memory of the sides, knees and shoulders." [5]

The task of architecture is to make visible "how the world touches us," as Merleau-Ponty wrote of the paintings of Paul Cézanne. [6] Architecture concretizes and frames human existence in "the flesh of the world." [7]

Bernard Berenson, developing Goethe's notion of 'life-enhancing,' suggested that when experiencing an artistic work we imagine a genuine physical encounter through "ideated sensations." The most important of these Berenson called "tactile values." In his view, the work of authentic art stimulates our ideated sensations of touch, and this stimulation is life-enhancing. [8] Genuine architectural works, in my view, also evoke similar ideated tactile sensations that enhance our experience of ourselves.

The retinally-biased architecture of our time is clearly giving rise to a quest for a haptic architecture. Montagu sees a wider change taking place in Western consciousness: "We in the Western world are beginning to discover our neglected senses. This growing awareness

388 Significance of the skin: Pierre Bonnard's scintillating *Nude in the Bath*, 1925. Private collection.
389 Architecture of the muscles: steps at the Heian Shrine Garden, Tokyo.

represents something of an overdue insurgency against the painful deprivation of sensory experience we have suffered in our technologized world."[9] Our culture of control and speed has favored the architecture of the eye, with its instantaneous imagery and distanced impact, whereas haptic architecture promotes slowness and intimacy, appreciated and comprehended gradually as images of the body and the skin. The architecture of the eye detaches and controls, whereas haptic architecture engages and unites. Tactile sensibility replaces distancing visual imagery through enhanced materiality, nearness, and intimacy.

We are not usually aware that an unconscious element of touch is unavoidably concealed in vision; as we look, the eye touches, and before we even see an object we have already touched it. "Through vision, we touch the stars and the sun," as Merleau-Ponty poetically writes.[10] Touch is the unconsciousness of vision, and this hidden tactile experience determines the sensuous quality of the perceived object, and mediates messages of invitation or rejection, courtesy or hostility.

MATTER AND TIME

"Architecture is not only about domesticating space," writes Karsten Harries, "(I)t is also a deep defense against the terror of time. The language of beauty is essentially the language of timeless reality."[11] Architecture's task to provide us with our domicile in space is recognized by most architects, but its second task—to mediate our relation with the frighteningly ephemeral dimension of time—is usually disregarded.

In its quest for the perfectly articulated autonomous artifact, the main line of Modern architecture has preferred materials and surfaces that effect flatness, immaterial abstractness, and timelessness. Whiteness, in Le Corbusier's words, serves "the eye of truth," mediating thus moral, objective values.[12] The Modern surface is treated as an abstracted boundary of volume, and has a conceptual rather than a sensory essence. These surfaces tend to remain mute, as shape and volume are given priority; form is vocal, whereas matter remains mute. The aspiration to geometric purity and reductive aesthetics further weakens the presence of matter, in the same way that a strong figure and contour reading diminishes the interaction of color in the art of painting; all real colorists in painting use a weak *gestalt* in order to maximize color interaction. Abstraction and perfection transport us into the world of ideas, whereas matter, weathering, and decay strengthen the experience of time, causality, and reality.

As a consequence of its own formal ideals, contemporary architecture usually creates settings for the eye that seem to originate in a sin-

390 Architecture and time: detail of Alvar Aalto's Villa Mairea, Noormarkku 1938–39.

391 Multi-sensory experience: the town of Casares in southern Spain.

390

391

gle moment of time and evoke the experience of flattened temporality. Vision places us in the present tense, whereas haptic experience evokes the experience of a temporal continuum. The inevitable processes of aging, weathering, and wear are not usually considered as conscious and positive elements in design; the architectural artifact often exists in a timeless space, an artificial condition separated from the reality of time.[13] The architecture of the modern era aspires to an ageless youth and a perpetual present. The ideals of perfection and completeness further detach the architectural object from the reality of time and the traces of use. Consequently, our buildings have become vulnerable to the effect of time—literally time's revenge. Instead of offering positive qualities of depth and authority, time and use attack our buildings destructively.

A particularly thought-provoking example of the human need to experience and read time through architecture is the tradition of designed and built ruins, a fashion that became a mania in 18th century England and Germany. While engaged in the construction of his own house in Lincoln's Inn Fields—which, by the way, incorporated images of ruins—Sir John Soane imagined his structure as a ruin by writing a fictitious study of a future antiquarian.[14]

There are architects of our period, however, who evoke healing experiences of time. The architecture of Sigurd Lewerentz, for instance, connects us with deep time; his works obtain their unique emotive power from images of matter, which speak of opaque depth and mystery, dimness and shadow, metaphysical enigma and death. Death turns into a mirror image of life; Lewerentz enables us to see our death without fear, and in the continuum of timeless duration—the "womb of time," to use Shakespeare's expression from *Othello*. Lewerentz' St. Peter's and St. Mark's churches are dreams of fired clay brick in the same way that Michelangelo's sculptures and buildings are dreams of marble; the observer is permitted to enter the unconsciousness of clay and stone.

THE LANGUAGE OF MATTER

392

Materials and surfaces have a language of their own. Stone speaks of its ancient geological origins, its durability and inherent symbolism of permanence; brick makes one think of earth and fire, gravity and the long traditions of construction; bronze evokes the extreme heat of its manufacture, the processes of casting and the passage of time as measured in its patina. Wood speaks of its two existences and time scales: its first life as a growing tree and the second as a human artifact made by the caring hand of a carpenter or cabinetmaker. These are all materials and surfaces that speak pleasurably of time.

In reaction to the loss of materiality and temporal experience, we again appear to becoming sensitive to messages of matter, as well as to scenes of erosion, and decay. Materiality, erosion, and ruins have been favored subject matters of contemporary art from Arte Povera and Gordon Matta-Clark to Anselm Kiefer and the films of Andrey Tarkovsky. The art of Jannis Kounellis expresses dreams and memories of matter, whereas Richard Serra and Eduardo Chillida's uniquely authoritative masses of forged iron and steel awaken bodily experiences of weight and gravity. These works directly address our skeletal and muscular system; they communicate from the muscles of the sculptor to those of the viewer. Contemporary art and architecture are again recognizing the sensuality and eroticism of matter. The popularity of earth as a subject and medium of artistic expression is another example of this growing interest in images of matter. The imagery of Mother Earth suggests that after the utopian journey towards autonomy, immateriality, weightlessness, and abstraction, art and architecture are returning towards archaic female images of interiority, intimacy, and belonging.

Collage and assemblage are favored techniques of contemporary artistic representation; these media enable an archaeological density and a non-linear narrative through the juxtaposition of fragmented images deriving from irreconcilable origins. Collage invigorates the experience of tactility and time. Collage and film are the most characteristic art forms of our century, and these modes of image-making have penetrated into all other forms of art, including architecture.

MATERIAL IMAGINATION

In his phenomenological investigation of poetic imagery, Gaston Bachelard makes a distinction between 'formal imagination' and 'material imagination.'[15] He suggests that images arising from matter project deeper and more profound experiences than images arising from form. Matter evokes unconscious images and emotions, but modernity at large has been primarily concerned with form. However, an engagement with the material imagination seems to characterize the entire "other tradition of Modernism," to use the title of Colin St. John Wilson's book.[16]

Alvar Aalto, in his development away from the retinality of the Modern Movement towards a multi-sensory engagement, made a distinct step towards "images of matter." Significantly, at the same time, he rejected the universalist ideal of the Modern Movement in favor of regionalist, organic, historical, and romantic aspirations. Aalto's episodic architecture suppresses the dominance of a singular visual image. His architecture is not dictated by a dominant conceptual idea down to the last detail; rather Aalto's work grows through separate architectural

393

394

392 A dream of stone: the Tomb of Giuliano de Medici by Michelangelo, 1526–33.
393 Image of memory and matter: Athens Wall, installation by Yannis Kounellis, 1985.
394 Imagination of form: Ledoux's Spherical House for a Bailiff, c. 1780.

scenes, episodes, and detail elaborations. Instead of an overpowering intellectual concept, the whole is held together by the constancy of an emotional atmosphere, an architectural key, as it were.

In the mid-1930s, Erik Gunnar Asplund, Erik Bryggman, and Alvar Aalto made remarkably parallel moves away from reductive Functionalist aesthetics towards a layered and multi-sensory architecture. Asplund described this change of ideals in a 1936 lecture: "The idea that only design which is comprehended visually, can be art is a narrow conception. No, everything grasped by our other senses through our whole human consciousness and which has the capacity to communicate desire, pleasure, or emotions can also be art."[17]

This transition signals a departure from the predominantly visual and masculine air of Modern architecture towards a tactile and feminine sensibility. The feeling of external control and visual effect is replaced by a heightened sense of interiority and tactile intimacy. Sensuous materiality and the sense of tradition evoke a benevolent experience of natural duration and temporal continuum. Whereas the architecture of geometry attempts to build dams to halt the flow of time, haptic and multi-sensory architecture makes the experience of time healing and pleasurable. This architecture does not struggle against time; it reifies the course of time and makes it acceptable. This architecture seeks to accommodate rather than impress, to evoke domesticity and comfort rather than admiration and awe.

THE ARCHITECTURE OF EXPERIENTIAL EVENTS

Whereas the usual design process proceeds from a guiding conceptual image down to the detail, this alternative architecture develops from experiential situations towards an architectural form. As drawings, in fact, these buildings might sometimes appear vague, fragmentary, or incomplete, as the design aims solely at qualities arising in the lived experiential situation. This is an architecture of sensory realism in opposition to single-minded conceptual idealism. Speaking of his cultural realism, Aalto writes: "Realism usually provides the strongest impulses [also] for my imagination."[18]

Architecture is usually understood as a visual syntax, but it can also be conceived through a sequence of human situations and encounters. Authentic architectural experiences derive from real or ideated bodily confrontations rather than from visually observed entities. Authentic architectural experiences, as I often state, thus have more the essence of a verb than a noun. The visual image of a door is not a true architectural image, for instance, whereas entering and exiting through a door are architectural experiences. Similarly, the window frame is

395 Imagination of matter: sensuous Sufi Fountain of Life.
396 Architecture of strong image: Lethbridge University in Alberta, Canada by Arthur Erickson, 1972.

not an architectural unit—whereas looking out through the window, or daylight filtering through it, are authentic architectural encounters.

In his description of the design process of the Paimio Sanatorium, Aalto formulates a design philosophy progressing from the identification and articulation of experiential situations: "…a building has to be conceived from inside outwards, that is, the small units and details with which a person is engaged form a kind of a framework, a system of cells, which eventually turns into the entity of the building. At the same time as the architect develops a synthesis from the smallest cells onwards, the opposite process exists and the architect keeps the entity in his mind."[19]

Using this method of analyzing experiential situations, Aalto conceived the Sanatorium as a carefully and empathetically studied instrument of healing for the benefit of human beings at their weakest, "the horizontal human being," as Aalto calls his hospitalized client.[20] Aalto's Sanatorium could well be the one building in the history of Modern architecture that contains the highest concentration of technical innovations, yet remains firmly rooted in human experiential reality.

FRAGILE ARCHITECTURE

Our culture aspires to power and domination. This quest characterizes Western architecture as well; architecture seeks a powerful image and impact. The Italian philosopher Gianni Vattimo, referring to a philosophical method that does not aspire to totalize the multitude of human discourses into a single system, introduced the notions of 'weak ontology' and 'fragile thought'—*il pensiero debole*—in *The End of Modernity*.[21] Vattimo's idea seems to be parallel to Goethe's method of "Delicate Empiricism" (*Zarte Empirie*), an effort "to understand a thing's meaning through prolonged empathetic looking and understanding it grounded in direct experience."[22] In accordance with Vattimo's notions, we can speak of a 'weak' or 'fragile' architecture, or perhaps, more precisely, of an architecture of weak structure and image, as opposed to an architecture of strong structure and image. Whereas the latter desires to impress us through an outstanding singular image and a consistent articulation of form, the architecture of weak image is contextual and responsive; it is concerned with sensory interaction instead of idealized and conceptual manifestations. This architecture grows and opens up, instead of the reverse process of closing down from the concept to the detail. Due to the negative connotations of the word 'weak,' we should, perhaps, use the notion 'fragile architecture.'

In an essay entitled "Weak Architecture"[23] Ignasi de Solà-Morales projects Vattimo's ideas on the reality of architecture somewhat differ-

397 Architecture of fragile image: garden of Katsura Detached Palace, Kyoto.
398 Fragile art: *Sycamore leaves*, Andy Goldsworthy, Leeds, Yorkshire, September, 1977.

ently from my interpretation, asserting that "In the field of aesthetics, literary, pictorial and architectonic experience can no longer be founded on the basis of a system: not a closed, economic system such as that of the classical age...the present-day artistic universe is perceived from experiences that are produced at discrete points, diverse, heterogeneous to the highest degree, and consequently our approximation to the aesthetic is produced in a weak, fragmentary, peripheral fashion, denying at every turn the possibility that it might ultimately be transformed definitively into a central experience."[24] He defines 'event' as the fundamental ingredient of architecture and concludes his essay as follows: "This is the strength of weakness; that strength which art and architecture are capable of producing precisely when they adopt a posture that is not aggressive and dominating, but tangential and weak."[25]

We could equally speak of a 'weak urbanism'.[26] The dominant trends of town planning have also been based on strong strategies and strong urban form, whereas the medieval townscapes, as well as the urban settings of traditional communities, have grown on the bases of weak principles. The eye reinforces strong strategies, whereas weak principles of urbanity give rise to the haptic townscape of intimacy and participation.

A similar 'weak structure' has also emerged in literature and cinema; the new French novel, *le nouvel roman*, deliberately fragments the linear progression of the story and opens it up to alternative interpretations. The films of Michelangelo Antonioni and Andrey Tarkovsky, on the other hand, exemplify a weak cinematic narrative, based on improvisation. Such a technique creates a deliberate distance between the image and the narrative, with the intention of weakening the logic of the story and thus creating an associative field of clustered images. Instead of being an external spectator of the narrative event, the reader/viewer is made a participant, one who accepts a moral responsibility for the progression of the events.[27]

THE POWER OF WEAKNESS

The idea of fragility suggests empathetic listening and dialogue. In the early 1980s, the Finnish painter Juhana Blomstedt entitled a series of his paintings *The Listening Eye*.[28] This title suggests a humbled gaze liberated from the desire for patriarchal domination. Perhaps we should also conceive architecture with a listening eye. Geometry and formal reduction serve the heroic and utopian line of architecture that rejects time, whereas materiality and fragile form evoke a sense of humility and duration.

The idea of weak image in architecture seems to run parallel with the idea of 'weak force' in physics, as well as with the weak processes of nature, when compared to the use of excessive physical violence in our technological processes.[29] Architecture is an art form of inherently weak impact compared with, for instance, the flood of emotions mobilized by theatrical, cinematic, and musical experiences. The strength of architectural impact derives from its unavoidable presence as the perpetual unconscious pre-understanding of our existential condition.

A distinct weakening of the architectural image takes place through the processes of weathering and ruination. Erosion strips away a building's layers of utility, rational logic, and detail articulation, and pushes the structure into the realm of uselessness, nostalgia, and melancholy. The language of matter takes over from the visual and formal effect, and the structure attains a heightened intimacy. The arrogance of perfection is replaced by a humanizing vulnerability. This is why artists, photographers, filmmakers, and theatre directors tend to utilize images of eroded and abandoned architecture to evoke a subtle emotional atmosphere.

In an essay on theater director Peter Brook's destructive manipulation of the architectural space for theatrical purposes, Andrew Todd writes: "The walls engage time in a complex way. There is an after-echo of the original bourgeois music hall form, and this is rendered profound, even tragic, by the opening up of the layers of time on the walls. The top skin, which seals the imagination at a specific style or period, has been scorched away, so the walls exist in an indeterminate time, partway between cultural definition and eschatological dissolution. But this is no dead ruin: Brook has not been afraid to bash the place around a little more, breaking holes, putting in doors … One can also speak of another virtual patina the walls have acquired through the accruing memory of Brook's work in there."[30] I have quoted elsewhere Rainer Maria Rilke's stunning chapter in *The Notebooks of Malte Laurids Brigge*, where the protagonist comprehends the life that has been lived in a demolished house through the traces it has left on the end wall of the neighboring building; in fact these are signs by which the young man reconstructs essential aspects of his childhood and self.[31]

A similar weakening of architectural logic also takes place in the re-use and renovation of buildings. The insertion of new functional and symbolic structures short-circuits the initial architectural logic of the structure and opens up emotional and expressive ranges of experience. Architectural settings that layer contradictory ingredients project a special charm. Often the most enjoyable museum, office, or residential space is that which is fit into an adapted existing building.

The ecological approach also favors an adaptive image, parallel to the inherent 'weakness' of ecologically adapted processes. This ecologi-

399

400

401

cal fragility is reflected in much contemporary art, for instance, in the poetic works of Richard Long, Hamish Fulton, Wolfgang Leib, Andy Goldsworthy, and Nils-Udo, all set in a subtle dialogue with nature. Here again, artists set an example for architects.

The art of gardening is an art form inherently engaged with time, change, and fragile image. On the other hand, the geometric garden exemplifies the attempt to domesticate nature into patterns of man-made geometry. The tradition of landscape and garden architecture can provide an inspiration for an architecture liberated from the constraints of geometric and strong image. The biological models—bio-mimicry—have already entered various fields of science, medicine, and engineering. Why should they not be valid in architecture? Indeed, the more subtle line of high-tech architecture is already heading in that direction.

IMAGES OF FRAGILE ARCHITECTURE

The architecture of the Japanese garden, with its multitude of parallel, intertwining architectonic themes fused with nature, and its subtle juxtaposition of natural and man-made morphologies, is an inspiring example of the aesthetic power of weak form. The remarkably sensitive architecture of Dimitris Pikionis' footpaths leading to the Acropolis in Athens, the abstracted waterfall of Lawrence Halprin's Ira's Fountain in Portland, Oregon, and Carlo Scarpa's meticulously crafted architectural settings—all are contemporary examples of an architecture that places us in a different relation to space and time than the architecture of eternal geometry. These are examples of an architecture whose full power does not rely on a singular concept or image. Pikionis' work is a dense conversation with time and history to the degree that the design appears as a product of anonymous tradition without drawing attention to the individual creator. Halprin's designs explore the threshold between architecture and nature; his designs have the relaxed naturalness of scenes of nature, yet they read as a man-made counterpoint to the geological and organic world. Scarpa's architecture creates a dialogue between concept and making, visuality and tactility, artistic invention and tradition. Although his projects often seem to lack an overall guiding idea, they project an impressive experience of architectural discovery and courtesy.

Alvar Aalto's Villa Mairea is, of course, an early masterpiece of the episodic architecture of fragile formal structure; it is made from a sequence of architectural parts or acts in the same way as a theatrical play consists of acts and a piece of music of movements.[32] The composition aims at a specific ambience, a receptive emotional state, rather than the authority of form. This architecture obscures the categories of

399 The strength of fragility: Wolfgang Laib, *The Mountains not to climb on*, 1990. Pollen from hazelnut. Installation Galerie des Beaux-Arts, Brussels.
400 Landscaping of Acropolis in Athens by Dimitris Pikionis, 1954–57.
401 Appropriateness and humility of design: a Finnish seal hunter's lunchbox. The boatlike object can float on bilgewater.

foreground and background, object and context, and evokes a liberated sense of natural duration. An architecture of courtesy and attention, it invites us to be humble, receptive, and patient observers. This philosophy of compliance aspires to fulfill the humane reconciliatory task of the art of architecture.

PERSPECTIVAL SPACE AND PERIPHERAL VISION

The historic development of the representational techniques depicting space and form is closely tied to the development of architecture itself. The perspectival understanding of space gave rise to an architecture of vision, whereas the quest to liberate the eye from its perspectival fixation has enabled the conception of multi-perspectival and simultaneous space. Perspectival space leaves us as outside observers, whereas multi-perspectival space encloses and enfolds us in its embrace. This is the perceptual and psychological essence of Impressionist and Cubist space; we are pulled into the space and made to experience it as a fully embodied sensation. The special reality of a Cézanne landscape, as well as of fragile architecture, derives from the way these artistic works engage our perceptual and psychological mechanisms.

While the hectic eye of the camera captures a momentary situation, a passing condition of light, or an isolated, carefully framed and focused fragment, the experience of architectural reality depends fundamentally on peripheral and anticipated vision; the mere experience of interiority implies peripheral perception. The perceptual realm that we sense beyond the sphere of focused vision is as important as the focused image that can be frozen by the camera. This assumption suggests that one reason why contemporary spaces often alienate us—compared with historical and natural settings that elicit powerful emotional engagement—has to do with the contemporary poverty of peripheral vision. Focused vision makes us mere outside observers; peripheral perception transforms retinal images into a spatial and bodily involvement and encourages participation. That is why a photographic image is usually an unreliable witness of true architectural quality; architects would do better if they were less concerned with the photogenic qualities of their works.

Even creative activity calls for an unfocused and undifferentiated subconscious mode of vision, one fused with integrative tactile experience.[33] The object of a creative act is not only enfolded by the eye and the touch, it has to be introjected, identified with one's own body and existential experience. In deep thought, focused vision is blocked and thoughts travel with an absent-minded gaze. In creative work, both the scientist and the artist are directly engaged with their corporeal and existential experience rather than with an external logistical problem.

THE MARGIN FOR TOLERANCE AND ERROR

The strong image in art aspires to the perfectly articulated and final artifact. This is the Albertian aesthetic ideal of a work of art "to which nothing can be added or subtracted."[34] By definition, a strong image has minimal tolerance for change and consequently contains an inherent aesthetic vulnerability in relation to the forces of time. A weak *gestalt*, on the contrary, allows additions and alterations; a fragile form possesses aesthetic tolerance, a margin for change. The criteria of tolerance also takes place on a psychological level; contemporary designs are often so constrained in their exclusive aesthetics that they create a hermetic and arrogant sense of isolation and autism, whereas a fragile structure projects a welcoming open-endedness and a sense of aesthetic relaxation.

The strong image is obliged to simplify and reduce the multiplicity of problems and practicalities in order to condense the shapeless diversity of the task into a powerful singular image. Such a strong image is often reached by means of severe censoring and suppression; the clarity of image frequently contains hidden repression.

Here I would like to stress that I am not condemning this architecture of such formal strength; I am merely critical of visually formalistic architecture. I suggest an alternative to the prevalent reductive aesthetics of Western architectural thought. There are architects today who combine conceptual strength with sensual subtlety, such as Tadao Ando, Peter Zumthor, Steven Holl, Rick Joy, and Kengo Kuma. In Luis Barragán's work as well, an apparently strong image glides into the elusive world of dreams.

John Ruskin believed that, "Imperfection is in some way essential to all that we know of life. It is the sign of life in a mortal body, that is to say, of a state of process and change. Nothing that lives is, or can be, rigidly perfect; part of it is decaying, part nascent ... And in all things that live there are certain irregularities and deficiencies, which are not only signs of life but sources of beauty."[35]

Aalto elaborated Ruskin's idea when he spoke of 'the human error' and criticized the quest for absolute truth and perfection: "One might say that the human factor (in the Finnish original, error) has always been part of architecture. In a deeper sense, it has even been indispensable to making it possible for buildings to fully express the richness and positive values of life."[36] Architectural design usually aspires to a continuity of ideas and articulation, whereas a fragile architecture seeks deliberate discontinuities. Aalto's design process, for instance, produces differences and discontinuities instead of a unifying logic. Elaborating Michel Foucault's critique of the Modernist sensibility,

Demetri Porphyrios identified Aalto's thinking as heterotopic, in opposition to the usual Modernist homotopic manner of thought.[37] Aalto himself uses the expression 'benign error,' referring to discontinuities in design logic.[38] He was a master of turning last minute design alterations or on-site mistakes into brilliant detail improvisations.

BEAUTY AS A PRECONCEPTION

Traditional architectural environments rarely read as outstanding singular aesthetic objects; they present variations on the unself-conscious themes of tradition. Even aesthetically awkward elements add up to attractive environments. The pleasurable experience of vernacular settings arises from a relaxed sense of appropriateness, causality, and contextuality, rather than from any deliberate aspiration for preconceived beauty.

In our culture of material abundance, lost in a spiritual desert, architecture has become an endangered art form. The discipline is threatened by quasi-rational, techno-economic instrumentalization, on the one hand, and the processes of commodification and aestheticization on the other. Paradoxically, works of architecture are simultaneously turned into objects of vulgar utility and objects of shrewd visual seduction.

The architecture of Modernity—and particularly of our consumerist era—has become too consciously engaged with aesthetic effects and qualities. Our culture has aestheticized politics as well as war, and aestheticization now also threatens the art of architecture. Erik Bryggman wisely cautioned against this already in the 1920s: "We should understand that beauty is not a mysterious veil thrown over a building but a logical result of having everything in the right place."[39]

Focused on visual imagery and detached from social and contextual considerations, the celebrated architecture of our time—and the publicity that attempts to convince us of its genius—too often has an air of self-satisfaction and omnipotence. Buildings attempt to conquer the foreground instead of creating a supportive background for human activities and perceptions. Contemporary architectural projects are often impudent and arrogant; we seem to have lost the virtues of architectural neutrality, restraint, and modesty. Authentic works of art, however, always remain suspended between certainty and uncertainty, faith and doubt. The task of responsible architects is to resist the current cultural erosion and to replant buildings and cities in an authentic existential and experiential soil. At the beginning of the new millennium, architectural culture would do well to nurture productive tensions between cultural realism and artistic idealism, determination and discretion, ambition and humility.

402 "The White House," an Anasazi
Indian structure, Canyon de Chelly,
Arizona.

LANDSCAPES OF ARCHITECTURE

Architecture and the Influence of
Other Fields of Inquiry
(2003)

"Thinking is more interesting than knowing, but less interesting than seeing." [1]

J.W.Goethe

•

An architect faces an immense landscape today: the art of construction with its complex cultural and disciplinary contexts, its deep history and desire for invention, its interrelations and interactions with numerous other fields, as well as its internal boundaries and contradictions. Unless one prepares a conceptual map of the territory to be traversed, confusion and disorientation will overtake the journey.

During my nearly forty years of architectural writing, I have often surveyed the essences and boundaries of architecture; here I intend to present a kind of a synopsis of my views. I have chosen to survey how our specific art form is situated in the fields of knowledge and expression, and to point out parallels and differences, and interdependencies and oppositions, in architecture's relation to other fields. Recognizable themes from my earlier writings are compressed in this survey, and here, too, I want to suggest frankly that we all have but one single story to tell, a story we continuosly reformulate throughout our lives. We all continually construct a single edifice in accordance with our own image.

ARCHITECTURE—AN IMPURE DISCIPLINE

The complexity of the phenomenon of architecture results from its 'impure' conceptual essence as a field of human endeavor. Architecture is simultaneously a practical and a metaphysical act: a utilitarian and poetic, technological and artistic, economic and existential, collective and individual, manifestation of our being. I cannot, in fact, name a discipline possessing a more complex, and essentially more conflicting, grounding in the lived reality and in human intentionality. Architecture is essentially a form of philosophizing by means of its essential characteristics: space, matter, structure, scale, and light. Architecture responds to existing demands and desires at the same time that it creates its own reality and criteria; it is both the end and the means. Moreover, authentic architecture surpasses all consciously set aims and, consequently, it is always a gift.

THE MULTIPLICITY OF THEORETICAL APPROACHES

During the past few decades, numerous theoretical frameworks originating in various fields of scientific inquiry have been applied to analyses of architecture: perceptual and gestalt psychology, anthropological and literary structuralism, sociological and linguistic theories, analytic, existential, phenomenological, and deconstructionist philosophies, and more recently, cognitive and neuro-sciences, to name the most obvious. Our discipline does not possess a theory of its own; architecture is usually explained through theories that have arisen outside its realm. In the first century B.C., in the most influential theoretical treatise in the history of Western architecture, Vitruvius acknowledged the necessary breadth of the architect's discipline and the consequent interactions with numerous skills and areas of knowledge: "Let him (the architect) be educated, skilful with the pencil, instructed in geometry, know much history, have followed the philosophers with attention, understand music, have some knowledge of medicine, know the opinions of the jurists and be acquainted with astronomy and the theory of heavens."[2] Vitruvius provides careful reasons why the architect needs to master each of these fields of knowledge. Philosophy, for instance, "makes an architect high-minded and not self-assuming, but rather renders him courteous, just and honest without avariciousness."[3]

THE FRENZY OF THEORIZING

In our time, however, theoretical and verbal explanations of buildings have often seemed more important than their actual design, and intellectual constructs often more important than the actual material and sensuous encounter of the built works. The uncritical application of various scientific theories to the field of architecture has caused more confusion than a genuine understanding of its specific essence. The over-intellectual focus of these approaches has detached architectural discourse from its experiential, embodied, and emotive ground; intellectualization has pushed aside the common sense of architecture. The interpretation of architecture as a system of language, for instance, with given operational rules and meanings, gave support to the heresy of postmodernist architecture. The view of architectural theory as a prescriptive or instrumental pre-condition for design should be regarded altogether with suspicion. I, for one, seek a dialectical tension between theory and design practice instead of a causal interdependence.

The extreme amount of logocentric theorizing—the hysteria of theorizing, I should say—during the past several decades calls for an explanation. Karsten Harries, one of today's significant philosophers deeply interested in architecture, has this to say about recent hyperactive theorization and philosophization: "One thing the widespread interest in philosophy, that has become so much part of the postmodern architectural scene, suggests is that architecture has become uncertain of its way. No discipline sure of itself will bother much with philosophy."[4]

NATURAL PHILOSOPHY OF ARCHITECTURE

Indeed, I well remember the innocently non-theoretical, pragmatic, and self-assured excitement of the late 1950s and early 1960s, as compared to today's air of uncertainty, frustration, and intellectualization. Architecture was regarded as a calling rather than as a profession; as we all remember, Le Corbusier considered architecture as a way of life rather than as a profession or a trade. We believed then—and I still do—that there is a tacit 'natural philosophy of architecture', which needs not to be—or, indeed, may not be—formulated and refined in words. Architecture develops autonomously within the realm of its very practice, and within its pragmatic as well as its idealistic aspirations.

Until the 1970s, a formal and formalist manner of analyzing and teaching architecture prevailed. Architecture was seen primarily as a rational engagement with function and technique and a visual exercise in geometry and proportion, taught through a visual elementarism deriving from Bauhaus pedagogy. During the past three decades this formalist approach has been challenged by experiential emphases often grounded in phenomenological philosophy; architecture has been increasingly regarded as a mental, embodied, and existential act. The experiential interest has also given rise to a quasi-poetic use of language and endless, but rootless, associations and metaphors. As the phenomenological geographer David Seamon warns us: "The phenomenological enterprise is a highly personal, interpretive venture. In trying to see the phenomenon it is very easy to see too much or too little."[5]

The sheer complexity of any architectural task calls for an embodied manner of working and a total introjection—to use a psychoanalytical notion—of the task. The real architect works, I believe, through his or her entire personality instead of manipulating pieces of pre-existing knowledge or verbal rationalizations. An architectural or artistic task is encountered rather than resolved. In fact, in genuine creative work, knowledge and prior experience has to be forgotten. The great Basque sculptor Eduardo Chillida—an artist who illustrated Martin Heidegger's book *Die Kunst und der Raum* (1969), by the way—once said to me in a conversation: "I have never had any use for things I have known before I start my work."[6] Joseph Brodsky, the Nobel poet, shares this view, in saying, "In reality (in art and, I would think, science), experience and the accompanying expertise are the maker's worst enemies."[7]

In creative work forgetting is as important as remembering, unknowing as important as knowing.

ARCHITECTURE AS PURE RATIONALITY

The seminal artistic question of the past decades has been 'What is art?' The general orientation of the arts since the late 1960s has been to be increasingly entangled, in fact identified, with their own theories. The task of architecture has also become a concern since the late 1960s, first through the leftist critique, which saw architecture primarily as an unjust use of power, redistribution of resources, and social manipulation. The present condition of excessive intellectualization reflects the collapse of the social role of architecture and the escalation of complexities and frustrations in design practice. The current uncertainties concern the social and human role of architecture as well as its boundaries as an art form.

With these observations an opposition emerges: architecture as a subconscious and direct projection of the architect's personality, on the one hand, and as an application of disciplinary knowledge on the other. This is the inherent dualism of architectural education, also.

The idea of transforming architecture from a subjective art to an objective science, a rational practice of rules, has been a periodically strong aspiration since Jacques-Nicolas-Louis Durand's system of architectural elements in the early 19th century all the way to Christopher Alexander's *A Pattern Language* and Peter Eisenman's *Visual Syntax*.[8] In order to make the notions of rationality and rationalization ambiguous, "rationalization" is one of the defense mechanisms in the theory of psychoanalysis. This means that rationalization is frequently used as a defense against some undesired and suppressed psychic contents. Rationalization may also be used as a defense against creative freedom.

SCIENCE AND ART

The relation of scientific knowledge and artistic knowledge, or instrumental knowledge and existential knowledge, requires some consideration in this survey. The scholarly and literary work of the unorthodox French philosopher Gaston Bachelard, who has been known to the architectural profession since his influential book *The Poetics of Space* (first published in French in 1958), mediates between the worlds of scientific and artistic thinking. I am indebted to Bachelard's thinking, and have made frequent references to it throughout my writings. Through penetrating philosophical studies of the ancient elements—earth, fire, water, and air, as well as dreams, day-dreams, and imagination—Bachelard suggests that poetic imagination, or 'poetic chemistry', as he says, is closely related to pre-scientific thinking and an animistic understanding of the world. In *The Philosophy of No: A Philosophy of the New Scientific Mind*, written in 1940 during the period when his interest was shifting from scientific phenomena to poetic imagery (*The Psychoanalysis of Fire* was published two years earlier), Bachelard describes the historical development of scientific thought as a set of progressively more rationalized transitions from animism through realism, positivism, rationalism and complex rationalism, to dialectical rationalism.[9] "The philosophical evolution of a special piece of scientific knowledge is a movement through all these doctrines in the order indicated," he argues.[10]

ANIMATED IMAGES

Significantly, Bachelard holds that artistic thinking seems to proceed in the opposite direction—pursuing conceptualizations and expression, but passing through the rational and realist attitudes towards a mythical and animistic understanding of the world. Science and art, therefore, seem to glide past each other, moving in opposite directions. Whereas scientific thought progresses and differentiates, artistic thought seeks to return to an un-differentiated and experientially singular, animistically charged world. Architecture is no exception in this respect. Buildings are given an animated life: they move and communicate, gesture and suggest, invite and reject. "The roofs of Paris lay on their backs with their small paws upright," the French writer Raymond Queneau writes, giving familiar buildings a life of their own.[11] Another French poet, Jean Pellerin, observes, "The door scents me, it hesitates."[12]

In addition to animating the world, the artistic imagination seeks imagery able to express the entire complexity of human existential experience through singular condensed images. This paradoxical task is achieved through poeticized images, ones which are experienced and lived rather than rationally understood. As I have often stated, Giorgio Morandi´s tiny still-lifes are a stunning example of the capacity of humble artistic images to become all-encompassing metaphysical statements. A work of art or architecture is not a symbol that represents or indirectly portrays something outside itself; it is a real mental image object, one that places itself directly in our existential experience and consciousness.

Although I am here underlining the difference between scientific and artistic inquiry, I do not believe that science and art are antithetical or hostile to each other. The two modes of knowing simply look at the world and human life with different eyes and aspirations. Stimulating views have also been written about the similarities of the scientific and the poetic imagination, as well as of the significance of aesthetic pleasure, for both practices.

THE POWER OF POETIC LOGIC

Architecture's task—to integrate irreconcilable opposites—is impossible, fundamental, and necessary. In fulfilment of this, the essential aims of architecture are bound to be mediation and reconciliation: the essence of an authentic architectural work is the embodiment of mediation and reconciliation. Architecture negotiates between differing categories and oppositions. Architecture is conceivable in this contradictory task only through understanding any design as a poetic manifestation; poetic imagery is capable of overcoming contradictions of logic through its polyvalent and synthetic imagery. As Alvar Aalto once wrote: "In every case [of creative work] one must achieve the simultaneous solution of opposites. Nearly every design task involves tens, often hundreds, sometimes thousands of different contradictory elements, which are forced into a functional harmony only by man's will. This harmony cannot be achieved by any other means than those of art."[13]

ARCHITECTURE IN OTHER ART FORMS

I have devoted many essays and a separate book to the architecture of painting and cinema and, along with others, I have also studied how architectural settings and situations are conveyed in poetry and fiction. Marilyn Chandler's book *Dwelling in the Text* has been inspiring in its study of architectural imagery in American fiction.[14] A considerable amount has also been written on the architectural essence of music and vice versa, not to speak of direct cross-inspirations between these two arts. The Pythagorean harmonics, that oldest of Western scientific traditions, seeks to unite the spiritual essences of music and architecture. I can confess that I was converted to Pythagoreanism by my professor and mentor Aulis Blomstedt already in the early 1960s.[15]

I am convinced that all art forms explore the existential essence of culture, life, and human consciousness, and all of them are bound to follow similar strategies and tactics. Moreover, all artistic expression is filtered through the human senses, and through our memory and imagination. For many years, I have relied on the phenomenologist Van den Berg's words—"All painters and poets are born phenomenologists"—to support my assertion that the same must be said of all artists and architects.[16] This view opens up a bottomless well for architectural inspiration and insight through the study of other art forms.

ARCHITECTURE OF PAINTING

When speaking of the evolution of Modern architecture, Alvar Aalto often said: "But it all began in painting." In 1947 he wrote, "... abstract art forms have brought impulses to the architecture of our time, although indirectly, but this fact cannot be denied. On the other hand, architecture has provided sources for abstract art. These two art forms have alternately influenced each other. There we are—the arts do have a common root even in our time ..."[17]

Painting is close to the realm of architecture, particularly because architectural issues are so often—or I should say, unavoidably—part of the subject matter of painting, regardless of whether we are looking at representational or abstract painting. In fact, this distinction is highly questionable altogether, because all meaningful art is bound to be representational in the existential sense.

Late medieval and early Renaissance paintings are particularly inspiring for an architect because of the constant presence of architecture. The painters' interest in architecture seems to be related with the process of the differentiation of the world and individual consciousness, the birth of the first personal pronoun 'I'. The smallest of details suffices to create the experience of architectural space; a framed opening or the mere edge of a wall provides an architectural setting. The innocence and humanity of this painterly architecture, the similarity of the human and the architectural figure is most comforting, touching, and inspiring: this is a truly therapeutic architecture. The best lessons in domesticity and the essence of home are 17th century Dutch paintings, in which buildings are presented almost as human figures. The mirrored images of the house and the human body were introduced into modern thought by the psychologist and analyst C.G.Jung, and have been expressed by countless artists.

I cannot think of a more inspiring and illuminating lesson in architecture than that offered by early Renaissance paintings. If I could ever design a single building with the tenderness of Giotto's, Fra Angelico's, or Piero della Francesca's houses, I would feel that I have reached the very purpose of my life.

The interactions between modern art and modern architecture are well known and acknowledged, but I have not yet seen an architecture inspired by J. M. W. Turner, Claude Monet, Pierre Bonnard, or Mark Rothko, for instance. Painting and other art forms have surveyed dimensions of human emotion and spirit unknown to architects, whose art conventionally tends to respond to rationalized normality. The work of numerous contemporary artists—Robert Smithson, Gordon Matta-Clark, Michael Heizer, Donald Judd, Robert Irwin, Jannis Kounellis, Wolfgang Leib, Ann Hamilton, James Turrell, and James Carpenter, among others—is closely related with the essential issues of architecture. These are all artists whose works have inspired architects and will continue to do so.

We can also study principles of artistic thinking and making in the writings of many of these artists. Henry Moore, Richard Serra, Donald Judd, Agnes Martin, James Turrell, all of whom write perceptively on their own work, have been meaningful for me. Artists tend to write more directly and sincerely of their work than architects, who frequently cast an intellectualized smokescreen across their writings.

THE ARCHITECTURE OF CINEMA

In its inherent abstractness, music has historically been regarded as the art form closest to architecture. Cinema, however, is even closer to architecture than music, not solely because of its temporal and spatial structure, but fundamentally because both architecture and cinema articulate lived space. These two art forms create and mediate comprehensive images of life. In the same way that buildings and cities create and preserve images of culture and particular ways of life, cinema projects the cultural archaeology of both the time of its making and the era that it depicts. Both forms of art define dimensions and essences of existential space; they both create experiential scenes for life situations.

Film directors create pure poetic architecture, which arises directly from our shared mental images of dwelling and domesticity as well as the eroticism or fear of space. Directors such as Andrey Tarkovsky and Michelangelo Antonioni have created a moving architecture of memory, longing, and melancholy, one that assures us that the art form of architecture is also capable of addressing our entire emotional range, ranging from grief to ecstasy.

THE WISDOM OF BOOKS

As a young man and aspiring architect, I organized my books in two categories: architecture books and other books. Later on, I realized that all good books are books about architecture in the essential sense that they depict the interaction of individuals with their settings, life histories, institutions and customs, as well as with other individuals, and that this is exactly the field in which architecture takes place. I realized that the essence of architecture is not in buildings as physical objects, but in their role as frames through which the world is seen and as horizons of experiencing and understanding the human condition. Buildings are mental instruments, not simply aestheticized shelters. The essence of architecture is essentially beyond architecture. The poet Jean Tardieu asks: "Let us assume a wall: what takes place behind it?", but we architects rarely bother to imagine what happens behind the walls we have erected.[18]

Somewhat later I came to yet another realization: the books I had categorized as 'non-architecture' seemed to reveal more important aspects of the human significance of architecture than the books written specifically about the art of building and architects. There is an obvious reason for this; architecture books deal with their subject matter as a closed, formalized and, usually, conventionalized discipline, whereas poetry, novels, and plays are engaged with the very mental ground from which architecture arises. This observation applies to all art forms: painting, sculpture, photography, theatre, dance, music, and cinema. They all reveal the essence of artistic aspiration and expression, and they valorize the existential condition behind artistic expression. All arts are expressions of the timeless human existential enigma—this gives Egyptian art, for instance, its voice by which to approach us, to have such a forceful impact across the abyss of four and a half millennia.

LITERARY LESSONS IN ARCHITECTURE

The best lessons in architecture I have read, however, can be found, for instance, in Anton Chekhov's correspondence, which etches into the reader's consciousness the essence of human character as well as the tragic and comic aspects of life. By example, Chekhov's work teaches the supreme virtues of condensation and simplicity in artistic expression. Rainer Maria Rilke's poetry and his novel, *The Notebooks of Malte Laurids Brigge*, as well as his letters, all reveal the nature of poetic sensibility and the osmotic interaction between the outer space of the world and the inner space of the mind. Rilke teaches us the irreplaceable values of solitude and silence as *sine qua non* conditions for creative work. Joseph Brodsky's essays, minutely detailed analyses of poems by Robert Frost, Anna Akhmatova, and Osip Mandelstam, for instance, expose an incredible archaeology of poetic images. Brodsky also teaches us how the tragic, the vulgar, and the commonplace are ennobled as they become condensed into the spiritual imagery of poetry. And, too, Brodsky convinces the reader of the significance of uncertainty and insecurity for the creative mentality. "Poetry is a tremendous school of insecurity and uncertainty," he writes, continuing, "Poetry—writing it as well as reading it—will teach you humility and rather quickly at that. Especially if you are both writing and reading it."[19] The poet's observation applies to architecture; it certainly humbles you, particularly if you are both making it and theorizing about it. In my personal case, the realm of uncertainty expands every day, and I have developed a great suspicion for individuals who are sure of themselves and of their field. In my view an arrogant and self-assured architect has not understood the meaning and depth of his trade.

I should add to my personal list of the most significant architecture books the works of Franz Kafka, Fyodor Dostoyevsky, Thomas Mann, Herman Hesse, and Italo Calvino. Calvino's *Invisible Cities* is, of course, pure architecture in literary form—written architecture, as it were—as are Jorge Luis Borges' short stories and Georges Perec's hilarious *Espéces d'espaces*. Simply, all good literature concerns the condition of architecture.

In Borges' *On Writing*, he explains the origins and meanings of his literary imagery.[20] For instance, in the horrifying short story "The End of the Duel," two gauchos, who had been hostile to each other throughout their lives, are both taken prisoners in a civil war and are forced to perform their final rivalry in a running race with their throats cut. Borges reverses our received understanding of the relation of reality and imagination: "Reality is not always probable, or likely. But if you are writing a story, you have to make it as plausible as you can, because otherwise the reader's imagination will reject it."[21] In architecture, likewise, a fantasy of spaces and forms is not needed, but rather a genuine understanding of human behaviour, experience, and imagination. Architecture's task is to reveal the essences of the real rather than to project mere fantasies. Borges also wisely warns us of the obsession with contemporaneity: "No real writer ever tried to be contemporary."[22] The desire to be novel and contemporary is equally disastrous in our craft.

As we read a poem, we internalize it, and we become the poem. When I have read a book and return it back to its place on the bookshelf, the book, in fact, remains in me; if it is a great book, it has become part of my soul and my body. The Czech writer Bohumil Hrabal gives a vivid description of this act of reading: "When I read, I don't really read; I pop a beautiful sentence in my mouth and suck it like a fruit drop or I sip it like a liqueur until the thought dissolves in me like alcohol, infusing my brain and heart and coursing on through the veins to the root of each blood vessel."[23] In the same way, paintings, films, and buildings become part of us. Artistic works originate in the body of the maker and they return back to the human body as they are being experienced.

DUALISTIC ESSENCE OF ARCHITECTURE

I have pointed out the inherent ties between various arts and architecture. Yet, the dissimilarities have to be identified with equal emphasis. During the past two and half decades, architecture and architectural education have sought inspiration from the fine arts, and products of art have been used for the purposes of inspiring and generating architectural structures. Indeed, architecture has frequently been presented as an art form, but this has eroded the soil of architecture just as disastrously as pretentious theorizing and the insensitive application of scientific theories.

My response to the question of whether architecture is or is not an art form is determined: architecture is an artistic expression and it is not an art, simultaneously. Architecture is an art in its essence as a spatial and material metaphor of human existence, but it is not an art form in its second nature as an instrumental artifact of utility and rationality. This duality is the very essence of the art of architecture. This dual existence takes place on two separate levels of consciousness, or aspiration, in the same way that any artistic work has its existence simultaneously as a material, disciplinary, and concrete execution, on the one hand, and as a spiritual, unconsciously conceived and perceived imagery, which carries us to the world of dreams, desire and fear, on the other. Architecture can be understood only through this very duality. "A painter can paint square wheels on a cannon to express the futility of war. A sculptor can carve the same square wheels. But an architect must use round wheels," as Louis Kahn once said.[24]

ONTOLOGICAL GROUND

In his book *ABC of Reading*, the legendary modernist poet Ezra Pound writes: "…music begins to atrophy when it departs too far from the dance…poetry begins to atrophy when it gets too far from music…"[25] Joseph Brodsky defines the origins of poetry similarly: "Literature started with poetry, with the song of a nomad that predates the scribblings of a settler."[26] The arguments of the two master poets focus on two simultaneous matters: the primordial connections between art forms, on the one hand, and the importance of the specific ontological ground for each art form, on the other. Each art form has its own ontological beginning; that is to say, it arises from a particular human act or manifestation or set of experiences, and if the art in question loses its connection, its umbilical cord, with its own original beginning, it loses its life force and impact.

The art form of architecture is born from the purposeful confrontation and occupation of space. It begins by the act of naming the nameless and through perceiving formless space as a distinct figure and specific place. I wish to emphasize the adjective 'purposeful'; utilitarian purposefulness is a constitutive condition of architecture. The task of architecture, however, lies as much in the need for metaphysical grounding for human thought and experience as in the provision of shelter from a raging storm.

ARCHITECTURE AS COLLABORATION

Architecture, as with all artistic work, is essentially the product of collaboration. Collaboration of course occurs in the obvious and practical sense of the word, such as in the interaction with numerous professionals, workmen, and craftsmen. But collaboration occurs as well with other artists and architects, not only with one's contemporaries amongst the living, but perhaps more importantly with predecessors who have been dead for decades or centuries. One's most important teacher may have died half a millennium ago. Any authentic work is set into the timeless tradition of artistic works and the work is meaningful only if it presents itself humbly to this tradition and becomes part of that continuum. Countless works made at all times, but particularly today, are too ignorant, disrespectful, and arrogant to be accepted as constituents of the esteemed institution of tradition.

The role of the dead in the collectivity of creative work was, of course, pointed out by the poet T. S. Eliot in his 1919 seminal essay "Tradition and the Individual Talent," part of the long list of compulsory reading for all students of architecture.[27] But rather than repeating this often quoted essay, I'll refer to Jean Genet's observations on the role of the dead in the creative collaboration, as part of his essay on Alberto Giacometti: "In its desire to acquire real significance, each work of art must descend the steps of millennia with patience and extreme caution and meet, if possible, the immemorial night of the dead, so that the dead recognize themselves in the work."[28]

THE WISDOM OF ARCHITECTURE

The artistic tradition is not a depository, however, from which to bor-row, quote, or steal without permission. Our tradition is an esteemed community of its own, a community of conversation, exchange, and mutual assessment and respect. We not only utilize the accumulated wisdom of architecture—Milan Kundera speaks of the 'wisdom of the novel,' and argues that all good writers consult this wisdom[29]—we also alter the reading of prior works. This reverse process of histori-cal influence is most often forgotten, but it calls for special sensitivity and responsibility. Aldo van Eyck, one of the seminal architects of the second half of the 20th century, an architect who demonstrated the importance of anthropological studies for architecture, was once asked to give a lecture on the influence of Giotto on Cézanne.[30] Instead of the suggested topic, however, he chose to give a talk on the influence of Cézanne on Giotto. He realized that the thinking and painting of Paul Cézanne made us all see Giotto´s work in a totally new context. Brodsky provides yet another view into this reversed time perspective of creative interaction "…When one writes verse, one's most immediate audience is not one's own contemporaries, let alone posterity, but one's predeces-sors."[31] I am mentioning this reverse interaction in order to emphasize the multi-directional and multi-dimensional nature of creative work. Creative works draw from, and advance towards, all possible directions simultaneously.

AESTHETICIZATION

The Modern Movement arrived occasionally at architecture´s boundary as the consequence of aestheticization, seeing architecture as a pure art. Particularly in our time, however, the process of aestheticization has produced projects and buildings that have moved outside the territory of architecture entirely and turned into objects of art—frequently poor art, at that.

Current philosophical discourse has reintroduced the issue of beauty and ethics; Elaine Scarry's small, elegant book, *On Beauty and Being Just*, exemplifies this new orientation of ethics.[32] I fully agree with Scarry´s argument for the primacy of aesthetic judgement—an idea which has been also condensed into powerful formulations by Joseph Brodsky: "Man is an aesthetic being before becoming an ethi-cal being,"[33] and "Aesthetics is the mother of ethics."[34] Brodsky even makes a thought provoking statement of the evolutionary role of beauty: "The purpose of evolution, believe it or not, is beauty, which survives it all and generates truth simply by being a fusion of the mental and the sensual."[35]

At the same time that we see the constitutive value of aesthetic aspiration and judgement, we should be critical of the dubious practice of aestheticization. In our consumer culture aestheticization has turned into the canniest strategy of manipulation; violence, human suffering, and inequality are aestheticized today—as well as politics and war. Indeed, our very lives are turning into aestheticized products, which we consume as nonchalantly as the newest material products of fashion.

In our craft, also, seductive beauty and aesthetic appeal have turned into conscious and explicit aims.

THE IDEA OF PARADISE

In the very same manner as in poetry, enchanting and touching beauty in architecture is a result of other concerns: a desire for simplicity, precision, or truthfulness, and most importantly for the experience of life and of being human in the presence and company of other human beings. Every great building opens a view into the essence of the human condition and to an idealized and better world. As Alvar Aalto asserted in 1957: "…Architecture has a second thought…the idea of creating a Paradise. That is the only purpose of our buildings…we wish to build a Paradise on earth for people."[36]

EDITOR'S NOTE

The essays presented in *Encounters* have been selected from a vast array of possible choices: the written lectures, articles, introductions, essays, and critiques authored by Juhani Pallasmaa extend as far back as 1967, and continue (will assuredly continue!) right beyond the current moment of this book's publication. The selection resulted from consideration of all such works—whether originally written in Finnish or in English—but focused from the start of the process on those essays with an architectural emphasis. A selection of the author's essays considering primarily aspects of the world of art (with some architectural pieces) has been published in 1993 in a small, fine work entitled *Maailmassaolon taide* [The Art of Being in the World] (Helsinki: Painatuskeskus, 1993), regrettably available only in Finnish. Equally, the reader will not find here a re-printing of material previously published in other books authored or edited by Juhani Pallasmaa; it is hoped, in fact, that the reader stimulated by these essays will seek out those longer considerations of art, design, and architecture. A selected bibliography of this material can be found on pages 373–376.

The essays are not arranged in chronological order; rather, they have been placed into thematic adjacencies that often juxtapose essays of the 1970s with essays of the 1990s, suggesting a latent set of consistent approaches and attitudes. The reader choosing to start at page one and proceeding directly to the final page may accomplish this task too mechanically—in fact, it is hoped that a reader will feel it possible to enter the book at almost any point and "encounter" a vivid way of thinking about architecture, almost without the need for a chronological reference. That the first essay dates from 1977, and the last from 2003 is simply a happenstance event.

However, that direct reader may notice a certain repetition of references and at times, even a repetition of phrasing. When this occurs, it is entirely intentional. Indeed, the essays have been edited to remove unnecessary repetition, and to reinforce still the sound of a series of resonating ideas. Those readers familiar with these essays through previous publication in journals and reviews, or through the remembered echoes of lectures, may find paragraphs displaced or removed entirely from their previous position—again, this has been done to achieve a greater smoothness and consistency. Finally, the essays have been edited for a consistency of tone, grammar, spelling, and punctuation, regardless of their original language of publication.

Many thanks are due to Diana Tullberg and Michael Wynne-Ellis, who translated and provided several of these essays a standard of precision and depth in their choice of the English words to match the Finnish original. The later essays were written directly in English by the author—another indication of their phenomenal character. With a final note of gratitude, it has been the editor's great privilege to assist in their collected publication.

Essays Source Notes

"The Two Languages of Architecture: Elements of a Bio-Cultural Approach to Architecture," *Abacus 2, The Yearbook of the Museum of Finnish Architecture* (Helsinki: The Museum of Finnish Architecture, 1980), 57–90.
Translation: English Centre, Diana C. Tullberg.

"Architecture and the Obsessions of Our Times: A View of the Nihilism of Building," first given as a lecture at the YAPA-SAFA meeting, Helsinki, September, 1982.
Arkkitehti, The Finnish Architectural Review 5–6 (1983), 22–26.
Translation: Harald Arnkil and Juhani Pallasmaa.

"Stairways of the Mind," *International Forum of Psychoanalysis 9* (2000), 7–18.

"The Place of Man: Time, Memory and Place in Architectural Experience," first given as a lecture at the SAFA Architect Days, Helsinki, November, 1982. *Arkkitehti, The Finnish Architectural Review 1* (1983), 26–34.
Translation: Diana C. Tullberg.

"The Geometry of Feeling: A Look at the Phenomenology of Architecture, part 1," *Arkkitehti, The Finnish Architectural Review 3* (1985), 44–49.
Translation: Diana C. Tullberg.

"The Rooms of Memory—Architecture in Painting: A Look at the Phenomenology of Architecture, part 2," first given at the State Artist Professor lecture day, Helsinki, May 3, 1985. *Arkkitehti, The Finnish Architectural Review 5* (1985), 22–29.
Translation: Diana C. Tullberg.

"Identity, Intimacy, and Domicile: Notes on the Phenomenology of Home," first given as a lecture at the "Dwelling in Scandinavia" Symposium, University of Trondheim, August, 1992. *Arkkitehti, The Finnish Architectural Review 1* (1994), 14–25.

"Lived Space: Embodied Experience and Sensory Thought," first given as a lecture at the University of Ljubljana, Ljubljana, Slovenia, November, 1999. *The Sacred in Architecture* (Ljubljana: The University of Ljubljana, 1999), 123–135.

"City Sense: The City as Perceived, Remembered, and Imagined," *Den Oversete By – det sansede København Overlooking the City—Copenhagen as perceived* (Charlottenborg: Arkitektens Forlag, 1995), 10–15.

"From Utopia to a Monument: The Centre Pompidou and the Future of Modernism," *Arkkitehti, The Finnish Architectural Review 3* (1977), 18–22.
Translation: Michael Wynne-Ellis.

"Avant-Garde vs. Derrière-Garde," *Creation and Re-creation: America Draws, exhibition catalogue* (Helsinki: The Museum of Finnish Architecture, 1980), 74–84.

"The Contemporary Avant-Garde and the Wisdom of Architecture," *Skala* (Copenhagen, 1993), 28–31.

"From Metaphorical to Ecological Functionalism," first given as a lecture at the Fifth Alvar Aalto Symposium, Jyväskylä, Finland, August, 1991. *Functionalism: Utopia or the Way Forward? Report of the Fifth Alvar Aalto Symposium* (Helsinki: The Museum of Finnish Architecture, 1992), 8–19.

"Immateriality and Transparency," first given as a lecture at the GPD Glass Processing Days, Tampere, Finland, June, 2003. First publication.

"Toward an Architecture of Humility," *Harvard Design Magazine* (Cambridge, 1998), 22–25.

"From Tectonics to Painterly Architecture," *Alvar Aalto: Points of Contact, exhibition catalog* (Jyväskylä: The Alvar Aalto Museum, 1994), 36–47.

"The Logic of the Image," *The Journal of Architecture, volume 3* (Winter, 1998), 289–299.

"Man, Measure, and Proportion: Aulis Blomstedt and the Tradition of Pythagorean Harmonics," *Acanthus, The Yearbook of the Museum of Finnish Architecture* (Helsinki: The Museum of Finnish Architecture, 1992), 6–31.

"Architecture and the Reality of Culture: The Feasibility of Architecture in a Post-modern Society," first given as a lecture at the SAFA Architect Days, Helsinki, 1986. *Arkkitehti, The Finnish Architectural Review 1* (1987), 66–76.
Translation: Diana C. Tullberg.

"Tradition and Modernity: The Feasibility of Regional Architecture in Post-modern Society," first given as a lecture at the "Nordic Tradition" conference, Copenhagen, 1988. *The Architectural Review 5* (May, 1988), 27–34.

"The Limits of Architecture: Towards an Architecture of Silence," first given as a lecture for the State Commission for Architecture, Helsinki, April 23, 1990. *Arkkitehti, The Finnish Architectural Review 6* (1990), 26–39.
Translation: Michael Wynne-Ellis.

"Six Themes for the Next Millenium: Architecture in the Post-historical Perspective," first given as The Herman Miller Lecture, The Royal Institute of British Architects, London, March 8, 1994. *The Architectural Review 7* (July, 1994), 74–80.

"Melancholy and Time," first given as a lecture at the "Permanence" symposium, Virginia Polytechnic Institute, Blacksburg, Virginia, March, 1996.
First publication.

"Hapticity and Time: Notes on Fragile Architecture," first given as the 1999 RIBA Discourse Lecture, The Royal Institute of British Architects, London. *The Architectural Review 5* (May, 2000), 78–84.

"Landscapes of Architecture," first given as the keynote lecture at the Association of Collegiate Schools of Architecture (ACSA) International Conference, Helsinki, August, 2003.
First publication.

Endnotes

THE TWO LANGUAGES OF ARCHITECTURE

1   Juan Pablo Bonta, *Architecture and its Interpretation: A Study of Expressive Systems in Architecture* (London: Lund Humphries Publishers Ltd., 1979), 31.

2   An excellent presentation of the ideas of the Enlightenment on architecture as a language. The examples given here are based on: Anthony Vidler, "The writing on the wall: architectural theory in the late enlightenment," *Architectural Design* vol, 48 (1978): 57–59.

3   Ernst Kris, *Psychoanalytic Explorations in Art* (New York: Schocken Books, 1964).

4   Joseph-Marie De Gerando, *Des signes et de l'art de penser, 1800,* as quoted in: Vidler, op. cit., 58.

5   Ozenfant's and Le Corbusier's view is set forth in: Bonta, op. cit., 31.

6   Ozenfant and Le Corbusier, as quoted in: Bonta, op. cit., 31–32.

7   Jacques-Nicolas-Louis Durand, *Précis des Leçons d'Architecture* (Paris: 1819).

8   Vidler, op. cit., 59.

9   Peter Eisenman's visual syntax is analyzed, for example, in Mario Gandelsonas, "From Structure to Subject: The Foundation of an Architectural Language," *Oppositions* (Summer, 1979), 17.

10 See, for instance: Edward T. Hall, *The Hidden Dimension* (New York: Doubleday, 1966).

11 The formulations of ethnoscience, structuralism, transformational linguistics, and paralinguistic research are mainly based on: Davydd J. Greenwood and William A. Stini, *Nature, culture, and human history: a bio-cultural introduction to anthropology* (New York: Harper & Row, 1977).

12 Christopher Alexander, Sara Ishikawa, Murray Silverstein, with Max Jacobson, Ingrid Fiksdahl-King, Shlomo Angel, *A Pattern Language: Towns, Buildings, Construction* (New York: Oxford University Press, 1977).

13 The well-known principal works of the author are: Edward T. Hall, *The Silent Language* (Westport: Greenwood Press, 1959) and Edward T. Hall, *The Hidden Dimension* (New York: Doubleday, 1966).

14 The ability of a nerve fiber to transmit information is approx. 20 bit/ sec. or, according to some estimates, a maximum of 100 bit/sec. As there are some 10^{15} nerve fibers in the brain, the conveying capacity of the brain is about 10^{17} bit/sec—yet we are only capable of conveying a maximum of c. 100 bit/sec. of conscious content. Thus the total information transmission capacity of the brain is 10^{15} times its conscious capacity. Matti Bergström, *Aivojen fysiologiasta ja psyykestä* [On the Physiology and Psyche of the Brain] (Helsinki, 1979), 77–78.

15 Hall (1966), op. cit., 33–34.

16 Oscar Newman, *Defensible Space: Crime Prevention through Urban Design* (New York: Collier Books, 1973).

17 See, for instance: Frode Strømnes, "On the architecture of thought," *Abacus*, *Yearbook 2* (Helsinki: The Museum of Finnish Architecture, 1981), 6–29.

18 Alexander Lowen, *The Language of the Body* (New York: Macmillan, 1967). Another general presentation of Lowen's views on therapy is: Alexander Lowen, *Bioenergetics* (New York: Penguin Books, 1975).

19 Kent C. Bloomer and Charles W. Moore, *Body, Memory and Architecture* (New Haven: Yale University Press, 1977).

20 For example: Claude Lévi-Strauss, *Structural Anthropology* (New York: Basic Books, 1963).

21 Noam Chomsky, *Language and Mind* (New York: Harcourt Brace Jovanovich, 1972).

22 *Testimony: the memoirs of Dmitri Shostakovich*, Solomon Volkov, editor, Antonina W. Bouis, translator (New York: Harper & Row, 1979).

23 The author's principal works are: Anton Ehrenzweig, *The Psycho-analysis of Artistic Vision and Hearing: An Introduction to a Theory of Unconscious Perception* (London: Routledge & Paul, 1967); Anton Ehrenzweig, *The Hidden Order of Art* (London: Paladin, 1973).

24 Bonta, op. cit., 26.

25 Hans Sedlmayr, *Art in Crisis, The Lost Center* (Chicago: H. Regnery Co., 1958), 3.

26 Bonta, op. cit., 200–201.,

27 Carl G. Jung et al. (eds.), *Man and his Symbols* (New York: Doubleday, 1968), 57.
    Other excellent books on the archetype are: Edward F. Edinger, *Ego & Archetype: Individuation and the Religious Function of the Psyche* (Baltimore: Penguin Books, 1974); Erich Neumann, *The Great Mother: an Analysis of the Archetype* (New York: Pantheon Books, 1955). The archetype has also been used as a basis for the analysis of modern art, as in: Erich Neumann, *The Archetypal World of Henry Moore* (New York: Pantheon Books, 1959).

28 Carl Jung, op. cit., 87.

29 Sinclair Gauldie, *Architecture* (London, New York: Oxford University Press, 1969) as quoted in: Bonta, op. cit., 226.

30 Stokes' profound essays are collected in: *The Critical Writings of Adrian Stokes* (London: Thames and Hudson, 1978).

31 Aniela Jaffé, "Symbolism in the Visual Arts," in: Jung, op. cit., 255–322.

32 Fourfold symbolism is discussed in detail in: Anna C. Esmeijer, *Divina Quaternitas: a Preliminary Study in the Method and Application of Visual Exeges* (Assen: Gorcum, 1978).

33 The story of the founding of Rome and other myths of the founding of cities in the Old World are presented in: Joseph Rykwert, *The idea of a town: the anthropology of urban form in Rome, Italy and the ancient world* (Cambridge: MIT Press, 1988).

34 The complex symbolism of the Dogon tribe is discussed in a fascinating book: Marcel Griaule, *Conversation with Ogotemmêli; An introduction to Dogon Religious Ideas* (London: Published for the International African Institute by the Oxford University Press, 1965).

35 Anton Ehrenzweig, *The Hidden Order of Art* (London: Paladin, 1973), 146.

36 Frank Stella as quoted in: Peter Leech, "Criticism and the Emblems of Art," *PN Review* 15, vol. 7, number 1.

37 Le Corbusier, *Towards a New Architecture* (London: The Architectural Press, 1959).

38 Nikolaus Pevsner, *An Outline of European Architecture* (Harmondsworth: Penguin Books, 1963).

39 Johnson's remark is quoted in: Richard Plunz, "A Note on Politics, Style and Academe," *Precis* (Spring 1980).

40 Le Corbusier, op. cit., the final chapter "Architecture or Revolution," 249–269.

41 Colin St. John Wilson, "Architecture–Public Good and Private Necessity," *RIBA Journal* (March, 1979).

42 Sedlmayr, op. cit., 2–3.

43 Stokes, op. cit., 2–3.

44 Richard Sennett, *The Fall of Public Man: On the Social Psychology of Capitalism* (New York: W.W. Norton, 1978).

45 Edinger, op. cit., 109, 117.

46 Edward T. Hall, *Beyond Culture* (New York: Random House, 1981).

47 Sir Christopher Wren, as quoted in: Norris Kelly Smith, "Crisis in Jerusalem," *Late Entries* vol. II (New York: Rizzoli International Publications, 1980).

48 Victor Hugo, as quoted in: Pekka Suhonen, "Talot ja kirjat" [Buildings and Books] *Teekkari* 2 (1959): 20–21.

ARCHITECTURE AND THE OBSESSIONS OF OUR TIMES

1 Peter Blake, *Form Follows Fiasco: Why Modern Architecture Hasn't Worked* (Boston: Little Brown, 1977); Hans Asplund, *Farväl till Funktionalismen!* [Farewell to Functionalism!] (Stockholm: Atlantis, 1980).

2 Asplund, ibid., 16.

3 Le Corbusier, *Towards a New Architecture* (London: The Architectural Press, 1959), 249–269.

4 Ludwig Wittgenstein, *Culture and Value*, Georg Henrik von Wright in collaboration with Heikki Nyman, editors (Oxford: Blackwell, 1998), 74.

5 Marshall McLuhan, "The Emperor's Old Clothes," Gyorgy Kepes, editor, *The Man-made Object* (New York: G. Braziller, 1966).

6 The following books touch upon architectural issues: Erich Fromm, *Escape from Freedom* (New York: Henry Holt and Company, 1994); Erich Fromm, *To Have or to Be* (New York: Harper & Row, 1976); Erich Fromm, *The Revolution of Hope, Towards a Humanized Technology* (New York: Perennial Library, 1968); Herbert Marcuse, *One-Dimensional Man* (Boston: Beacon Press, 1991).

7 A concise presentation of the notion of neurosis is in *Otavan suuri ensyklopedia* [The Great Otava Encyclopedia], part 6 (Helsinki: Otava, 1979). More profound publications on neurosis in Finnish are: P. Tienari, "Neuroosit" [Neuroses], *Psykiatrinen kuntoutus*

(Porvoo: WSOY, 1967); Achté, K., Alanen, Y. O., Tienari, P.: *Psykiatria* [Psychiatry] (Porvoo: WSOY, 1981).

8   Gaston Bachelard, *The Poetics of Space* (Boston: Beacon Press, 1969).

9   Alvar Aalto, undated draft for a speech, in: Göran Schildt, *Alvar Aalto, The Early Years* (New York: Rizzoli International Publications, 1984), 192.

10 Gotthard Booth, *The Shadow of the Conquest of Nature* (New York and Toronto: The Edwin Hellen Press, 1974).

11 Igor Stravinski, *Musiikin poetiikka* [The Poetics of Music] (Helsinki: Otava, 1968), 72.

12 Stravinski, ibid., 59.
    The sentence actually derives from the Catalan philosopher Eugenio d´Ors. Luis Bunuel also quotes the sentence in his memoirs, *My Last Sigh*.

13 Marcuse, op. cit., 17.

14 Erich Fromm, *Escape from Freedom* (New York: Henry Holt and Company, 1994).

15 A general presentation of the psychoanalytic theory including the notion of defences can be found in: Charles Brenner, *An Elementary Textbook of Psychoanalysis* (New York: Anchor Books, 1974).

16 Leonardo da Vinci, as quoted in: Stravinsky, op. cit., 75.

17 Jean Renoir, *Elämäni ja elokuvani* [My Life and Films] (Helsinki: Love-kirjat, 1974).

18 Stravinski, op. cit., 66–67.

19 Stravinski, op. cit., 75.

20 Louis Kahn, "I love beginnings," in: Alessandra Latour, editor, *Louis I. Kahn: Writings, Lectures, Interviews* (New York: Rizzoli International Publications, 1991), 288. "…If you ask brick what it wants, it will say: 'Well, I like an arch.'"

21 Marcuse, op. cit., 13.

22 Marcuse, op. cit., 57.

23 Marcuse, op. cit., 57.

24 Erhart Kästner, *Ölberge, Weinberge* (Wiesbaden: Insel-Verlag, 1953), as quoted in: Christian Norberg-Schulz, *Existence, Space and Architecture* (New York: Praeger, 1971), 21.

25 Fred Fischer, *Der Wohnraum* (Zürich: Verlag für Architektur im Artemis Verlag, 1965).

26 Bachelard, op. cit., 47.

27 Joë Bousquet, as quoted in Bachelard, op. cit., 26.

28 See Juhani Pallasmaa, "From Utopia to a Monument," *Arkkitehti, The Finnish Architectural Review* (3: 1977).

29 Demetri Porphyrios, *Sources of Modern Eclecticism: Studies on Alvar Aalto* (London: Academy Editions, 1982), 2–3.

30 Yi-Fu Tuan, *Landscapes of Fear* (Minneapolis: University of Minnesota Press, 1979).

31 Bachelard, op. cit., 25–26.

STAIRWAYS OF THE MIND

1   Le Corbusier's concept of the 'House-Machine,' a mass-produced industrial product, became a guiding Modernist idea.

    Le Corbusier, *Towards a New Architecture* (London: The Architectural Press, 1959).

2   Gaston Bachelard, *The Poetics of Space* (Boston: Beacon Press, 1969), 4, 46.

3   Maurice Merleau-Ponty, *Signs* (Evanston, Ill.: Northwestern University Press, 1982), 56.

4   Karsten Harries, "Thoughts on a Non-Arbitrary Architecture," in: David Seamon, editor, *Dwelling, Seeing and Designing: Toward a Phenomenological Ecology* (Albany: State University of New York Press, 1993), 47.

5   As quoted in: Bachelard, op. cit., 137.

6   Carl Jung's dream, as quoted in: *Environmental & Architectural Phenomenology Newsletter*, David Seamon, editor, Vol. 10, No. 2 (Spring 1999).

7   Curzio Malaparte, *Fughe in prigione* [Escape in Prison] (Milano: Aria d'Italia, 1954).

8   Rainer Maria Rilke, *The Notebooks of Malte Laurids Brigge*, M.D. Herter Norton, translator (New York and London: W.W. Norton & Co, 1992), 30–31.

9   Bachelard, op. cit., 224.

10 Alvar Aalto, "Taisteleva arkkitehtuuri" [The Fighting Architecture], in: Göran Schildt, editor, *Alvar Aalto: Luonnoksia* [Sketches] (Helsinki: Otava, 1972), 99.

11 Jorge Luis Borges, "The Immortal," *Labyrinths* (London: Penguin Books, 1964), 140.

12 Peter Wollen, "Arkkitehtuuri ja elokuva: paikat ja epäpaikat / Architecture and cinema: places and non-places," *Rakennustaiteen seura, jäsentiedote* (Helsinki), 4 (1996): 15.

13 Bachelard, op. cit., 25.

14 Joë Bousquet, *La neige d´un autre âge*, as quoted in Bachelard, op. cit., 26.

15 Gustave Flaubert, "The Dictionary of Received Ideas," *Bouvard and Pécuchet* (Harmonsworth: Penguin Books, 1983), 294.

16 Sigmund Freud, *The Interpretation of Dreams* (1900) (New York: The Modern Library, 1994), 183–184.

17 Sigmund Freud, "The Dream-Work: Representations by Symbols in Dreams," in *Complete Psychological Works*, vol. 5 (London: Hogarth Press, 1948). Quoted in: John Templer, *The Staircase* (Cambridge & London: The MIT Press, 1994), 10.

18 René Allendy, *Rêves expliques* (Paris: Gallimard, 1938), 176. As quoted in: Hans Biedermann, *Dictionary of Symbolism: Cultural Icons and the Meanings Behind Them* (New York: Meridian, 1994), 19.

19 Gaston Bachelard, *Air and Dreams: An Essay on the Imagination of Movement* (Dallas: Dallas Institute, 1988), 10.

20 Stanislas Klossowski de Rola, *The Golden Game: Alchemical Engravings of the Seventeenth Century* (London: Thames and Hudson, 1988).

21 The Bible, Genesis 28:10–22.

22 Borges, op. cit., 141.

23 Bachelard, *Air and Dreams*, op. cit., 15.

24 Borges, *Labyrinths*, op. cit., 78, 82.

25 John Templer, *The Staircase* (Cambridge, The MIT Press, 1994), 7.

26 The astonishing Dogon cosmogony is impressively documented in Marcel Griaule, *Conversation with Ogotemmêli; An introduction to Dogon Religious Ideas* (London: Oxford University Press, 1965).

27 Karsten Harries, "Thoughts on a Non-Arbitrary Architecture," *Dwelling, Seeing, and Designing*, David Seamon, editor (Albany: State University of New York Press, 1993), 47.

28 Edward F. Edinger, *Ego and Archetype: Individuation and the Religious Function of the Psyche* (Baltimore: Penguin Books, 1974), 107, 109, 117.

THE PLACE OF MAN

1   Gaston Bachelard, *The Poetics of Space* (Boston: Beacon Press, 1969), 4,6.

2   Bachelard, ibid., 72.

3   Alvar Aalto, quoted in: Göran Schildt, *Alvar Aalto: The Early Years* (New York: Rizzoli International Publications, 1984), 192.

4   Viktor von Weizsäcker, source unidentified.

5   Hans Sedlmayr, *Art in Crisis: The Lost Center* (London: Hollis & Carter, 1957), 1.

6   Mildred Reed Hall, Edward T. Hall, *The Fourth Dimension in Architecture: The Impact of Building Behaviour* (Santa Fe: Sunstone Press, 1995).

7   Charles Moore and Kent Bloomer, *Body, Memory and Architecture* (New Haven: Yale University Press, 1977), 107.

8   Moore and Bloomer, ibid., 105.

9   Bachelard, op. cit., 46.

10 Martin Heidegger, "Building Dwelling Thinking," *Basic Writings* (New York: Harper & Row, 1997), 334.

11 Wallace Stevens. "Theory," *The Collected Poems* (1923) (New York: Vintage Books, 1990), 86.

12 Herbert Marcuse, *One-Dimensional Man: studies in the ideology of advanced industrial society* (Boston: Beacon Press, 1991), 73: "...a whole dimension of human activity and passivity has been de-eroticized. The environment from which the individual could obtain pleasure—which he could cathect as gratifying almost as an extended zone of the body—has been rigidly reduced. Consequently the 'universe' of libidinous cathexis is likewise reduced. The effect is a localization and contraction of libido, the reduction of erotic to sexual experience and satisfaction."

13 Bachelard, op. cit., 17.

14 Alvar Aalto, undated manuscript for a speech, in: Göran Schildt, *Alvar Aalto: The Early Years* (New York: Rizzoli International Publications, 1984), 192.

15 Bachelard, op. cit., 91: "...primal images...bring out the primitiveness in us."

16 Gaston Bachelard, *Water and Dreams: An essay on the Imagination of Matter* (Dallas: Pegasus Foundation, 1983), 1.

17 Rudolf Schwartz, *Von der Bebauung der Erde* (1949), as quoted in Christian Norberg-Schultz, *Existence, Space & Architecture* (London: Studio Vista, 1971), 30.

18 Jarkko Laine, "Tikusta asiaa," *Parnasso* 6:1982 (Helsinki: 1982), 323–324.

19 Bachelard, *The Poetics of Space*, op. cit., 224.

20 Bachelard, ibid., 79.

21 Edward Edinger, *Ego and Archetype: Individuation and the Religious Function of the Psyche* (Baltimore: Penguin Books, 1974), 117.

22 Anton Ehrenzweig, *The Hidden Order of Art* (London: Paladin, 1973), 146.

23 Le Corbusier, *Towards a New Architecture* (London: The Architectural Press, 1959), 31.

24 Edinger, op. cit., 109.

25 Alvar Aalto, "From doorstep to living room," (1926) in Schildt, op. cit., 215.

THE GEOMETRY OF FEELING

1   Ludwig Wittgenstein, *Culture and Value*, Georg Henrik von Wright, in collaboration with Heikki Nyman, editors (Oxford: Blackwell, 1998), 74e.

2   Alberto Pérez-Gómez, *Architecture and the Crisis of Modern Science* (Cambridge: The MIT Press, 1990), 4.

3   Pérez-Gomez, ibid., 6.

4   Kyösti Ålander, *Rakennustaide renessanssista funktionalismiin* [Architecture from the Renaissance to Functionalism] (Porvoo-Helsinki: WSOY, 1954), 169.

5   Ezra Pound, ABC of Reading (New York: New Directions Publishing Corporation, 1987), 14.

6   Adrian Stokes, *The Image in Form*, Richard Wollheim, editor (New York: Harper & Row, 1972), 122.

7   Paul Valery, *Dialogues* (New York: Pantheon Books, 1956), 74.

8   Edmund Husserl, *The Crisis of European Sciences and Transcendental Phenomenology* (Evanston: Northwestern University Press, 1970); Edmund Husserl, *Phenomenology and the Crisis of Philosophy* (New York: Harper & Row, 1965).

9   Alvar Aalto, undated manuscript, in: Göran Schildt, *Alvar Aalto: The Early Years* (New York: Rizzoli International Publications, 1984), 193.

10 Gaston Bachelard, *The Poetics of Reverie* (Boston: Beacon Press, 1971).

11 Alvar Aalto, "From Doorstep to Living Room," in Schildt, op. cit., 214–218.

12 Schildt, op. cit., 215.

13 Juhani Pallasmaa, "Image and Meaning," Juhani Pallasmaa, editor, *Alvar Aalto: Villa Mairea 1938–39* (Helsinki: The Alvar Aalto Foundation and The Mairea Foundation, 1998), 70–103.

14 Cyril Connolly, *The Unquiet Grave*, as quoted in: Emilio Ambasz, *The Architecture of Luis Barragan* (New York: The Museum of Modern Art, 1982), 108.

15 Alvar Aalto, undated manuscript, in: Schildt, op. cit., 192.

16 Adrian Stokes, op. cit., 49.

17 Adrian Stokes, "Smooth and Rough," *The Critical Writings of Adrian Stokes*, Volume II (London: Thames and Hudson, 1978), 316.

18 Louis Kahn, "Form and Design," lecture, 1961, in: Alessandra Latour, editor, *Louis I. Kahn Writings,*

Lectures, Interviews (New York, Rizzoli International Publications, 1991), 114.

THE ROOMS OF MEMORY

1   Louis Kahn, "Form and Design," lecture, 1961, in: Alessandra Latour, editor, *Louis I. Kahn: Writings, Lectures, Interviews* (New York: Rizzoli International Publications, 1991), 116.
2   Gaston Bachelard, *The Poetics of Space* (Boston: Beacon Press, 1969), 6.
3   Colin St John Wilson, "Alvar Aalto and the State of Modernism," in: Kirmo Mikkola, editor, *Alvar Aalto vs. the Modern Movement* (Jyväskylä: K.J. Gummerus Osakeyhtiö, 1981), 114–115.

IDENTITY, INTIMACY AND DOMICILE

1   Max Frisch, *Homo Faber* (Helsinki: Otava, 1961).
2   Teilhard de Chardin, as quoted in: Juhana Blomstedt, *Muodon arvo* [The Significance of Form], Timo Valjakka, editor (Helsinki: Painatuskeskus, Kuvataideakatemia, 1995).
3   *Alvar Aalto Band I 1922–1962* (Zurich: Les Éditions d'Architecture Artemis, 1963), 108.
4   Gaston Bachelard, *The Poetics of Space* (Boston: Beacon Press, 1969), 25–26.
5   J.H. Van den Berg, *The Phenomenological Approach in Psychology* (Springfield, Ill.: Charles C. Thomas, 1955), 61, as quoted in: Bachelard, ibid., XXIV.
6   Jan Vrijman, "Filmmakers Spacemakers," *The Berlage Papers* 11 (January 1994).
7   Jean-Paul Sartre, *What is Literature?* (Gloucester: Peter Smith, 1978), 4.
8   Bachelard, op. cit., 17.
9   Bachelard, op. cit., 46.
10 Christopher Alexander Serge Chermayeff, *Community and privacy; toward a new architecture of humanism* (Garden City: Doubleday & Company, 1963).
11 Hall, *The Hidden Dimension.*
12 Bachelard, op. cit., 34.
13 Juhani Pallasmaa, "The Geometry of Feeling: a look at the phenomenology of architecture," *Arkkitehti, The Finnish Architectural Review,* March 1985, 44–49 (English translation, 98–100).
14 Juhani Pallasmaa, "Space and Image in Andrey Tarkovsky's Nostalghia," *Focus: Yearbook of the Faculty of Architecture* (Helsinki: Helsinki University of Technology, 1992), 13–14.
15 Anders Olofsson, "Nostalgia," *Tanken på en Hemkonst,* Magnus Bergh & Birgitta Munkhammar, editors (Stockholm: Alfa Beta Bokförlag, 1986), 150. Interview of Paola Volkova by Mikael Fränti in *Helsingin Sanomat* (9.12.1992), D 10.
16 For instance: Frode Strømnes, *A New Physics of Inner Worlds* (Tromsö: Institute of Social Science, University of Tromsö, 1976); Frode Strømnes, "On the Architecture of Thought," *Abacus, Yearbook 2* (Helsinki: The Museum of Finnish Architecture, 1981) 7–29; Frode Strømnes, *The Externalized Image, a study showing differences correlating with language structure between pictorial structure in Ural-Altaic and Indo-European filmed versions of the same plays.* (Helsinki: The Finnish Broadcasting Company, No. 211, 1982).
17 Rainer Maria Rilke, *The Notebooks of Malte Laurids Brigge*, M.D. Herter Norton, translator (New York: W.W. Norton & Company, 1992), 47–48.
18 Martin Heidegger, "The Origin of the Work of Art," *Basic Writings* (New York: Harper & Row, 1977), 163.
19 Bachelard, op. cit., XXXIV.
20 Bachelard, op. cit., 79.
21 Bachelard, op. cit., 91.
22 Lewis Mumford, *The City in History: Its Origins, Its Transformations, and Its Prospects* (New York: Harvest Books, 1972).
23 Bachelard, op. cit., 27.
24 Interview of J.M. Coetzee, *Helsingin Sanomat* (summer 1987).
25 Umberto Eco, "Postscript to the Name of the Rose," *Matka arkipäivän epätodellisuuteen* [Travels in Hyperreality] (Helsinki: WSOY, 1985), 349–352.
26 Peter Eisenman, "En Samtal med Carsten Juel-Christiansen," *Skala* 12/1987 (Copenhagen: 1987).
27 Bo Carpelan, *Homecoming*, David McDuff, translator (Manchester: Carcanet, 1993), 111.

LIVED SPACE

1   Liisa Enwald, editor, "Lukijalle," *Rainer Maria Rilke, Hiljainen taiteen sisin; kirjeita vuosilta 1900–1926* [The silent innermost core of art; letters 1900–1926] (Helsinki: TAI-teos, 1997), 8.
2   Juhana Blomstedt, *Muodon arvo* [The Significance of Form], Timo Valjakka, editor (Helsinki: Painatuskeskus, Kuvataideakatemia, 1995).
3   Private conversation between Eduardo Chillida and the author, Helsinki, 1987.
4   Jean-Paul Sartre, *The Emotions: An Outline of a Theory* (New York: Carol Publishing Co., 1993), 9.
5   Merleau-Ponty, "Cézanne's Doubt," *Sense and Non-Sense* (Evanston: Northwestern University Press, 1964), 9.
6   Maurice Merleau-Ponty describes the notion of the flesh in his essay "The Intertwining—The Chiasm," *The Visible and the Invisible*, Claude Lefort, editor (Evanston: Northwestern University Press, 1969): "My body is made of the same flesh as the world…and moreover…this flesh of my body is shared by the world…" (248) and: "The flesh (of the world or my own) is…a texture that returns to itself and conforms to itself" (146). The notion derives from Merleau-Ponty's dialectical principle of the intertwining of the world and the self. He also speaks of the 'ontology of the flesh' as the ultimate conclusion of his initial phenomenology of perception. This ontology implies that meaning is both within and without, subjec-

tive and objective, spiritual and material. See also: Richard Kearney, "Maurice Merleau-Ponty," *Modern Movements in European Philosophy* (Manchester and New York: Manchester University Press, 1994) 73–90.

7   Dr. Ilpo Kojo, "Mielikuvat ovat aivoille todellisia" [Images are real to the brain], *Helsingin Sanomat* (16.3.1996).

8   Andrey Tarkovsky, *Sculpting in Time* (London: The Bodley Head, 1986), 100.

9   Jean-Paul Sartre, *What is Literature?* (Gloucester: Peter Smith, 1978), 3.

10 Tarkovsky, ibid., 110.

11 Rainer Maria Rilke, *The Notebooks of Malte Laurids Brigge* (London: W.W. Norton & Company, 1992), 26.

12 Rilke, ibid., 27.

13 Göran Schildt, editor, *Alvar Aalto Luonnoksia* [Sketches] "Euroopan jälleenrakentaminen tuo pinnalle aikamme rakennustaiteen keskeisimmän probleemin," (Helsinki: Otava, 1977), 64.

14 Jean Genet, *L'atelier d'Alberto Giacometti* (Marc Barbezaf: L'Arbalft, 1963), as quoted in: Blomstedt, op. cit., 140.

15 Salman Rushdie, "Eikö mikään ole pyhää?" [Isn't anything sacred?], *Parnasso* 1 (Helsinki, 1996), 8.

16 Joseph Brodsky, *Watermark* (London: Penguin Books, 1992), 61.

17 Letter from George Nelson to the author 31.8.1982, Juhani Pallasmaa Architects, correspondence archive.

18 Italo Calvino, *Six Memos for the Next Millennium* (New York: Vintage Books, 1993), 1.

19 Calvino, ibid., 45.

20 Interview of Paola Volkova by Mikael Fränti in *Helsingin Sanomat* (9.12.1992), D 10.

21 Calvino, op. cit., 112.

22 Erich Fromm, source unidentified, most likely *Escape From Freedom*.

23 Interview in *Time Magazine*, 1990. Source not identified in detail.

24 Source unidentified.

25 Gaston Bachelard, *The Poetics of Space* (Boston: Beacon Press, 1964), XII.

26 Gaston Bachelard, *Water and Dreams: An Essay On the Imagination of Matter* (Dallas: The Pegasus Foundation, 1982), 107.

27 Martin Heidegger, "What Calls for Thinking?" *Basic Writings*, (New York: Harper & Row, 1977), 357.

28 Jacques Hadamar, "The Psychology of Invention in the Mathematical Field" (Princeton: Education in Vision Series, 1943).

29 Henry Moore, "The Sculptor Speaks," *Henry Moore on Sculpture*, Philip James, editor (London: MacDonald, 1966), 62–64.

30 Calvino, op. cit., 57.

CITY SENSE

1   Susan Sontag, *On Photography* (New York: Penguin Books, 1986), 24.

2   Sontag, ibid., 11, 16.

3   Maurice Merleau-Ponty, "The Film and the New Psychology," *Sense and Non-sense*, (Evanston: Northwestern University Press, 1964), 50.

4   Steen Eiler Rasmussen, *Experiencing Architecture* (Cambridge: The MIT Press, 1993), 224–237.

5   Rasmussen, ibid., 225.

6   Adrian Stokes, "Prologue: at Venice," *The Critical Writings of Adrian Stokes*, vol. II (Plymouth: Thames and Hudson, 1978), 88.

7   Italo Calvino, *If on a winter's night a traveller* (Orlando: Harcourt, 1979), 8.

FROM UTOPIA TO A MONUMENT

1   Edward T. Hall, *The Hidden Dimension* (New York: Doubleday, 1966), 105–106.

2   As quoted in: Andrew Rabeneck, "Beaubourg: Process & Purposes," *Architectural Design* (London), Vol. 47, No. 2 (1977), 104.

3   As quoted in: Dennis Crompton, "Centre Pompidou: A live center of information," *Architectural Design*, 110.

4   Rabeneck, ibid.

5   Louis Kahn, "Form and Design," lecture, 1961, in: Alessandro Latour, editor, *Louis I. Kahn: Writings, Lectures, Interviews* (New York: Rizzoli International Publications, 1991), 116.

6   Aulis Blomstedt, "Pensée et forme: etudes harmoniques" [Thought and Form: Studies in Harmony], exhibition in the Le Corbusier Foundation, Maison La Roche, Paris, 12.4.1977–16.8.1977.

7   Juhani Pallasmaa, editor, *Aulis Blomstedt: Pensée et forme, etudes harmoniques* (Helsinki: The Museum of Finnish Architecture, 1977), 15.

8   Erich Fromm, *Escape from Freedom* (New York: Farrar & Rinehart, Inc., 1941).

9   Alan Colquhoun, "Critique," *Architectural Design*, op. cit., 100.

10 Blomstedt, op. cit., 12.

11 Blomstedt, op. cit., 19.

12 Hasan Ozbekhan, "The Triumph of Technology: 'Can' Implies 'Ought'," in Nigel Cross, David Elliott & Robin Roy, editors, *Man-Made Futures: Readings in Society, Technology and Design* (London: Hutchinson, 1974).

13 Louis Kahn, "Spaces Order and Architecture," in: *Louis I Kahn*, op. cit., 76.

14 Letter from George Nelson to the author 31.8.1982, Juhani Pallasmaa Architects, correspondence archive.

AVANT-GARDE VS. DERRIÈRE-GARDE

1   Hans Sedlmayr, *Art in Crisis: The Lost Center* (London: Hollis & Carter, 1957).

2   K. Boulding, *The Image: Knowledge in Life and Society*. Quoted by: James W. Fernandez, "Persuasions and performances: the play of tropes in culture" (*Daedalus*, Winter 1972).

3   Gerald Allen, "Fission and Fusion: Free-style architecture," *Architectural Record* (December 1979).

4   Stanley Tigerman, "Late Entries to the Chicago Tribune Tower Competition of 1933," *Late Entries*, vol. II (New York: Rizzoli International Publications, 1980).

5   Richard Pluntz, "A Note on Politics, Style and Academe," *Precis* (Spring 1980).

6   Alexis de Tocqueville, *Democracy in America*, vol. II (New York: Vintage Books, 1954), 3, 5.

7   Allen, op. cit..

8   Sedlmayr, op. cit., 69.

9   Professor Oiva Ketonen, Academician, brought the books of F. J. Turner and Freeman Dayson to my attention.

10 Frederick Jackson Turner, *The Frontier in the American History* (New York: Dover Publications, Inc., 1996), 38.

11 Turner, ibid., 3.

12 As quoted in: Turner, op. cit., 11.

13 Charles Jencks, "Post-Modern Classicism and the Emergence of Architectural Humour," *Late Entries*, vol. II (New York: Rizzoli International Publications, 1980), 100.

14 Juan Pablo Bonta, "A Propos the Tribune Projects 1922," *Late Entries*, vol II (New York: Rizzoli International Publications, 1980), 96.

15 Richard Sennett, *The Fall of Public Man: On the Social Psychology of Capitalism* (New York: Vintage Books, 1978).

16 Gerald Allen, "The Reluctant Acceptance of Finity," *AIA Journal* (January 1980), 65.

17 Bonta, op. cit., 96.

18 Turner, op. cit., 32.

19 The project was heavily criticized by Christian Laine in his article "Using design as a weapon and bad joke," *The Chicago Sun-Times* (December 23, 1979).

20 Dimitri Shostakovich, *Dimitri Šostakovitsin muistelmat* [Memoirs of Dimitri Shostakovich], compiled by Solomon Volkov (Helsinki: Otava, 1979), 188.

21 Sedlmayr, op. cit., 66.

22 Norris Kelly Smith, "Crisis in Jerusalem," *Late Entries*, vol. II (New York: Rizzoli International Publications, 1980), 109.

23 Gerald Allen, op. cit., 94.

THE CONTEMPORARY AVANT-GARDE AND THE WISDOM OF ARCHITECTURE

1   Arthur C. Danto, "Narratives of the End of Art," *Encounters & Reflections: Art in the Historical Present* (New York: Farrar, Straus & Giroux, 1990).
    See also: Arthur C. Danto, *Beyond the Brillo Box: The Visual Arts in Post-Historical Perspective* (New York: Farrar, Straus & Giroux, 1992).

2   Michael Benedikt, *Deconstructing the Kimbell* (New York: Site Books, 1991), 7.

3   Milan Kundera, *Romaanin taide* [The Art of the Novel] (Helsinki: WSOY, 1986), 165.

4   Diane Ghirardo quoting Peter Eisenman in "Mind the Gap," *Architectural Review* (October 1988), 20.

FROM METAPHORICAL TO ECOLOGICAL FUNCTIONALISM

1   Arthur C. Danto, "Narratives of the End of Art," *Encounters & Reflections: Art in the Historical Present* (New York: Farrar, Straus & Giroux, 1990), 331–345.

2   Hans Belting, "Das Ende der Kunstgeschihte?" Referenced in: Danto, ibid., 331.

3   Alvin Kernan, *The Death of Literature* (New Haven: Yale University Press, 1990).

4   Pierre Boulez, as quoted in: Kalevi Aho, "Taiteilijan tehtävä postmodernissa yhteiskunnassa" [The Artist's Task in the Postmodern Society], *Synteesi 1–2* (Helsinki: 1991), 59.

5   Francis Fukuyama, "The End of History?" *The National Interest*, no. 16 (Summer 1989).

6   For instance: Juhani Pallasmaa, "Architecture and the Reality of Culture—the feasibility of architecture in a Postmodern society," *Arkkitehti, The Finnish Architectural Review* (Helsinki), 1 (1987): 66–76; Juhani Pallasmaa, "The Limits of Architecture—towards an architecture of silence," *Arkkitehti, The Finnish Architectural Review* (Helsinki), 6 (1990): 26–39.

7   Peter Eisenman, "The End of the Classical: the End of the Beginning, the End of the End," *Perspecta: The Yale Architectural Journal* issue 21 (Cambridge: The MIT Press, 1985), 155–172.

8   Aristotle, as quoted in: Danto, op. cit., 309.

9   Giorgio Vasari, *Lives of the Most Eminent Italian Painters, Sculptors and Architects* (London: H.G. Bohn, 1907).

10 Danto, op. cit., 309.

11 Leon Krier, "Vorwärts, Kameraden, Wir Müssen Zurück" [Forward, Comrades, We Must Go Back], *Oppositions* 24 (1981).

12 Thomas Lawson, "Nostalgia as Resistance," *Modern Dreams—The Rise and Fall and Rise of Pop* (Cambridge: The MIT Press, 1988), 163.

13 Quoted in Lawson, ibid., 105. Reprinted from *Store Days* (New York: Something Else Press, Inc., 1967).

14 Danto, op. cit., 333.

15 Referred to in: Diane Ghirardo, editor, *Out of Site: A Social Criticism of Architecture* (Seattle: Bay Press, 1991), 9.

16 Quoted in: Danto, ibid., 287–288.

17 Hans Belting, quoted in: Danto, op. cit., 7.

18 Referred to by Weiss in: *Modern Dreams*, op. cit., 141

19 Referred to in: Kernan, op. cit., 204.

20 Kernan, op. cit., 2.

21 Stanford Anderson, "The Fiction of Function," *Assemblage* 2 (February 1987): 19–20.

22 Hannes Meyer, "Building" (1928), in: Claude Schnaidt, *Hannes Meyer, Buildings, Projects and Writings* (Teufen AR/Schweiz: A. Niggli, 1965), 94.

23 Anderson, op. cit., 29.

24 William J.R. Curtis, *Modern Architecture since 1900* (Englewood Cliffs: Prentice-Hall, 1983), 182.

25 Sverre Fehn in a private conversation with the author, in conjunction with the Third Alvar Aalto Symposium, August 1985.

26 Fernand Léger, *Maalaustaiteen tehtävät* [The tasks of painting] (Jyväskylä: K.J. Gummerus, 1981), 63, 69.

27 Alvar Aalto, "The Humanizing of Architecture," excerpts in: *Alvar Aalto 1898-1976,* Aarno Ruusuvuori and Juhani Pallasmaa, editors (Helsinki: The Museum of Finnish Architecture, 1978), 120.

28 Lewis Mumford, "Function and Expression in Architecture," in: *Architecture as a Home for Man*, Jeanne M. Davern, editor (New York: Architectural Record Books, 1975), 155, 158.

29 Richard Neutra, referred to by Kenneth Frampton in his essay, "Reflections on the Autonomy of Architecture: A Critique of Contemporary Production," in: *Out of Site*, op. cit., 22.

30 Horatio Greenough, as referred to by Lewis Mumford, op. cit., 156.

31 Vincent P. Pecora, "Towers of Babel," in: *Out of Site*, op. cit., 73.

32 Lewis Mumford, op. cit., 153.

TOWARD AN ARCHITECTURE OF HUMILITY

1 Gianni Vattimo, *The End of Modernity* (Baltimore: The Johns Hopkins University Press, 1991).

IMMATERIALITY AND TRANSPARENCY

1 As quoted in: Hans Sedlmayer, *Art in Crisis: The Lost Center* (London: Hollis & Carter, 1957), 2-3.

2 Michael Wigginton, *Glass in Architecture* (London: Phaidon Press Ltd, 1996), 6.

3 Reyner Banham, "A Home Is Not a House," *Art in America* (April 1965): 109-118. Republished in: Joan Ockman, *Architecture Culture 1943-1968* (New York: Rizzoli International Publications, 1993), 371-378.

4 Marshall Berman, *All That Is Solid Melts Into Air—The Experience of Modernity* (London: Verso, 1990). First published by Simon and Schuster, New York, 1982.

5 Janine M. Benyus, *Biomimicry* (New York: William Morrow, 1997).

6 Walter Benjamin, "Surrealism", as quoted in Anthony Vidler, *The Architectural Uncanny* (Cambridge, and London: The MIT Press, 1999), 218.

7 Gaston Bachelard, *The Philosophy of No: The Philosophy of the New Scientific Mind* (New York: The Orion Press, 1968).

8 James Elkins, *What Painting Is* (New York-London: Routledge, 2000).

9 Gaston Bachelard, *Water and Dreams—An Essay on the Imagination of Matter* (Dallas: The Pegasus Foundation, 1983) 46.

10 Bachelard, ibid., 5.

11 Jorge Luis Borges, "The Draped Mirrors," in: Jorge Luis Borges, *Dream Tigers* (Austin: University of Texas Press, 2001), 27.

12 Following an ancient Chinese instruction, Leonardo da Vinci gives the following advice: "When you look at a wall spotted with stains, or with a mixture of stones, if you have to devise some scene you may discover a resemblance to various landscapes... or again, you may see battles and figures in action, or strange faces and costumes, or an endless variety of objects, which you could reduce to complete and well drawn forms. And these appear on such walls promiscuously, like the sound of bells in whose jangle you may find any name or word you choose to imagine." Quoted in: Robert Hughes, *The Shock of the New—Art and the Century of Change* (London: Thames and Hudson, 1980), 225.

13 As quoted in: Gary J. Coates, *Erik Asmussen, architect* (Stockholm: Byggförlaget, 1997), 230.

14 Alvar Aalto, Speech at the Helsinki University of Technology Centennial Celebration, December 5, 1972, in: Göran Schildt, editor, *Alvar Aalto in His Own Words* (Helsinki: Otava, 1997), 281-285.

15 André Breton, *Nadja* as quoted in Anthony Vidler, *The Architectural Uncanny* (Cambridge, and London: The MIT Press, 1999), 218.

FROM TECTONICS TO PAINTERLY ARCHITECTURE

1 For Alvar Aalto's early eclectic attitude, see: Igor Herler, "Early Furniture and Interior Designs," *Alvar Aalto Furniture*, Juhani Pallasmaa, editor (Helsinki: The Museum of Finnish Architecture, Finnish Society of Crafts and Design, Artek, 1984), 14-59.,

2 Alvar Aalto, "Motifs from Times Past," *Arkkitehti* 2 (1922) in: *Alvar Aalto: Sketches*, Göran Schildt, editor, Stuart Wrede, translator (Cambridge: The MIT Press, 1979), 2.

3 Alvar Aalto, "Stockholm Exhibition I (summary of an interview in *Åbo Underrättelser,* May 22, 1930)," in: Schildt, ibid., 16.

4 Alvar Aalto, "Rationalism and Man," (lecture at the annual meeting of the Swedish Craft Society), in: Schildt, op. cit., 48, 50.

5 Alvar Aalto, "The Humanizing of Architecture," *The Technological Review* (November, 1940), in: Schildt, op. cit., 77, 78.

6 Alvar Aalto, "Instead of an Article," *Arkkitehti* 1-2 (1958), in: Schildt, op. cit., 160.

7 For instance, Göran Schildt, "Alvar Aalto as Artist," *Alvar Aalto as Artist*, Juhani Pallasmaa, editor (Helsinki: The Mairea Foundation, 1982), 3-20.

8 Alvar Aalto, "From Doorstep to Living Room," *Aitta* 1/1926, Kustannusosakeyhtiö Otava, 1926. Reprinted in: Göran Schildt, *Alvar Aalto: The Early Years* (New York: Rizzoli International Publications, 1984), 214-218.

9 Schildt, op. cit., 216.

10 Alvar Aalto's manuscript fragment, presumably written as an introduction for a book he was planning. Göran Schildt, *Alvar Aalto: The Decisive Years* (Helsinki: Otava, 1986), 11-13.

11 Alvar Aalto, "Villa Mairean arkkitehtoninen selostus [The Architectural Explanation of the Villa Mairea]," *Arkkitehti* 9 (1939), 134-137.

12 Aalto, op. cit..

13 Paul Bernoulli's interview with Juhani Pallasmaa, May 21, 1989.

14 Alvar Aalto, "Koetalo, Muuratsalo [Experimental House, Muuratsalo]," *Arkkitehti* 9–10 (1953), 159.

THE LOGIC OF THE IMAGE

1 Among the numerous currently circulating exhibitions on Aalto's city planning, architecture, design, and paintings, the most significant are: *Alvar Aalto: Between Humanism and Materialism*, The Museum of Modern Art, New York; *Alvar Aalto in Seven Buildings*, The Museum of Finnish Architecture, Helsinki; *Alvar Aalto: Urban Visions*, The Museum of Finnish Architecture, Helsinki; *Alvar Aalto—Points of Contact*, The Alvar Aalto Museum, Jyväskylä; *Alvar Aalto and Red Brick—space, form, texture*, The Alvar Aalto Museum, Jyväskylä; *Alvar Aalto—the Artist*, The Amos Anderson Museum and The Alvar Aalto Foundation, Helsinki.
The numerous recent publications on Aalto include: Peter Reed, editor, *Alvar Aalto: Between Humanism and Materialism* (New York: The Museum of Modern Art, 1998); Timo Tuomi, Kristiina Paatero and Eija Rauske, editors, *Alvar Aalto in Seven Buildings* (Helsinki: The Museum of Finnish Architecture, 1998); Maija Holma, Markku Lahti, *Alvar Aalto: A Gentler Structure for Life* (Helsinki: Rakennustieto Oy, 1998); Louna Lahti, *Alvar Aalto, Ex Intimo—aikalaisten silmin* (Alvar Aalto, Ex Intimo—through the eyes of his contemporaries), (Jyväskylä: Ateena Kustannus Oy, 1997); Göran Schildt, editor, *Alvar Aalto in His Own Words*, (Helsinki: Otava, 1997).

2 At the time the Sanatorium was under construction, the Finnish Architects' Association even held semi-official meetings to discuss how to stop this daredevil before he would cause irreparable harm to the reputation of the esteemed profession.

3 In Aalto's defence, it is only fair to state that he initially specified a marble plate twice the thickness of the one eventually chosen by the municipality in order to reduce building costs. Moreover, a number of buildings around the world, contemporaneous with Finlandia Hall, have suffered from the same problems.

4 Alvar Aalto, "The Humanizing of Architecture," in: Schildt, *Sketches*, 77.

5 Gaston Bachelard, *Water and Dreams* (Dallas: The Pegasus Foundation, 1983).

6 Alvar Aalto, presumably a manuscript for a book on the art of towns that he was planning to write, in: Schildt (1997), op. cit., 49.

7 Alvar Aalto, lecture given at a meeting of the Society of South-Swedish Master Builders in Malmö, 1957, in: Schildt, op. cit., 215.

8 For a full description of the Villa Mairea, see: Juhani Pallasmaa, editor, *Alvar Aalto: Villa Mairea* (Helsinki: The Mairea Foundation and The Alvar Aalto Foundation, 1998).

9 In addition to the influential books of Tetsuro Yosida and Bruno Taut, published in the mid-1930s, the primary source for Aalto's Japanese motifs was, undoubtedly, the Zui-Ki-Tei (the House of the Promising Light) tea house built in the garden of the Ethnographic Museum in Stockholm in 1935. This connection was brought to my attention by Professor Fred Thompson.

10 One of the first critics to comment on Aalto's use of the ruin motif was: George Baird, *Alvar Aalto* (London: Thames and Hudson, 1970), 11–14.

11 Demetri Porphyrios, *Sources of Modern Eclecticism: Studies on Alvar Aalto* (London: Academy Editions, 1983).

12 For instance, David Michael Levin, editor, *Modernity and the Hegemony of Vision* (Berkeley and Los Angeles: University of California Press, 1993) and Martin Jay, *Downcast Eyes—The Denigration of Vision in Twentieth-Century French Thought* (Berkeley and Los Angeles: University of California Press, 1994).

13 Alvar Aalto, "Rationalismen och människan [Rationalism and Man]," lecture given at the annual meeting of the Swedish Society of Crafts and Design, May 9, 1935. Quoted in: Juhani Pallasmaa, editor, *Alvar Aalto Furniture* (Helsinki: The Museum of Finnish Architecture, 1984), 116.

MAN, MEASURE, AND PROPORTION

1 Aulis Blomstedt, journal entry. Unless otherwise stated, all the quotations and aphorisms in this article are from Aulis Blomstedt's journals. Selections from the journals were made by the author for the following exhibition catalogue: *Aulis Blomstedt, Architect: Thought and Form—Studies in Harmony* (Helsinki: The Museum of Finnish Architecture, 1980). As the journals and notes are mostly undated, it is not possible to provide accurate dates.

2 Aulis Blomstedt, "Tutkielma teollisen rakentamisen rakenneyksiköksi [Study for a structural unit of industrial building]," *Arkkitehti The Finnish Architectural Review* (November, 1954): 6.

3 Göran Schildt, editor, Stuart Wrede, translator, *Alvar Aalto: Sketches* (Cambridge: The MIT Press, 1979), 160. "The creator created paper for drawing architecture on. Everything else is, at least for my part, to misuse paper. Torheit—as Zarathustra would have said."

4 The founders of the journal were: Aulis Blomstedt, Eero Eerikäinen, Keijo Petäjä, Reima Pietilä, André Schimmerling, and Kyösti Ålander. It has been published in Paris since 1962 under the editorship of André Schimmerling.

5 *Otavan Suuri Ensyklopedia* [The Great Otava Encyclopedia] (Helsinki: Otava, 1979), 5490.

6 Finn Benestad, *Musik och tanke—Huvudlinjer i musik-estetikens historia från antiken till vår egen tid* [Music and Thought] (Ystad: Raben & Sjögren, 1978), 20–21.

7 *Otavan Suuri Ensyklopedia*, op. cit., 5491.

8 Rudolf Wittkower, *Architectural Principles in the Age of Humanism* (New York: Random House, 1965), 104.

9   Wittkower, ibid., 117, 119.

10 Rudolf Haase, "Harmonics in Architecture," *Abacus Yearbook 2* (Helsinki: The Museum of Finnish Architecture, 1980), 94.

11 György Doczi, *The Power of Limits: Proportional Harmonies in Nature, Art and Architecture* (Boulder & London: Shambala Publications, 1981), 96.

12 Haase, op. cit., 94.

13 Aulis Blomstedt, "Ihminen arkkitehtuurin mitta [Man—the measure of architecture]," *Arkkitehti* 2 (1971): 25.

14 Aulis Blomstedt revealed the musical aspects of his researches into proportions in his study *Module variations on the 180-centimeter measure* in 1957. He had clearly studied the connections between visual and musical ratios earlier on, but only dared publish them after the death of his respected father-in-law, the composer Jean Sibelius. Aulis Blomstedt's brother, Jussi Jalas, was a well-known conductor, and this probably increased his feeling that he was a layman in the field of music. Erkki Vanhakoski, who has compiled the list of Aulis Blomstedt's works, brought this idea to the attention of the author. The author also remembers how often after 1957 Blomstedt belittled his knowledge of musical theory and mathematics.

15 Wittkower, op. cit., 33.

16 Wittkower, op. cit., 110.

17 Wittkower, op. cit., 117.

18 Hans Kayser, *Lehrbuch der Harmonik* (Zürich: Occident Veriag, 1950), 176–177.

19 Aulis Blomstedt, "Mitta ja suhde [Measure and Proportion]," *Arkkitehti* 9 (1962): 175. Blomstedt hints at his artistic objectives becoming an end unto themselves in this article.

20 Haase, op. cit., 100.

21 Wittkower, op. cit., 14.

22 Wittkower, op. cit., 15.

23 Wittkower, op. cit., 16.

24 Wittkower, op. cit., 27.

25 H.E. Huntley, *The Divine Proportion—A Study in Mathematical Beauty* (New York: Dover Publications, Inc., 1970), 24–25, 30.

26 Robert Lawlor, *Sacred Geometry* (London: Thames & Hudson, 1982), 59.

27 György Doczi, among others.

28 Doczi, op. cit., 8–10.

29 Blomstedt (1971), op. cit., 25.

30 Blomstedt (1971), op. cit..

31 Huntley, op. cit., 157–159.
    The series derives its name from Leonardo Fibonacci (filius Bonacci), alias the Leonardo of Pisa (born c. 1175). The numbers in the series in his *Liber Abaci* are obtained by adding together two consecutive numbers to give the following number: 0, 1, 1, 2, 3, 5, 8, 13, 21, 34, 55, 89, and so on. The ratio of adjacent numbers in the Fibonacci Series approach the ratio of the Golden Section as the series progresses:
    2/3, 0.667
    3/5, 0.600
    5/8, 0.625

8/15, 0.615
13/21, 0.619
21/34, 0.618
The approximate value of the Golden Section is 0.618.

32 This matter frequently cropped up in the author's conversations with Aulis Blomstedt as, for example, in 1962 when arranging an exhibition at the Museum of Finnish Architecture on modular principles.

33 Hans Kayser, *Paestum: Die Nomoi der drei altgriechischen Tempel zu Paestum* (Heidelberg: Lambert Schneider Verlag, 1958), 13–15.
    Aulis Blomstedt made jottings in the margins of the relevant parts of his copy of this work, signed in 1959. Aulis Blomstedt's son, the architect Petri Blomstedt, brought this to the attention of the author.

34 Blomstedt (1954), op. cit., 2.

35 Aulis Blomstedt, "Moduulivariaatioita 180 cm mitasta [Module variations on the 180 centimeter measure]," *Arkkitehti* 4 (1957):72.

36 Published, for example, in *Le Carré Bleu 4* (Helsinki), (1961). The construction and its musical significance are explained in Blomstedt (1971), op. cit..

37 The harmonic proportions of the extension to the City of Helsinki's Finnish-language Adult Education Center were the subjects of Helena Sarjakoski's seminar paper in art history, *Aulis Blomstedt ja harmoniikka*, presented at the University of Helsinki on February 11, 1985. Since the original publication of this essay, Helena Sarjakoski's doctoral dissertation on Aulis Blomstedt's studies in harmony has been published in book format: Helena Sarjakoski, *Rationaalisuus ja runollisuus: Aulis Blomstedt ja suhteiden taide* [Rationality and poetry: Aulis Blomstedt and the art of proportions] (Helsinki: Rakennustieto Oy, 2003).

38 Blomstedt (1971), op. cit., 23.

ARCHITECTURE AND THE REALITY OF CULTURE

1   Göran Schildt, editor, Stuart Wrede, translator, *Alvar Aalto: Sketches* (Cambridge: The MIT Press, 1978), 160.

2   Oral quote from a lecture given by Professor Sverre Fehn at the *La tradizione moderna* symposium in Venice, September 23–25, 1982.

3   Henry Moore, *Henry Moore on Sculpture* (London: MacDonald, 1966), 62.

4   Frederic Jameson, "Postmodernism, or the Cultural Logic of Late Capitalism," *New Left Review* 146 (1989), 53–92.

5   Jussi Kotkavirta and Esa Sironen, *Moderni, Postmoderni* [Modern/Postmodern] (Jyväskylä: Tutkijaliitto, 1986), 27.

6   Jürgen Habermas, *The Philosophical Discourse of Modernity* (Cambridge: The MIT Press, 1992).

7   Joseph Rykwert, *The First Moderns—the Architects of the Eighteenth Century* (Cambridge: The MIT Press, 1983).

8   Ernest Mandel, *Late Capitalism* (London: 1978), as quoted in: Fredric Jameson, *Postmodernism or, the Cultural Logic of Late Capitalism* (Durham: Duke University Press), 35.

9   Interview with Fredric Jameson in *Helsingin Sanomat*, November 17, 1986.

10 Jameson, op. cit., 6–11.

11 Martin Heidegger, "The Origin of the Work of Art," *Basic Writings* (New York: Harper & Row, 1977), 163.

12 Victor Hugo, quoted in: Pekka Suhonen, *Talot ja kirjat* [Houses and books], Teekkari (1959): 20–21.

13 Hugo, quoted in: Suhonen, op. cit, 20–21.

14 Juan Pablo Bonta, "A Propos the Tribune Projects 1," *Late Entries* vol. II (New York: Rizzoli International Publications, 1980), 96.

15 Umberto Eco, *Travels in Hyperreality* (San Diego-New York- London: Harcourt Inc., 1986).

16 T.S. Eliot, "Tradition and Individual Talent," *Selected Essays* (New York: Harcourt, Brace, 1950).

17 Jean Baudrillard, "What are you doing after the orgy?" *Traverses* 20 (1984).

18 Tiina Arppe, presentation of Baudrillard in: Jussi Kotkavirta and Esa Sironen, editors, *Moderni/Postmoderni* (Helsinki: Tutkijaliitto, 1986).

19 Herbert Marcuse, *One Dimensional Man: Studies in the Ideology of Advanced Industrial Society* (Boston: Beacon Press, 1964).

20 Marcuse, ibid., 57.

21 Henryk Skolimowski, *Eco-Philosophy* (Boston: M. Boyars, 1981).

22 A comparison of Le Corbusier's and Meyer's houses—albeit with a different purpose—are presented in: William Hubbart, *Complexity and Conviction—Steps Toward an Architecture of Convention* (Cambridge: The MIT Press, 1980).

23 Karl Marx, Speech in London, 1856, as quoted in: *Moderni/Posmoderni*, op. cit., 18.

24 Baudrillard, in: *Moderni/Postmoderni*, op. cit., 185.

25 Jameson, op. cit.

26 Thierry de Duve, as quoted in: Jean-François Lyotard, "Vastaus kysymykseen: Mitä postmodernismi on? [Answer to the question: What is Postmodernism?]," in *Moderni/Postmoderni*, op. cit., 149.

27 *Suomen Kuvalehti* (Helsinki), 23 (June 6, 1986): 3.

28 Interview with Frank Gehry, "Collisions between spaces in built sketches," Pekka Suhonen, Marja-Riitta Norri, *Arkkitehti, The Finnish Architectural Review* 5 (1986): 33.

TRADITION AND MODERNITY

1 Le Corbusier, *Towards a New Architecture* (London: The Architectural Press, 1959), 89.

2 Umberto Eco, *Travels in Hyperreality* (San Diego-New York-London: Harcourt Inc., 1986).

3 *Aldo van Eyck*, Herman Hertzberger, Addie van Roijen-Wortmann, Francis Strauven, editors (Amsterdam: Stichting Wonen, 1982), 65.

4 See, for instance: Edward T. Hall, *The Hidden Dimension* (New York: Doubleday, 1966); Frode Strømnes, *A New Physics of Inner Worlds* (Tromsö: Institute of Social Science, University of Tromsö, 1976).

5 Frode Strømnes, "On the architecture of thought," *Abacus Yearbook 2* (Helsinki: The Museum of Finnish Architecture, 1980), 6–29.

6 T. S. Eliot, "Tradition and Individual Talent," *Selected Essays*, new edition (New York: Harcourt, Brace & World, 1964).

7 T.S. Eliot, "What is a Classic," *Selected Essays*, ibid.

8 Alvar Aalto, unfinished manuscript (c. 1926) in: Göran Schildt, *Alvar Aalto: The Decisive Years* (Helsinki: Otava, 1986), 11.

9 Kirsti Gallen-Kallela, *Isäni Akseli Gallen-Kallela* [My Father Akseli Gallen-Kallela] (Porvoo: Werner Söderström Oy, 1992), 612.

10 Milan Kundera, *Romaanin taide* [The Art of the Novel] (Helsinki: WSOY, 1986), 165.

11 Umberto Eco, "Postscript to the Name of the Rose," *Matka arkipäivän epätodellisuuteen* [Travels in Hyperreality] (Helsinki: Werner Söderström Oy, 1985), 331–364.

12 Kundera, op. cit., 160.

THE LIMITS OF ARCHITECTURE

1 As quoted in: Umberto Eco, *Travels in Hyperreality* (San Diego-New York-London: Harcourt Inc., 1986), 85.

2 Francis Fukuyama, "The End of History?" *The National Interest*, no. 16 (Summer 1989).

3 Fukuyama, ibid., 18.

4 Roberto Vacca, as quoted in Umberto Eco, *Matka arkipäivän epätodellisuuteen* [Travels in Hyperreality] (Helsinki: Werner Söderström Oy, 1985), 69.

5 Eco (1986), ibid..

6 Eco (1986), op. cit., 74.

7 Eco (1985), op. cit., 87.

8 Eco (1985), op. cit., 73.

9 Viktor von Weizsäcker, *Der Gestaltkreis* (Stuttgart: Georg Thieme, 1968).

10 Fredric Jameson, "Postmodernism, or the Cultural Logic of Late Capitalism," *New Left Review* 146 (1989), 53–92.

11 Donald B. Kuspit, editor, *The Anti-aesthetic: essays on postmodern culture*, Hal Foster, editor, 1st ed. (Port Townsend: Bay Press, 1983), 299.

12 Leonardo da Vinci, as quoted in: Igor Stravinsky, *Musiikin poetiikka* [The Poetics of Music] (Helsinki: Otava, 1968), 75.

13 Jürgen Habermas, *The Philosophical Discourse of Modernity* (Cambridge: The MIT Press, 1992).

14 Richard Rogers, "Pulling Down the Prince," *The Times* (July 3, 1989).

15 Herbert Marcuse, *One Dimensional Man. Studies in the Ideology of Advanced Industrial Society* (Boston: Beacon Press, 1964), 57.

16 Clement Greenberg, "Avantgarde ja kitsch [Avantgarde and Kitsch]," *Modernin ulottuvuuksia*, [Dimensions of the Modern] Jaakko Lintinen, editor (Helsinki: Kustannusosakeyhtiö Taide, 1989), 96.

17 Stravinsky, op. cit, 59.

18 *Modernin ulottuvuuksia*, op. cit., 96.

19 Eco (1985), op. cit., 88, 89.

20 Eco (1985), op. cit., 87–88.

21 William Faulkner, as quoted in: *The Anti-aesthetic: essays on postmodern culture*, Hal Foster, editor, 1st ed. (Port Townsend: Bay Press, 1983).

22 Roland Barthes, as quoted in: *The Anti-aesthetic: essays on postmodern culture*, Hal Foster, editor, 1st ed. (Port Townsend: Bay Press, 1983).

23 T.S. Eliot, "Tradition and Individual Talent," *Selected Essays*, new ed. (New York: Harcourt, Brace, 1950).

24 Rosalind Krauss, as quoted in: *The Anti-aesthetic: essays on postmodern culture*, Hal Foster, editor, 1st ed. (Port Townsend: Bay Press, 1983), 190–206.

25 *Alvar Aalto / Sketches*, Göran Schildt, editor, Stuart Wrede, translator (Cambridge: The MIT Press,1978).

26 Trotsky, as quoted in: *The Anti-aesthetic: essays on postmodern culture*, Hal Foster, editor, 1st ed. (Port Townsend: Bay Press, 1983).

27 Donald Kuspit, as quoted in *The Anti-aesthetic: essays on postmodern culture*, Hal Foster, editor, 1st ed. (Port Townsend: Bay Press, 1983).

28 Kuspit, "Ooppera on ohi [Opera is over]," *Modernin ulottuvuuksia*, op. cit., 294.

29 Kuspit, ibid., 300.

SIX THEMES FOR THE NEXT MILLENNIUM

1 Gianni Vattimo, *The End of Modernity* (Baltimore: The John Hopkins University Press, 1991), VI.

2 Karsten Harries, "Philosophy and Architectural Education," *Arkkitehtuurin tutkijakoulutus ja tutkimus* [Research Education in Architecture] (Helsinki: Helsinki University of Technology, Publications of the Faculty of Architecture 1994/6), 13–40.

3 David Harvey, *The Condition of Postmodernity* (Cambridge: Blackwell, 1990), 147.

4 Harvey, ibid., 240.

5 Fredrik Jameson, *Postmodernism, or The Cultural Logic of Late Capitalism* (Durham: Duke University Press, 1991).

6 Harvey, op. cit., 58

7 Harvey, op. cit., 61.

8 Martin Heidegger, *The Question Concerning Technology and Other Essays*, translated and with an introduction by William Lovitt (New York: Garland Publishing, 1977).

9 Italo Calvino, *Six Memos for the Next Millennium* (New York: Vintage Books, 1988), 1.

10 Calvino, ibid., 45.

11 Calvino, op. cit., 112.

12 Karsten Harries, "Building and the Terror of Time," *Perspecta: The Yale Architectural Journal*, issue 19 (Cambridge: The MIT Press, 1982), as quoted in: David Harvey, *The Condition of Postmodernity* (Cambridge: Blackwell, 1992), 206.

13 Italo Calvino, *If on a winter's night a traveller* (Orlando: Harcourt, Brace & Company, 1979), 8.

14 Calvino (1988), op. cit., 57.

15 Rainer Maria Rilke, *The Notebooks of Malte Laurids Brigge* (New York: Random House, 1983), 47–48.

16 Juhani Pallasmaa, "The Limits of Architecture—Towards an Architecture of Silence," *Arkkitehti, The Finnish Architectural Review* (Helsinki), 6 (1990): 26–39.

17 Max Picard, *The World of Silence* (Washington: Gateway Editions, 1988) 221.

18 Picard, ibid., 145.

19 Picard, op. cit., 231.

MELANCHOLY AND TIME

1 Joseph Brodsky, *Watermark* (London: Penguin Books, 1992), 44.

2 Joseph Brodsky, "Homage to Marcus Aurelius," *Campidoglio* (New York: Random House, 1994), 31.

3 Roger Scruton, *Modern Philosophy* (London: Mandarin, 1994), 316.

4 Gotthard Booth, *The Shadow of the Conquest of Nature* (New York and Toronto: The Edwin Hellen Press, 1974).

5 Salman Rushdie, "Eikö mikään ole pyhää? [Isn't Anything Sacred?]," (Helsinki) *Parnasso* 1:1996, 8.

6 Göran Schildt, *Alvar Aalto: The Early Years* (New York: Rizzoli International Publications, 1984), 192.

7 Interview of Heiner Müller in *Helsingin Sanomat* (summer, 1995).

8 Charles Taylor, *Autenttisuuden etiikka* [The Ethics of Authenticity] (Helsinki: Gaudeamus, 1995), 39.

9 Paul Virilio, *Katoamisen estetiikka* [The Aesthetics of Disappearance] (Tampere: Gaudeamus, 1994).

10 Michel Serres, *Conversations on Science, Culture and Time* (Ann Arbor: University of Michigan Press, 1995).

11 Germano Celant, *Unexpressionism—Art Beyond the Contemporary* (New York: Rizzoli International Publications, 1988), 5, 6, 10.

12 Remo Bodei, as quoted in: Celant, ibid., 5.

13 David Harvey, *The Condition of Postmodernity* (Cambridge: Blackwell, 1992), 240-242.

14 Daniel Bell, *The Cultural Contradictions of Capitalism* (New York: Basic Books, 1978), 107–111, as quoted in: Harvey, op. cit., 201.

15 Gaston Bachelard, "Introduction," *Water and Dreams: An Essay on the Imagination of Matter* (Dallas: Dallas Institute, 1983).

16 Cyril Connolly, *The Unquiet Grave* (Harmondsworth: Penguin Press, 1967), quoted in: Emilio Ambasz, *The Architecture of Luis Barragan* (New York, The Museum of Modern Art, 1976), 108.

17 Julia Kristeva, "On melancholic imagination," quoted in: Richard Kearney, *Poetics of Imagining* (London: Harper Collins, 1991), 187–188.

18 Brodsky, op. cit., 43.

19 Adrian Stokes, "Prologue: at Venice," *The Critical Writings of Adrian Stokes*, vol. II (Plymouth: Thames and Hudson, 1978), 88.

20 Brodsky, op. cit., 70.

21 Erich Fromm, source unidentified.

22 Jean-Paul Sartre, *What is Literature?* (Gloucester: Peter Smith, 1978), 3.

23 T.S. Eliot, "Tradition and Individual Talent," *Selected Essays* (New York: Harcourt, Brace & World, 1964).

1   For instance:
    Martin Jay, *Downcast Eyes—The Denigration of Vision
    in Twentieth Century French Thought* (Berkeley and Los
    Angeles: University of California Press, 1994);
    David Michael Levin, editor, *Modernity and the Hegemony
    of Vision* (Berkeley and Los Angeles: University of
    California Press, California, 1993).

2   Levin, ibid., 205.

3   Maurice Merleau-Ponty, "The Film and the New
    Psychology," *Sense and Non-Sense* (Evanston:
    Northwestern University Press, 1964), 48.

4   Ashley Montagu, *Touching: The Human Significance of
    the Skin* (New York: Harper & Row, 1986 [1971]), 3.

5   Marcel Proust, *Kadonnutta aikaa etsimässä*
    [Remembrance of Things Past] (Helsinki: Otava, 1968), 8.

6   Maurice Merleau-Ponty, "Cézanne's Doubt," *Sense and
    Non-Sense*, op. cit., 19.

7   The notion derives from Merleau-Ponty's dialectical
    principle of the intertwining of the world and the self. He
    also speaks of an 'ontology of the flesh' as the ultimate
    conclusion of his initial phenomenology of perception.
    This ontology implies that meaning is both within and
    without, subjective and objective, spiritual and material.
    See: Richard Kearney, "Maurice Merleau-Ponty," *Modern
    Movements in European Philosophy* (Manchester and New
    York: Manchester University Press, 1994), 73–90.

8   Bernard Berenson, *Aesthetics and History* (New York:
    Pantheon, 1948), 66–70, as referred to in: Montagu, op.
    cit., 308–309.

9   Montagu, op. cit., XIII.

10 As quoted in: Levin, op. cit., 14.

11 Karsten Harries, "Building and the Terror of Time,"
    Perspecta, The Yale Architectural Journal, issue 19
    (Cambridge: The MIT Press, 1982), as quoted in: David
    Harvey, *The Condition of Postmodernity* (Cambridge:
    Blackwell, 1992), 206.

12 Le Corbusier, as quoted in: Mohsen Mostafavi and David
    Leatherbarrow, *On Weathering* (Cambridge: The MIT Press,
    1993), 76.,

13 Mohsen Mostafavi and David Leatherbarrow, *On
    Weathering* (Cambridge: The MIT Press, 1993), 76.

14 John Soane, "Crude Hints," *Visions of Ruin: Architectural
    fantasies & designs for garden follies* (London: John
    Soane Museum, 1999).

15 Gaston Bachelard, "Introduction," *Water and Dreams:
    An Essay On the Imagination of Matter* (Dallas: Dallas
    Institute, 1983), 1.

16 Colin St. John Wilson, *The Other Tradition of Modern
    Architecture* (London: Academy Editions, 1995).

17 Erik Gunnar Asplund, "Konst och Teknik [Art and
    Technology]," Byggmästaren, 1936, in Stuart Wrede, *The
    Architecture of Erik Gunnar Asplund* (Cambridge: The
    MIT Press, 1980), 153.

18 Alvar Aalto, untitled manuscript for a lecture held in
    Turin, Milan, Genoa, and Rome in 1956, The Alvar Aalto
    Foundation. Published partly in Italian in: Alvar Aalto,

"Problemi di architettura," *Quaderni ACI* (Turin: Edizione
    Associazione Culturale Italiana, 1956).

19 Aalto, ibid., 3.

20 Aalto, op. cit., 4.

21 Vattimo introduced the notion in the late 1970s. The idea
    was developed in a volume of essays entitled *Il pensiero
    debole* edited by Vattimo in collaboration with Pier Aldo
    Rovatti. Vattimo also discusses the notion in his seminal
    The End of Modernity (Baltimore: The John Hopkins
    University Press, 1991).

22 "There is a delicate empiricism which makes itself
    utterly identical with the object, thereby becoming true
    theory." Goethe, *Goethe: Scientific Studies* (Princeton:
    Princeton University Press, 1934), p. 307. As quoted in:
    David Seamon, "Goethe, Nature and Phenomenology: An
    Introduction," David Seamon and Arthur Zajonc, editors,
    Goethe's Way of Science (Albany: State University of New
    York Press, 1998), 2.

23 Ignasi de Solà-Morales, *Differences: Topographies of
    Contemporary Architecture* (Cambridge: The MIT Press,
    1997), 57–70.

24 Solà-Morales, ibid., 58, 60.

25 Solà-Morales, op. cit., 70.

26 Simon Hubacker, "Weak Urbanism," *Daidalos* 72 (1999):
    10–17.

27 Juhani Pallasmaa, *The Architecture of Image: Existential
    Space in Cinema* (Helsinki: Rakennustieto, 2002),
    123–125.

28 Harald Arnkil, *Juhana Blomstedt* (Helsinki: Weilin+Göös,
    1989).

29 The power of a weak force in nature can be illustrated
    by comparing the toughest known material of nature
    with that of ours. None of the man-made metals or high-
    strength fibers of today can come even close to the com-
    bined strength and energy-absorbing elasticity of spider
    dragline. The line spun by the spider is five times stronger
    than steel, and much tougher than polyaramid Kevlar, the
    material used in bullet-proof vests and facial masks; it
    can absorb five times the impact force of Kevlar without
    breaking. According to an article in *Science News*,
    January 21, 1995, a web resembling a normal fishing net
    in its thickness of thread and the scale of the mesh could
    catch a passenger plane in flight. The spider line is pro-
    duced with low energy at spider body temperature whereas
    in the production of Kevlar petroleum derived molecules
    are poured into a pressurised vat of concentrated sulphuric
    acid and boiled at several hundred degrees Fahrenheit
    in order to force it into a liquid crystal form. The energy
    input is very high and there are extremely problematic
    toxic by-products.
    See: Janine M. Benyus, *Biomimicry* (New York: William
    Morrow, 1998), 132, 135.

30 Andrew Todd, "Learning From Peter Brook's Work on
    Theatre Space," (September 25, 1999) unpublished manu-
    script, 4.

31 Rainer Maria Rilke, *The Notebooks of Malte Laurids
    Brigge* (New York and London: W.W. Norton & Co., 1992),
    47–48.

32 Juhani Pallasmaa, editor, *Alvar Aalto: Villa Mairea 1938–39* (Helsinki: The Alvar Aalto Foundation and The Mairea Foundation, 1998).

33 For the role of unconscious vision, see: Anton Ehrenzweig, *The Hidden Order of Art* (London: Paladin, 1973).

34 Leon Battista Alberti, *The Ten Books on Architecture* (London: A. Tiranti, 1955).

35 John Ruskin, *The Lamp of Beauty: Writings on Art by John Ruskin*, Joan Evans, editor (Ithaca, N.Y.: Cornell University Press, 1980), 238, as quoted in Gary J. Coates, *Erik Asmussen, architect* (Stockholm: Byggförlaget, 1997), 230.

36 Alvar Aalto, "The Human Factor," in: Göran Schildt, editor, *Alvar Aalto in His Own Words*. (Helsinki: Otava, 1997), 281.

37 Demetri Porphyrios, *Sources of Modern Eclecticism: Studies on Alvar Aalto* (London: Academy Editions, 1982).

38 Alvar Aalto, Speech at the Helsinki University of Technology Centennial Celebration, December 5, 1972, in: Schildt, op. cit., 283.

39 Erik Bryggman, "Rural Architecture," in: Riitta Nikula, editor, *Erik Bryggman 1891–1955, Architect* (Helsinki: The Museum of Finnish Architecture, 1991), 279.

LANDSCAPES OF ARCHITECTURE

1   Source of the quote unidentified. The writer has received it from Steven Holl in the early 1990s.

2   Vitruvius (Marcus Vitruvius Pollio), *The Ten Books on Architecture* [De Architectura Libri Decem] (New York: Dover Publications, Inc., 1960), 5–6.

3   Ibid., 8.

4   Karsten Harries, "Philosophy and Architectural Education," *Arkkitehtuurin tutkijakoulutus ja tutkimus* [Research Education in Architecture] (Helsinki: Helsinki University of Technology, Publications of the Faculty of Architecture 1994/6).

5   David Seamon, "A Way of Seeing People and Place: Phenomenology in Environment-Behavior Research," in: S. Wapner, J. Demick, T. Yamamoto and H. Minami, editors, *Theoretical Perspectives in Environment—Behavior Research* (New York: Plenum Publishers, 1999), 172.

6   Private conversation between Eduardo Chillida and the author, Helsinki, 1987.

7   Joseph Brodsky, "A Cat´s Meow," *On Grief and Reason* (New York: Farrar, Straus and Giroux, 1995), 302.

8   Juhani Pallasmaa, "The Two Languages of Architecture: elements of a bio-cultural approach to architecture," *Abacus: Yearbook 2* (Helsinki: The Museum of Finnish Architecture, 1981), 58–91.

9   Gaston Bachelard, *The Philosophy of No: A philosophy of the New Scientific Mind* (New York: The Orion Press, 1968).

10 Ibid., 16.

11 Raymond Queneau, as quoted in: Georges Perec, *Tiloja, avaruuksia* [Espéces d´espaces] (Helsinki, Loki-Kirjat, 1992), 72.

12 Jean Pellerin, *La Romance du Retour*, N.R.F. 1921,18. As quoted in: Gaston Bachelard, *The Poetics of Space* (Boston: Beacon Press, 1969), 223.

13 Alvar Aalto, "Taide ja tekniikka [Art and Technology]," lecture, Academy of Finland, October 3, 1955, in: Göran Schildt, *Alvar Aalto Luonnoksia* (Helsinki: Otava, 1972), 87-88. Translation Juhani Pallasmaa.

14 Marilyn R. Chandler, *Dwelling in the Text: Houses in American Fiction* (Berkeley-Los Angeles-Oxford: University of California Press, 1991).

15 See: Juhani Pallasmaa, "Man, Measure and Proportion: Aulis Blomstedt and the Tradition of Pythagorean Harmonics," *Acanthus* (Helsinki, The Museum of Finnish Architecture, 1992), 6–31.

16 As quoted in: Bachelard (1969), op. cit., XXIV.

17 Kirmo Mikkola, *Aalto* (Jyväskylä, Gummerus, 1985), 42–45. The origin of the quote is unidentified.

18 As quoted in: Perec, op. cit., 50.

19 Joseph Brodsky, "In Memory of Stephen Spender," *On Grief and Reason* (New York: Farrar, Straus and Giroux, 1995), 473, 475.

20 Borges, *On Writing*, Norman Thomas di Giovanni, Daniel Halpern, Frank MacShane, editors (Hopewell, New Jersey: The Ecco Press, 1994).

21 Borges, ibid., 45.

22 Borges, op. cit., 53.

23 Bohumil Hrabal, *Too Loud a Solitude* (San Diego-New York-London: Harcourt, Inc., 1990), 1.

24 Louis Kahn, "Form and Design (1960)," in: Alessandra Latour, editor, *Louis I. Kahn: Writings, Lectures, Interviews* (New York: Rizzoli International Publications, 1991), 116.

25 Ezra Pound, *ABC of Reading* (New York: A New Directions Paperbook, 1987), 14.

26 Joseph Brodsky, "How to Read a Book," *On Grief and Reason* (New York: Farrar, Straus and Giroux, 1997), 101.

27 T.S. Eliot, "Tradition and the Individual Talent," in: T.S. Eliot, *Selected Essays* (New York: Harcourt, Brace & World, 1964).

28 Jean Genet, *L´atelier d´Alberto Giacometti* (Lárbelét: Marc Barbezat, 1963).

29 Milan Kundera, *Romaanin taide* [The Art of the Novel] (Helsinki: WSOY, 1986), 165.

30 Aldo van Eyck reported the incident to the author in a conversation in the early 1980s.

31 Brodsky, "Letter to Horace," *On Grief and Reason*, op. cit., 439.

32 Elaine Scarry, *On Beauty and Being Just* (New Jersey: Princeton University Press, 1999).

33 Joseph Brodsky, "An Immodest Proposal," *On Grief and Reason*, op. cit., 208.

34 Joseph Brodsky, ibid., 208.

35 Joseph Brodsky, op. cit., 207.

36 Alvar Aalto, "Arkkitehtien paratiisiajatus [The Paradise Idea of Architects]," lecture given in Malmö, Sweden in 1957, in: Göran Schildt, editor, *Alvar Aalto Luonnoksia* [Sketches] (Helsinki: Otava, 1972), 101–102.

Illustration Credits

The majority of these essays were initially presented as lectures in universities, or in similar scholarly contexts; each was usually presented accompanied by approximately 200 paired sequences of slides from the author's lecture slide collection. In the production and layout of this book, the essays have been illustrated by a selection of those initial lecture presentation images. Due to the quantity of the notational, diminutively sized images utilized, and to the scholarly nature of the book, individual reproduction permissions have not been sought. Rather, in the illustration credits listed below, the sources of the images have been precisely identified, whenever possible.

1   Zsa-Zsa Eyck, *Sigurdur Gudmundsson* (Malmö: Malmö Konsthall, 1991).
2   Photo Teemu Taskinen.
3   Photo Juhani Pallasmaa.
4   MacDonald Critchley, *Silent Language* (London: Butterworths, 1975).
5   Critchley, *Silent Language*.
6   Critchley, *Silent Language*.
7   Critchley, *Silent Language*.
8   Frans A. Stafleu, "Linnaeus and the Linnaeans," *Regnum vegetabile, vol. 79* (Utrecht: 1971).
9   Stafleu, "Linnaeus and the Linnaeans," *Regnum vegetabile, vol. 79*.
10   J.G. Heck, *The Complete Encyclopedia of Illustration* (New York: Park Lane, 1979).
11   J.H.L. Durand, *Leçons d'architecture. Partie Graphique des cours d'architecture* (Uhl Verlag, 1975)
12   Durand, *Leçons d'architecture. Partie Graphique des cours d'architecture*.
13   Le Corbusier et Pierre Jeanneret, *Oeuvre complète de 1910–1929* (Zurich: Editions Dr. H. Girsberger, 1937).
14   *Five Architects* (New York: Wittenborn & Company, 1972).
15   Karl-Georg Bitterberg, *Bauhaus* (Stuttgart: Institut für Auslandsbeziehungen; Helsinki: Suomen Rakennustaiteen Museo, 1983).
16   Le Corbusier et Pierre Jeanneret, *Oeuvre complète de 1910–1929*.
17   Robert Lawlor, *Sacred Geometry: Philosophy and Practice* (London: Thames & Hudson, 1989).
18   David Coxhead and Susan Hiller, *Dreams: Vision of the Night* (New York: Avon Books, 1975).
19   Anne Bancroft, *Zen: Direct Pointing to Reality* (London: Thames & Hudson, 1979).
20   Marie-Louise von Franz, *Time: Rhythm and Repose* (London: Thames & Hudson, 1978).
21   Drawing: Juhani Pallasmaa.
22   Joseph Rykwert, *The Idea of a Town* (New Jersey: Princeton University Press, 1976).
23   Rykwert, *The Idea of a Town*.
24   Source unknown.
25   Oliver Marc, *Psychology of the House* (London: Thames and Hudson, 1977).
26   Francis Huxley, *The Way of the Sacred* (London: Aldus Books, 1974).
27   John Michell, *The Earth Spirit: Its Ways, Shrines, and Mysteries* (New York: Avon Books, 1975).
28   Ajit Mookerjee and Madhu Khanna, *The Tantric Way* (London: Thames & Hudson, 1977).
29   Lama Anagarika Govinda, *Psycho-Cosmic Symbolism of the Buddhist Stupa* (U.S.A.: Dharma Publishing, 1976).
30   Govinda, *Psycho-Cosmic Symbolism of the Buddhist Stupa*.
31   Govinda, *Psycho-Cosmic Symbolism of the Buddhist Stupa*.
32   Govinda, *Psycho-Cosmic Symbolism of the Buddhist Stupa*.
33   Laleh Bakhtiar, *Sufi: Expressions of the Mystic Quest* (London: Thames and Hudson, 1976).
34   Source unknown.
35   Marcel Griaule, *Conversations with Ogotemméli—An Introduction to Dogon Religious Ideas* (London: Oxford University Press, 1965).
36   Source unknown.
37   Philip Rawson, *Tantra: The Indian Cult of Ecstasy* (London: Thames & Hudson, 1973).
38   J. Bronowski, *The Ascent of Man* (London: British Broadcasting Corporation, 1976).
39   Philip Rawson and Laszlo Legeza, *Tao: The Eastern Philosophy of Time and Change* (New York: Avon Books 1973).
40   David Sylvester, *Interviews with Francis Bacon* (London: Thames and Hudson, 1975).
41   Irmtraud Schaareschmidt-Richter, *Der Japanische Garten* (Fribourg: Office du Livre, 1979).
42   Source unknown.
43   Huxley, *The Way of the Sacred*.
44   Robert Graves, *New Larousse Encyclopedia of Mythology* (London: 1959).
45   Source unknown.
46   Erich Neumann, *The Great Mother* (New Jersey: Princeton University Press, 1974).
47   David Finn, *Henry Moore: Sculpture and Environment* (New York: Harry N. Abrams, Inc., Publishers, 1976).
48   Maria-Gabriele Wosien, *Sacred Dance: Encounter with the Gods* (New York: Avon Books, 1974).
49   Rawson, *Tantra: The Indian Cult of Ecstasy*.
50   Lawlor, *Sacred Geometry: Philosophy and Practice*.
51   Huxley, *The Way of the Sacred*.
52   Francis King, *Magic: The Western Tradition* (New York: Avon Books, 1975).
53   Susan Denyer, *African Traditional Architecture* (London: Heinemann, 1978).
54   Photo Bruce Greager.
55   Photo Bruce Greager.

56 Marc, *Psychology of the House.*

57 Jorma Hautala.

58 Marc, *Psychology of the House.*

59 Source unknown.

60 Huxley, *The Way of the Sacred.*

61 Arnold Toynbee, *A Study of History* (Great Britain: Oxford University Press, 1972).

62 Pierre Cassier, *Goya: A Witness of His Times* (Secaucus, New Jersey: Chartwell Books, 1983).

63 Photo Juhani Pallasmaa.

64 Photo Rauno Träskelin.

65 *Louise Bourgeois: Memory and Architecture,* exhibition catalogue (Madrid: Museo Nacional de Arte Reina Sofia, 1999).

66 *Louise Bourgeois: Memory and Architecture.*

67 Michael Juul Holm, Kjeld Kjeldsen and Tine Vindfeld, editors, *Arne Jacobsen – Absolutely Modern* (Denmark: Louisiana Museum of Modern Art, 2003).

68 Werner Blaser, *Mies van der Rohe: Crown Hall* (Basel: Birkhäuser-Publishers for Architecture, 2001).

69 Aarno Ruusuvuori, editor, *Alvar Aalto 1898-1976* (Helsinki: The Museum of Finnish Architecture, 1978).

70 Ruusuvuori, editor, *Alvar Aalto 1898-1976.*

71 Brian Brace Taylor, *Pierre Chareau: Designer and Architect* (Köln: Benedikt Taschen Verlag GmbH, 1992).

72 Christian Norberg-Schulz, *Modern Norwegian Architecture* (Oslo: Norwegian University Press, 1986).

73 Sarane Alexandrian, *Marcel Duchamp* (New York: Crown Publishers, Inc., 1977).

74 Donald Albrecht, *Designing Dreams: Modern Architecture in the Movies* (New York: Harper & Row, 1986).

75 Henri Stierlin, editor, *Architecture of the World: Mayan* (Köln: Benedikt Taschen Verlag GmbH).

76 Richard Weston, *Utzon* (Denmark: Edition Bløndal, 2002).

77 Peter Reed, editor, *Alvar Aalto: Between Humanism and Materialism* (New York: The Museum of Modern Art, 1998).

78 Stefano Zuffi, *Titian* (Milan: Arnoldo Monadori Arte, 1991).

79 Janine Barrier, *Piranèse* (France: Bibliothèque de l'Image, 1995).

80 Ernst Bruno, *The Magic Mirror of M.C. Escher* (New York: Ballantine Books, 1976).

81 Peter von Bagh, *Elämää suuremmat elokuvat* (Helsinki: Otava, 1989).

82 Patrick Humphries, *The Films of Hitchcock* (London: Bison Books Ltd., 1987).

83 Griaule, *Conversations with Ogotemméli.*

84 Lutz Heusinger, *Michelangelo* (Italy: Scala, 1989).

85 Photo Markku Komonen.

86 Stefano Zuffi, *Giorgione* (Milan: Arnoldo Mondadori Arte, 1991).

87 M.V. Alpatov, *Early Russian Icon Painting* (Moskva: Iskustvo, 1978).

88 William Rubin, *Picasso and Braque: Pioneering Cubism* (New York: The Museum of Modern Art, 1989).

89 Luciano Bellosi, *Giotto* (Italy: Becocci Editore, 1984).

90 Bellosi, *Giotto.*

91 Giulio Carlo Argan, *Fra Angelico* (Paris: Skira, 1955).

92 Argan, *Fra Angelico.*

93 Elsa Morante and Umberto Baldini, *Classici dell'Arte, vol. 38, L'opera completa dell'Angelico* (Milano: Rizzoli Editore, 1970).

94 David Sylvester, *Magritte* (New York: Harry N. Abrams, Inc., Publishers, 1992).

95 Jill Dunkerton, et al., *Giotto to Dürer: Early Renaissance Painting in the National Gallery*, Diana Davies, editor (New Haven and London: Yale University Press. London: National Gallery Publications Limited, 1991).

96 John Walker, *Turner* (New York: Harry N. Abrams, Inc., Publishers, 1983).

97 Source unknown.

98 Arthur J. Wheelock, Jr., editor, *Johannes Vermeer* (Washington: National Gallery of Art; The Hague: Royal Cabinet of Paintings Maritshuis; New Haven & London: Yale University Press, 1996).

99 Patricia Fortini Brown, *Venetian Narrative Painting in the Age of Carpaccio* (New Haven and London: Yale University Press, 1989).

100 Howard Hibbard, *The Metropolitan Museum of Art* (New York: Harrison House, 1986).

101 Richard Calvocoressi, *Magritte* (Oxford: Phaidon Press Limited, 1990).

102 Gregory Martin, *Bruegel* (New York: St. Martin's Press, 1978).

103 *L'opera completa di Carrà* (Milano: Rizzoli Editore, 1970).

104 Source unknown.

105 Jill Dunkerton, et al., *Giotto to Dürer: Early Renaissance Painting in the National Gallery.*

106 Françoise Bonnefoy, editor, *Edward Hopper* (Marseille: Musée Cantini; Paris: Éditions Adam Biro, 1989).

107 Andrej Tarkovskij, *Den förseglade tiden* (Stockholm: Albert Bonniers Förlag, 1993).

108 The Museum of Modern Art, *Walker Evans* (New York: The Museum of Modern Art, 1979).

109 Claude Roy, *Balthus* (Boston: A Bulfinch Press Book, 1996).

110 Giovanna Scirè Nepi, *Treasures of Venetian Painting: The Gallerie dell' Accademia* (London: Thames & Hudson, 1991).

111 Giulio Cattaneo and Edi Baccheschi, *Classici dell'Arte, vol. 60., L'opera completa di Duccio* (Milano: Rizzoli Editore, 1981).

112 Morante and Baldini, *Classici dell'Arte, vol. 38, L'opera completa dell'Angelico.*

113 Oreste del Buono and Pierluigi De Vecchi, *Classici dell'Arte, vol. 9., L'opera completa di Piero della Francesca* (Milano: Rizzoli Editore, 1981).

114 Bellosi, *Giotto.*

115 Maurizio Fagiolo Dell'Arco, *Classici dell'Arte, vol. 110, L'opera completa di De Chirico* (Milano: Rizzoli Editore, 1984).

116 Bonnefoy, *Edward Hopper.*

117 Morante and Baldini, *Classici dell'Arte, vol. 38, L'opera completa dell'Angelico.*

118 Martin, *Bruegel.*

119 Zuffi, *Giorgione*.

120 Cattaneo and Baccheschi, *Classici dell'Arte, vol. 60., L'opera completa di Duccio*.

121 Grigore Arbore, *Bellini* (Bucharest: Meridiane Publishing House, 1978).

122 Bellosi, *Giotto*.

123 Bonnefoy, *Edward Hopper*.

124 John Pope-Hennessy, *Angelico* (Firenze: Becocci Editore, 1983).

125 Calvocoressi, *Magritte*.

126 Arbore, *Bellini*.

127 *I maestri del colore, Rafaello, prima parte* (Milano: Fratelli Fabbri Editori, 1976).

128 Bruno Santi, *Botticelli* (Firenze: Becocci Editore, 1976).

129 Arbore, *Bellini*.

130 Alexandru Balaci, *Mantegna* (London, Abbey Library, 1980).

131 Gian Alberto dell'Acqua and Germano Mulazzani, *Classici dell'Arte, vol. 95, L'opera completa di Bramantino e Bramante pittore* (Milano: Rizzoli Editore, 1978).

132 Helmut Börsch-Supan, *Classici dell'Arte, vol. 84, L'opera completa di Caspar David Friedrich* (Milano: Rizzoli Editore, 1976).

133 Martin, *Bruegel*.

134 Gail Levin, *Edward Hopper 1882-1967: Gemälde und Zeichnungen* (München: Schirmer-Mosel, 1981).

135 Jill Dunkerton, et al., *Giotto to Dürer: Early Renaissance Painting in the National Gallery*.

136 Pierre Courthion, *Dutch and Flemish Painting* (New Jersey: Chartwell Books, Inc., 1983).

137 Jill Dunkerton, et al., *Giotto to Dürer: Early Renaissance Painting in the National Gallery*.

138 Bonnefoy, *Edward Hopper*.

139 del Buono and De Vecchi, *Classici dell'Arte, vol. 9, L'opera completa di Piero della Francesca*.

140 Balaci, *Mantegna*.

141 Dell'Arco, *Classici dell'Arte, vol. 110, L'opera completa di De Chirico*.

142 Morante and Baldini, *Classici dell'Arte, vol. 38, L'opera completa dell'Angelico*.

143 *I maestri del colore, Masaccio* (Milano: Fratelli Fabbri Editori, 1976).

144 Martin, *Bruegel*.

145 Morante and Baldini, *Classici dell'Arte, vol. 38, L'opera completa dell'Angelico*.

146 Source unknown.

147 Ronald Lightbown, *Botticelli* (Paris: Éditions Citadelles, 1990).

148 *I maestri del colore, Masaccio* (Milano: Fratelli Fabbri Editori, 1976).

149 Giovanni Fanelli, *Brunelleschi* (Firenze: Becocci Editore, 1985).

150 Bellosi, *Giotto*.

151 Bellosi, *Giotto*.

152 Dell'Arco, *Classici dell'Arte, vol. 110, L'opera completa di De Chirico*.

153 Bellosi, *Giotto*.

154 del Buono and De Vecchi, *Classici dell'Arte, vol. 9, L'opera completa di Piero della Francesca*.

155 Pere Gimferrer, *De Chirico* (New York: Rizzoli International Publications, Inc., 1989).

156 Bellosi, *Giotto*.

157 Balaci, *Mantegna*.

158 Pope-Hennessy, *Angelico*.

159 Arbore, *Bellini*.

160 Arbore, *Bellini*.

161 Gilles Néret, *à l'école des grands peintres, vol. 17, Cézanne* (Paris: Éditions de vergeures, 1982).

162 *L'opera completa di Carrà* (Milano: Rizzoli Editore, 1970).

163 Photo Juhani Pallasmaa.

164 Pippo Ciora, *Peter Eisenman: Opere e progetti* (Milano: Electa, 1994).

165 Ingo E. Walther, *Vincent van Gogh* (Köln: Benedikt Taschen Verlag GmbH, 1988).

166 Source unknown.

167 Lloyd Goodrich, *Edward Hopper* (New York: Harry N. Abrams, Inc., Publishers, 1989).

168 Source unknown.

169 Paige Rense, ed., *Architectural Digest: Celebrity Homes II* (Los Angeles: The Knapp Press Publishers, 1981).

170 Sylvester, *Magritte*.

171 Frame from Alfred Hitchcock's *Rear Window* (Photo Juhani Pallasmaa).

172 Tarkovskij, *Den förseglade tiden*.

173 Frame from Andrey Tarkovsky's *The Mirror* (Photo Juhani Pallasmaa).

174 Rene Passeron, *Rene Magritte* (Köln: Benedikt Taschen Verlag GmbH, 1985).

175 Robert Hobbs, *Edward Hopper* (New York: Harry N. Abrams, Inc., Publishers, 1987).

176 *Art in America*, July: 1992.

177 Ignasi de Solà-Morales, *Gaudi* (New York: Rizzoli International Publications, Inc., 1983).

178 *Encyclopedia of World Mythology* (London: Octopus Books, Ltd., 1975).

179 Albert Chatelet, *Early Dutch Painting in the Northern Netherlands in the Fifteenth Century* (Lausanne, Montreaux Fine Art Publications, 1980).

180 Peter Thornton, *The Italian Renaissance Interior 1400-1600* (New York: Harry N. Abrams, Inc., Publishers, 1991).

181 Source unknown.

182 Amy Stechler Burns & Ken Burns, *The Shakers* (New York: Aperture Foundation, Inc., 1987).

183 Jack Flam, editor, *Matisse: A Retrospective* (New York, Park Lane, 1990).

184 Photo Juhani Pallasmaa.

185 Photo Juhani Pallasmaa.

186 Photo Juhani Pallasmaa.

187 Georg Kohlmaier and Barna von Sartory, *Houses of Glass* (Cambridge: The MIT Press, 1986).

188 Leonardo Benevolo, *History of Modern Architecture* (Cambridge: The MIT Press, 1985).

189 Colin Davies, *High Tech Architecture* (London: Thames and Hudson Ltd, 1988).

190 Claude Mignot, *Architecture of the 19th Century* (Köln: Benedikt Taschen Verlag GmbH, 1994).

191 Selim Omarovich Khan-Magomedov, *Alexandr Vesnin* (New York: Rizzoli International Publications, Inc., 1986).

192 Davies, *High Tech Architecture.*

193 Kohlmaier and von Sartory, *Houses of Glass.*

194 *Renzo Piano: Mein Architectur-Logbuch* (Ostfilden-Ruit: Verlag Gerd Hatje, 1997).

195 Kohlmaier and von Sartory, *Houses of Glass.*

196 Kohlmaier and von Sartory, *Houses of Glass.*

197 *Renzo Piano: Mein Architectur-Logbuch.*

198 *Renzo Piano: Mein Architectur-Logbuch.*

199 Kohlmaier and von Sartory, *Houses of Glass.*

200 *Renzo Piano: Mein Architectur-Logbuch.*

201 Kohlmaier and von Sartory, *Houses of Glass.*

202 *Renzo Piano: Mein Architectur-Logbuch.*

203 Michael Raeburn and Victoria Wilson, editors, *Le Corbusier Architect of the Century* (Great Britain: Arts Council of Great Britain, 1987).

204 *Renzo Piano: Mein Architectur-Logbuch.*

205 *Aujourd'hui, art et architecture: Le Corbusier*, numéro 51 (Paris, 1965).

206 Jean-Louis Cohen, Monique Eleb and Antonio Martinelli, *The 20th Century Architecture and Urbanism: Paris* (Tokyo: A + U Publishing Co., Ltd., 1990).

207 Maurice Besset, *Le Corbusier* (Genève: Editions d'Art Albert Skira S.A., 1987).

208 Peter Gössel and Gabriele Leuthäuser, *Architektur des 20. Jahrhunderts* (Köln: Benedikt Taschen Verlag GmbH, 1994).

209 Juhani Pallasmaa, editor, *Daniel Libeskind, Architect: Micromegas, Architectural Drawings* (Helsinki: The Museum of Finnish Architecture, 1980).

210 Stanley Tigerman, *Late Entries, vol. 2* (New York: Rizzoli International Publications, Inc., 1980).

211 Tigerman, *Late Entries, vol. 2.*

212 Tigerman, *Late Entries, vol. 2.*

213 Tigerman, *Late Entries, vol. 2.*

214 Tigerman, *Late Entries, vol. 2.*

215 Tigerman, *Late Entries, vol. 2.*

216 Tigerman, *Late Entries, vol. 2.*

217 Tigerman, *Late Entries, vol. 2.*

218 Photo Arvi Ilonen.

219 Photo Arvi Ilonen.

220 Photo Arvi Ilonen.

221 *Andy Goldsworthy: In Collaboration with Nature* (New York: Harry N. Abrams, Inc., Publishers, 1990).

222 Richard Thomson, et al., *Toulouse-Lautrec* (New Haven and London: Yale University Press, 1991).

223 *National Geographic*, vol. 178, no 5, November 1990.

224 Kynaston McShine, *Andy Warhol A Retrospective* (New York: The Museum of Modern Art, 1989).

225 Arthur C. Danto, *Encounters and Reflections: Art in the Historical Present* (New York: Farrar, Straus & Giroux, 1990).

226 Jean-Yves Bosseur, *Musique: passion d'artistes* (Genève: Éditions d'Art Albert Skira S.A., 1991)

227 Gavin Macrae-Gibson, *The Secret Life of Buildings: An American Mythology for Modern Architecture* (Cambridge: The MIT Press, 1985).

228 Kirk Varnedoe and Adam Gopnik, *High & Low: Modern Art and Popular Culture* (New York: The Museum of Modern Art, 1991).

229 Source unknown.

230 Raeburn and Wilson, editors, *Le Corbusier Architect of the Century.*

231 Fiona Ragheb, editor, *Frank Gehry Architect* (New York: Guggenheim Museum Publications, 2002).

232 Raeburn and Wilson, editors, *Le Corbusier Architect of the Century.*

233 Joan Ockman, *Richard Meier Architect* (New York: Rizzoli International Publications, Inc., 1984).

234 Jean-Luc Daval, *Journal des avant-gardes* (Genève: Editions d'Art Albert Skira S.A., 1980).

235 Bitterberg, *Bauhaus.*

236 *Nils-Udo Bob Verschueren* (Brussel: Atelier 340, 1992).

237 *Andy Goldsworthy: In Collaboration with Nature* (New York: Harry N. Abrams, Inc., Publishers, 1990).

238 Photo Rauno Träskelin.

239 Haig Beck and Jackie Cooper, *Glenn Murcutt: A Singular Architectural Practice* (Australia: The Images Publishing Group Pty Ltd., 2002).

240 Kristiina Lehtimäki, editor, *Renzo Piano* (Helsinki: Building Information Ltd, 2000).

241 Felice Frankel and Jory Johnson, *Modern Landscape Architecture* (New York: Abbeville Press, 1991). Photo Felice Frankel.

242 Sergio Los and Klaus Frahm, *Carlo Scarpa* (Köln: Benedikt Taschen Verlag GmbH, 1999).

243 Courtesy of James Carpenter Design Associates.

244 Andrea Compagno, *Intelligent Glass Façades* (Basel: Birkhäuser Verlag, 1996).

245 Michael Wigginton, *Glass in Architecture* (London: Phaidon Press Ltd, 1996).

246 Wolfgang Pehnt, *Expressionist Architecture* (New York: Praeger Publishers, 1973).

247 Wigginton, *Glass in Architecture.*

248 Terence Riley and Joseph Abram, editors, *The Filter of Reason / Work of Paul Nelson* (New York: Rizzoli International Publications, Inc., 1990).

249 Yukio Futagawa, editor, *La Maison de Verre* (Tokyo: A.D.A. Edita, 1988).

250 Gössel and Leuthäuser, *Architecture in the Twentieth Century.*

251 Wilhelm Fraenger, *Bosch* (New York: Dorset Press,1989).

252 Joan Ockman, *Architecture Culture 1943-1968: A Documentary Anthology* (New York: Columbia Books of Architecture; Rizzoli International Publications, Inc., 1993).

253 Wigginton, *Glass in Architecture.*

254 Martin Pawley, *Design Heroes: Buckminster Fuller* (London: Grafton, 1990).

255 Paul Duncan, *Stanley Kubrick: The Complete Films* (Köln: Taschen GmbH, 2003).

256 Juhani Pallasmaa, editor, *Animal Architecture* (Helsinki: The Museum of Finnish Architecture, 1995).

257 John W. Nunley and Cara McCarty, *Masks: Faces of Culture* (New York: Harry N. Abrams, Inc., Publishers, 1999).

258 Charles Gibbs-Smith, *The Inventions of Leonardo da Vinci* (New York: Charles Scribner's Sons, 1978).

259 Tohio Nakamura, editor, *Louis I. Kahn* (Tokyo: A + U Publishing Co., Ltd., 1983).

260 James Elkins, *What Painting Is* (New York: Routledge, 2000).

261 Marianne Aav, editor, *Tapio Wirkkala: Eye, Hand and Thought* (Helsinki: Taideteollisuusmuseo, 2000).

262 Aav, editor, *Tapio Wirkkala: Eye, Hand and Thought*.

263 Museo Nacional Centro de Arte Reina Sofia, *Chillida* (Madrid: Museo Nacional Reina Sofia/Aldeasa, 1998).

264 Ernst-Gerhard Güse, editor, *Richard Serra* (New York: Rizzoli International Publications, Inc., 1988).

265 Mary Jacob, editor, *Gordon Matta-Clark: A Retrospective* (Chicago: Museum of Contemporary Art, 1985).

266 Richard Corlis, "Matrix Mania," *Time* (Amsterdam), Vol. 161, No. 19 (2003).

267 Wigginton, *Glass in Architecture*.

268 The Finnish Film Archive.

269 The Finnish Film Archive.

270 David Bellos, *Jacques Tati* (London: The Harvill Press, 1999).

271 Sylvester, *Magritte*.

272 *The Pritzker Architecture Prize: 2001 Jacques Herzog and Pierre De Meuron* (Los Angeles: Jensen & Walker, Inc., 2001).

273 *Stretto House: Steven Holl Architects / Introduction by Steven Holl* (New York: Monacelli Press, 1996).

274 Compagno, *Intelligent Glass Façades*.

275 Photo Rauno Träskelin.

276 Pirkko Tuukkanen-Beckers, *En contacto con Alvar Aalto* (Jyväskylä: Museo Alvar Aalto, 1993).

277 Tuukkanen-Beckers, *En contacto con Alvar Aalto*.

278 Bellosi, *Giotto*.

279 Tuukkanen-Beckers, *En contacto con Alvar Aalto*.

280 Reed, editor, *Alvar Aalto: Between Humanism and Materialism*.

281 Photo Rauno Träskelin.

282 Juhani Pallasmaa, editor, *Alvar Aalto Villa Mairea* (Finland: The Alvar Aalto Foundation and The Mairea Foundation, 1998).

283 Photo Rauno Träskelin.

284 Angelika Muthesius, editor, *Man Ray* (Berlin: Taco, 1989).

285 Rubin, *Picasso and Braque: Pioneering Cubism*.

286 Rubin, *Picasso and Braque: Pioneering Cubism*.

287 Tuukkanen-Beckers, *En contacto con Alvar Aalto*.

288 Photo Juhani Pallasmaa.

289 Photo Rauno Träskelin.

290 Jill Dunkerton, et al., *Giotto to Dürer: Early Renaissance Painting in the National Gallery*.

291 Göran Schildt, *Inhimillinen tekijä: Alvar Aalto 1939-1976* (Helsinki: Otava, 1990).

292 Photo Markku Komonen.

293 Reed, editor, *Alvar Aalto: Between Humanism and Materialism*.

294 Reed, editor, *Alvar Aalto: Between Humanism and Materialism*.

295 Peter B. MacKeith and Kerstin Smeds, *The Finland Pavilions: Finland at the Universal Expositions 1900–1992* (Finland: Kustannus Oy City, 1993). Photo Ezra Stoller.

296 Reed, editor, *Alvar Aalto: Between Humanism and Materialism*.

297 Reed, editor, *Alvar Aalto: Between Humanism and Materialism*.

298 Juhani Pallasmaa, editor, *The Language of Wood* (Helsinki: The Museum of Finnish Architecture, 1994).

299 Pallasmaa, editor, *Alvar Aalto Villa Mairea*.

300 Riitta Nikula, Marja-Riitta Norri and Kristiina Paatero, editors, *Acanthus 1992: The Art of Standards* (Helsinki: The Museum of Finnish Architecture, 1992).

301 Lawlor, *Sacred Geometry: Philosophy and Practice*.

302 Lawlor, *Sacred Geometry: Philosophy and Practice*.

303 Nikula, et al., editors, *Acanthus 1992: The Art of Standards*. Courtesy of the Aulis Blomstedt Estate.

304 Nikula, et al., editors, *Acanthus 1992: The Art of Standards*. Courtesy of the Aulis Blomstedt Estate.

305 Nikula, et al., editors, *Acanthus 1992: The Art of Standards*. Courtesy of the Aulis Blomstedt Estate.

306 Nikula, et al., editors, *Acanthus 1992: The Art of Standards*. Courtesy of the Aulis Blomstedt Estate.

307 Nikula, et al., editors, *Acanthus 1992: The Art of Standards*. Courtesy of the Aulis Blomstedt Estate.

308 Nikula, et al., editors, *Acanthus 1992: The Art of Standards*. Courtesy of the Aulis Blomstedt Estate.

309 Lawlor, *Sacred Geometry: Philosophy and Practice*.

310 Nikula, et al., editors, *Acanthus 1992: The Art of Standards*. Courtesy of the Aulis Blomstedt Estate.

311 Nikula, et al., editors, *Acanthus 1992: The Art of Standards*. Courtesy of the Aulis Blomstedt Estate.

312 Nikula, et al., editors, *Acanthus 1992: The Art of Standards*. Courtesy of the Aulis Blomstedt Estate.

313 Nikula, et al., editors, *Acanthus 1992: The Art of Standards*. Courtesy of the Aulis Blomstedt Estate.

314 Nikula, et al., editors, *Acanthus 1992: The Art of Standards*. Courtesy of the Aulis Blomstedt Estate.

315 Nikula, et al., editors, *Acanthus 1992: The Art of Standards*. Courtesy of the Aulis Blomstedt Estate.

316 Nikula, et al., editors, *Acanthus 1992: The Art of Standards*. Courtesy of the Aulis Blomstedt Estate.

317 Nikula, et al., editors, *Acanthus 1992: The Art of Standards*. Courtesy of the Aulis Blomstedt Estate.

318 Nikula, et al., editors, *Acanthus 1992: The Art of Standards*. Courtesy of the Aulis Blomstedt Estate.

319 Janus, *Jiří Kolár* (Milano: Grupo Editoriale Fabbri S.p.A., 1981). Courtesy of Béla Kolárova.

320 Ingo F. Walther and Rainer Metzger, *Vincent Van Gogh: L'ouvre complete–peinture*, vol 1 (Köln: Benedikt Taschen Verlag GmbH, 1990).

321 Centre Georges Pompidou, *Andy Warhol Retrospective* (Paris: Éditions du Centre Pompidou, 1990).

322 Edward Lucie-Smith, *Artoday* (London: Phaidon Press Limited, 1995).

323 Kirk Varnedoe, *Duane Hanson* (New York: Harry N. Abrams, Inc., Publishers, 1985).

324 Raeburn and Wilson, editors, *Le Corbusier Architect of the Century*.

325 Gössel and Leuthäuser, *Architektur des 20. Jahrhunderts*.

326 Khan-Magomedov, *Alexandr Vesnin*.

327 Gössel and Leuthäuser, *Architektur des 20. Jahrhunderts.*

328 Photo Juhani Pallasmaa

329 Photo Juhani Pallasmaa.

330 Source unknown.

331 Source unknown.

332 Source unknown.

333 Peter Gössel and Gabriele Leuthäuser, *Architecture in the Twentieth Century* (Köln: Benedikt Taschen Verlag GmbH, 1991).

334 Timo Valjakka, editor, *Synnyt: Sources of Contemporary Art* (Helsinki: Museum of Contemporary Art, 1989).

335 William J.R. Curtis, *Modern Architecture Since 1900* (London: Phaidon Press Limited 1996).

336 Gössel and Leuthäuser, *Architecture in the Twentieth Century.*

337 Jeanne D'Andrea, *Malevich* (Los Angeles: The Armand Hammer Museum of Art and Cultural Center, 1990).

338 Robert Hobbs, *Robert Smithson: Retrospektiivinen näyttely* (Tampere: Sara Hildénin taidemuseo, 1982).

339 Lars Nittve, editor, *Walter De Maria: Två mycket stora presentationer* (Stockholm: Moderna Museet, 1989).

340 Source unknown.

341 Mary Jane Jacob, *Gordon Matta-Clark: A Retrospective* (Chicago: Museum of Contemporary Art, 1985).

342 Ragheb, editor, *Frank Gehry Architect.*

343, Charles Jencks, *Post-Modernism: The New Classicism in Art and Architecture* (London: Academy Editions, 1978).

344 Photo Juhani Pallasmaa.

345 Photo Rauno Träskelin.

346 Klaus-Jürgen Sembach, Gabriele Leuthäuser and Peter Gössel, *Möbeldesign des 20. Jahrhunderts* (Köln: Benedikt Taschen Verlag GmbH).

347 Marja-Riitta Norri and Maija Kärkkäinen, editors, *An Architectural Present: Seven Approaches* (Helsinki: The Museum of Finnish Architecture, 1990).

348 Photo Arno de la Chapelle.

349 Photo Jouni Kaipia.

350 Gössel and Leuthäuser, *Architektur des 20. Jahrhunderts.*

351 Jencks, *Post-Modernism: The New Classicism in Art and Architecture.*

352 Source unknown.

353 Source unknown.

354 Gössel and Leuthäuser, *Architektur des 20. Jahrhunderts.*

355 Source unknown.

356 Miers Charles, editor, *Love for Sale: The Words and Pictures of Barbara Kruger* (New York: Harry N. Abrams, Inc., Publishers, 1990).

357 Source unknown.

358 Enrique X. de Anda Alanis, *Luis Barragan: Clasico del silencio* (Bogota: Colleccion Somo Sur, 1989).

359 *Symbol and Interpretation / Micromegas* (U.S.A.: Archantic Publications).

360 *Morandi* (Milano: Electa, 1990).

361 Lawrence Alloway, *Lichtenstein* (New York: Abbeville Press, 1983).

362 R.H. Fuchs, *Richard Long* (New York: Solomon R. Guggenheim Museum; London: Thames and Hudson, 1986).

363 Karen Lee Spaulding, editor, *Hamish Fulton: Selected Walks 1969-1989* (Buffalo: Albright-Knox Art Gallery, 1990).

364 Charlotte & Peter Fiell, *Modern Chairs* (Köln: Benedikt Taschen Verlag GmbH, 1993).

365 Arthur C. Danto, *397 Chairs* (New York: Harry N. Abrams, Inc. Publishers, 1988).

366 Charles Jencks, *Symbolic Architecture* (London: Academy Editions, 1985).,

367 Stechler-Burns & Burns, *The Shakers.*

368 Photo Juhani Pallasmaa.

369 Italo Calvino, *Six Memos for the Next Millenium* (New York: Vintage International, 1993).

370 Jill Dunkerton, et al., *Giotto to Dürer: Early Renaissance Painting in the National Gallery.*

371 Source unknown.

372 Postcard.

373 Photo Juhani Pallasmaa.

374 Kostas Papaioannou, *The Art of Greece* (New York: Harry N. Abrams, Inc., Publishers, 1989).

375 Curtis, *Modern Architecture Since 1900.*

376 Sarah Whitfield and John Elderfield, *Bonnard* (New York: The Museum of Modern Art, 1998).

377 Coosje van Bruggen, *John Baldessari* (New York: Rizzoli International Publications, Inc., 1990).

378 Photo Rauno Träskelin.

379 June Sprigg, *Shaker Design* (New York: Whitney Museum of American Art, 1978).

380 Curtis, *Modern Architecture Since 1900.*

381 Yukio Futagawa, editor, *Tadao Ando GA Architect 8* (Tokyo: A.D.A. Edita, 1988).

382 Hanne Finsen and Inge Vibeke Raaschou-Nielsen, *Hammershøi: Painter of Stillness and Light* (New York: Wildenstein; Washington: Philips Collection, 1983).

383 The Museum of Modern Art, *Walker Evans* (New York: The Museum of Modern Art, 1979).

384 Photo Juhani Pallasmaa.

385 Photo Juhani Pallasmaa.

386 Los and Frahm, *Carlo Scarpa.*

387 Source unknown.

388 Whitfield and Elderfield, *Bonnard.*

389 Photo Juhani Pallasmaa.

390 Photo Juhani Pallasmaa.

391 Photo Juhani Pallasmaa.

392 John Canaday, *Masterpieces by Michelangelo* (New York: Artabras Inc., 1979).

393 Gloria Moure, *Kounellis* (Paris: Éditions Cercle d'Art, 1991).

394 Source unknown.

395 Bakhtiar, *Sufi: Expressions of the Mystic Quest.*

396 Gössel and Leuthäuser, *Architecture in the Twentieth Century.*

397 Source unknown.

398 *Andy Goldsworthy: In Collaboration with Nature* (New York: Harry N. Abrams, Inc., Publishers, 1990).

399 Source unknown.

400 Agni Pikióni and Hannele Grönlund, editors, *Dimitris Pikionis* (Helsinki: The Museum of Finnish Architecture, 1993).

401 Photo Rauno Träskelin.

402 Photo Juhani Pallasmaa.

Bibliography

BOOKS WRITTEN AND / OR EDITED BY JUHANI PALLASMAA:

Juhani Pallasmaa, editor, *The Aalto House 1935–36* (Helsinki: The Alvar Aalto Foundation and The Alvar Aalto Academy, 2003).

Juhani Pallasmaa and Fang Hai, editors, *Juhani Pallasmaa–Sensuous Minimalism* (Beijing: China Architecture and Building Press, 2002).

Juhani Pallasmaa, *The Architecture of Image–Existential Space in Cinema* (Helsinki: Rakennustieto, 2001).

Juhani Pallasmaa, *Animal Architects: Ecological Functionalism of Animal Constructions* (Spanish-English-German edition) (Lanzarote, Islas Canarias: Fundación César Manrique, 2001).

Juhani Pallasmaa, editor, *Alvar Aalto: Villa Mairea 1938–39* (Helsinki: The Mairea Foundation and The Alvar Aalto Foundation, 1998).

Juhani Pallasmaa, *The Eyes of the Skin–Architecture and the Senses* (London: Academy Editions, 1996).

Juhani Pallasmaa with Andrei Gozak, *The Melnikov House* (London: Academy Editions, 1996).

Juhani Pallasmaa, editor, *Eläinten arkkitehtuuri–Animal Architecture* (Helsinki: The Museum of Finnish Architecture, 1995).

Juhani Pallasmaa, *Maailmassaolon taide–kirjoituksia taiteesta ja arkkitehtuurista* [The Art of Being-in-the-World–essays on art and architecture], Maija Kärkkäinen, editor (Helsinki: Painatuskeskus, 1993).

Juhani Pallasmaa, editor, *Alvar Aalto Furniture* (Helsinki: Otava, 1987/ Cambridge: The MIT Press, 1987).

Juhani Pallasmaa, editor, *Hvitträsk–Home as a Work of Art*, (Helsinki: Otava, 1987).

Juhani Pallasmaa, editor, *The Language of Wood* (Helsinki: The Museum of Finnish Architecture, Finnish Society of Crafts and Design, Association for Contemporary Art,1987).

Juhani Pallasmaa, editor, *Tapio Wirkkala* (Helsinki: Finnish Society of Crafts and Design, 1983).

Aarno Ruusuvuori, Juhani Pallasmaa, editors, *Alvar Aalto 1898–1976* (Helsinki: The Museum of Finnish Architecture, 1978).

INTRODUCTIONS IN BOOKS AND CATALOGUES:

"The Poetry of Reason," *Glenn Murcutt Portfolio* (Sydney: P. 01 Editions, in press 2004).

"Sculpted Light, Painted Matter, and Constructed Meaning," *Juan Navaro Baldeweg* (Madrid: Arquitectura Coam 337 Revista de Arquitectura y Urbanismo del colegio oficial de Arquitectos 2004), 2–3.

"Place and Image," *Marlon Blackwell: An Architecture of the Ozarks* (New York: Princeton Architectural Press, in press 2004).

"An Architecture of Resistance," *Contemporary Interpretations of the Kansas Vernacular Landscape*, Brian Carter, editor (TUNS Press, Canada, in press 2004).

"Constructing Essences," Linda Lee, editor, *Cathcart, Fantauzzi, van Elslander: Gravity, Pamphlet Architecture 25*, (New York: Princeton Architectural Press, 2003), 6–7.

"Arne Jacobsen"s Animated Geometry," Michael Juul Holm, Kjeld Kjeldsen, Tine Vindfeld, editors, *Arne Jacobsen–Absolutely Modern* (Humlebaek: Louisiana Museum of Modern Art, 2002), 8–13.

"Thought and Experience in Rick Joy's Desert Architecture," Clare Jacobson, editor, *Rick Joy: Desert Works*, (New York: Princeton Architectural Press, 2002), p.10–21.

"Una arquitectura del diálogo / an architecture of dialogue" (Angel Fernandez Alba), *Arquitecturacom 325* (Madrid: Revista de Arquitectura y Urbanismo del Colegio Oficial de Arquitectos de Madrid, 2001), p.43–48.

"Mindscapes," *William Curtis: Mental Landscapes* (Helsinki: The Alvar Aalto Academy, 2000), 5.

"Zen and the Art of Making Architecture: Concept and design in the work of Heikkinen-Komonen," William Morgan, editor, *Heikkinen+Komonen* (New York: The Monacelli Press, 2000), 9–19.

"Between Uniqueness and Uniformity," *Ung dansk arkitektur & design* (Copenhagen: Arkitektens Forlag, 1999), 14–19.

"Preface," *Body Latent*, (Helsinki: Helsinki University of Technology, Faculty of Architecture, 1995), 1.

"The Power of the Void," *Leonhard Lapin: Void and Space* (Helsinki: Helsinki University of Technology, Faculty of Architecture, 1995), 5

"Image in Wood–primordial and contemporary in Mauno Hartman"s Sculpture," *From Primitivism to Postmodernism in Nordic Sculpture* (Reykjavik: The Nordic House, 1995), 34–39.

"Tombs in Wood–Kain Tapper," *Exhibition catalogue Stuart Levy Gallery*, (New York: Stuart Levy Gallery, 1994), 9–10.

"The Thinking Hand" (preface), *Work: Record* (Helsinki: Helsinki University of Technology, Faculty of Architecture, 1994), 1.

"Black-bearded Venus," *Leonhard Lapin–architectons, graphics* (Tallinn: Tallinnan taidehalli 1991), 16–21.

"Sense and Sensation," *Paintings and Objects of Jim Wichmann* (Stockholm: Galerie Konstruktiv Tendens, 1990).

"Minoru Takeyama," Plym Distinguished Professorship in Architecture, School of Architecture, (Chicago: University of Illinois at Urbana-Champaign, 1989).

"Poetry of Reason," *Lund & Slaatto*, Ulf Grönvold, editor (Oslo: Universitetsforlaget, 1989), 6–11.

"Images in the Libeskind Macroscope," published in following publications:
  - *Between Zero and Infinity*, (New York: Rizzoli International Publications, Inc., 1981).
  - exhibition catalogue, (Zürich: Archantic Publications, 1981).
  - exhibition catalogue, (London: Architectural Association 1980).

"Five Artists from Today"s Finland—Between universal and unique," (Kamakura: Kamakura Museum of Modern Art, 1978).

ESSAYS PUBLISHED IN BOOKS, JOURNALS, AND CATALOGUES

"Roofness: Alvar Aalto's Architecture of the Roof," Jens Bernsen, editor, #5 The Fifth Facade (Copenhagen), issue 2004:1 (2004): .

"An Architectural Credo," Journal 3 (Dublin: Dublin School of Architecture, DIT, 2004), 58–61.

"Alvar Aalto's Image of America," Stanford Andersson, editor, Alvar Aalto in Context (Cambridge: The MIT Press, in press 2004).

"Geometry of Terror," Alberto Pérez-Gómez, Stephen Parcell, editors, Chora 4: Intervals in The Philosophy of Architecture, (London, Montreal & Kingston, Buffalo: McGill-Queen's University Press, in press 2004).

"Touching the World," Josep M. Egea, editor, 97.04 (on Santiago Paramón) (Barcelona: Actar, in press 2004).

"Monster in the Maze—The Architecture of the Shining," Stanley Kubrick, Kinematograph Nr. 20/2004 (Frankfurt: Deutches Filmmuseum and Deutches Architekturmuseum, 2004), 198–207.

"The idea of paradise," Lotus International 119 (Milan: Editoriale Lotus Srl, 2004), 6–13.

"Voices of Tranquility, Loss of Silence," Designing the Quietness, Barbro Kulvik, editor, (Helsinki: Japan Finland Design Association, 2003), 24–29.

"The World of Tapio Wirkkala," Marianne Aav, editor, Tapio Wirkkala: Eye, Hand and Thought (Helsinki: Design Museum and Werner Söderström Oy, 2002), 10–39.

"The Africa of the Mind: Reflections on the Geography of Architecture," Hannele Grönlund, Maija Kärkkäinen, Marja-Riitta Norri, editors, Before Next—Learning from Roots (Helsinki: The Museum of Finnish Architecture, 2002), 92–105.

"Architecture of the Forest: landscape, geometry and meta-phor," Approach 01, Graduate Studio Works, School of Architecture, Washington University in St. Louis, (St. Louis: Washington University in St. Louis, 2002), 51–57.

"The Art of Reason: Utility, Technique and Expression in Architecture," Gentle Bridges: Architecture, Art and Science (Basel·Berlin·Boston: Birkhäuser-Publishers for Architecture, 2003), 22–34.

"Lived Space, Embodied Experience and Sensory Thought," OASE #58, (Nijmegen, Summer 2002), 13–31.

"The Art of Wood 1: Wood in the Architecture of Finland," CRART, Craft & Art (Korea), No. 9 (May 2002), 64–67.

"Houses of Imagination," Jari Jetsonen, editor, Little Big Houses (Helsinki: Building Information, 2001), 124–129.

"Surface, Touch and Time," Alvar Aalto: The Brick (Helsinki: The Alvar Aalto Foundation, 2001), 13–27.

"Lived Space in Architecture and Cinema," Scroope 13: Cambridge Architectural Journal (Cambridge), (2001), 59–72.

"Lived Space: Embodied Experience & Sensory Thought," ARCHITALX, Volume four, Spring 2001 (Portland, Maine: Architalx Design Lecture Series, 2001), 10–15.

"Lived Metaphor," Primary Images of Architecture (St. Louis: Washington University in St. Louis, School of Architecture, 2001), 2–9.

"Image in Matter—form and feeling in Agneta Hobin's textile art," Form·Function (Helsinki) 4 (2001): 50–53.

"The Mind of the Environment," Birgit Cold, editor, Aesthetics, Well-being and Health (Ashgate, Burlington: 2001), 203–220.

"The Lived Image," a+a architecturanimation (Barcelona: Collegi d'Arquitectes de Catalunya, 2002), 56–79.

"Our Image Culture and Its Misguided Ideas about Freedom," Architectural Record (New York) 01, (2001): 51–52.

"Geography of Photography," Rax Rinnekangas: Spiritus Europaeus (Salo: Lurra Editions 2000).

"Lived Space in Architecture and Cinema," In Situ: Critical Explorations in Architectural Culture (Calgary: Faculty of Environmental Design, University of Calgary, 2000), 11–21.

"Hapticity and Time: notes on fragile architecture," Trace Four (Vancouver: Vancouver University of British Columbia, School of Architecture, B.C., 2000), 5–10.

"Hapticity and Time: Notes on Fragile Architecture," The Architectural Review (London), (May 2000): 78–84.

"From Frame to Framing," OZ, Volume 22 (Manhattan: College of Architecture, Planning and Design, Kansas State University, 2000), 4–9.

"Stairways of the Mind," International Forum of Psychoanalysis, Vol. 9, No 1–2 (April 2000), 7–17.

"Lived Space—Embodied Experience and Sensory Thought," The Sacred in Architecture (Ljubljana: Faculty of Architecture, University of Ljubljana, 2000), 123–135.

"Conceptual Knowledge, Compassion and Tacit Wisdom in Architecture," At fortaelle arkitektur, 70th Birthday publication of professor Nils-Ole Lund (Copenhagen: Arkitektens forlag, 2000), 84–99.

"Lived space in Architecture and Cinema," Festskrift Ben af Schultén 60 år (Helsinki: Gladius Oy, 1999), 93–102.

"Towards an Architecture of Humility," Harvard Design Magazine (Winter/spring 1999), 22–25.

"The Virtue of Humility," SD Space Design (Tokyo): 84–85 (1999).

"Function and Beauty in Animal Architecture," Marketta Seppälä, Jari-Pekka Vanhala and Linda Weintraub, editors, Animal, Anima, Animus (Pori: Pori Art Museum, 1998), 209–215.

"The Inner Space of the World: Existential Themes in Juhana Blomstedt's Art," Blomstedt: A Dream of Light (Turku: Wäinö Aaltonen Museum, 1998), 12–19.

"Out of the forest: six visual essays on the use of timber in Finnish building," Books from Finland (3: 1996), 182–189.

"Logic of the Image," The Journal of Architecture, Volume 3 (winter 1998), 289–299.

"The Space of Time," OZ, Volume 20 (College of Architecture, Planning, and Design, Kansas University, 1998), 54–57.

"Hitchcock"s Minimalism: Space and Image in Rope," Monument 25 (Australia: 1998), 88–95.

"Theory versus Practice," *Constructions of Tectonics for the Postindustrial World*, (Washington DC: Association of Collegiate Schools of Architecture, 1997), 11–13.

"Hegemony of the eye and the loss of the body," *Thesis* 6 (Weimar: Wissenschaffliche Zeitschrift der Bauhaus–Universität, 1997), 108–117.

"Una arquitectura de imágenes–An Architecture of Imagery," *Arquitectura Viva Monographs* 66 (1997), 12–19.

"Ecological Functionalism of Animal Architecture, Master Builders of the Animal World," *ILAUD International Laboratory of Architecture and Urban Design* (Milan: 1996), 50–53.

"The Geometry of Feeling–a look at the phenomenology of architecture," *Theorizing a New Agenda for Architecture– an anthology of architectural theory*, Kate Nesbitt, editor (New York: Princeton Architectural Press, 1996).

"Eye, World and Mind: Jorma Hautala's aesthetic project," *Jorma Hautala Teoksia* / Works (Helsinki: Porin Taidemuseo, 1995), 6–15.

"Builders of the animal kingdom–the essence of architecture," *Form·Function* (Helsinki) 2: (1995): 50–55.

"Phenomenology of Home," *The New Private Realm: the Berlage Cahiers* 3 (Rotterdam: 010 Publisher, 1995), 62–65.

"From Metaphorical to Ecological Functionalism," *Architecture: Urbanism* (Belgrad) 11:2 (1995): 39–44.

"El silencio del Norte–The Silence of the North," AV (Madrid) 55 (1995): 4–9.

"The fullness of asceticism," *Le Carré Bleu* (Paris) 2: 28–32.

"City Sense–byen som sanset, erindret og forestillet," *Den Oversete By–det sansede Köbenhavn* (The City as perceived, remembered and imagined) (Copenhagen: Arkitektens Forlag, 1995), 10–15.

"Identity, Intimacy and Domicile–notes on the phenomenology of home," *The Home: Words, Interpretations, Meanings and Environments*, Benjamin, N.D., editor, (Avebury: Aldershot, 1995) 131–147.

"Olemuslik Arhitektuur–Architecture of the Essential I," *Ehituskunst, Estonian Architectural Review* (Tallinn) nr 11, (1995): 52–59.

"Olemuslik Arhitektuur–Architecture of the Essential II," *Ehituskunst, Estonian Architectural Review* (Tallinn) nr 12, (1995): 53–59.

"Olemuslik Arhitektuur–Architecture of the Essential III," *Ehituskunst, Estonian Architectural Review* (Tallinn), nr 13 (1995): 46–59.

"Silence of the North–similarities and differences in contemporary Nordic architecture," *Arquitectura Viva*, Nr 55 (1995): 4–9.

"Gli animali architetti–Animal Architects," *Ottagono* (Industrial Design Quarterly), Nr. 177 (1995): 65–80.

"L"architettura dell"essenziale–Il funzionalismo ecologico delle construzioni animali/ Architecture of the Essential– Ecological Functionalism of Animal Constructions," *Spazio e società* (Space & Society) Nr 72/1995 (Milano: 1995), 40–55.

"Space and image in Andrei Tarkovsky's Nostalgia; notes on a phenomenology of architecture in cinema," *Chora 1: Intervals in the Philosophy of Architecture* (Montreal: McGill University Press, 1994), 143–166.

"An Architecture of the Seven Senses," *Questions of Perception–Phenomenology of Architecture*, A+U July (1994): 27–37.

"Six Themes for the Next Millennium," *Architectural Review* (London), July 1994, 74–79.

"Nutidig avantgarde og arkitekturens visdom/ Contemporary Avant-Garde and The Wisdom of Architecture," *Skala* (Copenhagen) nr. 28 (1993): 28–31.

"Image in Matter: Kain Tapper's recent sculpture," *Form·Function* (Helsinki) 1 (1992): 84–86.

"Space and Image in Tarkovsky's Nostalgia," *Focus* (Helsinki: Helsinki University of Technology, Faculty of Architecture, 1992), 13–24.

"Rum och bild i Andrej Tarkovskijs Nostalgia / Space and Image in Tarkovsky"s Nostalgia–notes on the phenomenology of architecture in cinema," *Arkitektur* (Stockholm) 4 (1992): 44–51.

"Culture, Identity, Environment," *Built environment–Identity– European Integration* (Helsinki: Suomen Unesco-toim-kunta, 1991), 107–117.

"Architecture in the making–Conception and experience in Alvar Aalto's architecture," Ben Farmer and Hentie Louw, editors, *Companion to Contemporary Architectural Thought* (London: Routledge, 1993), 409–415.

"Finnish Architecture after the Paris Spring and Alvar Aalto," *Synthesis: Architecture, Craftmanship and Design* (Helsinki, Association of Finnish Architects, 1990), 50–56.

"Alvar Aalto: Towards a Synthetic Functionalism," Peter Reed, editor, *Alvar Aalto–Between Humanism and Materialism* (New York: The Museum of Modern Art, 1988), 20–44.

"Tradition and Modernity," *The Architectural Review* (London), May 1988: 27–34.

"Language of Wood," *Form·Function* (Helsinki) 3 (1987), 6–15.

"An Architecture of the Forest," *Towards New Integration in Finnish Housing Architecture* (Helsinki, Association of Finnish Architects, 1987), 53–59.

"Architecture in Finnish Cultural Identity–Two Timely Masters," *Scandinavian Review* (New York), winter 1987: 59–73.

"Alvar Aalto: Image and Form," *Studio International*, Vol 200, Nro 1018 (London: 1987), 42–47.

"The Social Commission and Autonomous Architect–the art of architecture in the consumer society," *Harvard University Review* (New York: Rizzoli International Publications, Inc., 1987), 114–121.

"The Geometry of Feeling–a look at the phenomenology of architecture," *Skala* (Copenhagen) 4, (Juni 1986), 22–25.

"Finnish Architecture after the Paris Spring," *Byggekunst* (Oslo) 7 (1986).

"Villa Mairea, Fusion of Tradition and Utopia," Yukio Futagawa, editor, *Global Architecture* (Tokyo:1984).

"The Finnish Vision at Cranbrook," *Form·Function* (Helsinki) 2 (1984): 18–27.

"Rut Bryk: Journey to Landscapes of Tranquility," *Form·Function* (Helsinki) 2 (1983): 20–25.

"The Voice of Matter", *Form·Function* (Helsinki) 1 (1982), 12–19.

"Trends and Contradiction in Finnish Architecture," *Studio International* (London: 1982).

"Rediscovering a Tradition," *Urban Design International* (New York), 2, (1981), 18–23.

"Ageless Shapes," *Form·Function* (Helsinki) 1–2 (1980): 4–9.

"Towards a New Humanism—Aspects of Alvar Aalto's Architecture and Thinking," *Space Design* (Tokyo) 1+2, (1977).

"Architecture in Finland: Restlessness," *Projekt* (Poland), 4, (1972), 28–39.

INTERVIEWS:

"The Wisdom of Architecture," *Hunch: The Berlage Institute Report* No 6/7 (Rotterdam 2003), 383–6.

"Thought, Matter and Experience," conversation between Steven Holl and Juhani Pallasmaa, *el croquis*, 108 (Madrid: 2002), 6–27.

"The word made flesh—A discussion between an architect and a poet (Juhani Pallasmaa, Jyrki Kiiskinen)", *Alt'ing—The Scottish Journal of Architectural Research Number 1, March 1996* (The Rutland Press 1996), 75–78.

"And the Word and Space Were Made Flesh: Discussion entre un architecte (Juhani Pallasmaa) et un poéte (Jyrki Kiiskinen)," *Le Carré Bleu* (Paris), Nr. 3-4 (1994). 2–11.

BOOK REVIEWS:

"On Architecture, Aesthetic Experience and the Embodied Mind: Seven Essays," *Arkitektur 2–*2003 Mars (Stockholm: 2003), 73.

"Studies in Tectonic Culture: The Poetics of Construction in Nineteenth and Twentieth Century Architecture by Kenneth Frampton," *ARQ—Architectural Research Quarterly* (Cambridge), nr 4, vol. 1 (summer 1996): 90–92.

"Erik Asmussen, architect," *ptah* (Helsinki), 1–2, (1999): 68.

"Organic Functionalism" (review of Gary J. Coates, Erik Asmussen, architect), *ARQ Architectural Research Quarterly* (Cambridge), nr. 3, vol. 4 (2000): 281–282.

Alphabetical Index